From R
Labyrin
Los A

The Taming of the Demons

The Taming of the Demons

Violence and Liberation in Tibetan Buddhism

Jacob P. Dalton

Yale
UNIVERSITY
PRESS
New Haven & London

Published with assistance from the foundation established in memory of Philip Hamilton McMillan of the Class of 1894, Yale College.

Yale University Press books may be purchased in quantity for educational, business, or promotional use. For information, please e-mail sales.press@yale.edu (U.S. office) or sales@yaleup.co.uk (U.K. office).

Set in Electra type by Newgen North America.
Printed in the United States of America.

Library of Congress Cataloging-in-Publication Data

Dalton, Jacob Paul, 1969–
The Taming of the Demons : Violence and Liberation in Tibetan Buddhism / Jacob P. Dalton.
pages cm
Includes bibliographical references and index.
ISBN 978-0-300-15392-7 (cloth : alk. paper) 1. Tantric Buddhism—China—Tibet. 2. Violence—Religious aspects—Tantric Buddhism. I. Title.
BQ8915.8.D35 2011
294.3′4342—dc22 2010042341

A catalogue record for this book is available from the British Library.

This paper meets the requirements of ANSI/NISO Z39.48–1992 (Permanence of Paper).

10 9 8 7 6 5 4 3 2 1

Dedicated to my mother, Kate Wylie,
who has always been my loving audience

CONTENTS

ACKNOWLEDGMENTS

This book addresses a sensitive topic. The subject of violence, and perhaps even more so religious violence, can elicit strong reactions. The challenge for a study of this sort is to remain open to the frequently undecidable moral complexities of violence. Tibetan Buddhists themselves have a long history of nuanced engagement with the problem of violence. In the pages that follow, I have worked to do justice to this history by avoiding any demonizations or romanticizations of this rich and ancient religious tradition. In trying to avoid any such oversimplifications, I have benefited from the help of many teachers, colleagues, and friends.

The first glimmers of this project began in early 2000, when I was fortunate enough to read through the myth of Rudra's subjugation, which is appended to this study, under the guidance of Khenpo Pema Sherab. The abbot of Namdroling Monastery in Bylakuppe, India, Khenpo was visiting Dharamsala for five months to teach Prajñāpāramitā to the nuns of Shugsep. His extraordinary generosity made it a wonderful spring, and I thank him for all the time and attention he gave me.

I ended up excluding my translation of the Rudra myth from my doctoral thesis. After completing my Ph.D. at the University of Michigan, I was granted a three-year research position at the School for Oriental and African Studies in London. It was during this postdoctoral period that I began to conceive of the present project. Thanks to generous funding from the British Arts and Humanities Research Council, I spent these years working for the International Dunhuang Project, reading through the tantric Dunhuang manuscripts held in the British Library's Stein Collection. I would like to thank Susan Whitfield, Ulrich Pagel, and Burkhard Quessel for all they did to welcome me in these years.

I began writing this book in 2005, during my first year as an assistant professor in the Department of Religious Studies at Yale University. I am indebted to all my colleagues there for their kindness and generosity. Phyllis Granoff and Koichi Shinohara, in particular, gave me their friendship, the time to write, and much learned advice. I would also like to thank the American Council of Learned Societies for their support. As an ACLS Fellow in 2007–2008, I was able to concentrate more fully on my writing and to produce my initial draft.

Since then I have benefited from the valuable feedback of a number of colleagues. For this I thank Sam van Schaik, Harunaga Isaacson, Janet Gyatso, Georges Dreyfus, Iain Sinclair, and Shaman Hatley. My thanks also to my new colleagues at UC Berkeley for their comments, especially Alexander von Rospatt, Robert Sharf, and the Buddhist Studies graduate students. I was also helped by conversations with many colleagues and friends, especially Gene Smith, Benjamin Bogin, Kurtis Schaeffer, Bryan Cuevas, Frances Garrett, Stephen Jenkins, Franz-Karl Ehrhard, Dan Martin, Ron Davidson, and, of course, my dear wife, Alice, who fell asleep to my ravings on many a late night. Finally, I cannot say thanks enough to my advisor, Donald Lopez, who encouraged me throughout this process, read through numerous drafts, and responded tirelessly with a steady flow of creative and challenging advice. He has long since passed far beyond the call of duty, and I truly appreciate all the guidance he has given me over the past seventeen years.

The Taming of the Demons

Introduction

In 1895, in the Tibetan border region of Sikkim, Lieutenant Colonel L. Austine Waddell completed his study *Buddhism of Tibet or Lamaism, With Its Mystic Cults, Symbolism and Mythology.* With its publication, Waddell sought to lift "the veil which still hides [Tibet's] mysteries from European eyes," and thus to shed light on a "dark land" and its "sinister growth of poly-demonist superstition." Waddell's descriptions repeatedly criticized Tibetans for their corrupt and superstitious practices of sorcery and "sacrifice-offerings to devils." Today we may easily dismiss Waddell's prejudice as a product of his time, his Protestant upbringing, and the colonialist desires of the British Empire. Yet at the same moment, just a few hundred miles to the northeast, the Tibetan lama Rigdzin Gargyi Wangchuk was writing his own book, for Tibetan eyes, decrying the demonic corruptions he was encountering in his own borderland. Rigdzin Garwang (as he was also called) wrote in Nyarong in eastern Tibet, to warn his people of "the dangers of blood sacrifice." Like Waddell, Garwang criticized Tibetans for their involvements in sorcery and blood sacrifice, rituals that he similarly branded "ignorant" and "barbaric." Garwang's work thus at once challenges any facile dismissals of Waddell's views as mere colonialist fantasies, even as it contradicts his sweeping statements about the naïve and superstitious views of all Tibetans. Yes, some Tibetans were involved in violence, both symbolic and real, but they also harbored their own misgivings about the violent and bloody ritual practices that permeated parts of their religion, doubts that in many ways mirrored those of a Victorian-era son of a Scottish Presbyterian minister.

In fact, violence has always played a multivalent role in Tibetan Buddhism. It was plainly inadequate for Waddell to demonize the Tibetan tradition as nothing but corrupt demonolatry, yet neither should one ignore the tradition's darker aspects. Anyone traveling to Tibet today is inevitably struck by the prevalence of violent imagery. From frescoes of bloody scenes in temples and dark monastery halls filled with weapons, to local stories of demon subjugation and the masked dances that reenact them, it is clear that violence has played a crucial role in Tibetan Buddhism. Simultaneously condemned and revered, violence has a complex history in Tibet. As in the West, it has elicited in Tibetans a wide range of responses, from repulsion to fascination, from demonization to veneration. This book explores the ambiguities of violence within this variously mythologized culture.

The chapters herein offer a history of violence in Tibetan Buddhism. Violence has its own language in Tibet, a network of associations that have accumulated over many centuries and are still changing today in the harsh political climate of the Chinese occupation. This study traces the general contours of this language and its development from the ninth century to the present day. It cuts a path through the esoteric world of tantric myth and ritual, through historical darkness and dire prophesies, through Tibetan practices of lawmaking and temple building, through the Tibetan rhetoric of religious conversion, imperial collapse, and foreign invasion. The result will hopefully be a clearer understanding of the themes and influences that shaped Rigdzin Garwang's late-nineteenth-century composition and made it so similar to, yet different from, Waddell's own work.

A PAIR OF TEXTS: THE MYTH OF RUDRA'S SUBJUGATION AND THE LIBERATION RITE

The history of violence in Tibet is rooted in a fundamental pairing of myth and ritual, the myth of the demon Rudra's subjugation and the euphemistically named "liberation" (*sgrol ba*) rite. The myth describes the buddhas' battle with Rudra that culminates in them killing the demon, then reviving him as a worldly god bound by powerful oaths to protect the Buddhist teachings. From early on, the Rudra myth served to explain the origins of the tantras, esoteric scriptures that emerged in the seventh and eighth centuries C.E. The myth justifies in particular the tantras' teachings on compassionate violence as a path to buddhahood. It maintains that the extraordinary violence of tantric Buddhism was first necessitated by the appearance of Rudra (sometimes called Maheśvara), a terrible demon who grew to threaten all of Buddhism and plunge the universe into unthinkable suffering. Such a powerful manifestation of demonic ignorance could only be tamed by violent means, and more specifically by the methods taught in the tantras. The myth thus describes how, for the first time in this aeon, the wrathful buddhas of the tantras were sent forth to subjugate Rudra and thereby introduce the tantras into the world.

The same basic narrative has appeared in countless retellings. From the seventh-century *Sarvatathāgata-tattvasaṃgraha* to the eighth-century *Guhyagarbha* and *Cakrasaṃvara* tantras and innumerable renditions since, it has long served as the central myth of tantric Buddhism.[1] Some familiarity with the Rudra myth is essential for anyone seeking to understand the place of violence in Tibetan Buddhism. An annotated translation of the longest known version of the myth, drawn from a ninth-century tantra called today the *Compendium of Intentions Sutra* (Tib. *Dgongs pa 'dus pa'i mdo;* Skt. **Samāja-vidyā Sūtra*), is supplied in appendix A. The myth's narrative themes have been vital in shaping the history of violence in Tibet, so much so that each chapter of this book may even be seen as an exploration of a different aspect of the myth: the nature of evil, the place of demon taming, the liberation rite, Buddhist law, sacred space, Buddhist warfare, and conversion.

The ritual counterpart to the Rudra myth is the notorious liberation rite for ritual murder.[2] Rituals for exorcism and demon taming proliferated in the seventh and eighth centuries. By the second half of the eighth century the transgressive Mahāyoga tantras were emerging, and their rites of "liberation" quickly became paradigmatic. The Mahāyoga liberation rites took the violence of the earlier tantras to an extreme, as they purported to advocate not only the use of sympathetic magic to exorcize troublesome demons and spirits but the ritual killing of actual people. Many of the key passages recommended the use of an effigy, but others at least claimed to support the direct killing of live human beings.

Scholars of tantric Buddhism—traditional and modern alike—have long debated whether such transgressive claims were merely rhetorical or were taken literally and sometimes even acted upon. Conclusive proof of early tantric ritual killings may never be found; indeed, it is unclear what such evidence would even look like. In the case of Tibet, animal blood sacrifice is recommended by documents on early royal funerary rites,[3] and its practice is corroborated by ancient burial mounds excavated in Tibet; a single mound may contain dozens of animal skeletons, typically horses, cattle, sheep, goats, and dogs. Within the same funerary mounds, archaeologists claim to have recently found evidence of what may be human sacrifice.[4] Early Tibetan funerary sacrifices of this kind are generally associated with the pre-Buddhist religion of Tibet, so while interesting, they are not directly relevant to Buddhism and the questions surrounding the liberation rite.[5] Nonetheless, they do suggest that blood sacrifice of some sort was known in early Tibet.[6]

Given that firm archaeological evidence of live liberation is unlikely to emerge, the present study focuses solely on textual evidence and particularly on a text that appears in a largely unstudied tenth-century manuscript discovered in the famous "library cave" of Dunhuang.[7] Close examination reveals what appears to be, on its surface anyway, a remarkably detailed description of a Buddhist rite of human sacrifice. As chapter 1 reveals, however, surfaces are not to be trusted in tantric Buddhism, and it is quite possible that the entire procedure was supposed to be performed in the practitioner's imagination, perhaps with the support of an effigy. Liberation rites were to become well known in later Tibet, depicted in paintings and reenacted through dance and ritual performance, but they were almost always considered symbolic and directed against an effigy of the victim.[8] The Dunhuang version of the rite makes no mention of an effigy, as it directs the reader to arrange the victim on a mandala altar, purify him or her through a series of visualizations, and behead him or her with an axe. The head is then hurled into the mandala as a kind of offering, and its final resting position is interpreted to determine the success of the rite. While the rite's details are suggestive of a live ritual killing, they may well intend the use of visualization, or perhaps a lifelike three-dimensional effigy of some sort. As we shall see, such lifelike effigies are known in Tibetan Buddhism. Ultimately, whatever the manual's authors had in mind, their ancient ritual reveals a variety of themes and associations that have helped shape the Tibetan Buddhist tradition.

It should be emphasized here that later Tibetans were adamant about liberation not being performed on a live person, and their ritual manuals bear this out. The cases from Dunhuang studied herein represent the only known *possible* exceptions to this rule and are therefore anomalous. In focusing on these outliers, the present study is not suggesting that they should be taken as normative. Quite the opposite, it deploys them precisely because they represent the extreme, so as to explore the limits and the contours of this ancient practice and thus to shed light on its influences within the later tradition. Violence is excessive by definition and as such often functions within societies to define (reversely) those societies from without. The present study demonstrates how violence has functioned in Tibet as the other against which Tibetan Buddhism formulated itself. The extraordinary violence of the Rudra myth has for centuries provided the imagery and the language for Tibetans to explore their own relationship to violence, and similarly the liberation rite—and the *mere pos-*

sibility of an extreme, literal interpretation of the rite—has helped the Tibetan tradition forge itself, even if precisely as a tradition that does not engage in such practices. Outliers then, as these ancient manuscripts from a dark age may be, can tell us much about what is normative for a tradition.

TIBET'S "DARK AGE"

Both of these texts—the elaborate version of the Rudra myth translated in appendix A and the Dunhuang liberation rite translated and discussed in chapter 3—date from the so-called dark age of Tibetan history that spanned from around 842 to 986 C.E. Any discussion of violence in Tibetan Buddhism must consider the place of this mysterious period in the Tibetan cultural imagination. According to most standard histories, following the collapse of the Tibetan Empire in 842, Tibet was plunged into a century and a half of political chaos from which nearly no documents survive. During these years the Buddhist monasteries were forcibly closed, and later accounts describe a period of religious corruption, when violence, ignorance, and demons reigned. Not until the end of the tenth century did new centers of political and religious authority begin to be reestablished, allowing what has been termed the Tibetan "renaissance" to begin.[9]

For the later Tibetan tradition, the dark age, or the "age of fragmentation" (*sil bu'i dus*), as most Tibetans know it, came to epitomize all things evil, and not without some reason. The fragmentation of Tibetan society during these years resulted in a widespread breakdown of law and order; the royal tombs were sacked, and local wars were rife. But the age also took on a symbolic life beyond its historical realities. For later Tibetans, the period came to represent an archetypal era of demonic corruption. Modern scholars have observed how later Tibetans cast the earlier imperial period as a kind of "Tibetan Camelot" that embodied Tibet's highest political and religious ideals.[10] Less well recognized is how such glorifications of the empire were mirrored by a simultaneous revisioning of the age of fragmentation as the empire's polar opposite, an abyss of lawlessness and depravity.

Such wholly negative views of the age of fragmentation did much to obscure its historical importance in the early Tibetan assimilation of Buddhism. The present study suggests that the era was in fact marked by an eruption of religious creativity. The innovations that emerged during these crucial years were subsequently denied their historical importance by later historians, dismissed as the heretical distortions of ignorant Tibetans under the influence of demons. Nonetheless, many elements of the later Tibetan tradition—and many relating to tantric violence in particular—took root in this chaotic and obscure environment.

The age of fragmentation therefore has played two interrelated roles in the history of violence in Tibet. Initially, the period was marked by a proliferation of tantric Buddhism and its mythic and ritual themes of demon taming at the local and popular levels of Tibetan society. Later, as an increasingly darkened age, the period came to play a more symbolic role in the Tibetan imagination, as a fundamental time of demonic corruption and rampant violence to which Tibetans were forever in danger of reverting. The trajectories of this shift in the age of fragmentation's role, from real to symbolic, can tell us much about how violence has been understood in Tibet.

By questioning the traditional depictions of the age of fragmentation as completely dark, the present study might be mistaken to be arguing against the very idea of an age of fragmentation as a historical period distinct from the supposedly more enlightened periods that preceded and succeeded it. It is true that the Pugyal Empire faded only gradually from the mid-ninth to the early tenth centuries. As chapter 2 suggests, the period may not have been truly "dark," in a political sense at least, until the early tenth century and the rebellions of 901–905 C.E. and King Pel Khortsen's murder in 910. Thus the precise beginning of the age of fragmentation is difficult, if not impossible, to discern. Nor can the period easily be distinguished from the years that followed it. Continuities abound between the Buddhist traditions of Tibet's age of fragmentation and those of the so-called later dispensation (*phyi dar*) of the eleventh to thirteenth centuries. Ronald Davidson's recent study of the latter "renaissance" period characterizes it as a time of tantric innovation dominated by political fragmentation and local aristocratic concerns, yet the roots of many of these features may be traced back into the preceding century and a half of religious and political "darkness."[11] Precisely when the age of fragmentation ended may be even less clear than when it began.

Despite these problems, this study suggests that the age of fragmentation still has its uses as a historical tool. The age may not have been wholly exceptional, but neither was it an utterly indiscernible nonevent. Tibetan historians themselves distinguish the era, so as a unit of periodization it is already native to Tibet's own historiographic environment. And not without reason; it is an era that deserves recognition. The collapse of the Tibetan Empire that began around 842 C.E. had serious consequences for Tibet's Buddhist traditions. No longer did Tibetans receive the same kinds of tribute from the far reaches of Central Asia, no longer could they sponsor large-scale religious constructions, and no longer was a state-sponsored monastic elite able to control the shape of

Tibetan Buddhism. Each of these capacities would eventually return in subsequent centuries, but all were notably absent during the age of fragmentation. This was an era when the relatively centralized authority of the Pugyal imperial court and Buddhist monastic institutions was largely absent from Tibet. Both politically and religiously, then, the age of fragmentation was different from the imperial period that preceded it. And it differed too from the subsequent "later dispensation" period, an era of Buddhist "renaissance" marked by increased temple building, monasticism, and sectarianism. The present study therefore advocates for a reassessment, but not a rejection, of Tibet's age of fragmentation. Scholars of pre-medieval European history have redefined their own "dark age" as a nonpejorative but still useful concept. Just as they have become aware of the limitations and the potentially misleading connotations of their own dark age, scholars of Tibet must do the same.

This raises the question of whether it is appropriate to call Tibet's age of fragmentation a "dark age" at all. Given the present study's aim to provide, insofar as possible, a history of violence in Tibetan Buddhism *in Tibetans' own terms,* I have chosen to employ the more common indigenous phrase, "age of fragmentation." Notwithstanding this decision, "dark age" remains a surprisingly instructive conceptual tool, at least for present purposes. As already observed, it resonates nicely with Western historical and historiographical trends. Beyond this, however, its symbolic significance must also be considered, and here its true import emerges. As the present study demonstrates, metaphors of darkness figure heavily in Tibetan descriptions of the period. In the twelfth-century *Pillar Testament,* for example, the fateful era is described in the following prophetic terms:

> Then in three generations a king with the name of a beast of burden will come [*lang* means "ox"]. The excellent dharma will fade entirely. The teachings will decline and degenerate. In that age, all the peoples of Tibet who will be led by that king (Lang Darma) will end up going to the hells of unending torments. For a little over a hundred years the sounds of the excellent dharma will not be pronounced. The land of Tibet will become shrouded in darkness. For five generations it will remain like that. Then after several generations, the slight embers of the excellent dharma will be rekindled in this snowy kingdom.[12]

This same language of darkness appears throughout Tibetan historical writings and may even be detected in the titles of two of the period's most influential compositions, the *Armor against Darkness* and *Lamp for the Eyes in Contemplation,* both composed by Nupchen Sangye Yeshe in the late ninth and early tenth centuries. The "dark age," then, is a particularly revealing term for a study of violence such as this one. That said, the present study prefers the more emic term "age of fragmentation."[13]

EVIDENCE FROM DUNHUANG

Today Europe's dark ages are considered "dark" primarily due to the paucity of sources on the period compared to both earlier and later times. Here too we find parallels with Tibet's age of fragmentation, for hardly any documents survived the period. Fortunately for modern historians of Tibet, one small window onto the period has opened. In 1907, the Hungarian-born British explorer Sir Aurel Stein brought to light a huge cache of manuscripts and paintings that had remained hidden for nearly one thousand years in the Caves of the Thousand Buddhas, near the town of Dunhuang on the old Silk Road. Realizing what he had stumbled upon, Stein promptly loaded as many of the manuscripts as he could onto his camels and carried them back to London. A few months later the French sinologist Paul Pelliot heard about Stein's discovery and traveled to the cave himself, carrying away the bulk of the remaining manuscripts. Since that time, some one hundred years now, these two collections, the Stein Collection at the British Library in London and the Pelliot Collection at the Bibliothèque nationale in Paris, have revolutionized our understanding of Asian religious history.

The Dunhuang manuscripts are written in a variety of languages. Chinese documents compose the bulk of the collection, in addition to which there are several thousand Tibetan manuscripts, as well as works in Sanskrit, Khotanese, Uighur, and other Central-Asian languages. Over the past century it commonly has been assumed that the Tibetan manuscripts must date from the Tibetan occupation of Dunhuang (c. 786–848 C.E), when the Pugyal Empire was at the height of its power. In recent years, however, it has become increasingly clear that a large portion of the collection in fact dates from the tenth century, and this is particularly true of those items relating to esoteric, or "tantric," Buddhism.[14] This means that the Tibetan manuscripts from Dunhuang may reflect, in part, the kinds of religious concerns that characterized the Tibetan age of fragmentation. The fact that so many of the tantric manuscripts in particular date to the tenth century itself may be taken as an indication of the increased popularity of the tantras among Tibetans of the tenth century. Today the esoteric Dunhuang materials remain a surprisingly untapped resource, due in part to the difficulty of gaining access to the collection and to a prejudice among scholars of the early twentieth century against all things tantric. Both of these issues are starting to be addressed, thanks to recent digitization efforts and an upsurge of scholarly interest.[15] A number of preliminary studies on certain tantric manuscripts now cxist, yct to date little attention has been paid to the collection's significance as a whole and what it might tell us about Tibet's mysterious dark age. The present study represents an initial step in this direction.

Questions may be asked about the feasibility of using the Dunhuang collections to shed light on events in central Tibet: How can we be sure that the manuscripts reflect the religious trends of central Tibet and not merely the local traditions specific to the region around Dunhuang? Such a possibility should not be dismissed. However, it is notable how little reference is made in the *religious* materials from Dunhuang to any local people, places, or practices, and conversely how much is made of central Tibet and its Pugyal dynasty (and the vestiges of the dynasty that continued after its collapse). By the late ninth and the tenth centuries, Dunhuang was politically close to China. The Khotanese, for example, referred to Dunhuang as "China" and often sent envoys bearing tribute only as far as Dunhuang.[16] Yet the Tibetan Buddhists living around Dunhuang seem to have identified less with China than central Tibet. The Buddhist traditions represented in the Tibetan Dunhuang manuscripts share surprisingly little in common with the other traditions present in the region. The Dunhuang collection maybe a haphazard one, but the vast majority of the canonical works referenced therein also appear in the early catalogues of imperial-period translations, such as the Denkarma and Pangtangma.

The tantric manuscripts that are the particular focus of this study, moreover, are quite unlike anything seen in the Chinese manuscripts. The tantric forms that so occupied the Tibetan Buddhists of tenth-century Dunhuang simply are not seen among the Chinese manuscripts.[17] Tibetan Buddhists in Dunhuang may have studied Chinese, and the Chinese may have studied Tibetan, but generally speaking Tibetan Buddhism remained clearly distinct from Chinese Buddhism. Some of the scribes who penned the Tibetan tantric manuscripts even seem (given their names) to have been culturally Chinese, yet they did not translate their tantric interests into their native language. In Dunhuang, it seems that if one wanted to study the tantras, and especially the later Yoga and Mahāyoga tantras, one did so in Tibetan. Notwithstanding other modes of cultural exchange, within the Buddhist circles around Dunhuang, surprisingly strict sectarian boundaries were maintained between the Tibetan and Chinese religious traditions. The Tibetan Buddhists received their primary influences from the religious traditions of central Tibet.[18]

This is not to deny the existence of significant local innovations among the Tibetan Dunhuang manuscripts, but even these can be seen as representative of a wider trend toward alteration and localization that was typical of tenth-century Tibet. Take, for example, the possibly local interpretations seen in the arena of Tibetan Chan and the mixing of Chan with Mahāyoga ritual techniques.[19] The relevant manuscripts (PT699 being the principal example) may well reflect interpretations invented at Dunhuang, but as Nupchen's *Lamp for the Eyes in Contemplation* makes clear, similar innovations were also occurring in central Tibet. Even those variations that are particular to the Dunhuang collection still may be the *kinds* of changes that were being made in central Tibet around the same period, and for the purposes of this study that is the point: The collapse of the Pugyal Empire spurred new religious innovations throughout Tibet.

A HISTORY OF VIOLENCE

The present work opens with an analysis of the fundamental Buddhist doctrines relating to the topic of violence in Buddhism. Chapter 1, "Evil and Ignorance in Tantric Buddhism," begins by tracing a brief history of compassionate violence in Buddhism, from early works on *Abhidharma* and the *Vinaya* to the ritualized violence of the Mahāyoga tantras. Buddhists, it is argued, have long been aware of the extraordinary ethical complexities surrounding violence, moral convolutions that require interminable struggle and may remain irresolvable even when ethical clarity is absolutely demanded. This painful irresolvability of violence lies at the heart of the present study, and so it is here that we must begin. Over the course of several hundred years, Buddhist ethical theories that made allowances for the possibility of compassionate killing circulated throughout South Asia, particularly within the Mahāyāna. Such teachings on compassionate violence may have culminated in the tantras, but their seeds were present in much earlier doctrines. Already in the early tradition, the physical fact of killing was less important to one's karmic future than the mental intention that accompanied the act. This fundamental Buddhist emphasis on the mental state of the actor helped followers of the Mahāyāna explain the selfless violence of the bodhisattva, the compassionate hero of the Mahāyāna. Pure of intention and concerned solely with the welfare of all beings, the bodhisattva could even kill to reduce suffering in the world. Such teachings, in turn, provided the doctrinal foundations for the violent rhetoric and rituals of the tantras. From the seventh century, tantric rites grew increasingly elaborate, until the mid-eighth century, when the new Mahāyoga tantras introduced the so-called liberation rite and a whole new ethos of extreme behavior and transgressive violence.

In its second half, chapter 1 turns to the Rudra myth more specifically and its delicate distinction between moral and immoral violence. The lurid detail in which the myth describes Rudra's hideous appearance and cruel behavior betrays a powerful fascination with violence, even as the same details were clearly intended to produce revulsion and horror in the reader. Tantric Buddhism, it seems, despite its antinomian rhetoric of the sameness of all experiences, had a highly ambivalent relationship with violence. On the one hand, violence represented the awesome and righteous power of the avenging *heruka* buddha; on the other hand, it was something to be abhorred and avoided. These two kinds of violence—one wise and compassionate and the other ignorant and demonic—are difficult to distinguish, and yet if the Rudra myth tells us anything, their differentiation is crucial to the tantric Buddhist path.

The chapter argues that this subtle but fundamental distinction is embodied by the myth's two central characters, the wrathful buddha Vajrapāṇi and the demon Rudra. Within Indian society, the distinction between these two figures had partly been an interreligious one, with the enlightened Vajrapāṇi epitomizing the ideal Buddhist *tāntrika* and Rudra (Rudra and Maheśvara being epithets for the Hindu god, Śiva), representing the followers of tantric Śaivism. Tantric religion from early on was a pan-Indian movement that cut across religious boundaries. In the resulting environment of ritual and literary exchange, the lines that long had distinguished religious traditions were blurred and sectarian competition for royal patronage intensified. Literary and oral narratives of demon subjugation, of which our Rudra myth was in fact just one example, represented a popular strategy for establishing the superiority of one's own tradition over the demonic other. In our version of the myth, these sectarian tensions and intimacies are embodied in the nearly identical figures of Vajrapāṇi and Rudra.

Despite the closeness between these two figures, however, they do embody diametrically opposed forms of violence that must be distinguished, for not to do so, explain the commentaries, would lead one into the darkest of hells. At the heart of this dangerously subtle distinction between buddha and demon lies the most fundamental of philosophical moments, an instant in which one either recognizes the ground of all existence (*ālaya*) and attains enlightenment, or fails to do so and plunges into suffering. In this way the Rudra myth may be taken as an allegory for the entire Buddhist path, with Vajrapāṇi and Rudra representing both *nirvāna* and *saṃsāra,* identical yet opposite.

Against this doctrinal backdrop, chapter 2 takes up the themes of demon taming and Tibet's age of fragmentation. As suggested above, the late ninth and the tenth centuries saw the spread of tantric Buddhism at the local and popular levels. Under the Pugyal dynasty, access to the tantras had been strictly controlled, if not outright forbidden, by a conservative religious council under the direction of the court. The Dunhuang materials that date from this early period reflect these strictures and are mostly exoteric, sutra-based in content, whereas those that date from the tenth century exhibit a surge in interest in all things esoteric. Released from the watchful eyes of the "all-seeing" (*sarvavid*) imperial court, Tibetans were free to immerse themselves in the Buddhist tantras with a fervor that had considerable effect on the later Tibetan Buddhist tradition.

These, then, were formative years. With the collapse of the Pugyal court and its dependent monastic institutions, political and religious authority was dispersed, and Tibetans began to adapt the dharma toward their own ends. Lawlessness, violence, social fragmentation, and religious regionalization combined to put the tantras at the forefront of their interests. In India, tantric Buddhism had been entwined with new social patterns of political feudalism, pilgrimage, and local deities. Now in tenth-century Tibet, the pantheons, the myths, and the rituals of the Indian tantras were adapted and tied to specific sites in the Tibetan landscape, to create a new and often uniquely Tibetan Buddhist tradition. Groups of deities such as the demonic seven mother goddesses (*saptamātṛkā*) were identified with pre-Buddhist spirits native to the mountains, lakes, and valleys of Tibet; adaptations of the Rudra subjugation myth emerged that placed Tibet's autochthonous gods among the subdued demon's converted retinue; and tantric rituals were reworked to address the dangers of specifically Tibetan spirits.

These years also witnessed the spread of Buddhism at the popular level. It is increasingly clear that under the earlier empire, Buddhism (and especially tantric Buddhism) had been relatively limited in scope. Surprisingly little Buddhist activity can be reliably attributed to the early kings prior to Trisong Detsen (c. 742–800 C.E.). Traditional sources point to the seventh-century king Songtsen Gampo (died 649/650) as Buddhism's first major Tibetan patron, but recent scholarship suggests that many of this legendary ruler's best-known religious involvements are in fact pious fabrications or the result of historical conflations with later events.[20] Such revelations push the bulk of imperial-period Buddhist activities into a span of just seventy years, from about 770 to 840 C.E. During this short period, Buddhism remained a relatively limited affair largely specific to the royal court and its aristocratic supporters. Attracted by Buddhism's systematic reasoning and ethical order, as well as its ritual power, the court sponsored the construction of new temples and translation efforts. The resulting achievements were remarkable and did much to bolster the court's freshly acquired status as a major international power. Nonetheless, Tibetan

Buddhism during these early years remained a comparatively limited proposition that probably did not penetrate very deeply into the Tibetan populace before the empire collapsed.

Two centuries later, in the eleventh century, we find a radically different picture, with Buddhism enjoying far more widespread support among Tibetans at all levels of society. Suddenly (with some important exceptions, of course) everyone was Buddhist. Aristocratic families and a newly resurgent court in western Tibet deployed Buddhism as an authoritative discourse that was widely accepted by the Tibetan populace. Clearly something significant had happened in the intervening years. Through interpolation alone, we can see that the age of fragmentation must have been crucial to Tibet's conversion to Buddhism. This may have been a dark age—the light of the dharma may have gone out—from the perspective of monastic institutions and centralized authority, but it was no time of stagnation and decay.

In fact, the institutional darkness of the age and its remarkable creativity were two sides of the same coin. The political fragmentation of Tibet was precisely what allowed its populace to make Buddhism their own, freed from the controls of a centralized monastic authority. Yet that same fragmentation was also what later Tibetans found so threatening, even monstrous, about the period; the local innovations were by their very nature beyond the control and the confines of so-called orthodox Buddhism. The same creative "distortions" of the age that popularized Buddhism and thereby made possible the later Tibetan tradition were ultimately condemned by that same tradition. In the Rudra-taming myth, Rudra is described as the cause for tantric Buddhism to appear in the world, his demonic behavior giving rise to the extreme methods of the tantras. In a similar way, in Tibetan history the demons of the age of fragmentation gave rise to Tibetan Buddhism, defining and shaping it even as their influences were suppressed, concealed, and trampled underfoot.

With this historical background in place, chapter 3 provides a translation and study of the above-mentioned liberation rite from Dunhuang. The rite is first situated within the context of the larger manuscript in which it appears, then the translations themselves are provided, followed by a step-by-step explanation of the rite. Finally, a comparison is made between the rite and an Indian ritual of human sacrifice seen in the Śākta *Kālikā Purāṇa*. The chapter closes with a suggestion that the liberation rite as it appears in this ancient manuscript resembles in some ways a Buddhist ritual of human sacrifice.

Today, many within the Tibetan tradition might dismiss such a rite as a dark-age corruption, a distortion of true Buddhism, and given modern Tibetan sensibilities and today's definition of "true Buddhism," they might be right. Taken on its own terms, within its own historical context, however, the rite's deviation is not so clear. We can say with some confidence that the rite probably was not a corruption wrought solely by deluded Tibetan fanatics, but a practice that was known in India in some form and that was associated with the ritual tradition of the *Guhyasamāja Tantra*. There is nothing about the rite's overall form to suggest Tibetan authorship; its language and ritual details generally indicate an Indian origin, particularly when compared to the rite described in the *Kālikā Purāṇa*'s "Blood Chapter." That a second liberation rite sharing much in common with our own is described in another Dunhuang manuscript (Pelliot tibétain 840) only strengthens this conclusion. Certainly the rite was marginal and had its critics in India too, but to dismiss this ancient ritual too quickly as simply outside the fold and therefore irrelevant to "real" Buddhism is to overlook the force of its influence, especially on the later Tibetan Buddhist tradition.

That said, at precisely the same time from which our Dunhuang manuscript dates, Tibetan complaints against ritual abuses and "live liberation" (*gson sgrol*) in particular were emerging. A late-tenth-century pronouncement issued by the newly restored royal court in western Tibet speaks explicitly of similar practices, and labels them heretical "offering rites" (*mchod sgrub*) that were not properly Buddhist at all. In this rare and ancient manuscript from Dunhuang, we may have contemporary evidence of just how such rituals might have been performed.

Chapter 4 looks at King Yeshe Ö's late-tenth-century pronouncement. The edict has been well known to scholars of Tibetan Buddhism since its translation and publication in 1980, but it has yet to be considered within the context of the king's wider political project. Its complaints were expressly directed at the *tāntrikas* of Tibet, but Yeshe Ö is also known for reinstating the rule of law following Tibet's century-and-a-half-long age of fragmentation. His edict was actually just one in a series of such pronouncements, all of which were made in support of his newly established legal system. Understood within this wider context, the edict appears in a somewhat different light. While it may well have been motivated by a genuine revulsion felt by the king at the bloody violence of live liberation, it was also part of his legalist mission. Yeshe Ö was working to negotiate a new relationship between religious violence and the state. The Buddhist tantras bestowed upon their most accomplished practitioners the right to enact violence, and this presented a direct threat to the authority of the Tibetan court. Yeshe Ö reacted by insisting that live liberation remain outside legitimate Buddhist practice. True Buddhists, he maintained, would never offer sacrificial flesh to the buddhas, and when they do perform a violent rite, they always use an effigy. For Yeshe Ö, symbolic violence was one thing, real violence quite another. Questions of orthodoxy, lawful, and criminal religious practices are thus the focus of chapter 4.

Coming as it does in the middle of the book, chapter 4 serves as a kind of pivot for the study as a whole. The chapter references the framing narrative of Garwang and Waddell, each working in his respective borderland, and effects a movement from the real violence of the age of fragmentation to the symbolic violence of its image in later Tibetan history. The chapter also seeks to problematize the present study's own use of the term "sacrifice." In the West, this term carries significant ideological implications and often serves pejoratively to dismiss, exoticize, or demonize those deemed other.[21] And here we may be reminded of the modern Chinese attempts to demonize Tibetan Buddhists for their supposed involvements in human sacrifice.[22] "Sacrifice" is a dangerous term that can have its own violent and terrible consequences.[23] Seen as sheer barbaric religiosity, human sacrifice in particular represents the ultimate in cultish irrationality. It is beyond the pale of the law, whether religious or secular, and as such, the label of "sacrifice" carries a powerful ideological weight that needs to be contemplated.

Given the complex history of "sacrifice" in the West, one may wonder whether the term should be used at all in the present study. Certainly it can offer only an imperfect translation of the Tibetan *mchod sgrub* (literally "offering rite"), *dmar mchod* ("red offering"), and so on. For better or worse, the present study brackets the many questions surrounding the definition and translation of "sacrifice" and employs the term for its interpretive and comparative value. In doing so, however, the study's primary aim is to examine how Tibetans deployed their *own* terms, terms that in some ways resemble our own but in other ways differ dramatically (just as Waddell and Garwang's works are at once similar yet radically different).

Chapter 4 opens with a brief look at the role the *Kālikā Purāṇa*'s "Blood Chapter" played in colonial India. Around the turn of the nineteenth century, British scholars of religion repeatedly highlighted Indian involvements in human sacrifice and other violent religious practices to justify British rule and the imposition of British laws upon the Indian populace. Some eight centuries earlier, the Tibetan king Yeshe Ö held a similarly adverse view of "sacrifice" (*mchod sgrub*), as he applied the label to the live liberations that he held to be rampant in tenth-century Tibet. In so doing, Yeshe Ö sought to distinguish "sacrifice" from the Buddhist "liberation rite" properly performed. In late-tenth-century Tibet too, then, "sacrifice" played an ideological role in the justification of a new legal system. Bloody live liberation marked the extreme opposite of rational law, and as such it provided a justification for King Yeshe Ö's new legal system. A delicate interdependence thereby existed between demonic violence and the laws of Tibet's burgeoning western court in Gugé, between irrational religiosity and rational legal practice. It was an association that mirrored in many ways the ambivalent mythic relationship between Rudra and his enlightened vanquisher, two figures who—as seen in chapter 1—shared a common ground yet were absolute opposites.

After the tenth century, the Rudra myth and its liberation rite continued to shape the Tibetan Buddhist tradition in a variety of ways. Chapter 5 investigates their roles in the formation of Tibet as a Buddhist realm, focusing on the themes of temple building and the famous legend of Tibet's *rākṣasī* (*srin mo*) demoness. The eleventh and twelfth centuries saw temples spring up throughout Tibet, and the period's literature reflects a widespread interest in Buddhist architecture, building techniques, and Indian construction rituals. The *rākṣasī* legend was just one aspect of this broader movement to establish new Buddhist institutions across the Tibetan landscape. Situated within this larger historical context, the legend may be taken as an allegory for Tibet's conversion to Buddhism. As Janet Gyatso has observed elsewhere, the legend was part of a trend in which Tibetans were depicted as a demonic people in desperate need of subjugation.[24] According to this model, Tibetans were to remain silent and add nothing of their own (*rang bzo med pa*) to the Buddhist traditions they were importing from India. The age of fragmentation fit in here too, as a dire warning to all Tibetans of what could happen should their silent devotions to the authentic Buddhist teachings ever waver. A restrictive orthodoxy was being formed, through accusations of demonolatry and violent perversions of the dharma. In this invented world, Tibet's age of fragmentation, like the *rākṣasī*, lurked as a dark and pervasive demonic presence, pinned beneath the new tradition that was being built.

Chapter 6 traces the intertwining themes of darkness and violence into a still later period. The thirteenth century marked a major shift in Tibetan history. As the Mongols forced their way into Tibetan political life, and the *buddhadharma* finally faded from India, Tibetans found themselves no longer a barbaric people at the edges of civilization, but the residents of a major center for Buddhism in Asia. No longer did the principal threat to Buddhism lie within the Tibetan landscape; now it was located outside, in the border regions. Tibetans' earlier struggles to establish a Buddhist orthodoxy gave way to new concerns, and the literature of the period reflects this shift. The *Padma Chronicles*, for example, an authoritative new fourteenth-century biography of the early tantric master Padmasambhava, describes a Tibet that has come into its own. Here, Tibet is a center of Buddhist civilization, under threat from a demonic

Mongol horde stationed at its borders. It compares the Mongol Khan to Rudra, and his Tibetan vanquisher to the wrathful buddha Vajrapāṇi. Such mythic language was inevitably accompanied by violent ritual, sorcerous rites that Tibetans enacted against their Mongol enemies. In response to the Mongol depredations, Tibetans recast their violent tantric rites as large-scale performances for national defense that required dozens of lamas, elaborate preparations, and considerable financial support. In order to gain some insights into these ritual developments, *A History of How the Mongols Were Repelled*, by Sokdokpa ("the Mongol Repeller") Lodrö Gyeltsen (1552–1624), is examined.

By the sixteenth and seventeenth centuries, war magic had become a significant part of Tibetan politics. Chapter 6 closes with a look at the tumultuous events of this period, and especially at the Great Fifth Dalai Lama's involvements in such practices in his formation of the modern Tibetan state. In 1640 Gushri Khan invaded Tibet, and the Dalai Lama was solicited to lend his expertise in violent ritual to the war effort. In his history of the period, the Dalai Lama applies the language of liberation to the Mongol takeover, framing the Mongol Khan as Vajrapāṇi, and his Tibetan enemies as demons in need of subjugation. In light of such a mythic clash between good and evil, the Dalai Lama could only acquiesce to the khan's request, and between 1640 and 1641 he led a series of large-scale ritual performances in support of the Mongol king. By 1642 the Mongols had defeated their Tibetan enemies, and the Dalai Lama's Ganden Podrang government was quickly appointed as Tibet's new ruling power. Thus from the construction of temples in the twelfth century to the Dalai Lama's rise to power in the seventeenth, the Buddhist realm of Tibet was in multiple ways founded on the mythic and ritual themes of tantric violence.

The book ends with a brief seventh chapter that returns us to the late-nineteenth-century work of L. Austine Waddell, with whom this introduction began. Waddell (1854–1938) wrote his famous study, *The Buddhism of Tibet or Lamaism*, from the Tibetan border region of Sikkim, a hidden valley (*sbas yul*) known as the "Land of Fruits" ('Bras mo ljongs). The chapter looks at the development of such paradisiacal hidden valleys, typically located along Tibet's border, as an extension of the mandalic spatial models that flourished at the time of the Mongol invasions. Tibetan attitudes toward their border regions from the sixteenth century onward were marked by an ambivalence that viewed them as both Buddhist paradises promising spiritual renewal in dark times and demonic lands at the edges of civilization in desperate need of righteous subjugation. The chapter compares Waddell's writings on Tibet to those of his Tibetan contemporary, the lama Rigdzin Garwang (1858–1930), who composed *The Dangers of Blood Sacrifice* from his own border region in Nyarong in eastern Tibet. A comparison of these culturally distinct texts reveals much in common between European (and American) attitudes toward Tibet and Tibetans' own mixed attitudes toward the borders that define their cultural center.

Despite such curious parallels, however, violence has its own history and language in Tibet. It has followed its own uniquely Tibetan trajectories. From the mythic liberation of Rudra, to the fragmentation of the Pugyal Empire, to the Mongol invasions and the foreign depredations of the twentieth century, violence in Tibet has been shaped by many centuries of history. The ritual *cham* dances that are still performed throughout Tibet today unite and bear witness to these many semantic layers. The destruction of an effigy by fearsome Buddhist dancers may be a simultaneous reenactment of the liberation of Rudra, the ancient apostate king Lang Darma, the local spirits, and even the specter of Chinese occupation. Indeed, the identities of each of these demonic figures have shaped each other for so long that in many ways, they have become indistinguishable.

SUMMARY OF THE RUDRA MYTH

As Donald Lopez has observed, Western scholarship over the past century has swung from one extreme to another in its view of Tibet. At the turn of the twentieth century, scholars generally described Tibetan Buddhism (and tantric Buddhism more generally) as corrupt ritualism and demonolatry, "thinly and imperfectly varnished over with Buddhist symbolism."[25] All this changed with the second half of the twentieth century. Following China's invasion and annexation of Tibet, they recast Tibet as the pristine preserve of authentic Buddhism, a tradition of logical debate, ethical philosophy, and careful textual exegesis. Discussions of Tibet's dark side, like those of Waddell, were deemed tasteless Eurocentric anachronisms that served only to justify and promote the colonial order of the British and now the Chinese.[26] While the latter apologetic corrective may have seemed an improvement, the same fundamental prejudices remained intact; the same divide between Tibet's violent and bloody dark side on one hand and its high tradition of reason and nonviolence on the other was maintained; the focus merely shifted from one to the other. Only recently have scholars begun to consider the role of violence in Tibetan Buddhism in a more balanced manner, and the present study seeks to build upon their valuable efforts.[27]

The subject of violence in Tibetan Buddhism is extraordinarily complex and inevitably controversial. The present study traces just one narrative line through a myriad of possibilities. The resulting story is a construction, and in places probably an arbitrary one determined largely by the present author's own interests. Insofar as is possible, however, the study strives to understand its subject on its own terms, and it is toward this end that a complete translation of the most elaborate version of the Rudra-taming myth has been appended to this study. It is hoped that the myth's complex and often evocative narrative will provide a better understanding of the rich and varied culture of Tibet. Surely too, some familiarity with the myth will greatly enrich the reader's experience of the seven chapters that comprise this study. For this reason, the reader may wish to read the appended translation first, before continuing on to chapter 1. Many, however, will prefer to move directly into the body of this work, and for the latter a summary of the myth is provided here.

The myth appears in chapters 20–31 of the *Compendium of Intentions Sutra* (*Dgongs pa 'dus pa'i mdo*), the fundamental tantra of the Anuyoga class of tantras specific to the Nyingma school.[28] We first meet Rudra in a previous lifetime, in the aeon of the buddha Akṣobhya. The future Rudra, now a prince named Black Liberator, together with his personal attendant, Denpak, are both disciples of a Buddhist monk named Invincible Youth. It soon becomes apparent that the master and his servant have radically divergent interpretations of their teacher's words. Black Liberator grows angry at his servant's discord, banishes him from the country, and returns to his teacher to ask whose understanding was correct. When he is told that his servant had been right all along, Black Liberator becomes furious and exiles his teacher as well. He quickly plunges into a life of hedonism and "an ocean of errors" and spends the rest of his days wearing human skins and eating human flesh, living in charnel grounds, conducting orgies, and performing terrible asceticisms.

Upon his death, Black Liberator descends further into a series of violent and terrible rebirths that reach their nadir in the Avīci hell, where he is tortured incessantly. During a brief moment of reflection on why all this is happening to him, the buddha Vajrasattva appears to him and explains that it is all due to his own karma. This engenders an instant of remorse for his past deeds, a moment that frees him from the Avīci hell, though only into a neighboring hell that is almost as bad, where he remains for more millions of lifetimes. Finally the end of the aeon arrives in a great conflagration, but even this is not enough to pierce the thick fog of ignorance surrounding the future Rudra, and he continues to take rebirth in the newly formed universe. Gradually he rises up the rungs of rebirth, usually as one kind of demon or another, and ultimately is born into our world, on the island of Laṅka.

The infant's prostitute mother dies in childbirth, and the locals leave the illegitimate child on his dead mother's breast in the cemetery. There, the child subsists by devouring his mother's corpse followed by all the other corpses there, growing stronger and gaining power over the demonic beings inhabiting the cemetery. He soon becomes leader of all the evil beings there, and gruesome descriptions of his appearance and lifestyle close the first chapter of the myth.

The next chapter, 21, provides a teaching on karma in terms of nine mistaken views and the terrible rebirths to which each may lead. Chapter 22 returns us to Rudra, who continues to grow in strength by defeating increasingly powerful opponents. Having already overpowered the beasts and demons of Laṅka, the next target of his jealous fury is the demon-king of the island, Rāvaṇa, who is himself a Buddhist teacher with many followers. Rāvaṇa understands that he cannot defeat Rudra but foresees that a fearsome *heruka* buddha will be arriving soon for a final showdown at which the tantras will be taught for the first time in this aeon. Perceiving this, Rāvaṇa instructs his disciples to indulge the vile demon, and they all surrender to Rudra's wrath. Rudra now turns to the various Hindu gods and their wives, followed by the Buddhist *śrāvaka* monks, who are unable to withstand the terrible tests that Rudra demands. Finally, Rudra dismisses even Hayagrīva, the wrathful delegate of the *padma* buddha-family. The chapter ends by informing the reader that Invincible Youth, the teacher from the previous aeon, has now become the ultimate "thusness" (*de nyid*) Vajrasattva, while Denpak is now Vajradhara, the "regent" (*rgyal tshab*) Vajrasattva.

Chapter 23 is a detailed description of the emanation process by which the buddha-families arise out of emptiness to prepare the ground for the taming activities. Chapter 24 brings us to the first of the four activities that are standard in the later tantric ritual materials, that is, pacification, enhancement, coercion, and violence. First the buddhas send forth a peaceful emanation of Śakyamuni, but to no avail. Then they dispatch Hayagrīva again, this time to perform the enhancement activity. Upon being threatened by Rudra, Hayagrīva pretends to retreat, but actually transforms into a desirable snack that Rudra quickly devours. From within Rudra's belly, the *tathāgata* expands his body immensely, bursting out through the top of Rudra's head and through the soles of his feet. This causes Rudra such agonies as to purify him and prepare him for his eventual subjugation. Still, Hayagrīva himself is not able to perform the final deed, and he withdraws.

Once again, the buddhas call a meeting to discuss the need for the last two activities, those of coercion and violence. Their discussion culminates in the emanation of the menacing Chemchok (Skt. *Mahottara*) Heruka for this purpose. Now in chapter 26, the buddhas transform Denpak, Rudra's servant-of-old, into Vajrapāṇi, who will direct the proceedings. Vajrapāṇi appoints Hayagrīva to go to Laṅka to act as the witness for what is to come. Then all the buddhas focus their attentions into a single point (the Great Perfection, explains Nupchen's commentary), and Vajrapāṇi creates clouds of Vajrakīlaya emanations, who descend upon the mountain in Laṅka.

Now the taming begins in earnest. Chapter 27 opens with a description of Rudra's palace, a kind of anti-mandala, with Rudra and his queen, the goddess of desire, Krodhīśvarī, at the center surrounded by their terrifying minions. When Rudra leaves home with all his male retinue, the buddhas emit Vajrakumāra Bhurkuṃkūṭa ("Vajra-Youth Heaping Moles") for the activity of coercion. This buddha first consumes the sea of filth and blood surrounding Rudra's palace, thus purifying the ground. He then copulates with all the demonesses and goddesses remaining there, and they give birth to other Buddhist emanations—the *gaurīs, piśācīs*, and so forth—who will soon replace them in the newly purified mandala palace. Finally, the buddha takes on Rudra's likeness and appears before the queen. He seduces her and implants the seed-syllable *oṃ* in her womb. All the clouds of Vajrakumāras simultaneously dissolve into her womb, and Vajrapāṇi teaches the now-overpowered queen and her servants the *Compendium of Intentions*. This completes the activity of coercion.

When Rudra returns home, he senses something has changed. His queen soothes his agitation with the news that his own son is soon to be born. With *hūṃ* resounding *three times*, the Mahābhairava-Heruka of the *vajra* family is born from the queen. Rudra gathers his army to him with threats and exhortations to fight. The hosts of Hayagrīva, who are still watching from above, perform their nine dances to empower the *heruka*, and the three *herukas* of body, speech, and mind (*buddha, padma*, and *vajra*) thunder their exhortations for Mahābhairava to defeat the demonic horde. This alone is enough to overwhelm Rudra's entire retinue, and the demon is left alone, faced with the wrathful *heruka*.

Rudra makes a series of increasingly desperate attempts to fight, pronouncing his mantras and mutating into larger and larger forms, each of which is easily matched and surpassed by the buddha, until the demon collapses in a stupor. The *heruka* plunges a trident into Rudra's chest and swallows him whole. Within the *heruka*'s belly, Rudra is purified. He experiences the bliss of the *Gaṇḍhavyūha* buddhafield and perceives all the terrible sufferings he has caused. Then he is ejected through the *heruka*'s anus, whereupon he pleads for the buddha to liberate him once and for all. Swearing allegiance to the buddha, he offers his entire retinue up to him.

In the short twenty-eighth chapter, Rudra tells his followers the errors of his ways and prays to the buddha for forgiveness. In chapter 29, the *heruka* teaches

Rudra about his karma and finally destroys him, "liberating" him into emptiness with a mantra. He then reconstitutes Rudra once more, now in a completely purified state.

Finally, Rudra is ready to receive initiation into the purified mandala of the *Compendium of Intentions*, and the initiation ritual is described in chapter 30. At its close, Rudra is given his new name, Black Excellence (Legden Nakpo), and appointed as the chief protector of the Gathered Great Assembly (*Tshogs chen 'dus pa*) mandala. In chapter 31, the myth's last chapter, all of Rudra's followers are also granted initiation. Each is raised to the level of tantric realization appropriate to his or her capabilities and bound by vow to remain at the mandala's periphery as its protector.

1

Evil and Ignorance in Tantric Buddhism

The Rudra myth revels in a litany of violent imagery: in its account of the wild and bloodthirsty lifetimes that precede Rudra's final birth, in how the newborn demon eats his dead mother's flesh, in the details of his hideous visage, in the carnage and the disease he wreaks upon the world, in the descriptions of his vile palace, and in the conflagration of monstrous violence that ends his terrible reign. We are supposed to be repulsed by this dreadful demon and the bloody imagery intended to reflect the horrors of his evil ways. Yet the myth's violence is not entirely one-sided, for the compassionate buddha also appears in the same demonic form and is equally vile in his own horrific manner. He too has massive wings, nine hideous heads, and eighteen hands bearing an array of terrifying implements. He too is crawling with spiders, scorpions, and snakes. He too breathes fire and tramples beings beneath his feet. Surely we are not meant to be repulsed by the buddha as well. There must be more to this violent imagery than meets the eye; it must not be just for the purpose of portraying evil. That the buddha shares Rudra's terrifying aspect should give us pause.

Indeed, the myth itself states that a superficial understanding of the tantras was precisely what led Rudra to his evil and destructive end. During his previous life as Black Liberator, while studying the tantric teachings of uninhibited spontaneity, the demon-to-be took literally the words of his master, Invincible Youth, and thereby misunderstood their deeper meaning. His fixation on literal readings and surface appearances drew him into a downward spiral of egotism in which nothing else mattered. "Though he wore the outward costume of an excellent [monk]," the myth relates, "he followed a path of evil-hearted beings." Whereas his servant, on the other hand, "despite his outward appearance as one of low rank, remained on the path to ascertaining the excellent mind."[1] In the realm of the tantras and their antinomian teachings, one must proceed carefully. Appearances may not be what they seem.

Early Western condemnations of Tibetan Buddhism as bloody demonolatry, such as those of L. Austine Waddell, were driven in large part by scholars' own violent reactions against precisely the kind of imagery that fills the Rudra myth. Despite the strength of such visceral negative responses, however, the Rudra myth suggests that some forms of violence may be more complex. The extreme reactions that violence often engenders can obscure its nobler features. The superficial appearance of tantric violence, we are told, can mask a supremely compassionate intention. This chapter investigates the nature of this concealment, this disjuncture between the unsettling appearance of Buddhist violence and its hidden pacific intention. How can violence be both destructive and compassionate? How have Buddhists distinguished compassionate violence, this supremely dangerous form of virtuous activity, from its evil twin, the demonic violence we all fear and loathe? This chapter explores these questions, all the while attempting to remain open to the ambiguities that are inherent to violence.

Violence, as Hannah Arendt has observed, is instrumental by nature.[2] It is a means to an end and as such is neither good nor evil in itself. It is justifiable only in its end, in the purpose for which it is enacted. By means of violence, one may accomplish aims that are either positive or negative. Yet violence is not just any instrument; it is the ultimate of means, the activity of last resort in the Buddhist tantras. Its methods are dramatic, and its spectacular appearance can easily distract from and obscure its merely instrumental nature. The horror of violence thereby often seems gratuitous and fundamentally evil. In spite of its powerful appearance, though, violence remains merely a morally ambiguous means. The Rudra myth involves us in all these issues, in the tensions and the concealments that lie within violence itself, and it thereby provides an opportunity for us to investigate the Buddhist approach to violence in all its complexity.

COMPASSIONATE VIOLENCE IN THE SUTRAS

On the surface, killing is forbidden in Buddhism, as is clear from the very first precept to be observed by all Buddhist devotees (*upāsaka*): to abstain from killing living beings (Skt. *prāṇātighātād viratiḥ*). Yet what this has meant in practice has not been as simple as it might seem. The idea that killing may sometimes be permissible within Buddhism appears in the tantras, but it is by no means unique to these works. Violent rituals multiplied dramatically with the emergence of the tantras from the seventh century onward,[3] but already the earlier Mahāyāna sutras had made similar ethical allowances. Even certain non-Mahāyāna Abhidharma and Vinaya commentaries had left the door open for forms of killing that were not necessarily negative.[4] Such early sources distinguished moral from immoral killing on the basis of the mental intention (*cetanā*) that accompanied the act. Killing was only immoral if it was intentional, and conversely, unintentional killing did not break the first precept. As the *Samantapāsādikā*, a fifth-century collection of Pāli commentaries on the Vinaya, explains: "The intention to kill as a result of which one produces the activity that cuts off [a being's] life-faculty is called 'killing a living being'; 'the one who kills a living being' should be understood as the person [who kills while] possessing that intention."[5]

Of course, "intention" may be variously understood. In one sense, one may not intend to kill the mosquito with one's windshield, but in another sense one knows that it almost certainly will happen when one starts the car and heads down the road on a summer night. "Intention" would seem to require some careful definition. Here too, though, early Buddhists held a relatively liberal view. The Jains, in comparison, maintained a far stricter interpretation of violent intention. For them, the intention to do violence was intrinsic to everyone short of the Jain holy man who had fully comprehended the truth of existence.[6] Violence for the Jains was thus inherent to unenlightened, *samsāric*, existence, and all were guilty of constant involvement in it. For this reason, Jain monks might wear masks to prevent unintentionally inhaling flying insects or might sweep their path with a broom to prevent unintentionally stepping on ants. For Buddhists, however, only the far grosser forms of premeditated killing counted as sinful. Murderers could even be deemed karmically innocent due to temporary insanity, as in the *Milindapañha,* in which the Buddha in a previous life as the Brahmanical sage Lomasakassapa is described as having killed "hundreds of living creatures" for a great blood sacrifice. The text is careful to highlight, however, that the bodhisattva's terrible deeds were performed "when he was beside himself with passion, not when he was cognisant of what he was doing."[7] He did not *intend* to kill the creatures, it explains, "yet at the sight of Candavatī, the king's daughter, he became beside himself, unhinged, impassioned." It was only within this confused state that he made his bloody offerings, and so he remained faultless: "Evil done by one who is unhinged, sire, is not of great blame here and now, nor is it so in respect of its ripening in a future state. . . . So, sire, there is no punishment for a madman's crime, therefore there is no defect in what was done by a madman, he is pardonable."[8] Despite their insistence on strict adherence to the first precept, then, early Buddhists made significant allowances for all those who might kill in the course of leading a more-or-less-"normal" life.

The Mahāyāna exploited this ethical loophole still further. Where the Vinaya required an at least nominally literal adherence to its rules, the Mahāyāna allowed its bodhisattvas to transcend any potential moral transgressions simply by maintaining their supreme bodhisattva vow. This vow, to work for the enlightenment of all beings, became the primary marker of morality. As long as it was for the benefit of all beings, killing was permitted. This enhanced emphasis on the actor's motivation built upon the earlier Buddhist emphasis on the power of intention. Now an altruistic motivation could trump every other ethical concern. "Because of his or her intention," wrote the third-century Indian master Āryadeva, "both virtue and sin are entirely virtuous for the bodhisattva."[9]

The Mahāyāna attitude was illustrated most famously in the *Skill-in-Means (Upāyakauśalya) Sūtra*, a Mahāyāna work that may date from as early as the turn of the common era.[10] Here Mahākaruṇā ("Great Compassion"), a bodhisattva ship captain at sea on a long voyage, discovers a thief onboard who is about to murder his five hundred fellow passengers, all merchants. The captain finds himself in a moral quandary, for if he tells the merchants of the thief's plan, they will certainly kill the thief and thereby come to suffer terrible karmic consequences for their violent act. If he does nothing, five hundred will die and their murderer will suffer the karmic consequences. The only solution, he concludes, is for him to kill the thief himself and, in doing so, accept the karmic retribution that will follow his violent act, so as to save the thief from the much worse fate that would result from his own killing of five hundred men. Paradoxically (and not insignificantly), however, precisely in sacrificing himself for the good of another, the bodhisattva escapes the negative karma normally associated with killing, and indeed, as we well know, eventually attains buddhahood.[11] The thief, meanwhile, dies to be reborn in paradise.[12]

The paradoxical nature of the bodhisattva's self-sacrifice in this story shares much in common with other Indian narrative literature on giving (*dāna*).[13] When King Śibi, for instance, offers his eyes to a blind old Brahman in the *jātaka* tales, his pains are described in gory detail, yet through his awful act of self-sacrifice, the king gains a new set of superhuman eyes that can see through walls and for a hundred *yojanas* in every direction. In fact, throughout Buddhist narrative literature, the most terrible sufferings, when endured for the sake of others, become a blissfully cathartic purification of one's attachment to self, and the violence of the act is transformed into a creative moment of selfless, compassionate enlightenment. Through self-sacrifice, violence becomes precisely the opposite of what we might normally expect: absolute love.[14]

The eleventh-century *Bodhisattvāvadānakalpalatā* reflects the two opposing sides of compassionate violence. In his account of the bodhisattva Satyavrata's sacrifice of his body to a hungry tigress, the author, Kṣemendra, describes the act in terms that accentuate simultaneously its bloody violence and its compassionate beauty: "Then the tigress, stimulated by a desire for his blood, fell down upon his broad chest as he lay immobile, tearing into it with the glistening tips of her claws, which seemed to smile with joy, as if they were engraving into his chest the wonder of his noble conduct in this world. . . . And as his unblemished chest was torn apart by the sport of the tigress' rows of claws, it looked for a moment as if it were full of shooting rays of light whose purity was as bright as the moon."[15] The wonderfully incongruous language of the account highlights the tensions that are inherent in the idea of a compassionate violence. The more excruciating and bloody the act, the more compassionate the sacrifice. In this way the disjunction between the bloody violence and the bodhisattva's compassionate intention is both terrifying and beautiful.

In another version of the same basic story that appears in the *Suvarṇabhāsottama Sūtra,* Prince Mahāsattva is devoured by a tigress and reduced to nothing more than "bones devoid of blood, flesh, and sinews, with hair scattered in all directions." Yet, "for the onlookers this has the appearance of delicately scattered lotus petals."[16] Through the bodhisattva's self-sacrifice, the putrid body, full of blood, pus, stench, and rot, is transformed into an idealized body, perfectly beautiful, filled with light, and able to perform great miracles. Again, the bodhisattva's vow purifies the act of violence, turning it into a moment of virtuous creativity. Understood within this literary context, the *Skill-in-Means Sūtra*'s story of the ship captain may be seen as just one instance of a much larger ethical trend within Buddhist narrative literature, one in which the bodhisattva transcends the apparent negativities of violence and transforms them into pure virtue by means of a radical generosity with no expectation of return. In this sense, the Mahāyāna's unprecedented emphasis on the bodhisattva vow put the bodhisattva's act of giving at the center of its approach to moral violence.

Perhaps the best-known doctrinal formulation of this Mahāyāna approach appeared in Asaṅga's fourth-century *Stages of the Bodhisattva* (*Bodhisattvabhūmi*). According to Asaṅga, and in keeping with the story of the ship captain, the bodhisattva was permitted to kill beings if he did so for compassionate reasons, to prevent them from engaging in violent acts that would lead them to hell or other sufferings. Not only did such a bodhisattva act without sin, Asaṅga explained, he even produced considerable merit through his killing.[17]

Such an approach marked a departure from the earlier Buddhist approaches to violence. Compare, for example, the well-known tale of Migalaṇḍika, the "sham recluse," found in the Pāli Vinaya. The story opens with some monks who are cultivating the Buddha's teachings on the impure in its many aspects. While the Buddha is away on retreat, the monks begin to experience violent revulsion for their own bodies. Driven to suicide by their intense shame and self-loathing, they plead for the monk Migalaṇḍika to kill them. Migalaṇḍika fulfills their wishes, but as he washes his knife in a nearby river, he begins to feel remorse for his actions. At that very moment he is visited by a vision; across the waters floats a god sent by Māra, who encourages him with these words: "It is good, it is good, o worthy man; it is good for you, o worthy man; it is rightly gotten by you, o worthy man; much merit attaches to you because you liberate the unliberated."[18] Heartened by these words, Migalaṇḍika embarks upon a killing spree, "liberating" up to sixty monks every day for over two weeks. Finally the Buddha emerges from his retreat and asks, "Ānanda, how is it that the company of monks is so diminished?" On learning what has happened, he gathers the remaining monks and rebukes them, concluding that suicide is henceforth against the rules, as is the murder of another human being for any reason.

The story may well be an implicit critique of certain early Indian religious sects that practiced ritual killing under the guise of "liberation," and as we shall see, the Buddhist tantras took up precisely this language of liberation in justifying their own forms of ritual killing. In any case, the "sham recluse" Migalaṇḍika stood as a warning for anyone who might think to interpret murder as an act of compassionate liberation. According to this story, even when requested by the victim himself, and even if that victim is impure in nature and suffering terribly, murder cannot be virtuous. The Buddha's conclusions here contrast sharply with the Mahāyāna approach expressed by Asaṅga, a view in which violence was ethically ambiguous and ultimately should be judged on the basis of the motivations behind it. Whereas in the Pāli Vinaya killing was negative, or at best neutral, in the Mahāyāna it could be meritorious. Compassionate violence (under extreme circumstances) was a doctrinal possibility.

The Mahāyāna approach to violence had a further ethical repercussion. As Asaṅga observed in his *Stages of the Bodhisattva,* if killing with compassionate intention was meritorious, then the converse must equally be true; *not* to kill when it would benefit others (as in the case of the ship captain) must be a sin.[19] A number of Asaṅga's later commentators even included among their enumerations of the secondary infractions (*duṣkṛta*) of the bodhisattva code the failure of a bodhisattva to engage in any of the seven physical and verbal nonvirtues when they would help others.[20] Thus in certain cases, not to kill could be a worse crime than to kill. Moral killing was no longer determined by a *lack* of intention; now it could include even intentional killing. As long as one killed in order to benefit all beings and reduce suffering in the universe overall, even premeditated murder was acceptable, if not required; not to do so was a sin.

At this point we should perhaps remind ourselves that despite the philosophical conjecturing seen in the *Stages of the Bodhisattva* and the other texts discussed so far, the majority of Buddhists—Mahāyāna or otherwise—generally condemned killing. Not killing remained the first of the five precepts (*pañcaśikṣā*) and thus a foundation of Buddhist ethics. Not killing was the rule to which compassionate violence was still the exception. Nonetheless, even before the advent of the tantras and their violent rhetoric, the necessary doctrinal pieces were in place. Buddhists had long since made allowances for the possibility of a compassionate violence, and the tantras, with their wrathful rituals of exorcism and sorcery, simply codified the violent acts that had already been widely accepted as a possibility within exoteric Mahāyāna Buddhism. In this sense the Rudra myth may even be seen as a kind of tantric reformulation of the earlier Mahāyāna tale of the ship captain and the thief. Like the earlier tale, the Rudra myth too set an example for future Buddhists, for when and how compassionate violence might be permitted.

RITUAL VIOLENCE IN THE EARLY TANTRAS

The Rudra myth, of course, pushed the violence to an extreme, and this is not surprising given its literary setting; even today the tantras are infamous for their promotion of transgressive behaviors. By the late eighth century, ritualized sex and violence (*sbyor sgrol*) had become central to the identity of the Mahāyoga tantras. Followers of the tantras were said to sleep in cemeteries, rub cremation ashes on their bodies, eat human flesh, engage in sexual intercourse with outcaste women, kill indiscriminately, and the list goes on.[21] Our Rudra myth is just one example of this self-consciously antinomian language.

Today most scholars agree that tantric Buddhism proper began around the second half of the seventh century C.E. Its roots extend back into the late fifth and sixth centuries, and arguably all the way to the Vedas, but only in the seventh century did the self-proclaimed "tantras" begin to emerge. The tantras were framed as the ritual and esoteric counterparts to the exoteric and generally more doctrinally focused sutras. Like the sutras, the tantras claimed to be "the word of the buddha" (*buddha-vācana*), though they were more often ascribed to Vajrasattva, Vajradhara, Vajrapāṇi, or some other "cosmic" buddha, rather than to the historical Buddha Śākyamuni himself. In addition to an unprecedented focus on ritual and a rhetoric of secrecy, the tantras exhibited a fascination with violence, introducing a variety of rites that transformed Buddhist practice. The introduction was a gradual process, however, as tantric violence gained acceptance only slowly within more-orthodox circles.

The earliest violent rites often appeared embedded within a larger ritual triad, three types of fire offerings (*homa*)—offerings for pacifying, enhancing, and violence—a triad clearly imported, along with many other elements, from the earlier Vedic ritual tradition. The *Susiddhikāra* provides one such example. Probably dating from the first half of the seventh century, in later times this text would become central to the so-called Kriyā tantras, the lowest doxographical category of tantric texts that included many of the earliest tantras. Perhaps reflecting the still nascent state of violent ritual, the *Susiddhikāra* dedicates a single chapter to the three kinds of fire offering, entitled "The Section on the Ritual Manuals for Pacification, Enhancement, and Violence."[22] With compassionate intentions, the reader is instructed to perform the violent offering in a state of anger. Wearing red or blue robes sprinkled with water or blood, one should "smear [the ritual space] with [a mandala of] black earth, or alternatively smear it with the dung of a donkey, a camel, and so forth, or with ashes from a cemetery." Having scattered red or blue flowers upon the mandala as an offering, one prepares the necessary substances for oblation into the fire, items all foul and bitter in nature—one's own blood, dirt from the soles of one's feet, feces, human hair, thorns, and the like. One then digs a triangular hearth of specific dimensions, places sticks of wood cut from the base of certain trees, and lights them with a fire taken from a cremation pyre, from the house of an outcaste, or made by striking together bones or rocks. And finally, "taking cremation ashes, charcoal, chaff, and the like, or using the *homa* substances—salt, mustard, and so forth—fashion an effigy of your enemy. Proclaiming the name specific to that effigy, chop it repeatedly and perform the *homa* [that is, throw it into the fire]. Alternatively, one may crush its heart [underfoot] and then commence the *homa* activities having crushed its heart [underfoot]. As in the *homa*, one should crush the wrathful effigy while performing the recitations. Alternatively this accomplishment is also explained in the *kalpas* and the *dhāraṇī* ritual manuals."[23] The tantra goes on to warn that such rites are to be performed not against just anyone, but only in cases where they will bring greater benefit for all beings: "Such wrathful rites should be directed for the benefit of those who deprecate the words of the *sugata*, those who are inherently evil and hateful, those who harm the three jewels, those who hold wrong views, sinners, those who are immoral or argumentative, or those who injure the guru."[24]

As in the case of the ship captain, then, the rites are ultimately supposed to benefit the victims, as their immediate sufferings will save them from a more-dire future. The precise nature of the resultant sufferings may vary, as explained in the very next passage: "Such rites can cause limbs to fail, expel [one's enemies], or cause division [among friends]. They can produce serious illness, destruction, and torment, or they can cause [others] to become joyless. Or, they also may kill."[25]

It is notable that this final and ultimate result of killing is missing from the Chinese translation of the *Susiddhikāra*. Killing, in the Chinese version, was not part of the ritual bargain, at least not explicitly. This might seem a minor textual difference, were it not for the fact that soon after, in the same chapter, a related passage that *does* appear in the Chinese is conversely absent from the Tibetan. The Chinese passage insists that one should stop short of killing the victim and, if need be, reverse the ritual's effects by performing a pacification (*śāntika*) rite: "Once you have performed this rite, punished the person's wickedness, and consummated your wishes, if you see with eyes full of anger that he is becoming increasingly critically ill and will die before long, you should quickly perform the pacification and then slowly perform the enhancement. You should not continue with this [violent] rite."[26]

A Sanskrit version of the *Susiddhikāra* has not emerged, but two possible explanations may be offered for these textual differences. Either the Chinese translation preserves an earlier form of the Indian text that was later updated to make it more violent, once killing had become a more-accepted part of the tantric ritual repertoire, or (perhaps more likely) the Chinese translators went to considerable lengths to edit the original at multiple points in order to suppress the most violent aspects of the rite. In either case, it seems that ritual killing—even killing by indirect magic—encountered some initial resistance within some Buddhist circles (whether in India or China remains unclear). Violent rites had begun to appear, but some felt they should stop short of killing.

Only gradually, then, did ritual killing gain acceptance within Buddhist practice. The tale of the ship captain and the musings of Asaṅga had long since allowed for compassionate killing *in theory*, but it seems to have been quite another matter to put such doctrines into practice, much less into ritual practice, in a form that anyone might perform. The shift from the earlier narrative accounts and doctrinal expositions of Buddhist violence to the newly popular genre of ritual manuals, which provided practical instructions on how to enact these same kinds of violence, was an uneasy one. The new tantric rituals lent an immediacy and a reality to these teachings that many rejected. Similarly, in the case of demon taming, early Buddhists may have chanted sutras or prayed to the Buddha to pacify some worldly disturbance, but to enact the violent destruction of another being was beyond the pale. For a religion that had long prided itself on its advocacy of nonviolence and its rejection of blood sacrifice, such rites seemed downright un-Buddhist.

By the late seventh century the so-called Yoga tantras were beginning to emerge, bringing with them the latest developments in Buddhist ritual theory and practice. The most influential of these new works was the *Compendium of the Principles of All Tathāgatas* (*Sarvatathāgata-tattvasaṃgraha*). The *Compendium of Principles* gave the ferocious deities and the violent rituals that had appeared in earlier works a more-central role. One of its four sections was entirely dedicated to the *vajra* family of buddhas, and more specifically to the wrathful deity Trailokyavijaya, the "Conqueror of the Three Worlds."[27] This *vajra* section contained what would soon become the most influential rendition of the Rudra subjugation myth. Though not the earliest, it became the classic formulation that spread throughout Buddhist India, providing the narrative structure for innumerable retellings, including our own ninth-century version. The myth was deployed across the tantric literary spectrum to justify the many violent rites that proliferated in the years following its composition. The *Compendium of Principles* myth is significantly shorter than our own (translated in appendix A). It lacks any mention of Rudra's (there called Maheśvara) karmic origins in a past aeon, and opens instead with the bodhisattva Vajrapāṇi's wrathful manifestation atop Mount Sumeru in order to subjugate the miscreant demon. A series of insults and warnings are exchanged, until Maheśvara and his consort, Umā, are finally crushed underfoot by Vajrapāṇi. As in our own version of the myth, Maheśvara is then reborn in a purified form and initiated into the work's principal mandala, here called the *Vajradhātu maṇḍala.*[28]

Like the *Susiddhikāra* and other similarly early works, the new Yoga tantras also taught violent rituals for subjugating or exorcising demons. The new instructions were more complex, but the ritual core remained largely the same. The violent rites were couched within a now slightly expanded set of *four* ritual activities—pacification, enhancement, *coercion*, and violence. The *Compendium of Principles* does not provide much detail on what a Yoga tantra-style violent rite might have looked like, but we can turn to the Dunhuang manuscripts to get some possible ideas:

> If one wants to perform the activity of cutting and violence, one should perform as above, except that all the implements should be a dark blue-black. Cut thoroughly with [a weapon of] red sandalwood. At midday or midnight, face toward the southern direction. Seated in an assembly, perform the activities with a wrathful mind. [Recite the mantra:] "*Hūṃ ma ma a mu kan pari-vidhana cinta cinta hūṃ ni a hūṃ phaṭ hūṃ ma ma a mu kan a ta yā maraya hūṃ ni a hūṃ phaṭ.*" Always place the object of accomplishment in front

> [of yourself], and protect. Having led forth the evil one, take the effigy or a thread-cross made from *kuśa* grass and enact the weapon or the many *mudrās* [upon it]. For the fire offering, do the same. Then raise up [the victim] with your mind. Wash with milk and bestow the sacrament, [reciting,] "*Oṃ vajra samaya hūṃ*." Then having completed the activity, perform the worship and praises. Offer the desirable objects and mentally undo the boundaries. Bind the root *mudrā* and pray with the verse, "Having definitively accepted me, protector endowed with awareness and mantra, please proceed into bliss." While reciting those words, imagine that he, along with his retinue, departs. Then protect yourself by doing the *mudrās* and the associated mantras at the five bodily points. Having protected the deity and the equipment, act happily.[29]

As in the earlier *Susiddhikāra*, the destruction of an effigy remains at the heart of the rite. Only the surrounding ritual context has changed to include many of the standard Yoga tantra ritual elements. One must use the right kind of implements, perform the proper *mudrās* and recite the corresponding mantras, and after the destruction is complete, one should make offerings, release the ritual space, dismiss the deities, protect one's body, and engage in celebration (typically in the form of songs and dancing).

In the second half of the eighth century, the violent rhetoric of the tantras increased still further with the emergence of the so-called Mahāyoga ("Greater Yoga") tantras. With these works, tantric transgression reached its zenith. Spontaneous and mad behavior was promoted as a rapid, if dangerous, path to direct enlightenment. Ritualized forms of sex and violence (*sbyor sgrol*) were central to these new antinomian texts. On prescribed days of the month, Mahāyoga practitioners were exhorted to celebrate ritual *gaṇacakra* feasts, described in the tantras as Dionysian gatherings around food, alcohol, sex, and sometimes blood sacrifice. Such was the literary matrix from which our own Rudra myth emerged.

The *Guhyasamāja Tantra* offers a classic example of a Mahāyoga tantra. In its fifth chapter, the five precepts of abstinence and pure conduct are turned on their heads. Each of the precepts—not to kill, not to lie, not to steal, not to engage in sexual misconduct, and not to become intoxicated—is here transformed into its opposite: "Those sentient beings who kill people, who take pleasure in telling lies, and who covet the wealth of others, those who enjoy constant sex, and who eat feces and urine—those are [worthy] vessels for accomplishment."[30] And as with the normal precepts, any violations of these tantric vows may be purged by means of confession. Thus the *Confession for the Root and Branch Downfalls of the Vajrayāna*, another tantric text attributed to King Indrabhūti, includes a confession for one who has neglected his or her vow to kill: "I confess," it reads, "that I have not annihilated and been loving toward those persons who do not believe in, or who despise and deprecate, the lama, the three jewels, and the Vajrayāna of Secret Mantra."[31] In this way the tantras mirrored exoteric Buddhism, repeating and inverting its doctrines and rituals, and thereby confounding its normative divisions of sacred and profane.

The extent to which such violent transgressions were actually practiced remains unknown. Western scholars have disagreed over how to interpret these kinds of passages. Some have suggested that they were taken literally, but the tradition's abundant commentarial literature tends to take such teachings metaphorically, as veiled references to more-acceptable Buddhist ideas.[32] To kill one's father and engage in intercourse with one's mother may, for example, simply mean to destroy all concepts and rest in the space of emptiness. It is certainly relevant that many Indian tantric adherents appear to have been monks themselves, well trained in the canonical teachings of the sutras. In all likelihood, both approaches probably existed among the tantric Buddhists of early medieval India, with most preferring to understand them figuratively and a few actually performing the rites. Whether the occasional literalist should be labeled a heretic depends, of course, on one's perspective, and this is an issue to which we shall return in later chapters.

In either case, whether the violent language of the tantras was taken metaphorically or literally, its *literary* function remained essential. As literature, the tantras and their associated ritual manuals bestowed fearsome powers upon their followers, by depicting them as religious radicals who transcended all societal taboos. Thus the *possibility* that the violent language of the tantras might be taken literally fed their power and increased their appeal. The mere perception, whether true or not, that the followers of the Mahāyoga tantras were the kind of people who might perform such outrageous acts was enough to make them dangerously liminal beings who dwelt beyond society's norms. This literary effect would have been as real for the tantric practitioner as it was for members of the wider society.

The tantras thus created a mystique around their followers, an air of danger, secrecy, and power that made them feared but, on certain occasions, required. Known for their magical abilities, *tāntrikas* were called upon by villagers and kings alike to perform their formidable rites.[33] People who might sleep and eat in the cemeteries among dead bodies, wild animals, and ghosts must be mad, but also in some way fearsome. These were experts in all things demonic, from protective rites and exorcisms to divination and sorcery. Their power lay precisely in their supposed transgressions. Thus Rudra's dominion over the triple world of demons, gods, and humans is described at the beginning of our myth's twenty-fourth chapter as the direct result of his "mistaken ascetic practices" (*log pa'i dka' thub*). Likewise, while he was still in his childhood cemetery, the simple act of Rudra's eating human flesh gave him "an automatic power (*rang bzhin gyi mthu*) by which the hosts of *mātṛkās*, *piśācas*, and *pretas*, as well as the hordes of non-humans, came under his control." Similar wording appears too in a Dunhuang manuscript that contains a lengthy discussion of the transgressive Mahāyoga practices. There it is claimed that the euphemistically named "ambrosias" of feces, semen, and human flesh, if eaten regularly, would bestow automatic powers (*rang gzhin gyis grub pa can gyi rdzas*). "Henceforth by those means," it asserts, "one will no longer suffer from illness. Moreover, one will become accomplished at clairvoyance, flying, invisibility, teleportation, and the like."[34]

That both of these passages emphasize the "automatic" nature of the powers gained is a testament to the sheer force of the transgressions involved. These were acts that were chosen specifically for their shock value within the traditional Indian culture of the period, particularly within the royal courts, and this alone made them powerful. Concerns with ritual purity had been central to Indian society from at least the time of the *Laws of Manu* (first century B.C.E. to second century C.E.), and the laws and strictures that accompanied them were basic to royal authority. Though such ritual concerns had been nominally rejected by early Buddhists, the vocabulary of purity and pollution continued to pervade Buddhist doctrinal discussions,[35] and with the rise of the Kriyā-style rituals in the sixth and seventh centuries, the Brahmanical purification rites had fully returned to the tradition. Thus when the Mahāyoga tantras expressly advocated overturning these laws, they struck at the heart of these Indian sensibilities. Their claims alone, not to care about the fundamental rules that governed Indian society, were powerful enough to place their adherents beyond the worldly realm and to gain them the respect and patronage of kings.

While the violence of the tantras' language may account, in part, for their status within Indian society, there was nothing uniquely Buddhist about this literary function. Śaivas, Śāktas, Vaiṣṇavas, and others used nearly identical narratives, rituals, and imagery to portray themselves as similarly powerful beings. The same basic strategies were shared by tantric groups across the religious spectrum, and for this reason whatever marked the Buddhist tantras as uniquely Buddhist had to be located elsewhere, outside this vital literary function. The transgressive language of the tantras may have been key to their power, but in and of itself it could not determine the sectarian affiliations of these controversial works. For the Buddhists to differentiate their particular forms of tantric violence from those of others, they had to claim some crucial, if invisible, difference. Earlier Mahāyāna authors had distinguished their own compassionate violence from ordinary deluded violence by highlighting the beneficent intentions that underlay it. Now the tantras had to make a similar distinction, by stressing the importance of a similarly hidden element within their own violent myths and rituals. It is to this subtle distinction that we now turn.

DISCERNING ORTHODOX VIOLENCE: BUDDHA VS. RUDRA

It is important to recognize just how widespread the tantric turn was in early medieval India. It was by no means limited to Buddhism. Ritual techniques largely identical to those of the Buddhists had developed simultaneously—and in many cases earlier—across the Indian religious field, in Śaiva, Vaiṣṇava, and Jain circles alike. As Ronald Davidson recently observed, competition for royal patronage was fierce both within and between these different tantric sects.[36] India's political world had fragmented following the collapse of the Gupta Empire in the fifth century, and the feudal systems that replaced it were mirrored in the religious world by intense rivalries between religious groups. As the tantric ritual technologies were widely adopted, the new ritual resemblances that resulted can only have heightened sectarian anxieties. The common acceptance of similar tantric practices by Buddhists, Brahmans, and other religious groups blurred many older ritual distinctions. Thrust into this new world of feudal politics, Buddhists had to struggle to distinguish themselves from their close competitors.

To some degree, the Rudra-taming myth reflects these burgeoning sectarian rivalries. Rudra and Maheśvara are both epithets of the god Śiva, so by destroying Śiva and binding all the Brahmanical gods into service, the buddhas were not only providing a model for subsequent rituals of demon taming; they were also demonstrating Buddhism's superiority over Brahmanism, and Śaivism in particular. Certainly the social realities of early medieval India were not the only factors driving the Rudra/Maheśvara narrative. Buddhist accounts of demon taming were popular long before the advent of the tantras. Śākyamuni's subjugation of Māra on the night of his enlightenment represents just one particularly obvious example, and Māra's continuing influence in the tantras is apparent where the *Compendium of Principles* describes him as a bodhisattva produced out of the violence (*maraṇa*) and the firmness of Vajrasattva's meditative concentration.[37] Even specifically Rudra-focused subjugation narratives were well known from an early date. The *Xianyu jing*, a Chinese collection of Buddhist tales dating from the early fifth century, includes a popular story in which the monk Śāriputra subjugates the demon Raudrākṣa so that the Jetavana monastery garden could be constructed. The tale is depicted in several Dunhuang cave murals, all from the Northern Zhou to early Tang dynasties.[38] Thus already by the fifth century a number of the Rudra myth's key elements were in place; already Raudrākṣa had been portrayed as a powerful magician and leader of a band of local heretics who required taming before a given site could be claimed for a new Buddhist monastery.

Despite the influence of such popular tales on our own Rudra myth, there can be little doubt that real sectarian tensions also contributed to its narrative.[39] With the advent of the *purāṇas* and the tantras in the early medieval period, demon-taming narratives proliferated still further, recounted by Śaivas, Vaiṣṇavas, and Buddhists alike. In Śaiva versions, Śiva played the role of tamer, subjugating the gods and demons of India.[40] The Buddhist myth simply turned the tables, imitating much of the content but recasting Rudra as the worldly demon in need of taming by wrathful buddhas, while working Buddhist ritual elements, doctrines, and symbols into the narrative mix.

The degree of imitation between Buddhist and Śaiva tantric circles is made explicit at numerous points in our myth. The depiction of Śiva-Rudra's palace that opens chapter 27 is clearly meant to mirror descriptions of Buddhist mandalas found in the Mahāyoga tantras. Only the inhabitants of the mandala's central core have been replaced with Śaiva characters. Normally populated by the principal buddha and his consort, along with representatives from each of the other four buddha-families in his or her respective cardinal direction, the center is now dominated by Rudra and his consort. Even more blatant, though, is how the wrathful *heruka* buddha defeats Rudra by mimicking his physical appearance and even his mantra, adding only the single syllable *hūṃ* at the end. Thus on folio 207, Rudra shouts his spell, "*Rulu-rulu bhyo*," and mutates "into a wrathful appearance with three heads, six arms, and four legs." To which the buddha responds by imitating Rudra's appearance and replying, "*Rulu-rulu hūṃ bhyo*." The tantra explains that, "Pronouncing the five seed [syllables] of [Rudra's] *saṃsāric* [mantra] empowered with [the further *hūṃ*,] the indestructible syllable of his blessing, [the buddha] thereby stole [Rudra's] speech emanation." Finally, when Rudra and his demonic horde are initiated into the Buddhist mandala, the buddha adopts the horde and takes Rudra's ornaments as his own.[41] The myth's authors were well aware of both the tensions and the similarities between the Buddhist and Śaiva tantric traditions.

The ambivalent relationship between the buddha and Rudra became a topic of much debate among later Tibetan commentators. In Tibet, of course, the Indian social realities behind the myth's characters were no longer of much relevance; now the main concerns were more philosophical than sectarian.

Almost every major Tibetan commentary on the myth included a discussion of how Rudra should best be understood, whether he is ultimately identical to or different from the buddha, and the question was usually asked in terms of whether he is an emanation (*sprul pa*) of the buddha or a fully autonomous being (*rang rgyud pa*). In the end, the tradition reached a more-or-less-unanimous decision not to decide. The relationship between the buddha and Rudra, and thus too between just and unjust violence, was simply too complex to answer definitively. An early example of one such discussion is found among the writings of Katok Dampa Deshek, the twelfth-century founder of Katok monastery. A portion of it is reproduced here to provide some sense of the issues at stake:

> In the *Parinirvāṇa Sūtra* it says, "Child of good lineage, do not think of that demonic evildoer in the time of that age as different from yourself." Thus even a demon is without autonomy. Because he is asserted as an emanation of the *bhagavat* himself, even Rudra is without autonomy. In the end, he is an emanation of the buddha himself. On the other hand, if he were solely an emanation and not autonomous, there would also be problems. . . . If Rudra were only an emanation, then by implication the three negative rebirths [of animals, ghosts, and hell beings] would also have to be emanations, and that would be a problem. To someone who thinks that might be acceptable, [we would point out that] if the three negative rebirths were merely emanations, there would be the problem that the ripening of virtuous and sinful karma must be false, and thus it would contradict the general teachings. Therefore Rudra must be said to be both autonomous and an emanation. We do not it find a problem that Rudra is an emanation, and we [also] find it suitable that Rudra be taken as autonomous for the purposes of this myth.[42]

From the ultimate perspective of the tantras, then, Rudra in all his horrific aspects is no different from the buddha. This is precisely the kind of outrageous claim for which the tantras are so infamous (though here the cited source is notably the Mahāyāna *Parinirvāṇa Sūtra*). Yet, as Dampa Deshek observes, such a transgressive and antinomian statement threatens the very foundations of Buddhist doctrine. By challenging any meaningful distinction between buddha and Rudra, good and evil, happiness and suffering, or virtue and sin, the myth is in danger of undercutting "the general teachings" of Buddhism on causality and the very order of the universe. All moral judgment might become impossible. Despite this fearsome prospect, Dampa Deshek is clearly unwilling to dilute the tantras' rhetoric of radical transgression and concludes that the only solution is to accept the possibility of both perspectives being true. However paradoxical it may seem on its surface, Rudra's violence is both identical to and different from the buddha's. The distinction between compassionate and demonic violence is at once absolutely necessary and impossible.

This is the central point of the Rudra myth. Indeed, this fundamental quandary, which lies at the root of the Mahāyoga tantras and their violent teachings, marks precisely the point over which the buddha and Rudra diverge. As close as these two forms of violence—Buddhist and Śaiva—may appear, they are understood by orthodox Buddhists to be infinitely distant. Rooted in the subtlest of distinctions, they are also polar opposites. Their differences mean everything, distinguishing good from evil, *nirvāṇa* from *saṃsāra*, and buddhas from demons, yet the vast gulf that divides them originates, according to the myth's own narrative, in a mere instant of misrecognition, in a moment that occurred in the distant past of time immemorial.

The Rudra myth opens with the aeon called "Joyous" (Ānanda) in the buddhafield of "Manifest Joy" (Abhirati), where we are introduced to three characters: a Buddhist teacher named Invincible Youth and his two students, a wealthy householder named Black Liberator and his servant Denpak. Under the guidance of Invincible Youth, the two students train together in the tantric "path of yoga." In accordance with the common tantric espousal of spontaneity in action, Invincible Youth explains that his path consists of simply "whatever occurs in the present" (*da lta nyid du 'byung ba dag*). Pleased with this idea, Black Liberator reflects back his understanding of this pithy teaching, saying, "I too will adopt your path in which nothing is prohibited." To this, the teacher grants his approval: "Yes. Very good. Do so."

Not long after this seminal event, Black Liberator and Denpak begin to realize they have arrived at very different readings of this same teaching. The problem, we are told, is that Black Liberator has taken the teacher's words literally, while his servant has comprehended the ultimate meaning behind the words. Thus Black Liberator becomes attached to a life of extreme hedonism, while Denpak recognizes the key point of suchness, of resting in the natural state of things. On the surface, their two approaches seem identical. Sharing as they do the same fundamental instructions, their differences are inexpressible in words. Yet the karmic results of their respective understandings diverge quickly and dramatically. From that very moment, Black Liberator commences his descent into the hells that eventually culminates in his rebirth as Rudra, while Denpak rises inexorably to become Vajrapāṇi, the enlightened tamer of the future Rudra.

At this point the myth's ninth-century Tibetan commentator, Nupchen Sangye Yeshe, enters into an extensive discussion on how to understand this crucial moment of divergence. He explains that because of Black Liberator's disagreement with his teacher and servant,

> the technique was severed and he became enraged with his master, which was a sin of immediate retribution and a fundamental transgression. These were the cooperating causes and conditions. . . . [As for] the associated cause, it was his not understanding the secret meaning due to his being obscured by intrinsic ignorance, that is, his not realizing the hidden secret. He was drawn into partiality, agreeing [only] with himself without examining by means of reasoning, scripture, and pith instructions. And therefore he practiced perverted practices, which were the conditions.[43]

In order to unpack this rather dense passage, some background may be in order. Nupchen reads the myth's opening chapter as an overall account of the causes for Rudra's eventual appearance in the world.[44] In clashing with his teacher, Nupchen explains, Black Liberator activated the so-called cooperating cause for his future demonhood. This combined with the "associated cause," that is, Black Liberator's misunderstanding of the tantric teachings due to his "intrinsic ignorance." To these later were added the common conditions, that is, the various nefarious practices in which he subsequently engaged. Thus Black Liberator's downfall was twofold. It was both a ritual downfall, as he broke his vows of obedience to his master, and a doctrinal one, as he misunderstood the hidden meaning of the tantras due to his original intrinsic ignorance (Skt. *sahajāvidyā*; Tib. *lhan cig skyes pa'i ma rig pa*).

Nupchen explains his use of this latter technical term elsewhere in the same commentary. Chapter 55 of the *Compendium of Intentions* falls under Nupchen's discussion of Atiyoga (otherwise known as Dzogchen, or the "Great Perfection"). The chapter focuses on the procedure by which all of existence unfolds out of an originary mind of enlightenment. It explains the process in terms of the eight consciousnesses of Indian Yogācāra thought. The chapter is lengthy and complex, but in brief, it describes how the foundation (*ālaya*) is either realized or not as identical with the mind of enlightenment.[45] Recognition is enlightenment, but nonrecognition brings the foundation consciousness (*ālaya-vijñāna*), afflicted thought (*kliṣṭa-manas*), mind and the five sense consciousnesses, and the rest of *saṃsāra*. In this sense, the foundation encompasses both enlightenment and ignorance, good and evil. As Nupchen writes, "It is the fundamental basis for the afflicted and for the completely pure."[46] "By the power of realization or non-realization," adds Nupchen's early twentieth-century commentator, "[the foundation] appears as the two kinds of divisions into good and evil."[47] The ramifications of Nupchen's early Atiyoga approach to the foundation and the eight consciousnesses would continue to be developed for centuries to come. As later Tibetan writers on Dzogchen observed, the gradual unfolding of consciousness into increasingly coarse forms may be understood as either a cosmogonic process, describing the origin of beginningless *saṃsāra*, or a phenomenological one, tracing the momentary emanation of concepts out of emptiness.[48] In this sense, the universe is collapsing and being reborn at every instant, the phenomena of *saṃsāra* withdrawing into the foundation and, propelled and shaped by our own fears and karmic predispositions, reemerging once more in its variegated forms as wisdom and ignorance, good and evil.

The crucial statement for our purposes, however, appears near the beginning of Nupchen's discussion of this process, where he explains, "Mistaking the foundation arises from intrinsic ignorance."[49] Intrinsic ignorance, then, is behind this most fundamental of errors, the nonrecognition of the foundation, and in this sense intrinsic ignorance is the subtlest of all forms of ignorance, one that pervades all of existence.

Returning once more to Nupchen's analysis of Rudra's causes, his point may now be discerned, for Liberator's original mistake too was caused by intrinsic ignorance: "His not understanding the secret meaning [of the tantras was] due to his being obscured by intrinsic ignorance." Nupchen is saying, in effect, that the cause for Rudra's appearance in the world was Black Liberator's misinterpretation of the tantras, itself a mythic allegory for the fundamental moment of error that lies at the root of all cyclic existence, the misrecognition of the foundational *ālaya*.[50] Faced with the undifferentiated potential of the foundation, ignorance discriminates self from other, enlightenment from suffering, buddha from demon, and good from evil. In the same way, when confronted with the uninhibited spontaneity (and thus too the violence) of the tantras, teachings that point beyond the dualistic judgments of *saṃsāric* existence, Black Liberator latched on to a superficial misinterpretation. He discriminated between his own selfish desires and those of others in a misreading that would eventually lead him to become the violent and demonic hedonist Rudra. Nupchen thus understands the Rudra myth as a narrative account of the very nature of *saṃsāric* existence, a violent universe rooted in a seminal moment of intrinsic ignorance when beings mistake their own projections onto the foundation for the foundation itself, when Rudra misunderstood the Mahāyoga teachings.

CONCLUSIONS

For early Tibetans like Nupchen, compassionate violence and demonic violence should be distinguished by understanding where the paths of Black Liberator and Denpak originally diverged. In many regards, the violent teachings of Rudra, and thus by implication of the Śaivas too, may have seemed like those of the Buddhist tantras in many regards, but the good Buddhist knew that the intentions behind them were diametrically opposed. Black Liberator performed a literal interpretation of the tantras; Denpak looked past the words to enact the hidden intention that lay beyond.

As in the earlier Mahāyāna sutras, the legitimate violence of the tantras required the proper intention of selfless compassion. Unlike the sutras, however, the tantras emphasized the secret nature of this intention, and concealment in general. We have seen how the tantras were powerful because they focused not on the sacred, but on the profane. This same focus, however, involved them in concealment and deceptive appearances. Because of their transgressions, filth, sexual practices, and violent rites, the tantras were held by their adherents to be the highest and most effective of all the Buddhist teachings, and yet they were also the most vulnerable to misinterpretation. Their transgressive language was both supremely direct and highly allusive, simultaneously rising above social norms and concealed within them. This dangerous disjunction is summarized well by one Dunhuang manuscript:

> Just as the king of the realm rules directly, the master who teaches the meaning of the tantras cuts directly to the blissful union between the words. He teaches to be appropriate that which is inappropriate for those inferior ones who are like lambs clambering up rocks. Thus [for him,] negativities themselves are good qualities. He teaches the dharma in crowded places. Using common language full of meaning, he understands its inner resplendence. He teaches with a mind that is like a hidden tortoise. Understanding the hidden secret is the quality of such a master.[51]

The compassionate intention of the tantras was to be found not through a literal reading of their words, but in the "blissful union" that lay hidden *between* the words. It was not in the words themselves, nor did it exist completely separate from them. The Rudra myth used common language that was "full of meaning," vulgar (and sometimes violent) forms that exceeded their own appearance. In this way the language of the tantras exploited the disjunction between the destructive appearance of compassionate violence and its hidden intention. One could never quite be sure the transgressive *tāntrika* was truly acting for the benefit of others, for his actions, on their surface, appeared otherwise. Was he demon or was he buddha? It was dangerously unclear, and this ambivalence was precisely what made him so powerful.

Despite the apparent similarities between the violent methods of the Buddhists and those of Rudra, early Tibetans insisted there was a crucial difference, a distinction that was in many ways invisible, concealed as it was beneath the outrageously transgressive rhetoric of the Mahāyoga tantras. The vast gulf that was held to separate orthodox and heterodox tantric violence was only to be fully understood, they claimed, in the subtlest of moments, in one's fleeting encounter with the foundation consciousness. The infinite chasm that divided the violence of buddhas from that of Rudra was thus also a hair's breadth. Compassion and hate, good and evil may be as different as night and day, but when they take up the instrument of violence, they are dangerously close.

2

Demons in the Dark

The character of Tibetan Buddhism during the early imperial period of the seventh to ninth centuries is well illustrated by the story of how the religion first arrived in Tibet: It literally *fell from the sky*. One day, as the great king Lhato Tori stood upon his palace roof, a golden casket containing the *Karaṇḍavyūha Sūtra* descended out of the sky and into his waiting hands.[1] What place could be farther from the earth, or more heavily inscribed with signs of royal and divine providence than the roof of the imperial palace? The sky itself long had been seen by Tibetans as the royal family's ultimate source of authority. Already in the *Old Tibetan Chronicle* (Pelliot tibétain 1287), the earliest Pugyal kings are described as semidivine beings who descended on cords of light from their ancestral lands in the heavens to rule the Tibetan people, ascending again once their sons were old enough to ride a horse. Similarly the *Karaṇḍavyūha*, the primary sutra dedicated to Avalokiteśvara, the "patron deity" of Tibet, and the probable literary source for the popular Tibetan mantra *oṃ maṇi padme hūṃ*, has long enjoyed close mythological ties to the Pugyal imperial line.[2] The three great Buddhist kings of the imperial period are even considered emanations of this same bodhisattva, Avalokiteśvara. Every aspect of the story, from the king and his palace to the sky and the title of the received text, bear the marks of Tibetan royal authority. Buddhism during this earliest period of Tibetan history may well be described as a top-down affair. As the nascent Pugyal Empire rose to power in the seventh and eighth centuries, it found itself surrounded on all sides by Buddhist countries. Yet the first signs of Buddhism did not come from the north, south, east, or west, but from above. For these early Tibetans, Buddhism represented a universal religion that transcended borders and promised to bestow immediate international status upon all who adopted it.

Following the empire's collapse in the mid-ninth century, however, a different kind of Buddhism began to emerge. With the closure of Tibet's monasteries and the fragmentation of Tibetan society, Buddhists could no longer depend on royal patronage. Forced to forge alliances with local rulers, they adapted the myths and rituals of the Indian tantras and tied them to specific sites in the Tibetan landscape. In the historical darkness of the late ninth and tenth centuries, Buddhism began to spread at a more grassroots level, colonizing the very soil of Tibet. This chapter takes up the theme of demon taming and explores its role during this "dark age" of Tibetan history.

According to the traditional histories, Buddhism arrived in Tibet in two waves, first during the "early dispensation" (*bstan pa snga dar*), when the Tibetan Empire was at its height, and then again in a "later dispensation" (*phyi dar*) following the rise of a new royal court in the late tenth century. These two periods of growth were separated, so the story goes, by a century-or-more-long "age of fragmentation" (*sil bu'i dus*), spanning from the mid-ninth century to the late tenth.[3] During these intervening years, the nascent traditions of Tibetan Buddhism were persecuted, monasteries fell into ruin, and the teachings were hopelessly corrupted by benighted Tibetans under the influence of demonic forces. According to tradition, this age of fragmentation was precipitated by the actions of a demonic king, Lang Darma (aka Wui Dumten). This king, we are told, single-handedly changed the course of Tibet's religious history when he sided with the evil, and by now much-embittered, Bonpo priests of Tibet's native religion against the Buddhists of the royal court. Soon after taking the throne, Lang Darma closed down the monasteries, persecuted the Buddhists, and drove many underground or into exile. It was not long before Lang Darma was assassinated by a Buddhist loyalist named Lhalung Pelgyi Dorje, but the nativist faction within the court already had gained too strong a hold over Tibet. The political situation continued to deteriorate, and Tibet was plunged into anarchy and darkness.

Scholars have recently questioned this traditional depiction of events.[4] Using documents from Dunhuang and elsewhere, they have argued that it may actually have been only the Buddhist monastic establishment that suffered, and then only from a collapse of royal patronage caused less by anti-Buddhist sentiment (though that may well have been a factor) than by the shrinking fortunes of the Tibetan Empire. Some have even suggested that Lang Darma may in fact have been a supporter of Buddhism and that the final collapse of the empire is better attributed to a disagreement over succession that followed his death.[5] Indeed, it was only with Darma's sons that the royal lineage split into the Yumten and Ösung lines. Nonetheless, whatever the political realities may have been, the

Buddhist monasteries were closed, and the only forms of Buddhism to continue through the ensuing years of political fragmentation were those less dependent on monastic institutions, in particular the esoteric teachings of the tantras.[6]

Given new evidence from Dunhuang, we may now take such recent arguments a step further to suggest that the age of fragmentation not only witnessed the *continuity* of nonmonastic Buddhism but also fostered a wide range of creative changes and developments. It seems that despite the closing of the state-sponsored monasteries in the mid-ninth century, Buddhism continued to flourish throughout the ninth and tenth centuries at the local level.[7] Compared to Tibetan writings of the later dispensation, the Dunhuang manuscripts that date from this age of fragmentation reflect a remarkable level of assertiveness on the part of Tibetans, a boldness not often seen after the tenth century.[8] With the return of monastic centers of authority, a new conservatism took hold among Tibetans of the new and old schools alike. The earlier late-ninth- and tenth-century interpretations were labeled corrupt, even as the authority of the new (*gsar ma*) Buddhists relied on the widespread acceptance of Buddhism that had been made possible by precisely those same "corrupt" interpretations.

The forms Buddhism took during these "dark" years may have been distortions in the view of *later* Tibetans, but these same corruptions were fundamental in shaping Tibetan Buddhism. Freed from the watchful eye of the imperial court and the monastic orthodoxy, Tibetans of the age of fragmentation were able to make Buddhism their own. The themes, the imagery, and the strategies they developed during these inchoate years formed the cultural foundations upon which Tibetan Buddhism would be built. Only by excavating these foundations and shedding some light on the age of fragmentation can we gain a clear appreciation of the Tibetan adaptation of Buddhism.

The importance of this period has been overlooked due largely to the paucity of sources, but also to the lingering influence of the Tibetan tradition's own historical accounts. Most modern scholars writing on early Tibet have chosen to follow the tradition's lead and focus on the significance of the early imperial period. Kapstein's recent book, *The Tibetan Assimilation of Buddhism,* for example, tells us that early Tibetans were interested in Buddhism for its international reputation, its orderliness, its rationality, and its systematic morality: "Monastic, clerical Buddhism, with its trained scholars and scribes, its language sciences and methods of translation, its libraries and catalogues, its systematicization of reasoning and debate, provided medieval Tibet with an ideal model of organized knowledge. In a sprawling empire in which the management of knowledge must have been felt as an ever more urgent concern, part of the charisma attributed to Buddhism stemmed from its particular mastery over the arts of the written word, its mastery of reason."[9] While all of this may be true, following the collapse of the Pugyal dynasty and the subsequent fragmentation of Tibetan society, a very different set of interests emerged. The adaptations of Indian tantric themes seen during these years were quite unlike those that characterized the earlier imperial period.

THE POLITICAL REGIONALIZATION OF TIBET

The death of the great Buddhist king Relpachen (aka Tritsug Detsen) in 841 C.E. marked the beginning of the end for the Tibetan Empire. According to the Chinese *Tang Annals*, Relpachen died with no heir. His successor was thus chosen from among his brothers. There is some disagreement between Chinese and Tibetan sources on when exactly Lang Darma took the throne; the Chinese say 838, while the Tibetans say 841. Relpachen apparently suffered from a serious illness during the last three years of his reign, so it may be that control of the realm during these years fell to his brother Lang Darma, who thereby became the de facto ruler until his own official enthronement in 841.[10]

In any case, by 841 considerable tensions surrounded Lang Darma's succession, and he ruled for little more than a year before being killed in 842. Darma was probably an unpopular king. The *Tang Annals* describe his rule in these terms: "He was fond of wine, enjoyed hunting, and had a taste for women; he was cruel and perverse, and lacked generosity; the disorder of the state did nothing but increase."[11] But apart from such personal foibles, the extent of Darma's overtly anti-Buddhist activities remains unclear. As is well known, the Tibetan tradition depicts him as a demonic king (in some cases, with horns on his head) bent on destroying Buddhism, but evidence from Dunhuang describes him differently, possibly even as a patron of Buddhism.[12] Even the later Tibetan sources admit he supported Buddhism in his first six months of rule and began his purges only after that.[13] These same Tibetan sources are unanimous that the Buddhist monasteries were forcibly closed during Lang Darma's reign. Yet even here we find room for doubt, and it seems that the final demise of institutional Buddhism may not have occurred until after Darma's death, as the empire fragmented into two royal lines.[14] For now, a clear answer remains impossible. We may note that Buddhists in China were undergoing their own persecutions around the same period. In Chang'an, for example, in 842, the year of Darma's death, more than three thousand monks were forcibly returned to lay life.[15]

How we interpret Darma's relationship to Buddhism further determines how we understand the reasons behind his assassination. Tradition claims he was killed by the tantric master Lhalung Pelgyi Dorje in an act of righteous vengeance (sometimes framed as a case of ritual "liberation") for his persecutions of the faith. But again a more sympathetic reading is suggested by the *Tang Annals*, which have Darma killed by his disgruntled chief minister, Bagyel Tore, who was still embittered over Darma's questionable accession to the throne.[16]

The tensions surrounding the throne's succession finally came to a head with Darma's death. Once again, there was no clear heir apparent. Some endorsed Namde Ösung, the son of Darma's younger queen, while others supported another candidate named Yumten. The latter, as the son of the elder queen, would have been the rightful heir had there not been significant questions regarding the legitimacy of his birth. The disagreements grew, and Dunhuang documents confirm that a period of violent conflict arose around this time.[17] Before long, central Tibet was divided between the two heirs, with the Yoru, or "left horn" (roughly south of the Tsangpo River), going to Ösung, and the Üru, or "center horn" (roughly north of the Tsangpo), going to Yumten.

The division of the empire left it in a chaotic and much-weakened state. Following the deaths of the two rival kings, Ösung in 893 and Yumten in c. 877, their holdings were transferred to their respective sons, Pel Khortsen and Tride Göntsen. Pel Khortsen (881–910) is often described as a weak leader. It was during his rule that Tibet's aristocratic clans desecrated the royal tombs in 901 and launched their final rebellions of 904 and 905, the latter continuing for some five years and culminating in Khortsen's murder in 910.[18] By this point, Khortsen's reputation was so badly damaged among the ruling clans that the electoral council passed over his son and turned instead to Yumten's son, Tride Göntsen. For a brief moment it seems that, in name at least, Tride Göntsen was king of all Tibet, but the title no longer sufficed.[19] Despite his good standing relative to Pel Khortsen, the authority of the throne had sunk too low, its power long since having been fragmented between Tibet's various regional principalities. Shortly after, following Tride Göntsen's death, control of the western regions of Tsang returned to the nominal control of the Ösung line, and over the following years the broken empire splintered still further into an ever-proliferating number of minor kingdoms.

As we shall see, Tibetans often view their political history through a lens of sorcery and demonology, and the age of fragmentation is no exception. Traditional accounts of the two final rebellions and the resulting collapse of imperial authority attribute them, in true Tibetan fashion, to the actions of a vengeful spirit. "All this was the doing of the *yakṣa* spirit, Drenka Pelyon," writes one sixteenth-century historian, Pawo Tsuglag Trengwa.[20] Earlier, the story goes, during Lang Darma's demonic reign, the monk Drenka Pelyon is said to have served as a virtuous minister to Relpachen, only later to be murdered by Darma's own chief minister, Bagyel Tore.[21] Haunted by the injustices done to him and to Buddhism in general, Drenka Pel is said to have lingered in the world for some fifty years as a vengeful spirit, nursing his bitterness until he was able to instigate the rebellions against the same royal line that had betrayed him.[22] Disturbed by the rebellions' chaotic aftermath, the local gods and demons of Tibet convened a council to resolve the matter. Yarlha Shampo and the other ancestral deities of the aristocratic clans appealed to Drenka Pel to create a system of regional principalities (*rje dpon tshan*) arranged around their respective divine mountains. The demon acquiesced, and a new social order of fragmented clan power was formed.

A number of political realities may be detected within this narrative. Earlier, in the seventh century, when the early Pugyal kings first brought Tibet's clan-based regional provinces under control, it is said that they too had united the corresponding ancestral mountain deities, binding them by oath to support the imperial regime.[23] Now, as the empire's power disintegrated, these same gods were released from their vows of allegiance and resurfaced to shape Tibetan society once more.

Within the ensuing environment of fragmented political power, Buddhists found themselves forging new ties with local patrons. They accomplished this in a number of ways, creating new myths and rewriting rituals in order to tie the ancestral deities of the ruling clans into a new, more-localized and nonmonastic Buddhist tradition. The fragmented political environment of these dark years encouraged a wide range of local adaptations in Buddhism that set the stage for the renaissance that was to come. In the eleventh century, as monastic institutions and a more-settled social order gradually returned, the same local ties that Buddhism had forged in the chaos of the preceding century and a half remained strong. The very landscape of Tibet had been converted.[24] Central to this conversion were the narratives and rituals of tantric Buddhism, and it is to these that we now turn.

THE AGE OF FRAGMENTATION AS A TANTRIC AGE

Even the traditional Tibetan histories agree that something unprecedented took place during this period of fragmentation, that certain nonmonastic forms of Buddhism continued to develop. More specifically, they say that Tibetans became fascinated (and sometimes even unhealthily obsessed) with the tantras.[25] The late-ninth-/early tenth-century master Nupchen Sangye Yeshe is portrayed as the embodiment of this esoteric movement, a lone protector of tantric Buddhism in benighted times. Though later sources extend Nupchen's lifespan

Figure 1: Nupchen Sangye Yeshe (photo of mural at Mindroling Monastery, Benjamin Bogin)

back into the imperial period, it is clear that he really lived somewhat later, when the age of fragmentation was, politically at least, at its darkest.[26] Nupchen's biography paints a dramatic picture of how these years and Nupchen's role came to be seen by later Tibetans (fig. 1). The following passage describes the chaotic events of the early tenth century, when the aristocratic clans rose up in a series of rebellions against the already fragmented royal court. For unknown reasons, Nupchen was drawn into the conflict. Only his expertise in violent sorcery was able to save him, and the tantric teachings he promoted, from extinction:

> [During these years,] occasions for "liberating" fiendish beings into the *dharmadhātu* by means of violent *abhicāra* presented themselves repeatedly. The circumstances for such things took the form of a series of three rebellions. As it says in [Nupchen's] *Sayings*, "Defilements emerged in the central (Dbus) province of Tibet. . . . I, Sangye Yeshe, and others like me, at the meditation hut called 'Sky of Yama' atop the black peak at Drak, spun a disruptive whirlwind, destroying thirty-seven towns around Drak. . . . I, the little monk

Nup, and others like me, generated a heartfelt intention to practice according to the dharma. I did not allow myself the anger that was practiced by [my] enemies. In order to protect the Buddha's teachings, after their anger was born, I thought to demonstrate the power of the white [dharma] and trained in the various books on black magic."

In the *Great Beard of Nup* it says, "Then when I was sixty-one in the wood male rat year [904], when my obstructing [*skeg* constellation] had befallen me, the second rebellion took place. I could not stay at Drak, so I fled to Nupyul Rong. . . . Nor could I stay there, so I occupied Nyemo Chekhar."

Thus when the rebellion began, he fled from Drak Yongdzong to Nupyul Rong. Unable to stay there too, he occupied and resided at Nyemo Chekhar in Tsang province. But he was surrounded by the army, so that the entire hillside before him was filled with soldiers. Hearing that they were making evil preparations to kill him, he flew high into the sky and spoke these words:

"All you scheming rebels, listen! May all the gods and demons of existence act as [my] mediators and witnesses! To the vow-bound, [I offer] continuous heaps of offerings. In order to seek out and protect the nectar-like excellent dharma, I have wandered throughout the world since I was thirteen years old. I have traveled to India and Nepal seven times, where I continually attended to the learned. In order to maintain the dharma as my work, I have provided for the gods. I have cultivated a mind of enlightenment for the welfare of beings, without distinguishing between the purposes of myself and others. I have fled, but to no avail; you pursued me. All the oceans of the vow-bound protectors of the teachings, all the power-wielding *vidyādharas* and *siddhas*, and all the powerful demons of Tibet, my companions without evil and without fault: turn back these rebels who have treated me this way!"

So saying, he flapped his robes three times, whereby all the vow-bound ones manifested and said, "With our power we can pulverize even Mt. Meru. We can hold a mountain on our laps. We can drain an ocean in one gulp. We can play the sun and the moon like cymbals. We can turn heaven and earth upside down. However, [these present events] are the karmic results of this master's [Nupchen's] previous lives. We did not help at those earlier occasions, so how can we destroy the world now?"

So, pulling a teak ritual dagger from the hem of his robes, [Nupchen pronounced] the life-mantras of those vow-bound ones, stabbing and rolling [the dagger], then recited, *ri pha gi māraya phaṭ!* ("Mountain over there, kill them!")[27] Thereby fire erupted from the mountain, incinerating and destroying all the armies.

To create the merit necessary for purifying that sin, he composed his *Lamp for the Eyes in Contemplation*. To his personal enemies it seemed like a savage

> act of *abhicāra*, but [Nupchen] had perfected the [practices of] "union and liberation" which embrace one's purposes in compassion. Thus the subjugated were liberated through violence, that is, there was no doubt that they were raised into the primordial buddhafield.[28]

Many of the links between the age of fragmentation and violent tantric ritual are spelled out here. In the eyes of the later tradition at least, these were desperate times, and at such moments only the violent rites of the tantras can be relied upon. Nupchen is portrayed as a solitary and persecuted protector of the faith. His training in the dark arts made him a Buddhist beacon of hope, someone with enough esoteric power to control the local gods and demons of Tibet and save the teachings.

One may also hear in such an account echoes of the Rudra myth. Rudra's mythic conquest of the universe led to its own age of darkness that made necessary the original appearance of the Buddhist tantras and their rites of violent liberation. Similarly, Tibet's age of fragmentation saw the demonic king Lang Darma destroying Buddhism, leading Tibetans astray, and forcing Nupchen's last resort—the violent liberation of his enemies. Just as the buddhas first tried to tame Rudra by means of pacification, enhancement, and coercion (the first three of the four tantric ritual activities), Nupchen is portrayed as having exhausted all other options. ("I have provided for the gods. I have cultivated a mind of enlightenment for the welfare of beings, without distinguishing between the purposes of myself and others. I have fled, but to no avail; you pursued me.") In all these ways, the rhetoric surrounding Nupchen's violent acts seems to have been drawn from that of demon taming, and perhaps even from the Rudra myth itself. The myth's influential narrative themes and imagery may be seen here shaping Tibetan history.

It remains unclear how much this story reflects actual events and Nupchen's own perceptions of his role within early Tibet. Nupchen's biography, from which the above passage is extracted, was compiled much later, in the seventeenth century, by the second head of Dorje Drak Monastery, Pema Trinle, but it purports to draw on earlier sources, some of which (including the *Sayings* and portions of the *Great Beard of Nup*, quoted above)[29] may have been composed by Nupchen himself. We also may detect some indication of Nupchen's mood in the titles he chose for his two major works: *Armor against Darkness* and *Lamp for the Eyes in Contemplation*. It seems he may indeed have viewed himself as something of a protective beacon in a time of darkness. Yet it is also sure that Nupchen was not entirely alone. Other tantric practitioners were active in his time. Another member of the Nup clan, Nup Namkhe Nyingpo, is also described fighting to protect the Buddhist teachings. By threatening the use of violent sorcery, he is said to have forced the demonic king Lang Darma to back down and agree not to oppose the lay tantric practitioners.[30]

Nupchen's own writings provide further evidence of the popularity of tantric activity in the late ninth century. In his *Armor against Darkness*, Nupchen complains repeatedly about his Buddhist contemporaries, and it is always about their miscomprehension of the tantras:

> One great person of today is [said to be] "the foundation of the dharma." But this person thinks that in Atiyoga there is a need to perceive something. In the pith instructions of this person who perceives a method [where there is none], he claims to be liberated, yet it is clear he has not attained confidence in the meaning of thusness. That blind man is like one who wishes to open a treasury casket with a bone.[31]
>
> The Conqueror said that the entities of *saṃsāra* are [themselves] the reality of suchness, but the mantrins of today don't see the meaning of this. They rejoice in their intellectualizations, which are like grains poured into a worn out sack. Through their own experience, in which they have not seen the great meaning, they say that non-action is not a basis for dharma nor an adequate object of practice, and they claim beginners must think and analyze. Such people are devoid of the great method and not worthy of immediate engagement (*gcig char 'jug pa*). Alas, such cause for compassion.[32]
>
> These [three vehicles of Mahāyoga, Anuyoga, and Atiyoga] should not be established as systems with views. . . . Nowadays there are a lot of heretics claiming to be on such a path.[33]

The classes of Mahāyoga, Anuyoga, and Atiyoga represented the cutting edge of tantric practice in Tibet at the turn of the tenth century, and these were the teachings that fascinated Nupchen and his age-of-fragmentation contemporaries. Nupchen's own writings thus confirm the later tradition's depictions of these years of fragmentation as a time when tantric practices proliferated, the difference being that where later Tibetans of the resurgent western court viewed these practices as dangerous and requiring significant prior training, Nupchen saw them in a more positive light, as powerful methods that should be embraced by all those brave enough to do so. Nupchen's approach thus contrasts with the kinds of cautionary language that took hold in certain circles following the tenth century. The teachings that Nupchen criticized as corruptions of the true dharma—teachings on the importance of perceiving something in meditation, of having a well-reasoned philosophical view and an orderly method—were what some later and more-orthodox Tibetans saw as crucial foundations that needed to be restored in the period of the later dispensation. Clearly what counted as "orthodox" was in dispute during these contentious years, and Nupchen's early tenth-century views were opposed by many who came later.[34]

Nupchen's complaints about his Tibetan contemporaries and their confused approaches to the tantras reflect tensions that were characteristic of the era. Lacking the scholarly authority of monastic institutions to decide questions of interpretation and legitimacy, Tibetans of the age of fragmentation were left to fend for themselves. Charismatic teachers could form new tantric communities and teach as they liked, establishing themselves as local sources of authority. Later writings bear witness to the existence of several such groups. In the late tenth century, for example, a teacher by the name of Buddha Star King (Sangs rgyas kar rgyal) inspired a large following with his meditative and magical abilities.[35] The Star King's notoriety eventually forced the famous translator Rinchen Zangpo (958–1055) to defeat him with a wrathful gaze that brought the levitating teacher crashing to the ground in an unconscious state. Such "outbreak teachings" (*rdol chos*) were apparently popular enough to pose a threat to the authority of the later court. Similar tensions also surrounded the so-called Four Children of Pehar, a set of eleventh-century teachers, all of whom, the later tradition claims, were possessed by demons and propagated an assortment of dangerously antinomian methods.[36] While both of these movements—the Star King and the Four Children—date from just after the age of fragmentation, similar tantric communities were surely typical of the late ninth and tenth centuries.

Indeed, as we leave Nupchen and move farther into the tenth century, the growing popularity of tantric practice is well attested in the documents from Dunhuang. It is increasingly clear that much of the Dunhuang collection, and in particular those manuscripts relating to the tantras, date from the tenth century, well after the collapse of the Tibetan Empire.[37] The Dunhuang collection thus sheds some much-needed light on the age of fragmentation, and its contents reveal a proliferation of locally produced tantric treatises and ritual manuals. While the sutras and sutra-based commentaries from Dunhuang remain relatively conservative, sticking close to the Indian tradition or at least to those doctrinal innovations that date from the imperial period, the tantric manuscripts include numerous variations, many of which are uniquely Tibetan. If the Dunhuang collection reveals anything about the Tibetan assimilation of Buddhism, it is the central role that tantric myth and ritual played in this process.

PT840 paints a particularly vivid picture of the extraordinary popularity tantric practice enjoyed during the tenth century at the local level:

For every hundred disciples there are a thousand masters,
Yet no one listens to the sublime dharma.
There are ten masters in every village,
And no limit to the number of *vajra* masters.
Everyone thinks they have been accomplished as a deity.
In the end, how could so many groups
Not destroy the *vajra* body?[38]

Clearly, even before the return of Buddhist monastic institutions at the end of the tenth and the eleventh centuries, tantric authority was already hotly contested.

Another glimpse of how Tibetans of the tenth century perceived their own age is provided in a series of prayers that appear in ITJ752. The prayers portray the period as one of political and religious strife, and they look to the tantras for salvation:

> May those past generations of yogins who have died remember their vows; may they fulfill them now, in this time of corrupted vows. Having become beings with *vajra*-like body, speech, and mind, may they come to our assistance. May the troubles in the Tibetan kingdom be pacified quickly, and may the life of our dharma-protecting king be long and his rule be powerful. Further, may all those with evil intentions, those oppressive enemies such as those who are enemies of the Vajrayāna and those who obstruct the virtuous gathered within our mandala, may they be taken as suitable for taming, and converted in accordance with the subjugation methods of the four activities by someone on the level of a noble one. The time has come for violence toward these evil ones who cannot be tamed peacefully, who have violated the teachings and broken their vows. May they be conclusively eliminated by means of violent activity, in accordance with the power of the vows. May all those who previously have accepted the vows and the sacramental substances have their obscurations completely purified. May those who are suitable for decisive liberation by means of the supreme yoga "attain the realm."[39]

Here, then, we have direct evidence of violent ritual being called upon in an attempt to reassert order during a period of political fragmentation and religious chaos. Those who are making trouble for Tibet are labeled "enemies of the Vajrayāna," and the solution, we are told, is to kill them by means of violent tantric ritual. Desperate times, the prayers seem to say, call for desperate measures, and the tantras provided the necessary means.[40] With their emphasis on violence, demon taming, and political order, the tantras provided a range of powerful strategies to the Tibetans of the late ninth and tenth centuries.

In his work on the "Tibetan Renaissance" of the eleventh to thirteenth centuries, Ronald Davidson has observed, "While the sociopolitical forms inherent in tantric maṇḍalas might seem tailored to royal use, in fact its distribution of power through a complex feudal system of quasi-independent vassals was problematic, and the tantric ritualization of Tibet during the renaissance later enacted and validated the emperors' fears of fissiparous forces."[41] Given the evidence from Dunhuang, we may suggest that the "tantric ritualization" of Davidson's renaissance period had its roots in, and indeed to a large extent was already well under way during, the age of fragmentation that preceded it. The tantras' ability to bestow authority upon priests and local rulers alike, all the way down to the village level, made them ideally suited for the fragmented society of late-ninth- and tenth-century Tibet.

All this is quite unlike what we know of the earlier imperial period, which Davidson has described as "the period of the great *sūtra* translations."[42] Under the empire, a strict "religious council" (*mdun sa*) had carefully controlled the translation and dissemination of the tantras.[43] The restrictions seem to have targeted the Mahāyoga tantras in particular. The early ninth-century *Grammar in Two Volumes*, a guide for the imperial translators of the day, explained the prohibitions in the following terms:

> By regulation, the mantra-tantras are to be kept secret. It is furthermore unacceptable to explain or show them to those who are unsuitable. Until now they have been translated and practiced, but for this reason their enigmatic language has gone unexplained, and they have been taken literally, their practices perverted. While it is noted that the collection and translation of mantra-tantras has occurred, henceforth with regard to *dhāraṇī-mantras* and higher teachings, unless permission for translation is granted, the mantra-tantras and the words of the mantras are not to be collected or translated.[44]

At the time of the *Grammar*'s writing, it seems that the tantras were being practiced by some at least, and that the court felt such practices needed to be restricted. Other sources suggest some regulations may have already been in place by the second half of the eighth century, so that the *Grammar*'s prohibitions may have been intended to reinforce earlier rules.[45] In any case, it seems that the court did sponsor the translation of certain tantras, but their dissemination was severely limited to members of the royal court and its circle of aristocratic supporters. The *Pangtangma*, a mid-ninth-century imperial catalogue of the available Tibetan translations, closes with a note that the "inner" tantras (here apparently corresponding to the Mahāyoga tantras, as the Yoga tantras do appear in the catalog itself) were "put in a separate list," a list that perhaps not surprisingly has long since disappeared.[46]

Even when the tantras were circulated, however, there is some evidence to suggest that they were carefully censored, with their most violent sections removed. Drakpa Gyeltsen (1147–1216) would claim that this is precisely what happened in the case of the imperial-period translation of the *Sarvadurgatipariśodhana Tantra*, which even today lacks two sections on the violent fire offering ritual.[47] These, after all, were the handbooks to the empire's secret power. In India, the tantras lent literary and ritual authority to the rulers of the early medieval period, and perhaps for the same reasons, they were also adopted by the new Tibetan court. Tibet's first monastery, Samye, the great Buddhist symbol of Tibetan imperial power founded around 779 C.E. by King Trisong Detsen, was said to have culminated on its top floor in a recreation of the mandala from the *Sarvadurgatipariśodhana Tantra*.[48] At its center stood an image of the All-Seeing (Sarvavid) Vairocana, the Buddhist patron deity of the Pugyal dynasty.[49] Clearly the tantras such as the *Sarvadurgatipariśodhana* and the violent rites they described were crucial to Tibetan imperial power and therefore needed to be carefully restricted.

With the empire's fall, however, the restrictions were lifted, and Tibetans eagerly adopted and adapted the myths and rituals of the Indian tantras toward their own particular ends. Compared to the court-driven Buddhism of the imperial period, the age of fragmentation witnessed a tantric conversion of Tibet at the popular and local levels.[50]

EARLY BUDDHIST ENCOUNTERS WITH THE GODS AND DEMONS OF TIBET

Local gods and demons were probably central to Tibetan religious life long before Buddhism's arrival, but the precise nature of the ritual practices that surrounded them remains obscure. Today's followers of the non-Buddhist Bon religion are known for their expertise in the spirit world, and Bon is often understood by Western and Tibetan scholars alike as "the pre-Buddhist religion of Tibet." Nevertheless, Bon practices have changed dramatically from what they were in the seventh and eighth centuries, having been deeply affected by their contacts with Buddhism. Documents from Dunhuang suggest that the early Bonpo were responsible for overseeing the Pugyal royal funerary rites, in addition to other related functions within the court, such as healing illnesses.[51] It is unclear, however, just how widespread the Bonpo were at this early point and to what extent their rituals may have overlapped with other Tibetan practices that were popular prior to Buddhism's arrival. In any case, Buddhists quickly adopted the term "Bonpo" as a blanket pejorative to refer to non-Buddhist medicine men, exorcists, and prognosticators of all sorts. The imperial-period Tibetan translation of the Chinese *Eight Brilliances Sūtra* (Ch. *Bayang jing;* Tib. *Snang brgyad kyi mdo*) provides some good examples of the way the Bonpo were portrayed by early Tibetan Buddhists. Numerous copies of this work appear in the Dunhuang collections, and all warn repeatedly against false teachers, here in the Tibetan, cast as Bonpo:[52] "Son of good family, only the unwise believe in the Mo Bon. In the hope of good luck, they cast divinations, but the virtuous do not do this."[53] And elsewhere, "The Bonpo kill and oppress, then claim they are 'creating happiness.' They make prayers to spirits and demons which bring nothing but harm and affliction for themselves."[54] Such admonitions indicate that many early Tibetan Buddhists took a hard line against the entire range of popular pre-Buddhist ritual practices involving the native gods of Tibet.

Similar tensions also characterized relations between the early followers of the tantras and those of Tibet's native spirits. One of our earliest pieces of evidence on this subject is the early ninth-century treatise the *Questions and Answers of Vajrasattva* by Nyen Pelyang. This work consists of a series of fifty-one questions and answers on a range of topics relating to the theory and practice of the new Mahāyoga tantras. Such catechetical works were common in early Tibetan Buddhism, their dialectical nature being useful for resolving the difficult cross-cultural religious issues that arose in the initial Tibetan encounters with Buddhism, and indeed a number of "Question and Answer" texts are found among the Dunhuang manuscripts.[55] In Pelyang's *Questions and Answers of Vajrasattva*, the thirty-sixth question speaks directly to the place of native spirits in the new Tibetan religious environment:

> Question: There are yogins worshipping the gods and demons of Tibet. Is this in agreement with the system of Yoga, or not?
>
> Answer: For one who has pledged to Samantabhadra-Vajrasattva,
> The worship of mundane gods and *nāgas* as higher beings,
> Is like a king performing the acts of a commoner.[56]
> Do not beseech [such beings even] for your provisions; it conflicts with the purpose of Yoga.[57]

This is a decided condemnation of anyone worshipping the gods of Tibet. While its prohibitions imply that some early Tibetan *tāntrikas* probably did continue to worship local gods, the passage also indicates that such open-minded behavior may have come under increasing attack from Buddhists in the imperial period. In his colophon to the same work, Pelyang makes it explicit that he was writing for the benefit of two of central Tibet's prominent aristocratic clans, the Nanam and the Dong. Within these high circles at least, and all the more as the Pugyal dynasty reached the apex of its power in the early ninth century, it seems that Tibeto-Buddhist syncretism was frowned upon. Native Tibetan and Buddhist religious practices found ways to coexist alongside one another,[58] but the Buddhist assimilation of Tibetan rituals and pantheons likely remained minimal during these early years. For many early Tibetan Buddhists, the autochthonous spirits of Tibet were at best a waste of time and at worst a cause of great suffering.

Such was the sad state of affairs for Tibet's native gods during the waning years of the empire. Following the empire's collapse, however, a very different social environment emerged. A newly fractured political authority allowed and fostered new, more uniquely Tibetan forms of Buddhism. Freed from the controls of the royal court, Buddhism began to be assimilated into the Tibetan culture on a wider and more popular level. A number of documents from Dunhuang indicate that, for some at least, the imperial court's concerns about tantric Buddhism and prohibitions against Tibetan syncretism faded into the background. While evidence remains scant, we can infer from what we have that, as Buddhism spread into the countryside and left behind the authority of the imperial court, a kind of religious opening occurred. By the tenth century, new texts had begun to emerge that combined Buddhist teachings and practices with the traditional Tibetan fascination with the spirits of the Himalayan plateau.[59]

BINDING THE AUTOCHTHONOUS SPIRITS OF TIBET

It is well known that the Tibetan landscape is believed to be inhabited by countless dangerous beings, and that local tales of demon subjugation are omnipresent, shaping the sacred places of Tibet and imbuing them with power. Evidence from Dunhuang suggests that these motifs, which are so basic to Tibetan Buddhism, have many of their roots in the age of fragmentation. Concerns with controlling spirits and demons seem to have driven Tibetans' fascination with the violent myths and rituals of the Buddhist tantras. Their need for control over these invisible forces could only have been exacerbated by the seemingly endless decades of social and political chaos that Tibetans were experiencing. Within this historical context of lawlessness and fragmentation, the Buddhist themes of demon subjugation proliferated throughout Tibet.

The well-known image of the massive *rākṣasī* (or "*sinmo*") demoness of Tibet, barely restrained by the Buddhist temples of the seventh-century king Songtsen Gampo, illustrates the situation well: The gods and demons of the Tibetan landscape were seen as volatile beings, held in check only by the oaths they had sworn to their Buddhist masters. They were liminal beings whose behavior was extreme and ambivalent. The vows that bound them may have been strong, but they were still just that—vows that had been accepted only reluctantly and usually under threat of violence. These were powerful beings who always might break their vows.

The importance of the tantric vow in controlling these dangerous spirits cannot be overestimated. The vow is a crucial part of tantric ritual and is reinforced with threats of extreme violence. The vows are administered by means of a sacramental drop of sexual fluids or, more typically, perfumed water that is ingested, so that the same term (Skt. *samaya;* Tib. *dam tshig*) refers to both the tantric vow and the sacramental drop. In this sense the tantric vow *is* the drop and the drop *is* the vow. After the sacrament is swallowed, it works its way into one's heart, where it remains for the rest of one's life. As long as the vow is maintained, this internal sacrament provides protection, but should the vow be broken, the drop will turn to poison and cause terrible and often graphically described agonies.[60]

When confronted with a demon, this is the goal then—to coax the spirit into accepting such a vow of allegiance. This may require extreme measures, for fierce beings often need a forceful hand. The buddhas' violent subjugation of Rudra is an example of what might be necessary, and in this sense the Rudra myth provided Tibetans with a model for how to treat their own native gods and demons. They should be regarded with compassion, but always with the threat of violence clearly present in the background. The ideal encounter may not necessitate violence, as the demon will hopefully recognize the benefits of his or her submission, but the alternative should always be made evident. A lively description of such an ideal encounter appears in the following passage from Dunhuang:

> One may also enter [a spirit] into servitude. After praying for the *siddhi*, one prays for success in making that particular [spirit] enter into servitude. One writes down the letters [of the spirit's name]. Then, clearly visualizing oneself in the *mahāmudrā* [that is, in the form of the deity], one should give the commands and summon [the spirit].
>
> Without letting one's mind slip from its concentrated state, ask, "Are you (insert the name . . .)?" If the reply is, "Yes, I am," then demand, "Now henceforth show yourself! Of what tasks are you capable?" [And to whatever the

> reply may be,] say, "Those tasks of which you are capable, I will make you perform them! The foods and the gifts of the vow-bearer shall be granted if you do as I say. I give you this name, (insert the name . . .). Whenever I use this name to command you, you are to do as I ask without deception! I will be your benefactor. Drink these vow-waters! If you perform as you are sworn, they will provide the highest bliss and well being, but if you do not perform as you promise, these vow-waters will become *vajra*-fires and consume your body and voice. You will experience all sorts of sufferings, and you will be separated from that which is dear and precious."
>
> Whichever is appropriate—inwardly the *amṛta*, or outwardly water perfumed with sandalwood or saffron water—is blessed with the mantras for all the activities and then poured. Both the questioner and the vow-holder should be covered, that is, they should both take it, as [the vow's] completion by one may not be evident to the other. Furthermore, both should perform this ritual for the conferral of the *siddhi* identically and at the same moment, though due to the power of their respective merits, the prophecies and the receptions of the *siddhis* may arise one before the other. Thus the attainment of a prophesy of seeing or the attainment of the *siddhis* will indicate clear companionship, that it has been accepted.[61]

The demon, then, should see one as a beneficent master and friendly companion, but a formidable one deserving of unswerving devotion. He or she should be addressed directly and forcefully, with the threatening content of one's demands matched by the abrupt tone of one's language. Just as Rudra had to be killed and revived before he could be forced to accept his tantric vows, the local demons of Tibet, too, had to be treated with a combination of violence and compassion.

The Rudra myth may describe the prototypical act of violent demon subjugation at a cosmological level, but historically it has operated very much at the local level, being the subject of innumerable regional adaptations. Known tantric masters forced named demons at specific sites to submit to Buddhism. Every place and each demon required its own particular stories and rituals, for without these violent conversions, the Tibetan landscape would be a chaotic and dangerous place.

The Tibetan universe is infused with spirits—spirits that live in the rocks, trees, and mountains, spirits that live in one's body, spirits that wander the landscape, spirits that live underground and in the sky, spirits that cause illness and natural disasters. Spirits demand recognition and respect, yet they are forever changing names, being associated with multiple locations, appearing in different groups, eluding classification, and manifesting according to shifting iconographies. This demonic realm is unruly and contrasts sharply with that of tantric ritual, which is guided by metaphors of power and control, with the practitioner seated as a virtual sovereign at the center of the mandala palace, ruling over the realm by threat of violence. In this sense, the mandala acts as a constitutive mirror, simultaneously reflecting and inverting the spirit world into an ordered utopia. Like the demons, the *tāntrika* too changes his name, transforms his appearance, and shifts his place, but his world is an ordered one that conforms to carefully established Buddhist norms. Tantric Buddhism thus offered both ritual methods for controlling, and overarching narrative schemes to explain, the spirits' roles in Tibetan life. The pattern may be observed throughout Asia, Indian Buddhism providing a wide range of new, tried and tested strategies for organizing a protean demonic realm into a more obedient and ordered universe.

The link between tantric demon subjugation and the orderly mapping of the spirit world is perhaps best seen in the Dunhuang manuscript ITJ711, titled *An Explanation of the Tantras and Their Narrative Setting.* The text is a commentary of Tibetan authorship, on a prayer that commonly appears in the *dhāraṇī* collections (*gzungs 'dus*) found at Dunhuang. The prayer is titled *An Invitation to the Great Gods and Nāgas*, and, as its title suggests, its invitations are directed to the mundane gods and spirits of the Indian pantheon, from Indra to the demonic seven mothers (*saptamātṛkā*), to come and observe the *dhāraṇī* recitations that will follow.[62] Thus the prayer's closing line reads, "Listen all [of you] to these words of the profound conqueror. . . ." The Dunhuang commentary to the prayer provides the narrative background to these ritual invitations. The result is a brief account of the origins of the Buddhist tantras, which begins as follows:

> Originally in the so-called "southern land" there was a great city called Vaiśālī. In that land, there was a monk who had received ordination from the son of the healer-king in the palace of the Akaniṣṭha heaven. He accomplished seven *samādhis* on his deity over the course of seven days, receiving the *siddhi* of [long] life, the *siddhi* of power, the *siddhi* of greatness, the *siddhi* of fulfilling wishes, and the *siddhi* of attaining power over action. All was attained.
>
> Then he came into the world to explain the dharma before those fortunate enough to be gathered there, and when he looked in the ten directions he saw all sentient beings to be afflicted. That noble one gazed with compassion.
>
> Then it says, "With devotion I prostrate and go for refuge to the unsurpassable lama, the three jewels, and to the supremely powerful supreme one of greatness."[63]
>
> Regarding this [opening sentence]: the buddha is birthless; the dharma is beyond words; the *saṃgha* is the father and the mother of the three times. As nothing surpasses those three, one should go to them for refuge. Aḥ.

> As for their having for refuge: Previously five hundred demonic sons, upon seeing the splendor of that noble *tathāgata*, became extremely fearful. "A la la!" they exclaimed, and went for refuge. "Whose splendor [did they witness]?" you may ask. He was a mind emanation of Ārya Vairocana, a *heruka* who caused a great rain of *vajras* to fall from the sky, *vajras* that were blazing with fire. The sons of the demonic gods were afraid and went for refuge. The mantra he used for overpowering them was, "*Oṃ samaye heye svāhā!*"[64]

The text goes on to comment on the next line in the *Three Sequences* prayer, which begins what is essentially an extended list of the mundane gods and demons of India, calling upon them one by one to present themselves. The commentary (and therefore, by implication, the prayer itself) ends with all the gods and demons having been subjugated and prepared to receive the initiations and teachings of tantric Buddhism: "Because Matraṅgara Rudra enjoyed sexual union with fallen women of the charnel grounds, he requested an explanation of the teachings on union. The *heruka* said, 'Son of good family, thus it is . . . ,' and he took [the form of] a white man on a white horse and explained the great teaching on union for seven days. Then all the demons prostrated and paid homage. Thus they went for refuge, and thus they are called 'the conquered.'"[65] In this way the commentary explains the efficacy of the invitation prayer to be a result of the earlier subjugation of Rudra, the implication being that by reciting the *Three Sequences*, one calls upon the gods and demons to fulfill their previous vows to the victorious *heruka* buddha.

This tenth-century reformulation of the Rudra myth is of particular interest, however, for its uniquely Tibetan elements. Halfway through, while describing the gods of the sun and the moon, the commentary suddenly introduces the following discussion:

> Regarding the sun and the moon: The sun was a goddess and the moon was a demon. Together the demon and the goddess rested in union, and three fruits arose from their liberation and ripened into the three, A and E and *Hūṃ*.
>
> Regarding these three that arose: The first to arise came from an egg. On being seen, he was called Candraputra in Sanskrit and "Great Son of the Moon" in Tibetan. Who was this? Having initially emerged as an egg from the mother's womb, he was born and went into the sky. For that reason the Buddhist community call him a great son of a god, and the Bonpo call him a "sky god." His essential life force is [the syllable] *ste*.
>
> Below that, another birth was led forth from the mother's foot as she stamped on the earth. After she stamped her foot, he emerged from her foot. Then, digging a hole, he slipped into it. In Sanskrit he is called a *de'i*. In Tibetan, *teu rang*. His life force is *tri*.

Below that, the next one was pressed downward and trampled underground by the mother. His senses were impaired. His name was 'Gong po. His heart force is *tī*.[66]

While the specifics of this passage do not match those seen in other early Tibetan cosmogonic myths, a number of aspects are similar. The importance of the primeval egg to early Bonpo beliefs has been noted by a number of modern scholars, as it was already by the twelfth-century Tibetan author Nyangrel Nyima Özer.[67] Further correspondences are found in the Bonpo text *The Appearance of the Little Black-Headed Man*, where too the third of three offspring born from eggs is born with no physical senses,[68] and later in the same account three children are born to a demon and a woman.[69]

Also in our text, however, the ancient Tibetan tripartite universe of heaven, earth, and underworld (*gnam-sa-'og*), where the sky gods, the *teu rang*, and the demons dwell, is being tied to Indian cosmology, possibly even to the three realms of *khecara, bhūcara*, and *nāgaloka*.[70] Here the autochthonous spirits of Tibet are explicitly identified with the mundane (*laukika*) gods of India, with each bearing both a Tibetan and a Sanskrit name. In this way, the gods and demons of Tibet are granted a position in the new Buddhist universe, to dwell among Rudra's subjugated horde. This process, by which local gods were incorporated into the Buddhist pantheon as lesser "mundane" deities capable of bestowing worldly benefits but not enlightenment, was of course well known throughout Asia from an early date. The tantras only codified the procedure, with the Rudra myth providing the basic narrative, and the mandala, the spatial template.

In the Rudra myth, the gods of India, once tamed, are relegated to the edges of the mandala. The tantric mandala thus makes a permanent place for these mundane beings, though it is one of definite subservience. The gods of India, from Brahmā and Indra to the local spirits, are positioned around the mandala's outskirts, whence they are to serve the buddhas who dwell at the center. This was a shadowy place, where violence was rife[71] (fig. 2). "The outskirts of the mandala are taught to be a black ground," explains one manuscript; "they have the nature of unending aggression due to the great violent compassion for the sake of sentient beings,"[72] and within this darkness, continues a somewhat later text, demonic beings lurk:

Crows, owls, and vultures of many varieties, male and female jackals, male and female hawks, demonesses with fierce and terrifying faces, lion-faced and tiger-faced, snakes with bull heads, two-faced [monsters], and so on, moving in every direction. There are skeletons impaled upon spears, hanging corpses,

Figure 2: Charnel grounds. “The outskirts of the mandala are taught to be a black ground,” explains one Dunhuang manuscript. (Himalayan Art Resource, Item 792)

> half-burned and decapitated. There are skulls, legs, limbless torsos, grimacing heads, and [scattered] bones. There are also some *vidyādharas* and bands of *yogins* and *yoginīs* observing their vows, as well as [supernatural beings]—vicious spirits, zombies, demons, and others screaming, "Kili kili!"[73]

Here at the dark edges, among these bloodthirsty creatures and gruesome carnage, Tibetans of the ninth and tenth centuries found something familiar, and it was here that they made their home, binding their violent local gods to the ordered universe of Indian Buddhism.

BRINGING BUDDHISM TO TIBET: PADMASAMBHAVA AND THE *SAPTAMĀTṚKĀ*

The relocation of Tibet's mundane gods to the edges of the Buddhist mandala was not just some vague theory of equivalence between cosmological groups. It involved practical realities that had consequences at the local level, focused projects that created new narratives relating to specific spirits associated with particular sites. Following the collapse of the Tibetan Empire, the tantric traditions flourished at a more local level, and the adaptation and localization of the Rudra myth for specific sites became paradigmatic.

Over the course of the age of fragmentation, one figure emerged as central to the relocation of Buddhism's mythic universe onto Tibetan soil. If the theme of demon subjugation is crucial to Tibetan culture, Padmasambhava is Tibet's demon tamer *par excellence*. Padmasambhava is often credited as the principal person responsible for bringing Buddhism to Tibet. The Indian master is said to have been invited by the king Trisong Detsen (c. 742–800 C.E.) for his expertise in handling the local non-Buddhist spirits who were opposed to the introduction of this foreign religion. Whatever the original historical realities of Padmasambhava may have been, his legend spread widely and its growth followed the thematic channels of tantric myth and demon subjugation. Today the influences of the Padmasambhava legend appear everywhere. Tibet's geography is dotted with countless sacred sites where the tantric master is said to have subjugated local Tibetan spirits and converted them to Buddhism. From the tantric deity Vajrakīlaya, used for pinning demons to the ground in all kinds of Tibetan rituals, to reenactments of the violent subjugation of demons commonly performed at Tibet's masked dance festivals, Padmasambhava stands at the center of tantric violence in Tibet.

Though most of the rich legends that surround Padmasambhava today developed long after his departure, it is likely that a Buddhist master by the name of

Sambhava did visit Tibet around the late eighth century.[74] The early evidence for the existence of such a historical person suggests he may indeed have been an expert in the demon-taming techniques of the Mahāyoga tantras. One of the relatively few works that can be attributed to the master with at least some reliability is the *Garland of Views*, a commentary to the thirteenth chapter of the *Guhyagarbha Tantra*,[75] the *Guhyagarbha* being a Mahāyoga tantra well known in Tibet for its connections to the so-called liberation rite for the ritual killing of demonic beings. Another text that may have been authored by Padmasambhava appears in the Dunhuang collections. ITJ321 is a commentary on another Mahāyoga tantra, the *Lasso of Means, a Lotus Garland*,[76] and here the author makes repeated and direct references to liberating beings who are "attached to wrong views."[77] Such evidence suggests that there may have been an actual person behind the Padmasambhava legends and that he may have had some knowledge of the tantric rites of violent subjugation.

Nevertheless it is also clear that the historical activities of this personage paled in comparison to those of his legend. Some sense of the historical reality that was Padmasambhava can be gleaned from the above-mentioned *Lasso of Means* commentary. The attribution of this work to Padmasambhava depends in large part on a short verse appended to the Dunhuang manuscript that praises the scholarly merits of the master. An interlinear note attributes the verse to an Indian *master*, Śāntigarbha, a contemporary of Padmasambhava who was also active at the court of the Tibetan king Trisong Detsen. "Śāntigarbha examined this work," it says, "and having found it to be without errors, he praised Padmasambhava. . . ."[78] Relatively little is known about this Śāntigarbha. Various sources say he specialized in medicine and the rituals associated with the tantric deity Yamāntaka. He is also said to have presided at the consecration of Samye, Tibet's first Buddhist monastery. In any case, from the perspective of the later Tibetan tradition, it is remarkable that the opinion of a relatively insignificant figure such as Śāntigarbha would have any relevance for one of Padmasambhava's stature.

Ultimately to search for an original Padmasambhava is probably less illuminating than to trace his continually changing manifestations through Tibetan history. Indeed, our earliest evidence on Padmasambhava already reveals a marked mutability to the legend. PT44, for example, is a late-tenth-century booklet devoted to the ritual traditions of the wrathful deity Vajrakīlaya.[79] It relates how *Ācārya* Sambhava, as he is called, practiced meditation, battled demons, and performed miracles at the Asura cave at Yangla Shö. Additional evidence from Dunhuang suggests, however, that even this early account draws upon a number of narrative themes found in earlier textual traditions,

Figure 3: Kongla Demo, "the leader of the seven"
(Department of Culture, Royal Government of Bhutan)

so that the story should be considered already a product of the mythification of Padmasambhava.[80] From the ninth to the eleventh centuries, the Indian master's role in the Tibetan imagination grew and evolved dramatically, so that by the time of his first complete biography, the twelfth-century *Copper Island* by Nyangrel Nyima Özer (1124–1192), Padmasambhava had become the single most important figure in Tibetan narratives of their early conversion to Buddhism. A study of our earliest evidence can provide insights into how these Tibetan conversion narratives took root and developed during the dark years of the late ninth and tenth centuries.

The Dunhuang manuscript PT307 contains our earliest discussion of the master's activities in Tibet. The account makes explicit how Tibetans of the tenth century understood the Padmasambhava legend as an adaptation of the Rudra subjugation myth. Here we see the cosmological battle between the tantric *heruka* buddha and Rudra being relocated into the Tibetan landscape. The passage in question appears in a short work on the female protectors in the wrathful mandala of Śrī Mahā Heruka. It begins with descriptions of a series of seven demonesses native to Tibet:

> Dorje Kundrakma has a black-colored body. To many she appears pleasing, [in which case] if their *samaya* is kept, she wears dharma robes and is adorned with various additional ornaments, displaying a beautiful and lovely form. Or she may be displeasing, [in which case,] if the *samaya* is kept, she is black with [her hair in] a top-knot and riding a mule. She is also called Kongla Demo. She is the leader of these seven [fig. 3].
>
> Dorje Kuntu Zang has a white-colored body. For her seat, she sits upon a white all-knowing horse, and she relishes the saliva from vows. She is also called Shamey Gangkar ("fleshless white snow mountain").[81]
>
> Dorje Kunselma has a pink-colored body. She usually wears black robes and rides a blue horse. She is also called Lhari Yama Kyol ("the slate bearer of Lha ri").
>
> Dorje Yeshe Chok has a pink-colored body. She wears an assortment of clothes. She rides an emanation of a female *dzo*. She is also called Dala Tsenmo ("queen of the herders").
>
> Dorje Dronma usually wears robes. For her seat, she rides an emanated *myan*. She is also called Kharak Khyungtsun ("revered garuḍa of Kha rag").[82]
>
> Dorje Ö Chakma has a red-colored body and usually wears clothes. For her seat, she rides an emanation of a wild (*kham yu*) female yak. She is also called Changi Sertang Yige Khordulma ("tamer of the wheel of letters, the golden tone of the north").
>
> Dorje Yudronma has a blue-colored body. As her throne she rides an emanated blue horse. She is also known as Lhoi ting ting ("chime of the south").
>
> These seven are also known as *ḍākinīs*, the powerful women, the seven great mothers, or the seven great *rākṣasīs*. Originally, the two types of *maṇḍalas* were arranged and arose, and then in the chapter on the taming of Matraṅgara Rudra, their vows were bestowed and their activities appointed. The great charnel ground was opened and the seven protective guardians were addressed by the *heruka*. Furthermore, they form an assembly that is large but seems small. Thereafter they were also sacred consorts to the noble one.
>
> After that, both the Indian master Padmasambhava and Lang Pelgyi Senge subjugated and suppressed them. Bestowing upon these ladies of Tibet *vajras* to hold, they gave them names for being in the company of [the buddha] Vajradhara. Since then, they have aided and supported those who accomplish

> the secret mantra in accordance with the scriptural systems, and they have been entrusted as the eternally unfailing guardians of Tibet.
>
> They are also sisters. These women who are greater than the great have promised; they are avowed. They rejoice in the saliva from vows. They are pleased by the remainder offerings. They strive to act unremittingly for meditators and for the pure substances. They wield a variety of terribly fearsome weapons. At other times they wield lovely and beautiful implements.
>
> Great leader Dorje Kundrakma, fleshless white snow mountain Dorje Kuntu Zang, glorious one of Lhari, Kunselma, queen of herders Dorje Yeshe Chok, revered garuḍa of Kharag, Dorje Dronma, golden tone of the north Dorje Ö Chakma, chime of the south Dorje Yudronma: For the welfare of sentient beings, perform according to the vows you took in the presence of the noble ones. If the precious jewels are deceived or if the vows are violated, then the devastations will be unbearable—one's mind will burn and one will shudder with horror at the hell fires. Keep me in mind! Come here! Perform completely the activities of pacification, enhancement, coercion, and violence. Accomplish without fault.[83]

As noted above, the Tibetan landscape is dotted with innumerable sacred sites where Padmasambhava is said to have subjugated and converted the local Tibetan pre-Buddhist spirits. It is no exaggeration to say that these conversion narratives represent the dominant way in which the Tibetan assimilation of Buddhism has been understood by Tibetans themselves. PT307 is our earliest reference to such narratives, and significantly, it dates from the age of fragmentation.

The relationship between Padmasambhava and the seven female deities described here should be considered in light of the *saptamātṛkā* ("seven mothers"). Carvings of these seven mothers are prominently displayed throughout northern India and the Kathmandu Valley of Nepal. Even more pertinent are the widespread systems of holy sites (*pīṭha*) and temples associated with the seven mothers are common.[84] The *saptamātṛkā* sites played an important role within eighth-century Indian tantric circles and were closely associated with violent ritual. The *Mahāvairocana-abhisaṃbodhi Tantra*, for example, describes the mythic origins of the seven mothers in the following terms: "When Indra and the gods fought with the Asuras, when the gods were unable to defeat the Asuras, seven goddesses called the Mothers emerged from Indra, Brahmā and so on, and these seven goddesses drank the blood drawn by swords before it fell to the ground and also quelled the harmful Asuras. When doing malevolent rites with the mantra of the Seven Mothers . . . , you will cause people to die."[85] In a similar vein, the *Guhyasamāja Tantra* recommends that wrathful subjuga-

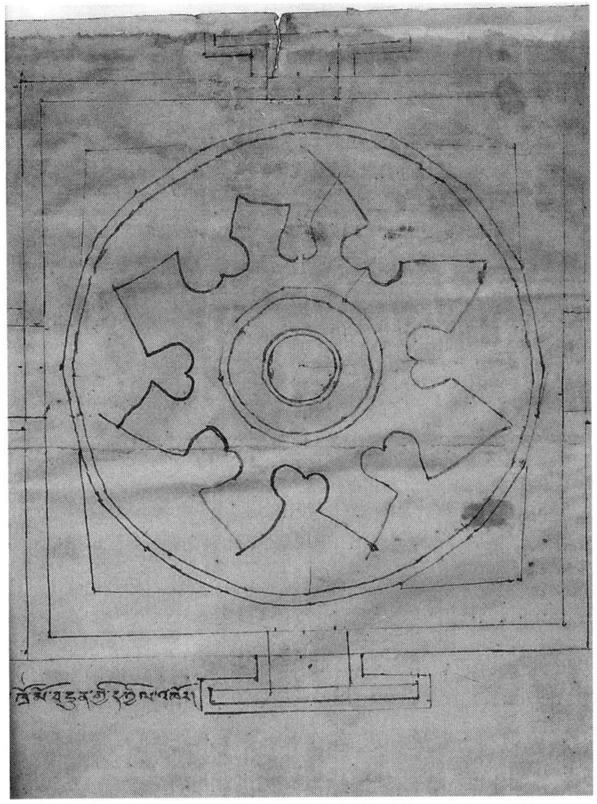

Figure 4: The Mandala of the Seven Wrathful Mothers
(ITJ 727; Courtesy of the British Library)

tion rites be performed "in the shrines of the *mātṛkā*" (Skt. *mātṛgṛhe;* Tib. *ma mo gnas*).[86]

The importance of the *saptamātṛkā* was clearly recognized by the tenth-century Buddhists of Tibet; references to the "seven mothers" (*ma bdun*) appear throughout the Dunhuang manuscripts. They play a recurring role in the commentary to the *Three Sequences* prayer examined above, and elsewhere they attend to the buddhas as their mundane servants.[87] The scroll ITJ727 even contains a simple line drawing of a mandala (fig. 4) dedicated to the "seven wrathful women," along with a prayer that enjoins the seven mothers to fulfill their tantric commitments by destroying all enemies and obstacles.[88] Throughout these Tibetan sources there is nothing to indicate that these are references to anything other than the normative Indian set of seven mothers. In PT307 however, we see the seven goddesses transformed and transplanted into the

Tibetan landscape, each bearing a Tibetan name and each associated with a specific place in Tibet.

Whatever their Indian precedents, in Tibet the seven mothers came to be seen as pre-Buddhist spirits tied to specifically Tibetan sites, usually sacred mountains, valleys, or lakes. Innumerable lists of such local "pre-Buddhist" spirits are found throughout later Tibetan literature, and many make specific reference to the seven goddesses.[89] A "Cult of the Seven Mothers" (*Ma bdun bka' brgyud pa*) even flourished along the Tibet-Nepal border regions well into the nineteenth century.[90] It is important to note, however, that none of these later references to the seven mothers date from before the influence of Buddhism. Despite the claim made in PT307 and elsewhere that this was a pre-Buddhist grouping of goddesses, it is unlikely that such a set existed in Tibet before Buddhism's arrival. Rather, it probably appeared in response to the Indian *saptamātṛkā*, in age-of-fragmentation works such as the one we see here. The individual members of the group may well have been drawn from the wider pantheon of local Tibetan spirits, but the set of seven mothers as such was almost certainly invented under the influence of Indian Buddhism.

The seven goddesses in PT307 thus share their names with other native Tibetan deities found in similar groupings. Various versions of twelve *tenma* "earth" goddesses, for example, include many of the same names.[91] Indeed, such lists of local spirits are countless and appear throughout Tibetan literature.[92] Nebesky-Wojkowitz's voluminous yet still-partial 1956 survey is overwhelming, to say the least. Faced with the pervasive overlapping between the lists found therein, one might be tempted to dismiss them as meaningless chaos. Yet we are left with the Tibetans' own persistent interest in these lists, and this alone makes them significant testaments to the Tibetans' need to control and order the unruly gods of their chaotic landscape.

Thus the purportedly "pre-Buddhist" seven mothers were not that at all. Instead, they were formulated as a group in direct response to the Indian *saptamātṛkā*. We have already observed that the incorporation of local gods into the Indian pantheon was commonplace across the Asian continent. Here, however, we see something slightly different. Here Tibetan gods, qua the seven mothers, were invented in order to provide local correlates for the Indian deities. In this sense the pre-Buddhist Tibetan landscape was being retroactively reshaped to "prepare" it for the imminent arrival of Buddhism and all its Indian trappings.

The Rudra myth played a particularly important role in this shaping process. PT307 makes explicit the connection between the tantric myth and Padmasambhava's own legendary taming activities in Tibet. Thus from an early date Tibetans looked to the tantric subjugation myth to understand their own conversion to Buddhism. We have seen how in India, Rudra was another name for the Hindu god Śiva, a fact that has caused some scholars to speculate that Śaiva-Buddhist competition may have contributed to the myth's popularity there. PT307 reveals how the Indian narrative of the Buddhist conversion of Śiva was adopted by the Tibetans and applied to their own non-Buddhist deities.

Of all the many versions of the Rudra subjugation myth, our PT307 passage probably refers to the one found in chapter 15 of the *Guhyagarbha Tantra*, a Mahāyoga work that exerted a strong influence over early Tibetan Buddhism. Padmasambhava's bestowal of *vajras* upon the seven sisters is likely a reference to the chapter's closing lines in which all the women in Rudra's demonic host are addressed: "Then the great joyous Bhagavat, having bestowed the *vajra* into their hands, conferred the name initiation, then arrayed them around the outer edges of the *maṇḍala*."[93] In the same way in our Dunhuang manuscript, the Tibetan goddesses are given *vajras* to carry as symbols of their new roles as the Buddhist guardians of Tibet and given new Buddhist names bearing the prefix "Dorje" (Skt. Vajra). Thus Kongla Demo is renamed Dorje Kundrakma ("Vajra Renown"), and so on.

PT307's reference to the "two types of *maṇḍalas*" that were "originally arranged" is probably also an allusion to the Rudra-taming narrative of the *Guhyagarbha*, this time to the peaceful and wrathful Māyājāla mandalas that open its fifteenth chapter.[94] "After that" (*de slan*), PT307 explains, Padmasambhava and the Tibetan Lang Pelgyi Senge subjugated the seven mothers of Tibet. This temporal ordering of events thereby brings the buddhas' original mythic "opening" of the wrathful mandala (through their taming of Rudra) into historical time. The implication, it seems, is that the buddhas' violent subjugation of Rudra opened the ritual space for the subsequent taming of Tibet's gods and demons. The Rudra narrative thus functioned simultaneously as a mythic ideal to be emulated in later ritual practice *and* as a quasi-historical event that made possible the performance of the subjugation rites. It stood with a foot in both worlds, in the mythic realm of the buddhas and in the historical landscape of Tibet.

THE LOCALIZATION OF TANTRIC RITUAL

Tibet's age-of-fragmentation conversion narratives, then, often took the form of localized adaptations of the Rudra myth. These uniquely Tibetan versions of the Indian subjugation myths were further mirrored in the ritual sphere by new Tibetan ritual manuals. While the Rudra myth was being tied to specific Tibetan sites through mythic and historical narrative, new localized versions of tantric ritual manuals were also appearing. One remarkable example of these ritual appropriations is found in a fragmentary manuscript from Dunhuang.

ITJ931 describes a ritual that exhibits several distinctively Tibetan features. The rite in question usually appears as part of a larger sequence of site rituals (*sa chog*) for preparing the space for the construction of a mandala.[95] Generally speaking, matters of place and ritual space are addressed in the early preparatory stages of tantric practice, before the ritual proper begins. One of the first steps is often to dig a hole in the soil to test for signs of the site's suitability.[96] Precisely where to dig, however, is a sensitive question, for there is always the danger that one might inadvertently injure the local spirit who dwells beneath the ground. For this reason a diagram is created along with instructions on how to determine the exact position of the local guardian spirit within this grid. The spirit's location depends on the day of the year, such that the spirit gradually spins under the ground, turning one degree each day to arrive full circle back where she began every 360 days, or one year. In tracing the roots of this rite, we should first observe that it was surprisingly widespread. A similar ritual associated with house building was practiced throughout much of Southeast Asia.[97] Later Buddhist and Hindu architectural works refer to it as the *vāstunāga* ritual, as in the *Samarāṅgaṇasūtradhāra*, and we may detect a possible early Brahmanical source for the rite in the myths surrounding the demon Vāstupuruṣa.[98] The adaptation of the ritual found in ITJ931, however, betrays uniquely Tibetan features.

Whereas the Indian versions generally do not mention the names or locations of any specific deities and thus may be applied anywhere,[99] ITJ931 specifies by name a series of local spirits native to the Tibetan landscape and tailors the rite to the characteristics of each. The first spirit discussed is Tsangkun, possibly associated with the place Tsangkun Yog, which appears in the Sino-Tibetan treaty of 821(/3), where it is said to be located on the Tibet-China border,[100] while another spirit named Chiu (Pyi'u), we are told, dwells in the valley of Chiu. Each local spirit, the manuscript explains, turns in its own inimitable way, requiring its own particular analysis. Each resides in a different direction according to the season and year, rather than according to the day as seen in the Indian renditions of the rite.[101] Tsangkun, for example, dwells in the western direction in the pig, mouse, and ox years, in the northern direction in the tiger, rabbit, and dragon years, and so on, while Chiu is found in the southwest in the first summer month, in the west in the middle summer month, and in the east in the final summer month. Thus in addition to adapting the rite for specific spirits native to the Tibetan landscape, ITJ931 makes use of the Sino-Tibetan–style calendrical system, which associates each year with one of twelve specific animals.[102]

In short, ITJ931 describes a popular Indian rite that was meticulously adapted for Tibetan purposes. Through this manuscript we catch a glimpse of the local and practical concerns of tenth-century Tibetans and how those concerns translated into specific, idiosyncratic adaptations of Buddhist ritual. The manuscript is unusual not only for its uniquely Tibetan elements, but for how it complicates particular aspects of the proceedings, dividing a monolithic rite of Indian Buddhism into discrete variants so as to tailor them to individual places in the Tibetan landscape. The resulting localizations are absent from the post-tenth-century versions of the rite. Following the reestablishment of royal and monastic centers of authority, Tibetans could not take the same liberties with the original Indian rites that they had during the age of fragmentation, when they were free to remake Buddhist ritual toward their own objectives.

CONCLUSIONS

The Dunhuang manuscripts exhibit a variety of strategies for binding the local gods and demons of Tibet to the myths and rituals of the Buddhist tantras. Many of the strategies were already implicit in the tantras themselves, as they had been central to the genre's earlier successes in India, but others were uniquely Tibetan innovations. One manuscript adds the autochthonous *teu rang* spirits of Tibet to the mundane retinue of tamed gods that dwell at the mandala's edge, while another relocates the *saptamātṛkā* from India to new homes in the "pre-Buddhist" Tibetan landscape, and still another ties a popular Indian site ritual to particular places in Tibet, adapting it differently for each of a series of specific local spirits.

Such localizations of Buddhism turned the earlier top-down, court-driven approach of the imperial period on its head. Buddhism's more rational aspects, its moral laws and its international prestige, may initially have been emphasized in early Tibet, but the tenth-century manuscripts examined here reveal a markedly different set of concerns. During the earlier imperial period, the royal court was attracted to Buddhism's more utopian and displaced cosmologies and sought to raise Tibet onto the international stage. In the subsequent age of fragmentation, however, quite the opposite movement is seen, as Buddhism was localized, brought down into the Tibetan soil at specific sites, and recreated as a new and uniquely Tibetan tradition. Whereas the imperial court strove to raise a recently unified Tibet into a utopian realm of international Buddhism that resided nowhere, the Tibetans of the age of fragmentation situated Buddhism in the local landscape, tying it to specific lakes, mountains, and valleys. In this sense the sociopolitical realities of these two periods—unified and fragmentary—were clearly reflected in the kinds of Buddhism that developed—utopian and localized.

Again, the story of King Lhato Tori on his palace roof summarizes the situation well: When the *Karaṇḍavyūha Sūtra* descended out of the sky and into the king's hands, nobody in Tibet could understand what it was. The Buddhist teachings had arrived fully formed out of the sky, but Tibetans could not recognize them. Out of the blue, they lacked any context, and the revered *Karaṇḍavyūha* remained a mere sacred symbol. For generations to come, Tibetans are said to have worshipped the text as a holy object, but only later did they learn how to read and comprehend its contents. For Tibetans to fully embrace Buddhism, it had to grow from the soil, not fall from space.

Thanks to the manuscripts from Dunhuang, we can catch glimpses of what happened during the mysterious years of late-ninth- and tenth-century Tibet, and what we see is quite unexpected. Rather than a time of decay, this so-called dark age was when Buddhism plunged its roots deep into the Tibetan soil. Social fragmentation combined with the demonic landscape to provide a perfect ecosystem for the tantras to flourish. Here, at the outer reaches of the Indian Buddhist mandala, in earth enriched by the droppings of jackals and decaying human flesh, the roots of the tantras took hold. The growth of Buddhism during these years was of a qualitatively different sort, to extend the plant analogy further, both from the initial seeds of the imperial period that preceded it and from the lush flowering of the renaissance that followed. The growth that took place during the intermediate years of fragmentation may have been invisible to the watchful (and sometimes withering) gaze of later monastic authorities,[103] but the proliferation of roots in the darkness marked a crucial stage in the development of Tibetan Buddhism, one that determined to a large degree the shape of the Buddhism that was to come.

3

A Buddhist Manual for Human Sacrifice?

Certainly the most violent text to emerge from the library cave of Dunhuang is a ritual manual for the performance of the notorious "liberation rite" (*sgrol ba*). Many early Mahāyoga writings from Dunhuang and elsewhere mention the liberation rite, but none is so explicit or detailed as this manual.[1] The rite is actually described twice in the same manuscript, and taken together the two passages paint a relatively complete picture of the proceedings. The instructions have the victim brought in and placed at the center of the ritual altar so that he faces west; the weapon is blessed and the victim purified, before being beheaded with an axe. Finally, the position in which the head comes to rest is interpreted to determine the rite's success.

The description is unusual, as it supplies so much detail yet makes no mention of an effigy. Liberation rites were central to early Mahāyoga practice, and they went on to play an important role throughout Tibetan culture, but they almost always suggest as an indirect performance, to be directed against an effigy of paper, cloth, or dough.[2] The Dunhuang manual, however, remains silent on the matter, and several details suggest that a live person may be intended. The ritual lacks a summoning rite, by which the victim's consciousness is usually called into the effigy.[3] But perhaps even more significant are the manual's instructions to fling the severed head onto the mandala platform and then divine the victim's next rebirth from how the head comes to rest; if it splits open, the rebirth will be a good one.[4] To be used in such a procedure, an effigy would have to be three-dimensional, not simply a drawing on paper, and fragile. Three-dimensional effigies are indeed well attested in Tibetan Buddhism, and the offering of such effigies' heads may even be observed in some modern rituals. In the Gathered Great Assembly (*Tshogs chen 'dus pa*) festival performed annually at Namdroling monastery in South India, for example, a painted dough effigy of Rudra is chopped up in the course of a ritual dance and its head preserved in a triangular box, to be thrown into the flames of a wrathful fire offering the following day.[5] Thus, while the casting of the victim's head in our Dunhuang rite is suggestive of a direct killing, it is by no means conclusive. A further but similarly ambiguous piece of evidence appears in another Dunhuang manuscript that also may describe a live liberation rite. PT840 goes a step further by listing as offerings both the victim's head and his blood.[6] Were an effigy intended here, it would have to be both three-dimensional and filled with blood. Again, however, such effigies are not unheard of: "In some cases," writes Nebesky-Wojkowitz in his study of Tibetan ritual dance, "the *liṅga* contains a bladder filled with blood. After piercing the bladder, some of the blood is sprinkled by a dancer in the four main directions as an offering."[7] Still another possibility is that the rite may have been intended as an imagined one, with the gruesome oblations all to be offered in one's mind.[8] Ultimately, it is impossible to say for sure whether our Dunhuang liberation rite is one of sympathetic magic or live human sacrifice. We can only conclude that these ancient instructions are highly ambiguous and that they at least *could* be read to involve the ritualized killing of an actual person. As we shall see in our next chapter, some Tibetans of the tenth century are purported to have read liberation rites of this sort in just such a way.

Tibetan historical sources do contain stories of face-to-face murders that are justified as instances of Buddhist "liberation." The best known is certainly the 842 assassination of King Lang Darma by the tantric expert Lhalung Pelgyi Dorje.[9] According to legend, the apostate king was killed with a knife or an arrow, depending on the version. The tale's historical accuracy is highly doubtful,[10] yet it has exercised a strong effect on the Tibetan imagination and is at least partly indicative of how the liberation rite has been understood in Tibet. The basic story was already well known by the mid-twelfth century, when it appeared in both the *Door for Entry into the Dharma* by Sonam Tsemo (1142–1182) and *The Flower's Essence: A Religious History* by Nyangrel Nyima Özer (1136–1204), and before long it had become the best-known case of "liberation" in Tibetan history, with Pelgyi Dorje in effect playing the role of Vajrapāṇi, saving Buddhism from the depredations of the Rudra-like demonic king, Lang Darma.[11]

Despite the popularity of the story, the vast majority of Tibetan liberations were performed by magical means. Even a character as transgressive as the eleventh-century tantric master Ra Lotsawa, who is credited with having killed dozens of Buddhist teachers and translators, is said to have employed the indirect *abhicāra* rites of Yangdak Heruka, Vajrabhairava, and others.

In the *Guhyasamāja Tantra* itself, the canonical work from which our Dunhuang manual was purportedly derived, the most explicit section on liberation recommends the destruction of a paper effigy.[12] A case of direct *abhicāra* is extremely rare, much less a detailed description of such a rite.

INTRODUCTION TO THE MANUSCRIPT

The manuscript containing the liberation manual is one of the longest in the Tibetan Dunhuang collections. Today it is divided into three parts, with two parts held in the Pelliot Collection at the Bibliothèque nationale and one in the Stein Collection at the British Library (fig. 5). Thus it begins in Paris, continues in London, and then concludes back in Paris.[13] Like much of the tantric material excavated from Dunhuang, the manuscript probably dates from the tenth century. It is in fact a compilation of seventeen distinct works, all probably based on the *Guhyasamāja Tantra*.[14] The *Guhyasamāja* was foremost among the transgressive Mahāyoga tantras that emerged in India during the second half of the eighth century, and it has been one of the most influential tantras in Tibetan history. It was also by far the most popular tantra among the tantric Buddhists of tenth-century Dunhuang.

The manuscript in question opens with a series of three offering rites: an offering to the mundane spirits and gods, a general offering (*spyi gtor*), and a ransom offering (*glud gtor*).[15] Immediately following these three rites is another, more-elaborate offering ritual for worshipping the mandala of the wrathful deity

Figure 5: A Buddhist Manual for Human Sacrifice?
(ITJ 419; Courtesy of the British Library)

Śrī Heruka.[16] Together, the four offering rites reveal how this ancient manuscript may have been used within the Tibetan Buddhist circles from which it emerged. Strictly speaking, the manuscript as a whole is less a ritual manual than a series of teachings on both ritual and doctrinal issues. The teachings appear, however, to have been transmitted within the context of a ritual, so that offerings were made and obstacles were cleared prior to the teachings being given.[17] For this reason the three initial offering rites conclude with the instruction, "In all temples, these offerings should be explained using words that are themselves a bestowal of the dharma."[18] Apparently there were even sponsors for these at least nominally secret tantric teachings, for the first two offering rites are dedicated to unnamed patrons: "May this [offering] fulfill the wishes of the patron, whoever they may be" [19] and "May the patron named . . . [insert name] . . . attain the level of a noble one through this accumulation of merit and wisdom."[20] In short, these esoteric teachings appear to have been intended for a relatively public setting, perhaps taught in a temple, to a gathering of tantric practitioners and with the material support of a wealthy donor.

After the initial offerings, the manuscript opens with an abbreviated version of the myth of Śrī Heruka's subjugation of the demon Rudra. This is followed by a series of nineteen questions and answers on the details of tantric theory and practice.[21] After this comes a long treatise on tantric ritual, then a brief text on the five vows, and then a treatise on the rites of sexual union and violent liberation (*sbyor sgrol*). Here in the latter work, we find our first discussion of the liberation rite. This is followed by four more short works: an explanation of the tantric *gaṇacakra* feast, verses of praise for the deity Vajrasattva, a short *sādhana*, and some mantras. At this point we encounter our second description of the liberation rite, after which the manuscript ends with a number of short works on the ten activities, a typology of *vajras*, various sets of deities and goddesses, an extensive discussion of ritualized sexual union, and some closing mantras.[22]

In addition to the two main passages mentioned here, several other brief discussions of the liberation rite appear elsewhere in the same manuscript, in particular in the series of nineteen questions and answers. The eighteenth of these, for example, expresses concern that the rite be performed only by a qualified master:

> Question: During the liberation rite, which methods make for good qualities, and which for faults?
>
> Answer: The performance of what is called "liberation" presses harmful demons at their heart into unsurpassable enlightenment. For one who is expert in the mantras, the *mudrās*, and the *samādhis* [necessary] for performing this, and for whom habituation to the subtle *vajra* has been experienced, there is

> no transgression, and so there is "attainment of the realm." This is not so for ordinary people who perform it, just as in the case of performing [ritualized sexual] union.[23]

The practitioner of this liberation rite, then, should be one who has received the necessary ritual training and who, perhaps more importantly, has habituated to "the subtle *vajra*." Only such a high state of realization will ensure that the practitioner is not simply committing murder and thus transgressing the normative Buddhist prohibitions against killing. In chapter 1 we have explored the dangerous proximity of illegitimate to legitimate violence within the Buddhist teachings. Here we see concerns at these same dangers being expressed, and once again the mental state of the actor makes all the difference.

Precisely what it means to be habituated to "the subtle *vajra*" (Tib. *rdo rje phra mo*; Skt. **sūkṣma-vajra*) is addressed in the eleventh question of the same text. There we read,

> Question: Regarding this so-called "habituation to the subtle *vajra*," if the *mahāmudrā* is clearly attained, is that it or not?
>
> Answer: Though the *mahāmudrā* [that is, the union of one's own body with that of the deity] may be clearly performed, if during one's meditation one thinks about how clear the *mahāmudrā* is, then that cannot be called "being habituated to the subtle *vajra*." And even when [performing] just the proper *samādhi*, one with the thoughts of a proud person who thinks he is powerful in this way is not habituated to the subtle *vajra*. One can tell that someone is like that if he fashions himself in the likeness of an expert. Obsessed with the external and internal signs [of accomplishment], he seeks to discriminate between their varieties. He engages in practice with no realization and hoping only for power. This is a great abyss of error.[24]

In order to perform the liberation rite, one has to be expert in cultivating a nondual, nonconceptual mental state within which union with the deity and other ritual practices may be performed.

Elsewhere in our manuscript, cultivating "the subtle *vajra*" is associated with the so-called subtle yoga practice in which a tiny five-colored jewel is visualized at the tip of one's nose. Such a practice is a well-known element of the *Guhyasamāja* ritual system, and variations on the theme appear throughout the tantra itself.[25] In the present manuscript, the following description appears in the context of a rite of sexual union:

> Upon the head of oneself abiding in the *mahāmudrā* is a [yellow] *oṃ*. At the throat, a [red] *aṃ*, and at the heart a [white] *hūṃ*. At one's waist is a [blue] *svā*. On the soles of one's feet a [green] *hā* is arranged. From those, light-rays

> radiate and regather, whereby a *vajra* at one's heart becomes a body the size of a mere mustard seed [the wisdom body in five colors]. Moving from within the interior, it emerges at the tip of one's nose and radiates light-rays. Then they regather. Constantly cultivate "like that," as it says. The brightening is what is called "habituating to the subtle *vajra*." Meditate in that way.[26]

Given the sexual context of this passage, we may wonder whether the "nose" (*shangs*; elsewhere sometimes *sna*) here might be a euphemism for the penis. Such a reading is encouraged just one folio side farther on, where we find a reference to the "*vajra* nose" (*rdo rje shangs*), the *vajra* being the more common tantric term for the penis. A sexualized interpretation of the "nose" is also seen in the notes to the Dunhuang manuscript of the *Guhyasamāja Tantra* and is likewise common in the later Ārya tradition of *Guhyasamāja* exegesis.[27] According to such a reading, cultivating "the subtle *vajra*" might refer to the state of dwelling in sexual union while visualizing a drop (*bindu*) containing a miniscule assembly of buddhas at the tip of the penis, which results in a blissful intensification, or a "brightening," of one's meditative experience. Whether from focusing on the tip of the penis or the actual nose, the resulting nonconceptual brightness is the state within which one is supposed to perform the liberation rite.[28]

Question nine tells us still more about the mental state of the properly qualified practitioner. This question asks about the three "heats" associated with each of the rites of the tantric feast, liberation, and sexual union. "Heat" in this context is a sign of accomplishment, an experience that results from intense meditative practice. The three heats of liberation consist of heat, near heat, and the great heat. Of particular interest is the last: "As for the measure of descending into the great heat: While planning and executing the activities, [one performs] the yoga of resting in the excellent. A mass of blazing *vajras* goes into the sky and so forth. The wrathful gods and goddesses of compassionate means become manifest. The activities are performed, then the oblations are taken and 'the realm is attained,' whereupon the marks of faith in everything are immediately demonstrated."[29] Within this meditative state, then, one performs the liberation rite. Indeed, this is precisely how the first of our two descriptions of the rite begins, by instructing that the practitioner "descends into heat."

DESCRIPTION OF THE RITE

At this point we should turn to the two Dunhuang passages in question.[30]

TRANSLATION OF PASSAGE 1:[31]

Here a brief discussion of liberation is in order: Initially the master descends into heat, whereby it is said, "the activities are completed." If the master is not endowed with heat, it is said that one should "practice by means of the ten activities." If neither option is possible, the performance of the [liberation] activity will not overpower the eight great terrors (**mahābhairava*), whereby those who assemble [to perform the rite] will immediately become extremely unhappy, and even if great compassion is felt, they will wander through the realms of *saṃsāra*. Because great negativities may arise, anyone who fabricates or lacks the necessary confidence and heat, or does not have the relevant scriptural and oral instructions, should not be taught how to perform this activity.

Thus a master for whom the two activities discussed above are possible, at one of the specified times, should consecrate the site and arrange the shrine with the outer and inner offerings. The master grants initiation and blesses the gathered assembly, then commands them to cultivate the meditative concentrations on the various deities. Recite in unison the heart mantra of Śrī Heruka 108 times, "*oṃ rulu rulu hūṃ bhyo hana hana hūṃ phaṭ*," then present the inner offering cakes. Worship Śrī Heruka and his retinue and all the powerful ones in the assembly. These activities must be accomplished. Prayers should be made that there be no obstructions from evil spirits and that the accomplishments be attained. Transgressions of the sacrament on any side should be repaired.

Present the outer offering cakes. When performing the offerings, feasts, and worship for all those [mundane gods such as] Brahmā, Indra, the great kings, the directional guardians, the serpent king, and so on who do not abide in the secret sacrament, at that time a sacramental vow should be bestowed upon them, so that they do nothing to obstruct or harm [those present], or to obstruct or harm [the attainment of] the *siddhis*. Establish the protective [ritual] boundaries against the outside, and when [selecting] the group of insiders, establish the boundaries by means of meditative concentration so that those who are not included in the secret sacrament will not perceive [what will occur]. Perform the blessings. Then the master should [physically] expel, and establish the boundaries against, those who are not included in the sacrament.[32] This is the yogin's coercion activity.[33] Those who remain gathered then transform themselves into the manner of powerful wrathful deities. Propitiate for a long while and do the recitations and meditations.

Then at the center of the *maṇḍala*, at the center of a crossed *vajra* that rests atop a wind *maṇḍala*, whoever is to be held with compassion is placed so that he faces toward the west.[34]

Those present in the group, having entered together into meditative concentration, then imagine that all their karma and afflicted karmic imprints are incinerated by a conflagration. All their karmic imprints are shaken and loosened by devastating gales, then washed away and purified by apocalyptic floods.

Then it is time for the so-called "mixing of the internal and the external." Using a paste of white mustard seeds that purifies the negative rebirths, do the recitations and smear it on the object of compassion [that is, at key points on the victim's body],[35] purifying his karmic imprints. Through the activities of [sexual] union too, the imprints may be purified and "the object will be offered." The being who is to perform the liberation transforms himself into *Tāraka-sūrya. His right eye becomes the sun, whereby [the victim's] karmic imprints are incinerated by a conflagration. His left eye becomes the moon, whereby all [the victim's] karmic imprints are washed away and purged by apocalyptic floods. "Ha ha!" The winds of his loud laughter loosen and scatter [them afar]. That object of compassion is completely pure, like a crystal egg.[36]

Then imagine a shining crescent moon atop [the victim's] head.[37] Invite the noble ones[38] who gather in the *maṇḍala* assembly, and without stopping the activities for purifying his karmic imprints, perform in unison the meditative concentrations for the deed.

Then above the neck of that object of compassion, imagine that Kālarātrī appears. Black with matted hair and riding a white mule, she brandishes and shakes an iron net, performing her activities without the passage of time. She is the "Lady of Death." Holding aloft the demonic iron axe, imagine that one performs the activities of this Lady of Death. From her, imagine that a dark blue *krong* syllable appears atop [the victim's] head.

The being who is to perform the liberation enters the meditative concentration of Ṭakkirāja, then liberates with the weapon while reciting, "[. . .]."[39] From the *krong* atop [the victim's] head, many blades cleave and chop.[40] Then the consciousness emerges and is offered to the principal deity. Each time it meets with the mouths of the principal deity and all his retinue, *siddhis* are granted and the object who is the cause [that is, the victim] is fed into the unmistaken.

Do the meditations and recitations, obtain the meditative concentration of the deity, and keep in the mind the number of times the consciousness shakes. Having made the thoughts clear in his mind, the master revives the consciousness, then flings it [and the head] onto the *maṇḍala* and analyzes the signs. Once in the midst of the *maṇḍala*, if [the head] does not stop shaking, then the *siddhis* have been attained. If [the head] faces in the direction of the *maṇḍala*, all the noble ones are pleased. If [the head] splits at the crown, that is good. If it looks to the right or the left, the performance of the yogin's activities has been unobstructed. If it faces toward the doors of the *maṇḍala* or faces downward, the *siddhis* were not attained and there has been some interference from obstacles, so it will be necessary to perform the suppression by means of the outer assembly.

TRANSLATION OF PASSAGE 2:[41]

Regarding the activity of liberation: There are five kinds of causes for worship: (i) someone who deprecates the teachings of the Mahāyāna, (ii) one who insults a noble one, (iii) one who comes into the *maṇḍala* without having received the sacraments, (iv) one with false views, or (v) one who threatens the survival of the Mahāyāna teachings. The liberation of such a being should be undertaken with a foundation of great compassion.

At the five locations [on the body] of whomever is chosen, place the five seed [syllables] of the wrathful buddhas. This is the method for [ensuring that the victim] will not be reborn in the three realms,[42] called "the five kinds of ornaments for the mind." Placing *oṃ* at the crown of the head cuts off the path to [rebirth with] the demi-gods. Placing *hrīḥ* on the tongue cuts off the path to the humans. Placing *hūṃ* at the heart cuts off the path to the animals. Placing *drang* at the secret place cuts off the path to the ghost realm. Placing *a* on the soles of the feet cuts off the path to the hells. These paths having been cut off, [only] the path to the gods remains open. Then the many assemblies of nobles ones are invited.

Regarding which [deities] are suitable for performing the respective activities: Noble *Tāraka-sūrya[43] performs the act of liberation. Mahākrodha Vidyārāja offers the object [of compassion]. Yamāntaka pleases the assembly of the many peaceful and wrathful deities, the Heruka lord of the assembly and so forth.

Then at the cranial aperture at the top of the head stands the heart syllable, a dark blue *krong*, the heart mantra for the *vajra* weapon. From that [syllable] come blessings so that the [victim's] body is chopped [as if] by many blades.

Then the being who is to perform the liberation transforms into *Tāraka-Sūrya. His right eye is empowered as a sun, the fiery light-rays of which incinerate [the victim's] karmic imprints. His left eye is empowered as a moon, from which the floods of the apocalypse wash away [the victim's] karmic imprints. "Ha ha!" The winds of his loud laughter loosen and scatter [them afar]. Having been purified, [the victim] is imagined to be utterly pure, like a crystal egg.

Pronouncing, ". . ." perform the liberation with the weapon.

Then without interrupting the survival of the consciousness,[44] offer it up to the lips of the many assembled [deities], to the central [*heruka*] and so on. [The consciousness] gathers, dissolving into the jeweled stomachs of Vajrasattva and the others.

Then emerge into the *vajra*-path, proclaimed as the place of indivisibility, and offer the five fruits in the manner of the five families. Then visualize the four limbs and the head (making five in all) and the five internal organs as the ten wrathful gods and goddesses, and worship them. All the sentient beings who are on the [Buddhist] path are blessed as deities and then called as

> guests. They all act in the manner of vultures. Then just as they are satisfied by the flesh and the blood, in the same way they all are satisfied by the teachings of the Vajrayāna and are established in the level of Samantabhadra.
>
> All mistaken and afflicted teachings are not other than the teachings of the vehicles. Therefore not even the names of the demons and the evil spirits really exist. With regard to the three realms, all the sentient beings present in that *maṇḍala* are meditated upon and worshipped as an enlightened assembly of wrathful gods and goddesses.

The two descriptions thus combine to provide a full picture of the rite, though they introduce some technical issues that may require some further explanation. As already observed, the officiating master initially enters the proper meditative state, or "descends into heat." If unable to accomplish this at will, the master is to perform "the ten activities." The latter are discussed elsewhere in the same manuscript,[45] and seem to constitute a basic ritual for worshipping the buddhas and receiving their blessings, a rite that presumably culminates in the attainment of a level of meditation equivalent to that of "descend[ing] into heat." The entirety of the proceedings that follow are thus to be accomplished while maintaining this same meditative state. If, even after the ten activities, the master is still unable to descend into heat, he is instructed not to continue with the rite. Otherwise, the text warns, an endless series of negative rebirths will result.

The master then prepares the ritual space, consecrating the site and arranging the appropriate offerings upon a shrine. He initiates all those present into the wrathful mandala (presumably that of the *Guhyasamāja* ritual system), after which each person cultivates himself as his respective deity within that imagined mandala, and recites the mantra of the central deity, Śrī Heruka. The assembled then present to the deities of the mandala the "inner" offering cakes, a traditional oblationary form usually fashioned out of dough. They then pray for protection against any possible obstructions and repair any past transgressions of the vows by means of further confession and prayers.

This is immediately followed by the "outer" offerings, a set of presumably lesser oblations that are directed at the mundane gods who reside outside the mandala palace. Being mundane gods, they are bound by vow not to create difficulties for the liberation rite that will follow. The ritual space is then sealed and protective boundaries are established, a process that typically involves the visualized construction of an adamantine "pavillion" enclosing the ritual space. Finally, anyone present who still has not received the necessary initiations is expelled.

Now the "object of compassion" (either the actual victim or the effigy) is brought in and placed at the center of a mandala that has been constructed at the heart of the ritual space. The term "mandala" here likely refers to some sort of altar platform, as is commonly seen in early tantric Buddhism.[46] The placing of human subjects upon such platforms is also attested elsewhere, as for example in the ritual section of the *Mahāpratisāravidyārājñī*, in which a sick person is placed at the center of a "mandala" in order to be cured.[47] In the case of the liberation rite, the platform in question may well have been triangular, the shape most commonly associated with violent ritual activity.[48] The victim is thus positioned upon the mandala, facing west, the direction of Sukhāvatī, *Amitābha*'s buddhafield, to which the victim's consciousness will hopefully depart.

The victim himself should represent a threat to the Buddhist teachings by being guilty of one of five possible crimes, and our second passage enumerates these five. Similar lists of appropriate targets for liberation are common in tantric literature, with tenfold lists being particularly popular in later Tibet. The fivefold list is reminiscent of the earlier nontantric set of "five sins of immediate retribution" (*pañcānantaryāṇi*), five sins said to send the offender straight to hell at death. The five crimes for liberation may represent a tantric response to these earlier five sins, though it should be noted that enumerations of seven or ten crimes are also seen in the earliest stratum of Mahāyoga materials.[49] Having been identified as guilty of one of the five crimes, the victim is determined to be a "field" for liberation.

Then come a series of purificatory rites. First, all those present imagine themselves as being cleansed of all their karmic negativities, then the victim is purified through the application of a white-mustard-seed paste at five key points on his body (or the body of his effigy), each corresponding to one of the six possible realms of rebirth, excluding the highest realm of the gods.[50] As each daub is smeared upon the body, the appropriate syllable is recited: *oṃ* for the demigods, *hrīḥ* for the humans, *hūṃ* for the animals, and so forth. Thus five possible exits are blocked. Later Tibetans commonly say that one's rebirth is determined by where on the body one's consciousness emerges. Normally a purificatory practice of this sort ensures that the consciousness will emerge only from the top of the victim's head, but here the crown has been blocked as the exit to the demigods. Here the rite also seems to conflate the god realms—the only path remaining open—with enlightenment, as represented by the mandala visualized above the victim's head, presumably positioned to receive the consciousness as it emerges.[51]

Next a final purification of the victim's mental impurities is performed, in conjunction with the ritual master's imaginative transformation of himself into the wrathful buddha Ṭakkirāja.[52] The *Guhyasamāja Tantra* includes a brief description of this deity. "The great wrathful Ṭakkirāja," it reads, "has three terrifying faces and four supremely terrifying arms."[53] The mere appearance of this fearsome buddha, our Dunhuang manual explains, with his apocalyptic gaze and wild laughter, completes the cleansing of the victim's karmic imprints. From his right eye burst flames that incinerate the impurities, from his left eye flood waters that wash them away, and the winds of his laughter blow away any that remain, leaving him thoroughly purified.[54]

The goddess Kālarātrī (Dus 'tshan ma) is then summoned. Ferocious in form, she appears in the space directly above the victim's neck, riding a white mule. With the mantra-syllable *krong*, she empowers and propels the liberating weapon, driving it with the force of many blades.[55] It is perhaps relevant that the same goddess appears in a similarly terrifying form in the *Sauptikaparvan* of the *Mahābhārata*, where she presides over Aśvatthāman's sacrificial slaughter of Dhṛṣṭadyumna and his sleeping army.[56]

Proclaiming a version of Ṭakkirāja's mantra, the master then beheads the victim. As the victim's consciousness emerges, presumably from the severed neck, the master carefully directs it up to the mouth of the *heruka* buddha at the center of the mandala, where it is eaten.[57] Purified, it dissolves into the buddha's "jeweled stomach," and thus too into enlightenment. The same ingestive imagery is seen in the mythic description of Rudra's own liberation. There, the *heruka* buddha's stomach is likened to a blissful buddhafield, and Nupchen Sangye Yeshe's ninth-century commentary adds the following: "[The buddha] ate the flesh, drank the blood, and having arranged the bones, ate the three poisons as offerings. He hacked and cut off the limbs, ripping out the heart and sense organs. Drawing out the internal organs, he swallowed them, and all was purified in his stomach."[58]

According to the tradition, here begins the crucial moment that determines the success or failure of the rite, and it hinges on the master's ability to link his consciousness to that of the victim and guide it into enlightenment, or at least to a better rebirth. It is notable that the moment is cast in terms of a bloody sacrificial feast.

At this point the second of our two passages instructs the master to "emerge into the *vajra*-path," which under most circumstances would involve the performance of a rite of sexual union. The subsequent feasting then takes place within the meditative state that this union produces, as the ten parts of the victim's dead body—his four limbs, head, and five internal organs—are transformed into the ten wrathful gods and goddesses and "worshipped."[59] All lesser beings on the Buddhist path (that is, not those deities who dwell within the mandala, as those have already received the choicest share of the sacrifice) are then invited to feast upon the victim's bodily remains and receive it as blessings.

Finally, one imagines the victim's consciousness to be revived and ejected once more into the mandala. Again we see parallels with the Rudra myth, as this second ejection would seem equivalent to the tantric initiation that is bestowed upon Rudra following his own resuscitation. As discussed above, this second ejection of the victim's consciousness is accompanied by a simultaneous hurling of the head—be it real, effigial, or imaginary—onto the mandala platform.[60] The position in which the head lands is then interpreted to divine the victim's rebirth. The offering of the head into the mandala may be in part a macabre play on the flower-tossing rite of many tantric initiation ceremonies, in which the initiate throws a flower into the mandala. Where the flower lands on the mandala determines which deity the initiate is karmically predisposed to take as her tutelary *yidam* (the deity that she will henceforth worship).[61]

It is important to remember that many Indians and Tibetans of the day would have been horrified by a ritual such as this. Indeed, as we have seen, this was to some degree the point. Even as the Mahāyoga tantras advocated the transgression of societal norms, they depended on the existence of the very values they claimed to disregard. In chapter 1 we have observed how the Rudra subjugation myth purposefully dwelt at length upon the most terrifying and disturbing aspects of its narrative. The liberation rite may similarly have been intended to horrify, to challenge some of society's most unquestioned truths. It was the ultimate extreme, and in precisely this sense it was the Mahāyoga practice *par excellence*. Given the centrality of the practice, at least rhetorically, to these transgressive tantras, we may not be surprised to learn that similar rites were performed in the other contemporaneous tantric traditions of India, and it is to one of these that we now turn.

A COMPARISON OF THE LIBERATION RITE AND THE *KĀLIKĀ PURĀṆA*'S "BLOOD CHAPTER"

Tantric religion was a pan-Indian development, and the Buddhist tantras shared much in common with those of other sects. Even as Buddhists, Śaivas, Vaiṣṇavas, and others competed for patronage, they exchanged a wide range of ideas and practices, at times even drawing from the same well of oral and written sources. The liberation rite from Dunhuang may represent an example of such intersectarian sharing, for a comparison of the rite's details with a similar Śākta ritual reveals a number of striking similarities.

Ritual slaying appears in a variety of Hindu tantric sources, but there too effigies are typically employed (thus *māraṇa*, "slaying," is one of the six ritual acts (*ṣaṭkarman*) commonly listed in Śaiva sources).[62] A description of a rite of human sacrifice (*mahāpaśu*) does appear, however, in chapter 71 of the *Kālikā*

Purāṇa. The *Rudhirādhyāya*, or "Blood Chapter," describes a sacrificial rite in which either an animal or a human being may be offered to the wrathful goddess Kālī. The rite first came to the attention of Western scholars in 1799, when W. C. Blaquiere, a magistrate working in Calcutta, published his English translation in *Asiatick Researches*.[63] The *Kālikā Purāṇa* appears to have undergone numerous redactions. In its received form it is a relatively late text, dating from the sixteenth century or later, but portions of it likely date from considerably earlier.[64]

Like the Dunhuang liberation rite, the *Kālikā Purāṇa*'s ritual of human sacrifice directs the practitioner to arrange the victim at the sacrificial site, facing him in a specific direction, "so that he faces north" in the *Kālikā Purāṇa*,[65] and west in our liberation rite. Next the sacrificial victim is prepared by touching different parts of his body and reciting prayers: "Worship the deities on each of his limbs,"[66] we are told in the *Kālikā Purāṇa*, while in the liberation rite, key points on the victim's body are daubed with a mustard paste while reciting a mantric syllable over each.

The purification complete, the sacrificial weapon is then selected. The *Kālikā Purāṇa* recommends, "cutting with an axe or a knife is said to be the best."[67] A similar recommendation is also made in the liberation rite, where a "demonic iron axe" (*bdud lchags kyi sta re*) is specified (or a *kartari* in PT840).[68] The similarities grow still more striking with the appearance of Kālarātrī.[69] In both rituals, this fearsome black goddess is called upon to bless and empower the axe, and she then presides, hovering over the proceedings, so that the killing takes place in her name. In the *Kālikā Purāṇa*, "Having empowered the sword with her mantra, Kālarātrī shows her favor for the destruction of the enemies,"[70] while in the liberation rite, "Holding aloft the demonic iron axe, imagine that one performs the activities of this Lady of Death."

When the time comes for presenting the sacrificial oblations to the gods, whether to Kālī or to the *heruka* buddha and his mandala assembly, in both cases the severed head is offered.[71] Here, however, is a significant difference, for in the Śākta rite the victim's blood is offered along with his head.[72] This double offering stands in contrast to that of our liberation rite, in which the head is accompanied instead by the victim's mental consciousness. We will return to this point below.

Finally the position in which the severed head comes to rest is interpreted for signs of success, and once again the *Kālikā Purāṇa* describes a similar divination: "Listen to the good and bad omens for one's animals and so on, as indicated by where the man's severed head falls: If the man's head falls toward the northeast or southwest, there will be loss and destruction for the kingdom.

If the man's severed head falls in the following directions, the following omens are indicated: If in the east, prosperity; if in the southeast, increase; if in the south, danger; if in the west, profit; if in the northwest, a son will be obtained, if in the north, riches."[73]

The parallels between these two ancient works are thus many and striking. It seems safe to say that this ancient liberation ritual manual that has emerged from the darkness of the Dunhuang caves was not entirely unique among the tantric circles of medieval India.

LIBERATION AS SACRIFICE

A comparison of the Buddhist and Śākta versions of this violent ritual allows us to suggest something even more significant: From a structural standpoint, the *Guhyasamāja* liberation ritual closely resembles a rite of *sacrifice*. Such an idea sharply contrasts with the well-known Buddhist proscriptions against blood sacrifices of any kind, let alone *human* sacrifice. Historically, the Brahmanical traditions have touted various forms of sacrifice as their central religious practice, and few would disagree that the rite described in the *Kālikā Purāṇa* is a blood sacrifice. Yet many Tibetan Buddhists might be appalled at the suggestion that their own well-known liberation rite is, in one of its earliest forms at least, a rite of human sacrifice.[74]

Technically speaking, the *Kālikā Purāṇa* does not refer to its blood offering as a "sacrifice" (the most common translation of the Sanskrit term, *yajña*), at least not directly; rather it prefers the term *balidāna*, or "oblation offering." It is clear, however, that many ancient Indians considered the *bali* a type of sacrifice. In a well-known passage from the *Laws of Manu*, the *bali* is listed as one of the five "great sacrifices" (*mahāyajña*) to be carried out daily by householders: "The sacrifice to the Veda is to teach; the sacrifice to the ancestors is the libation; the sacrifice to the gods is the *homa*; the sacrifice to the spirits is the *bali*; and the sacrifice to humans is hospitality."[75] To label all five of these offerings "sacrifices" is perhaps to stretch the meaning of sacrifice, but it remains true that many Indians, ancient and modern, would probably not object to calling the human *balidāna* described in the *Kālikā Purāṇa*'s "Blood Chapter" a sacrifice, nor more specifically that, as a *bali*, the rite represents a form of sacrifice meant for satisfying the *bhūta* world of ghosts, spirits, and demons.

Tibetans might argue that their liberation is framed differently from Vedic and Brahmanical sacrifice, that the Buddhist emphasis on ethics and the welfare of the victim's consciousness is irrelevant to a sacrificial offering and thus puts their liberation rite in a class different from the earlier Vedic rituals. In fact, however, the Vedic texts also assert that the sacrificial victim ascended to heaven upon death. "You do not die, nor are you hurt," reads the *Ṛgveda*, "By easy paths, you go to the gods."[76] Later too, compassionate rhetoric appeared in the tantric Śaiva tradition. In the *Netra Tantra*, for example, the immolation of the victim (*paśus*) liberates his soul from suffering and into a state of union with his lord, Śiva.[77]

Certainly from a Western perspective, the Dunhuang liberation rite includes many elements that are characteristic of sacrifice. In accordance with Edward Tyler's early (1871) model of sacrifice, it is an offering. It includes a communal meal (William Robertson Smith). It is exorcistic (Frazer); it is consecratory (Hubert and Mauss); and as an act of violent transgression, it is "aneconomic, gratuitous, indeed excessive" (Derrida).[78]

Thus many of the ritual elements seen in this Dunhuang manual are probably best understood as remnants, at least, of the rite's sacrificial origins, even if they have been sanitized to bring them into line with the ideologies of normative Buddhism. After immolating the victim, for example, the practitioner offers him up to be *eaten* by the wrathful deities of the mandala and then by the other ravenous gods and demons of the spirit world. Although the Buddhist reading prefers to emphasize the offering of the consciousness over that of the flesh and blood, the gory facts remain. Nonetheless, the offering of flesh into the mandala remained popular enough to require repeated condemnations by Buddhist teachers in later Tibet and its border regions. The late-nineteenth-century work *The Dangers of Blood Sacrifice*, by Rigdzin Gargyi Wangchuk, forbids those practices in which "the killed flesh is placed in the *maṇḍala*."[79]

When seen as sublimated aspects of Buddhist human sacrifice, the details of the Dunhuang liberation rite suggest a further connection between the sacrificial offering of blood and the ejection of the victim's consciousness. We have noted above that the rite replaces the *Kālikā Purāṇa*'s offering of the head and the blood with one of the head and the *consciousness*.[80] This shift from blood to consciousness may be understandable if we consider both blood and consciousness to represent the essential spirit of the sacrificial victim, the "vital sap" that is to be offered.[81] Both the victim's consciousness in the liberation rite and the blood offering in the *Kālikā* rite should emerge from the victim's severed neck.[82] Here we may be reminded of a standard practice in the animal sacrifice rites of modern India and Nepal, in which the arteries in the victim's neck are clamped immediately following the decapitation. The dead victim is then brought near to the image of the oblatory deity, and the artery is released so as to spray the image with the carefully preserved, still-warm blood as an offering.[83] In a similar way in the liberation rite, "without interrupting the survival of the consciousness, one offers it up to the lips of . . . the central deity." Elsewhere too, another Dunhuang discussion of the liberation rite identifies the victim's mind as "the choice share" that is to be offered into the mandala.[84] And finally, a parallel between the victim's blood and his life force may be seen in the animal sacrifices of the Magar of northwestern central Nepal. Oppitz has described how the Magar distribute the animal's meat among themselves, while giving the spirits only a little of the animal's blood mixed with flour. "As the Magar say," writes Oppitz, "the supernaturals receive the essence of the sacrifice, *shya si*, 'the breath and life of the meat,' whereas the humans receive its material substance."[85] Here too, then, blood and spirit are correlated substances.

A sacrificial reading of the Dunhuang manual's ritual logic thus reveals a possible strategy by which the Buddhists of early medieval India may have domesticated the kinds of human sacrifice rites practiced by the *tāntrikas* of other religious sects. By shifting the ritual focus from the victim's blood to his consciousness, they cleansed the offering of its more overtly sacrificial appearance, to focus instead on the more ethical rhetoric of compassionate violence that reemphasized the victim's metempsychotic welfare over the simple gratification of the gods.

The successful offering of the consciousness into the mandala is referred to by the technical phrase "offering into the realm" (*gnas bstabs*). This marks the crucial moment in the liberation rite, and discussions of the phrase appear in a number of other tantric texts. Of particular relevance is an example from chapter 23 of the Mahāyoga tantra, the *Lasso of Means*. As the chapter's title makes clear, it contains a teaching on the "Ritual for Offering into the Realm" (*gnas bstabs pa'i cho ga*). It describes the actual moment of offering in terms that are remarkably similar to our Dunhuang passages: "For those on whom the wrathful liberation has been performed, meditate on closing their gates to the five [lower] rebirths by means of the five seed[-syllables]. At that time gather their consciousness with a *hūṃ*. Having inhaled it into your stomach, send it into the Akaniṣṭha land, ejecting it with a '*phaṭ*' into the womb of she who performs union with the aforementioned deity."[86]

Anyone familiar with Tibetan ritual who reads this description of drawing the consciousness into one's belly in order to eject it with a forceful "*phaṭ*" up and out through the top of one's head and into a buddhafield will inevitably be reminded of the well-known "transfer of consciousness" (*'pho ba*) rite. In later Tibet a similar, though often more elaborate, rite became popular, for propelling one's consciousness at death, up the subtle body's central channel and into an ideal rebirth.[87] Here, in the liberation rite's "offering into the realm," we see an early version of the transfer-of-consciousness ritual.[88] It is notable that the later transfer-of-consciousness rite may be performed not only upon oneself, but in order to eject the consciousnesses of others as well. Thus, in modern Tibet, for example, the rite functions as a standard part of the funerary sequence. The early liberation rite thus may be seen to straddle a variety of interrelated rituals, from violent curses to the transfer of consciousness and Buddhist funerary practices.[89] All of these later practices may be understood, in some sense, as ritual sublimations of the original sacrifice.

Despite Buddhism's well-known and much-repeated prohibitions of blood sacrifice, this tenth-century manuscript from Dunhuang seems—on its surface—to describe just such a rite. Even assuming it intends an effigial rite, through the lens of this ancient manual, vestiges of sacrifice appear throughout the Tibetan tradition. As in Christianity and so many other religions, human sacrifice through its powerful tropes strongly influenced Tibetan Buddhism, its ritual logic informing a wide array of later practices.[90] Some form of the liberation rite presented here likely originated in late-eighth- or early ninth-century India (after which the transmission of Buddhism into Tibet was interrupted). The tenth-century manuscript in which it appears includes a number of additional Buddhist texts, and none describes anything but the usual fare of early Mahāyoga practice. The ritual procedures were common enough to be translated into Tibetan and preserved thousands of miles to the north in a cave near Dunhuang, and here too we may note, once more, the existence of a second detailed description of the liberation rite, also with no effigy mentioned, that appears in the Dunhuang manuscript PT840. Indeed, offering rites like the one seen in these Dunhuang manuscripts seem to have been practiced across the religious spectrum of tantric India, as indicated by the existence of the *Kālikā Purāṇa*'s own remarkably similar "Blood Chapter." The Dunhuang liberation rite thus embodies a tradition of tantric practice that seems to have enjoyed some popularity, at least in certain circles, and that even in later years continued to haunt the Buddhism of Tibet.

A millennium ago the original body of this valuable manuscript was sacrificed to the sands of time. In 1908 its three limbs, PT36, ITJ419, and PT42, were scattered across the world, landing in the great capitals of London and Paris, and they remain to this day in London buried in a vault beneath the ground. Only now, by reassembling its limbs, can we see clearly this ancient text's original form and begin to appreciate the extent of its influence within the history of Tibetan Buddhism.

4

Sacrifice and the Law

In 1777, William Coates Blaquiere set sail from England with his father, Jacob Blaquiere, an employee of the East India Company. Following his arrival in India, William became an interpreter for the Supreme Court and Justice of the Peace in Calcutta, and by the 1780s had risen to the post of police magistrate. Apparently a student of the Sanskrit language, in 1799 he published his translation of the *Kālikā Purāṇa*'s infamous "Sanguinary Chapter" (or "Blood Chapter") in the fifth volume of the recently inaugurated *Asiatick Researches*. Unfortunately, Blaquiere provided no preface to his translation, nor did he ever publish with the journal again, so we have little direct knowledge of his motivations for publishing the work. His interest in such a bloody topic is not entirely surprising. As police magistrate, he must have been confronted with violence on a regular basis, but more significantly, his British colleagues in the Calcutta legal system and the East India Company shared a similar fascination with the violent rituals of the Hindus.

Just five years before Blaquiere's article, in 1794, Sir William Jones had published his own landmark translation of the *Laws of Manu* (*Mānava Dharmaśāstra*), entitled *Institutes of Hindu Law, or, the Ordinances of Menu*. Jones arrived in Calcutta six years after Blaquiere's arrival in 1777, and as judge on the Supreme Court of Bengal, founder of the Asiatic Society, and renowned philologist, he surely exerted a significant influence on his younger contemporary. Unlike Blaquiere, Jones was explicit about what motivated his work. He published in order that the rule of British law would "be conformable, as far as the natives are affected by them, to the manners and opinions of the natives themselves; an object, which cannot possibly be attained, until those manners and opinions can be fully and accurately known."[1] Through his work, he hoped that the British would come to understand their colonial subjects and thus rule them more effectively. In fact, of course, the *Laws of Manu* was nearly two thousand years old, and its rules were rarely observed in late-eighteenth-century India outside a small class of Brahmans. Its translation may have shed light on India's ancient past, but it told its British readers little about the laws and customs of contemporary India.[2] Nonetheless, it was used to justify the British occupation of India.[3] Its "dreadfully cruel" punishments and "idle superstitions" paved the way for rule by "a country happily enlightened by sound philosophy and the only true revelation."[4] Elsewhere Jones explained, "The cruel mutilations, practiced by the native powers, are not only shocking to humanity, but wholly inconsistent with the mildness of our system."[5] Indians' approach to violence and the law was deeply irrational and misguided, so much so that the "protection for their persons and places of abode, [and] justice in their temporal concerns" were far better kept in the hands of the British courts.[6]

Such was the audience that received Blaquiere's publication of the *Kālikā Purāṇa*'s "Blood Chapter." The chapter's sacrificial rites were seen not as practices of the distant past; such horrors were still rife among the peoples of India. In his widely read 1817 *The History of British India*, James Mill cited Blaquiere's translation when he wrote, "It is abundantly ascertained that the Hindus at one time, and that a time comparatively recent, were marked with the barbarity of human sacrifices. It even appears that the remainder of that devotional service is now in existence. . . . The British Government has interfered to prevent the sacrifice of children by throwing them to the sharks in the Ganges."[7] Such barbaric behaviors served to justify the civilizing influences of British law and morality. "Among rude nations," Mill continued, "it has almost always been found, that religion has served to degrade morality, by advancing to the place of greatest honour, those external performances, or those mental exercises, which more immediately regarded the deity; and with which, of course, he was supposed to be more peculiarly delighted."[8] Cultish ritual killings meant to please one's deity thus marked the lowest degradation of proper moral behavior. Though such "abominable rites" pay lip service to morality in "pompous strains," they were ultimately deluded and must be prohibited by rule of law.[9]

The early nineteenth century saw a spate of such vilifications of Indian religious practices. Perhaps best known were the sensationalized debates over *sati*, or widow burning, that spanned a half century and culminated in the 1829 prohibition of the practice. As recent scholarship has observed, such debates were as much over legal and religious authority as they were about the suffering of the women involved.[10] The sacrificial rites of the *Kālikā Purāṇa*'s "Blood Chapter" may well be understood similarly, as contentious practices that the British exploited to demarcate the depraved ritual acts of Indians as distinct from the enlightened morality of their own law. In the language of the British courts the bloody violence of sacrifice served an ideological purpose, justifying the imposition of a new legal system that prohibited such abominations. Sacrifice represented the opposite extreme to Britain's moral rule.[11]

Somewhere around 990 C.E., King Yeshe Ö (947–1024) of western Tibet issued a public edict addressed to the *tāntrikas* of Tibet.[12] The 108-line pronouncement voiced the court's opposition to what it saw as a rampant abuse of tantric ritual. Of particular concern were corrupt performances of the liberation rite: "According to the orders of the earlier bodhisattva kings [of the imperial period]," the edict read, "such false teachings were prohibited. . . . But these days, as our karma has diminished and the rule of law has become weak, . . . sacrifices have become widespread, so that people are being 'liberated' alive."[13] The complaint is revealing for its suggestion that live liberation rituals resembling the one described in our last chapter were indeed performed in tenth-century Tibet, but the edict is perhaps more significant for the language it employs. The abuses of tantric ritual are blamed on the lawlessness of the period and the overall weakness of the Tibetan state. The solution was thus already implicit in how Yeshe Ö framed the problem: Tibet needed a new and more effective legal system.

As Tibetans emerged from a century and a half of political fragmentation, King Yeshe Ö's new western court was striving to assert its authority over the various local forms of Buddhism that had taken root in the preceding years of chaos. The royal family's initial arrival in the western regions in the mid-tenth century, under the leadership of Kyide Nyima Gön (grandfather to Yeshe Ö), was described by later Tibetans as a "conquest by the lawful," whereby "the three regions of Upper Ngari were subdued by the royal law, as if by a golden yoke."[14] Now, at the end of the tenth century, Yeshe Ö was reinforcing the court's military presence in the region with a series of new legal statutes and decrees that he presented at ceremonial events and public gatherings and then circulated throughout the land. The fifteenth-century *Royal Annals of Ngari* summarizes Yeshe Ö's lifework by saying, "In general he greatly diffused the Buddhist teachings, and in particular he prepared many [copies of] his writings on Buddhist law and secular law."[15] Yeshe Ö's 990 edict prohibiting live liberation should thus be understood within this context, as part of a broader effort to reestablish the rule of law in the kingdom. Of particular concern were the violent practices of the tantras. The performance of tantric ritual killings had to be brought under the rule of law. This was a dispute not just over ritual interpretation and moral outrage but over authority and specifically over the authority to kill, a struggle between the royal court on the one hand and local religious practitioners of tantric violence on the other.

It is perhaps worth noting that despite Buddhism's insistence on the importance of compassion, its teachings sometimes appear to have done little among Indian and Tibetan rulers to prohibit corporal and capital punishment. The Mahāyāna *Sūtra of the Manifested Teaching on the Methods That Are within the Bodhisattva's Field of Activity* does voice concern over more extreme forms of corporal and capital punishment, but the extent to which such restrictions were observed remains unclear. Aśoka is often represented as the prototypical Buddhist ruler, but even he is described in the *Aśokāvadāna* as torturing his (evil) wife and former associates to death, flying into a fury and killing eighteen thousand heretics, and so on. And this is *after* his conversion to Buddhism and his heartfelt expressions of regret for the bloodthirsty ways of his youth.[16] More concretely, the disjunction between Buddhist rhetoric and royal practice may be detected in the fifth-century travel diaries of Faxian. During his visit to Madhyadeśa, the Chinese pilgrim reports that the realm was prosperous and happy. "The King," he writes approvingly, "in the administration of justice, inflicts no corporal punishment, but each culprit is fined in money according to the gravity of his offense; and even in cases where the culprit has been guilty of repeated attempts to excite rebellion, they restrict themselves to cutting off his right hand."[17] The good Buddhist king, it seems, refrained from all corporal punishment . . . except in some cases. While the Buddhist teachings may have tempered the actions of some kings, their effects appear often to have been limited. And whatever the case may have been in India, when we turn to Tibet, it is clear that legal punishments of extraordinary violence were common practice into the twentieth century.[18]

Perhaps recognizing the incompatibility of politics and Buddhist ethics, many Buddhists considered it an impossibility that a king might remain true to the moral requirements of the *buddhadharma*. "The dharma of release, where calm prevails, and the dharma of kings, where force prevails—how far apart are they!" exclaims Śākyamuni in the *Buddhacārita*.[19] Similarly Śāntideva (c. 685–763 C.E.), who is supposed to have been born a prince, is said to have renounced his throne to avoid administering the violent punishments (*daṇḍa*) that kingship inevitably entails.[20] For many, the laws of Buddhism and those of the secular world were mutually exclusive. For others, however, the perfect union of religion and state was considered a real possibility, as Yeshe Ö's project attests.

Within this context, tantric "liberation" and the ritual killings it could engender were seen as serious threats to Yeshe Ö's new legal system. Such killings, if we are to believe the histories, had become disturbingly common among the tantric communities that had formed during the "dark years" of the late ninth and tenth centuries. The "eighteen robber monks" comprised just one such group that was active in western Tibet during the reign of Yeshe Ö. The group had studied the tantras under a visiting Indian master named *Prajñāgupta, and by the early eleventh century they had become notorious for kidnapping victims, stretching them out on the ground between ritual stakes, and sacrificing them to the *ḍākinīs*.[21] Such dramatic descriptions are reminiscent of British accounts of the Indian Thuggee cult, a criminal gang that rose to infamy in the eighteenth century and was eventually suppressed by the British in the 1830s. The Thuggees (or "Thugs") were a secretive group of murderous thieves who would infiltrate traveling caravans, gain their trust, and rob and kill them in remote locations. Such a criminal network may really have existed, but its cultish religiosity was to a large extent a British invention. The Thuggees were supposed to have sacrificed many of their victims to the tantric goddess Kālī, but such practices were likely mere British imaginings.[22] Similarly, perhaps, violent Tibetan groups like the "eighteen robber monks" may well have presented a real challenge to the western court's authority and its efforts to establish the rule of law in the region, but Tibetan accounts of their cultish practices, whatever their historical accuracy, fed into a wider ideological trend. Descriptions of such groups' involvements in tantric ritual killings went on to play a significant symbolic role in the Tibetan imagination, one that went well beyond the political events of the tenth century. For later Tibetans, blood sacrifice came to represent a powerful image of demonic barbarism, but it was an image to some extent shaped by the late-tenth-century legal concerns of Yeshe Ö and the Gugé court.

In ancient India, the dispensation for inflicting punishment had been seen as the sole preserve of kings, as is made abundantly clear in India's oldest and most fundamental legal treatises, the *Dharma Sūtras*.[23] Similarly in the West, as Max Weber observes in his 1918 *Politics as a Vocation*, "the monopoly on the legitimate use of physical force" is an essential attribute of a state's sovereignty.[24] Late-tenth-century Tibet was no exception, and the religious violence spawned by the Buddhist tantras had to be controlled. Yeshe Ö's edict of 990 sought to shift tantric authority away from the local groups that had taken hold in the valleys of Tibet, and back to the royal court.

Yeshe Ö was not the first Tibetan ruler to establish a legal system. Traditional histories attribute Tibet's earliest legal codes to the seventh-century king Songtsen Gampo (c. 605–649/650). The *Old Tibetan Chronicle* describes Songtsen's reign in the following terms: "Earlier in Tibet there was not even an alphabet, but when this king arose, the great government and legal systems of Tibet, the ministerial ranks, the levels of power, the awards for good service and the punishments for criminals, the contracts for grazing, tilling, and irrigation rights for farmers and nomads, the systems of weights and measures, and so on—all these good conceptions of Tibetan customs originated during King Tri Songtsen's reign. All the people honored and were grateful for his kindness, and they called him Songtsen Gampo ('Songtsen the Wise')."[25]

The source for this account, the *Old Tibetan Chronicle* (PT1286/1287), dates from the second half of the ninth or the tenth century, and it is notable that such early evidence says little about the place of Buddhism in Songtsen's legal system.[26] In this regard the *Chronicle* is unlike later post–tenth-century sources, which unanimously cast the seventh-century ruler's legacy in strongly Buddhist terms.[27] According to Nyangrel's twelfth-century *Religious History*, for example, King Songtsen's laws were rooted in the ethical teachings of the dharma and represented a perfect union of law and religion. In a parallel passage to the *Old Tibetan Chronicle* description cited above, Songtsen is quoted as saying, "'I am a religious ruler, and as long as there are no religious laws at my court and for the common good of Tibet, people are going to keep practicing the ten nonvirtues which will lead them into the three negative states and rebirth in a realm in which there is no escape from suffering.' . . . Hav[ing] pronounced many [legal] edicts, that king created harmony in the world. He enacted the purposes of sentient beings, so that everyone became content. 'This king is true-hearted and wise,' they said, and so he was known as Songtsen the Wise."[28]

In this way later Tibetans portrayed the legal system of the early empire as a Buddhist one, a perfect union of religion and state (*chos srid zung 'brel*). Such an ideal union would come to dominate later Tibetan political theory, shaping Tibet's affairs in a variety of ways, from the influential "priest-patron" (*mchod yon*) relationship to the Ganden Podrang government of the Dalai Lamas. Tibetan sources regularly trace this Tibetan ideal to Songtsen Gampo, but as an explicit legal and historical reality, it may be better represented by the person of Yeshe Ö.

The later rulers of the imperial period, including the great Buddhist kings Trisong Detsen and Relpachen, certainly were more affected by Buddhist thought than Songtsen Gampo. We have already seen in chapter 2 how the early kings identified themselves with the buddha Vairocana, and evidence of similar portrayals of the kings as bodhisattvas appear in several other early texts, including Buddhaguhya's famous letter addressed to Trisong Detsen.[29] Perhaps more concretely, the *Sutra of the Manifested Teaching on the Methods That Are within the Bodhisattva's Field of Activity*, a treatise on Buddhist ethics that has been described as a Mahāyāna response to the Brahmanical *Arthaśāstras*, was translated during the late eighth and early ninth centuries, as were several of the texts contained in the "Treatises on Worldly Affairs" (*thun mong ba lugs kyi bstan bcos*) section of the Tibetan *Tengyur* canon.[30] All of these works may well have affected Tibetan rulership. Thus the relationship between the Buddhist religion and Tibetan governance had already taken root, at least to some extent, by the early ninth century. Nevertheless, it remains unclear just how far this relationship went. The early kings do not appear to have made significant revisions of Tibet's legal codes on the basis of their new religious interests.[31] The Sino-Tibetan treaty of 821/823, inscribed on a stone pillar outside the Jokhang temple in Lhasa describes Trisong Detsen as, "knowing everything pertaining to religion and state" (*chos srid ci la yang mkhas*), yet the same treaty provides clear evidence of the limitations of Buddhist influence within the political sphere. The treaty was solemnized by a sacrifice of animals and, according to the *Tang Annals*, the smearing of the victim's blood upon the lips of all those present—excluding, notably, the Buddhist priest present.[32] Thus even in the final decades of the empire, the realities of Tibetan politics were at times kept carefully apart from those of the Buddhist order. To find an example of a more complete union of Tibetan Buddhist religion and state, we must turn instead to the reign of Yeshe Ö.

Yeshe Ö did not, however, intend a simple theocracy in which secular and religious authorities were united in one person. Such was already the trend in the fragmented society of the tenth and eleventh centuries, as local chieftains cast themselves as inheritors of both local clan power and tantric lineages; Drokmi Lotsawa (born 993) and Marpa Lotsawa (eleventh century) are two well-known examples.[33] Yeshe Ö sought to do something different, to unite the various clans and tantric masters of Tibet under a single umbrella of Buddhist law. His strategy may have been partly pragmatic; the authority of his own royal line was, after all, still divided between his and the now-two Yumten branches in central Tibet headed by Tride Göntsen and Tsana Yeshe Gyaltsen, and Tibet's tantric lineages were even more fraught with competing claims. To trump both of these common strategies for local control (that is, familial and tantric), Yeshe Ö turned elsewhere and sought to construct a new level of translocal authority. For him, the Buddhist clergy stood above all other forms of authority. "If any subject, monk or layman, contravenes the legal decrees," he proclaimed in one of his missives, "kings and ministers are not to use whatever high authority they have, but must rather attempt a reconciliation regardless of the circumstances. In brief, no one is allowed to break the great laws of religious law."[34] Yeshe Ö offered a transcendent Buddhist legal system that found its authority in the institutions of principled monasticism.

Thus according to Yeshe Ö's 988 "Legal Decree," issued just prior to his famous edict, religion and state were to be divided, their powers distributed between two leaders—a secular king (*mnga' bdag*) and a religious grand lama (*bla chen*). The king was to administer the laws and govern Tibet, but the grand lama was to decide questions of religion.[35] Despite this nominal separation of powers, Yeshe Ö ensured that both secular and religious authority remained entirely in the hands of the royal family, for the grand lama was none other than the retired king. According to Yeshe Ö's system, each heir to the throne could be installed only after the previous king had entered the priesthood. In this way, the ultimate source of the ruler's secular authority lay in the monastic establishment, headed by the king's own father. Secular and religious laws were separate but entwined, with the former based in the latter, in the moral authority of Buddhism, and, perhaps significantly, in the king's familial obligations to his father. Even as he distinguished religion and state, then, Yeshe Ö realized their union. The monastic establishment provided an ethical model that was simultaneously otherworldly and intimately connected to the very worldly affairs of the royal court.

Yeshe Ö's system was not some ideal never followed; it continued to determine the political structure of the kingdom for generations to come. After Yeshe Ö, the secular throne passed to his younger brother, Khore, then to Khore's son, Lhade, and to his son, Öde, and as each ascended the throne, his predecessor (if still living) would retire to the church.[36] The practical flexibility of the system became clear only with Öde's death, when no lay member of the family was available, and Öde's son, the famous monk Jangchup Ö, was forced to take the throne. Throughout these years, the independence of the monastic branch appears to have been maintained. A 1042 inscription at Tabo Monastery insists that, "Everybody, be he king, minister, lord, or layman, by physically harming or verbally abusing a monk, whether he be immoral or moral, will accumulate immeasurable bad karma."[37]

In other respects, however, Yeshe Ö's ambitious project fell short. For centuries, his Gugé Kingdom would remain strongly dedicated to monastic Buddhism, but it would never achieve anything approaching the glory of the early Pugyal Empire.[38] The political fragmentation of the late ninth and tenth centuries and the new social forces that had taken shape within that environment ran too deep; the regional independence of Tibet's chieftains had become the norm. As during the late ninth and tenth centuries, local chieftains of the later dispensation period continued to bolster their authority with the myths and rituals of the tantras, often playing dual roles as local kings and tantric masters, holders of secret lineages and powerful practices.[39] Not even the allure of Tibet's glorious imperial past and a sophisticated union of religion and state could reunite them. The tantric themes that had taken root during the age of fragmentation could not be deracinated, and they continued to determine Tibet's political realities.

Despite the limitations of Yeshe Ö's immediate political achievements, his privileging of Buddhist ethics and principled monasticism over the teachings of the tantras did much to lay the rhetorical groundwork for the Kadam and Geluk schools' later successes, successes that resulted in large part from these schools' own reputations for moral and monastic rigor. The early Kadampa built their name on their monastic purity and scholasticism, and thereby provided a significant counterbalance to the continuing popularity of the tantras in the later dispensation period. Founded by Dromtönpa (1005–1064), the Kadam school emphasized the teachings of Dromtön's Indian teacher, Atiśa, who was invited to Tibet by King Jangchup Ö, Yeshe Ö's grandnephew. In this sense, a line of influence—a kind of lineage of Tibetan sutra-based ethical rhetoric—might be traced from Yeshe Ö's legal concerns in the tenth century, through early Kadampa monasticism, to the eventual rise of the Dalai Lamas and the Ganden Podrang in the seventeenth century. Perhaps here, then, in Yeshe Ö's ethical and legalistic rhetoric, the extent of his project's influence upon later Tibetan history may best be appreciated.[40]

Yeshe Ö's edict outlawing abuses of the tantras in general and ritual killings in particular should be understood within this ideological and legalistic context. His edict was in fact the last in a series of at least four proclamations that were issued in quick succession, and all four strove to institute the rule of law, both Buddhist and secular, in western Tibet. In 986, the king issued his "Great Edict" (*bka' shog chen mo*), in which he made Buddhism the state religion and ordered his subjects to adopt its teachings and ritual forms. He followed this two years later, in 988, with a "Legal Decree" (*chos stsigs*) which set forth a new legal system that combined religious law (*chos khrims*) with secular law (*rgyal khrims*). Soon after, probably later in the same year, Yeshe Ö's chief minister, Zhangrung, gathered the regional leaders of Tibet at the new Gugé court to issue a further "pronouncement" (*bka' stsal*), emphasizing the need for Tibetans to emulate the early imperial kings by following the laws of both Buddhism and the state. To promote the king's new legal system, Zhangrung distributed copies of the new laws and encouraged all those present to circulate them throughout every district.[41] Only after these three earlier proclamations did Yeshe Ö issue his edict for the *tāntrikas* of Tibet. The order of these events makes some sense; laws, after all, have to be introduced before they can be enforced. Buddhism needed to be instituted as the state religion and the rule of law had to be established before a cleansing of the religion could begin.

Of particular significance for Yeshe Ö's assault on Buddhist heretics were the earlier imperial prohibitions of tantric practice among the public. Thus he wrote, "The early *bodhisattva* kings remained in accordance with the word of the Buddha and prohibited false teachings."[42] Yeshe Ö thus proposed to return Tibet to the days of old, when monastic Buddhism reigned supreme and tantric ritual was the preserve of the court. He sought to reverse Tibetans' unregulated age-of-fragmentation involvements with the tantras and their violent practices, and restore Buddhism to its former institutional self. We have seen how some Tibetans of the age of fragmentation had already been demonizing tantric excess. Unlike them, however, Yeshe Ö looked to purge the tantric corruptions he saw not by means of ritual violence, but through ritual prohibitions, moral restraint, and ethical purity. Whereas Nupchen Sangye Yeshe and the Buddhists of the age of fragmentation prayed "for violence toward these evil ones who cannot be tamed peacefully, who have violated the teachings and broken their vows," Yeshe Ö recommended something different:

> You ought to believe in the results of karma.
> Karma does not deceive; it follows after you.
> It does not ripen as the four elements, and
> The sufferings of the evil negative rebirths are unbearable,
> So reject these evil practices and practice what is in the *tripiṭaka*![43]
> Those who wish and desire to be Mahāyānists
> Must gather the two accumulations and abandon notions of subject and object.
> They must practice the ten perfections of generosity and so forth.
> They must achieve all the practices of a *bodhisattva*.
> With love and compassion they must accomplish the welfare of living beings.
> If you practice in that way, then you will be a Mahāyānist![44]

With such moralistic language, Yeshe Ö targeted the nonmonastic tantric communities that had flourished in the social fragmentation of the late ninth and tenth centuries. His edict was explicitly addressed to the *tāntrikas* of central Tibet, "you tantrists who live in the villages,"[45] and it complained of the "Bajiwa" (*'Ba ji ba*), Buddhist heretics who claimed for themselves the highest enlightenment and to have transcended all distinctions of sacred and profane, moral and immoral. These were corrupted people who dwelt in cemeteries and offered flesh to the buddhas, who drank alcohol, ate meat, and engaged in sexual intercourse: "You say 'we are Buddhists,' but in practice you are less compassionate than a demon. You are greedier for meat than a hawk or a jackal.

You are lustier than a donkey or a bull. You crave fermented drink more than the flies in an old house. You distinguish pure from impure less than a dog or a pig. By making offerings of feces and urine, semen and menses, you will be reborn in [the 'neighboring hell' of] Swamp of Rotting Corpses. Alas!"[46]

It is important to recognize that Yeshe Ö was probably not wholly against the tantras. Certainly his successors at Gugé continued to study them, though within a more controlled environment than had some earlier Tibetans. No Tibetan could deny that the tantras by that time played a central role in Indian Buddhism, or that transgressive language abounded in them. Indeed, apart from the obviously negative valuation Yeshe Ö gives the tantric transgressions he enumerates, the above description is in fact fairly typical of many canonical tantras. As observed in chapter 1, the line between orthodox and heterodox tantric practice is a fine one, and here again, the critical issue was one of interpretation and the authority of the interpreter.

Yeshe Ö, in his critique of Tibet's *tāntrikas*, employed the same cautionary language seen in the Rudra myth, language that had become well known by the late tenth century. Like Rudra, the village *tāntrikas* were fixated on external appearances and superficial readings of the tantras: "Ignorant of the hidden intention, you take the teachings literally. Such 'Mahāyānists' will surely be reborn as demons."[47] And like Rudra, these local *tāntrikas* were still caught in webs of their own ignorance, subtle obscurations that clouded their understandings of the tantras: "Not even the noble Maitreya, crown prince of the tenth [bodhisattva] level, is untainted by the [subtlest] 'obstructions to [all] objects of knowledge.' Are degenerate beings such as you nobler than he? Caught in the mires of the five sensual objects and women, it is astonishing that you claim to be the *dharmakāya*."[48] These were evil beings, who "must either have been deceived by demons or simply be mad."[49]

The alternative Yeshe Ö offered these misguided *tāntrikas* was normative, exoteric Buddhism—the moral truths of cause and effect, a gradual path of self-improvement, generosity, and laboring for the welfare of others. These were the teachings of exoteric, monastic Buddhism, and in the years following the release of his edict, Yeshe Ö oversaw the establishment of new monastic communities throughout his kingdom. Many of the local *tāntrikas* were encouraged to submit to the *vinaya* and join the ranks of the ordained. The king was not opposed to the tantras per se, just to what he saw as their malpractice, and tantric practice was therefore permitted to continue within these new monkish, and more easily controlled, institutional settings. Tantric ritual was thus worked into monastic training and firmly grounded in Buddhist logic and ethics.[50] When the tantric rites were performed, they were to be imagined. The liberation rite, in particular, was not to be taken literally and performed on live victims; an effigy was mandatory.

The use of an effigy was central to Yeshe Ö's more conservative conception of ritual violence. When the king complained that, "sacrifices have become widespread, so that people are being 'liberated' alive," he was making a careful distinction between ritual killings that targeted a live victim and those that employed an effigy. With this criterion, his edict distinguished "sacrifice" (*mchod sgrub*) from "liberation" properly performed. The direct killing of a person was to be rejected as a brutal case of "sacrifices"; liberation required an effigy. As the edict's sixteenth-century commentator, Sokdokpa, explains, "Summoning the spirit of an enemy into an effigy, one liberates him. To 'liberate' a person directly is not attested [in the tantras]."[51]

Yeshe Ö's distinction between sacrifice and liberation may also have rested in part upon the identity of the rite's perceived beneficiary. The Tibetan term the king used for "sacrifice," that is, *mchod sgrub*, means more literally something like "ritual offering," and as such it emphasizes the ritual feature of oblational worship. The term would thus seem to imply that, in Yeshe Ö's view, "liberation" was performed for the good of the victim, to save him from his own bad karma, whereas sacrifice, or "ritual offering," was first and foremost an offering (Skt. *pūjā*), a rite performed primarily for the benefit of the deity receiving the oblations. Certainly the buddhas' imagined feasting upon the victim continued to play a role in the later and more sublimated forms of the liberation rite, such as the Tibetan *'chams* dance or the sky burial, but this particular aspect discomfited some Tibetans. As the early twelfth-century master Gampopa (1079–1153) explained, "Inflicting violence upon sentient beings and then offering them to the three jewels is like a father cutting a child's flesh and feeding it to the mother. This is senseless."[52] The more bloody culinary aspects of the liberation rite's "offering into the realm," in which the buddhas voraciously devour the victim, seem to have been, for Yeshe Ö at least, wrongheaded. Only harmful demons crave the flesh of sacrifice. And even the converted mundane deities of Tibet were horrified by such practices. "As the flesh-eating demons are worshipped," complained the king, "plagues have appeared among humans and animals. As the smoke of burning human flesh is sent forth, the local deities and *nāgas* have been repelled."[53] These two aspects, then—the use of an effigy and the specification of the primary beneficiary—were fundamental to the distinction Yeshe Ö drew between sacrifice and liberation, two disturbingly similar yet diametrically opposed practices.

In these ways, Yeshe Ö drove a wedge between the liberation rite and "sacrifice," further effacing the historical and ritual connections between them. In his view, sacrifice constituted a misguided interpretation of the liberation rite, one that was largely unique to ignorant Tibetans and the corrupt state of religious and secular law in tenth-century Tibet. Certainly, he contended, it could not be found among the legitimate Buddhists of India. "If other kingdoms heard about the kinds of practices performed by you village *ta¯ntrikas*, it would be cause for shame,"[54] he wrote. By making such claims, Yeshe Ö sought to redefine tantric Buddhism. Sectarian lines were beginning to be drawn. Liberation with an effigy may be Buddhist, but sacrifice was a demonic Tibetan distortion.

For Yeshe Ö, then, "sacrifice" was no neutral term of simple description; it was an ideological label reserved for the practices of others. In the king's eyes, the bloody demonolatry of sacrifice was clearly distinct from liberation and the other legitimate ritual practices recognized by the court. By labeling the direct liberation of a live victim a "sacrifice," Yeshe Ö placed it squarely outside the Buddhist law.

How today the Dunhuang liberation rite should be understood is thus a complex question. One might be tempted to describe it as an example of Buddhist human sacrifice, but Tibetans would see this as oxymoronic. They know well that Buddhists do not practice blood sacrifice. From the *Buddhacārita,* the early Indian biography of the Buddha that repeatedly emphasizes Śākyamuni's opposition to Vedic sacrifice, to the *Sayings of Wa,* the late-tenth- or eleventh-century history of the Pugyal Empire that is filled with tales of Buddhist outrage at early Tibetans' pre-Buddhist involvements in blood sacrifice, the prohibition of sacrifice was well known as a key marker that distinguished Buddhist from non-Buddhist.[55] King Yeshe Ö may well have agreed that a literal performance of the Dunhuang manuscript PT42/ITJ419 would qualify as human sacrifice, but he would not have seen it as Buddhist. At stake here are the limits of authentic Buddhism, the very definition of what is properly "Buddhist." While Tibetans may agree with us that ritual killing is beyond the pale, a bloody and barbaric sacrifice, they would disagree that such a practice could ever be Buddhist. With more at stake, they are not surprisingly more protective of Buddhism's boundaries. Here we may be reminded of the uncomfortable parallels between the writings of Waddell and Rigdzin Garwang, the late-nineteenth-century authors who both saw demonolatry and barbarities all around them in their respective border regions, but who differed markedly on the relationship of those practices to true Buddhism.

As the ideological weight of the term "sacrifice" becomes clear, one may even wonder whether it can ever be a neutral or appropriate label for anything we find in other cultures. "I know of no ethnographic monograph published in the last twenty years," J. Z. Smith has observed, "in which the term sacrifice appears in the index. My conclusion is that there is no 'sacrifice' until we invent it. We imagine it and then go out and find it."[56] Sacrifice, then, is a constructed category that may well be ill suited for describing the liberation rite.

At the same time, however, curious parallels do exist between our own modern deployment of the term "sacrifice" and Yeshe Ö's use of *mchod sgrub*. Both terms function to distinguish a demonic and corrupt practice from one's own pure, rational, and ethical civilization. In many ways, Yeshe Ö's application of the term was clearly different from our own and reflected his own unique cultural and historical position, yet his juxtaposition of live liberation against true law and morality, and his interest in justifying his own legal and political project, bear significant comparisons with our own uses of the ancient and bloody label of "sacrifice."

None of this is to suggest that Yeshe Ö's edict was solely a case of self-serving political expediency. Even aside from the real ethical outrage the king may well have felt at his contemporaries' violent ways, his rhetoric was well within the normative Buddhist tradition. In opposing ritual killing and blood sacrifice, he was reiterating a long-standing Buddhist position.[57] Nonetheless, his appeal to this normative language came at a particular point in history, as Tibetans were emerging from a century of political fragmentation and religious decentralization. In calling upon Buddhism's well-known critiques of sacrifice to help reinforce his own legal system against the social chaos of the age of fragmentation, the king was laying the groundwork for a new rhetorical trend in Tibet, and the contours of his language were in many ways indicative of what was to come.

Yeshe Ö's purgative rhetoric of tantric corruption and moral decay also built upon the similarly dire language that had already taken root in the age of fragmentation. After Yeshe Ö, this rhetoric continued to flourish in Tibet, as it became a powerful tool used widely by Tibetan Buddhists of the eleventh century and beyond. At the Gugé court in particular, Yeshe Ö's royal descendants continued to follow his example and develop his rhetoric still further. Some fifty years after Yeshe Ö's edict was pronounced, the great Indian teacher Atiśa would arrive in Gugé at the invitation of Yeshe Ö's grandnephew, Jangchup Ö. Atiśa would teach to the new king's interests, by composing his famous *Lamp for the Path of Enlightenment* and other works that repeatedly echo Yeshe Ö's edict and its emphasis on Buddhist ethics and a rigorous grounding in exoteric scripture and scholasticism. In his *Jewel Garland of Dialogues*, for example, Atiśa would write,

> Many sentient beings whose minds remain impure—
> Having failed previously to accomplish the cause, the two accumulations—
> Have failed to experience the taste of the *tripiṭaka*,

Despite having encountered the teachings of the Mahāyāna.
They've discarded at will pure ethical discipline, which is the basis . . .
They claim to be Mahāyānists,
While belittling the profound [law of] karma and its effects;
They consume whatever reaches their mouth at whatever time—
Meat, alcohol, and garlic—a butcher's diet![58]

The parallels with Yeshe Ö's edict are obvious enough. From Atiśa's language of purity and ethical discipline, to the need for the two accumulations of merit, to the central importance of the laws of karma and training in the monastic canons, both works follow a similar rhetorical pattern.

Over the centuries that followed, Yeshe Ö, Atiśa, and the Gugé court in general came to be identified with monastic ethics and upright Buddhist behavior. Yeshe Ö's rhetoric of a lawful, moral, and rational Buddhism over and against one of tantric excess came to dominate much of Tibetan Buddhism, even as tantric ritual and narrative themes continued to infiltrate nearly every corner of the religion. The resulting strains channeled tantric violence into new, more-acceptable forms, as the ongoing tensions between law and the tantras produced a wide array of Tibetan innovations, from new artistic forms to unprecedented systems of myth and ritual. In these ways and along these lines, in the years that followed the tenth century, the bloody violence of the age of fragmentation moved increasingly from the real to the symbolic.

In chapter 3 we observed the close resemblances between the liberation rite described in the tenth-century manuscripts from Dunhuang and the ritual of human sacrifice found in the *Kālikā Purāṇa* of India. Now we can see that the two texts share similar legacies too. Both drew the attention of later critics, Tibetan and British, respectively. Both were held up as examples of misguided demonolatry, irrational corruptions that threatened the moral order of "the only true revelation," as William Jones put it. Both were used to justify the imposition of new legal systems upon peoples deemed cruel and barbarous. The British rulers of colonial India, as described at the beginning of this chapter, used the *Kālikā Purāṇa*'s "Blood Chapter" to condemn Indians for their lawless behavior. The Tibetan ruler of late-tenth-century Gugé presented the liberation of living beings as evidence of Tibet's benighted state of anarchy. In each case, the specter of bloody sacrifice served to justify a rational rule of law, at least as understood by its advocates. The similar uses to which the rhetoric of violence was put by regimes separated by both time and culture raise larger issues of the role of religious violence, and its proscription, in the realms of law and empire.

5

Foundational Violence

Even as Tibetans of the later dispensation demonized the innovations of the age of fragmentation as violent excesses, they relied on them in founding their new Buddhist tradition. A new (*gsar ma*) Tibetan Buddhism was being built, an elaborate edifice that rested upon the earlier demonic "corruptions" of tantric Buddhism. Throughout the eleventh and twelfth centuries, Buddhist temples were being erected and Buddhist geographies constructed, using the narratives and ritual themes of demon taming that had been developed in the preceding years of darkness. In this sense, the violence of the earlier age of fragmentation was not solely destructive; it was creative as well. The violent foundations that had been laid in the preceding years of fragmentation continued to shape the Tibetan Buddhist imagination, producing innovative new myths and historical narratives.

This chapter investigates the creation of Buddhist Tibet, of a pan-Tibetan Buddhist identity, from the entwined themes of tantric violence and religious darkness. Chapter 2 has already argued that the late ninth and tenth centuries were far more important to the formation of Tibetan Buddhism than the tradition has maintained. The present chapter examines more precisely how the age of fragmentation came to be obscured by later Tibetans, how the earlier age-of-fragmentation rhetoric of religious corruption and demonization continued to spread alongside the promise of the new Buddhist traditions of the later dispensation. The darkening of the age of fragmentation, it is suggested, may be seen as part of a wider effort to create a new Buddhist orthodoxy in Tibet.

By the turn of the eleventh century, Buddhism was firmly rooted in Tibet. At all levels of society Tibetans had adopted en masse the religion's terms and symbols, and new contests of authenticity and power inevitably followed. A restricted and restrictive orthodoxy was being formed, in part through accusations of demonolatry and violent perversions of the dharma.[1] The later dispensation of the eleventh and twelfth centuries was marked by aristocratic clans and wealthy landowners claiming exclusive rights over powerful lineages and authentic Buddhism. Vital to their successes were their common demonizations of Tibet and Tibetans, and a multifaceted rhetoric of tantric corruption.

Within this restrictive and condemnatory environment developed some of the most famous and influential of all Tibetan legends, and the extraordinary creativity of this period should also be recognized.[2] One work was of particular importance. The *Pillar Testament* was a revealed history that described King Songtsen Gampo's seventh-century construction of the Rasa Trulnang cathedral in Lhasa and a related network of "border-taming temples." The *Testament* was therefore a tale of temple construction, and as such it was a true product of its time. The eleventh and twelfth centuries witnessed a burst of temple building across central and western Tibet, and themes of architecture and construction dominated the Buddhist literature of the period. The extent of their influence may also be seen in Nyangrel Nyima Özer's *Copper Island*, a twelfth-century revealed biography of the Indian master Padmasambhava. Here Padmasambhava's subjugation of the native gods and demons of Tibet was retold in an elaborate narrative, framed as a whole by the construction of Samye Monastery. The work built upon the earlier narrative strategies of localization that had accumulated around the Indian master during the two preceding centuries, and like the examples we have from Dunhuang, it told a story of demon subjugation writ large, applied to the whole of Tibet.

In their interest in temple building, the *Pillar Testament* and its later-dispensation literary counterparts such as the *Copper Island* were concerned with opening and defining Tibet as a sacred space, a new Buddhist landscape of chosenness and power. Theirs was, however, a space within and beneath which demons inhered, and in this regard their authors followed the metaphorical leads of the Rudra myth. In the myth, Rudra's ghastly palace of skulls atop blood-soaked Mount Malaya had provided the original setting for the tantras to be taught. Similarly for Tibetans of the later dispensation period, tantric violence provided the sacred space within which Buddhism flourished. From preliminary rites for pinning down local gods, to the mapping of Tibetan geography, the violent imagery of Rudra's sacrificial liberation remained formative. No ritual could be performed until the space had been seized from the local spirit, no temple could be built until the site had been forcefully secured, and no Tibet could be converted without the subjugation of its local gods, demons, and peoples.[3]

TEMPLE CONSTRUCTION AND THE *PILLAR TESTAMENT*

According to traditional sources, monastic Buddhism returned to central Tibet in the late tenth century with the famous "ten men of the Central and Tsang provinces."[4] Seeking fresh monastic ordination lineages, these ten men had journeyed to far reaches of northeastern Tibet, where institutional Buddhism had survived the late ninth and tenth centuries relatively intact.[5] Once back, the men set to work restoring the crumbling temples of the imperial period, and by the turn of the eleventh century their pupils were beginning to build new temples as well.[6] Construction continued at a remarkable rate throughout the eleventh and twelfth centuries, and the new temples played a central role in shaping the religion and politics of the period. New regional districts (*tsho*) were developed, each with its own central temple ruled over by a local Buddhist master. The new districts were constructed over the remnants of older aristocratic systems of territorial control, with the local rulers often belonging to the same clans that had dominated the regions under the earlier imperial regime. Tibetan political power thus became a blend of clan-based and religious lineages centered on the new temple sites.[7]

Territory and temple building were thus vital themes, themes that were both reflected in the literature of the period. The *Pillar Testament* is a composite work, probably dating from the late eleventh to mid-twelfth centuries but traditionally attributed to Songtsen Gampo (died 649/650), the first of the three great kings of the early imperial period.[8] Its original scrolls are said to have been discovered in the mid-eleventh century by the influential Bengali teacher Atiśa (c. 982–1054), during his visit to the Rasa Trulnang cathedral (often referred to today as the Jokhang) at the heart of Lhasa. The *Pillar Testament* itself describes the Rasa Trulnang's construction in an elaborate legend that became extraordinarily well known over the centuries following its revelation. Despite the account's popularity, however, its historical accuracy is questionable. Songtsen Gampo may well have been responsible for building the famous Rasa Trulnang and perhaps even some of its affiliated border temples, but the details of the account more likely reflect the concerns of the eleventh and twelfth centuries than those of the seventh.[9] Like many Tibetan works of the later dispensation, the *Pillar Testament* reflects the period's fascination with temple construction and architectural detail. It claims, for example, to have been discovered inside a supporting pillar in the Rasa Trulnang temple, while another twelfth-century account of the scroll's discovery shifts the location from a pillar (*ka ba*) to a central beam (*gdung bar*).[10]

Biographies of the period are similarly littered with discussions of pillars, beams, walls, geomancy, and foundations, with construction metaphors even defining the organization of the new Buddhist communities. Lume Sherab Tsultrim, one of the leaders of the "ten men," for example, is said to have built his congregation around his four most worthy disciples, who became known as his four "pillars,"[11] while Zurchungpa's (1014–1074) twelve main disciples are described as the "four pillars and eight beams" of his community.[12] Within this well-defined literary environment, certain narrative sequences became recurring tropes. The building site came to serve as a proving ground for Buddhist masters, where new teachers displayed their miraculous powers by effortlessly laying foundations, moving massive pillars, and stabilizing walls. Buddhist construction efforts were repeatedly said to have enjoyed success by day but to have been destroyed by local spirits by night. Zurche Śākya Jungne (1002–1062), in founding his clan's new temple in Ukpalung, for example, saw his daily work dismantled each night by disruptive demons, and Nyangrel's account of the eighth-century construction of Samye reads the same way.[13]

True to the zeitgeist, the *Pillar Testament* also contains many of the same stock motifs. Once again, local spirits resist Songtsen's construction efforts with the same daily strategy: "By day the workers would build it, but by night the gods and demons would destroy it. It was destroyed seven times in this way, so that construction could not progress."[14] The *Pillar Testament*'s account of Songtsen's temple-building projects was thus typical of the literature of the period and is best understood less as a reflection of historical fact than of its twelfth-century context.

TIBET'S *RĀKṢASĪ*-DEMONESS AS A PURANIC DISMEMBERMENT MYTH

According to the *Pillar Testament*'s narrative, the problem underlying Songtsen's building woes was discovered through a series of three geomantic consultations performed by his Chinese bride, Kongjo: "I have determined," she announces, "that the country of Tibet resembles a *rākṣasī*-demoness lying on her back. The center of Lhasa resembles the heart of the demoness, and the Otang lake is reckoned as her heart-blood."[15] The demoness, splayed supine across the Tibetan landscape (fig. 6), is one of the best-known images in Tibetan Buddhism. First introduced in the *Pillar Testament*, it was copied a century later into the influential *Collected Precepts on Maṇi*, whence it entered the Tibetan popular imagination.[16] It was a powerful image that had deep roots in Indian Puranic and early tantric mythology.

The Tibetan king makes several attempts to overcome the obstacles presented by the supine demoness, but only with Kongjo's third and final consultation does the solution that would ultimately succeed become clear:

Figure 6: The *rākṣasī*-demoness of Tibet. "The body of the demoness had to be pinned to the earth by these twelve outlying temples." (© Rubin Museum of Art / Art Resource, NY, Item 65719)

> Unable to build [further] because whatever was built like that [by day] was damaged or destroyed by the [native] spirits and demons [by night], the great king Songtsen Gampo and the Chinese [princess] Kongjo discussed [the situation] and made a geomantic probe. [It] was recognized that this land of snowy Tibet, configured as a supine *rākṣasī*-demoness, should be suppressed at the pivotal foci of her head and her four limbs, at the two shoulders, the two hips, the elbows, the two knee-joints, and the two hands and feet. It was understood that the four district-[suppressing] temples should be erected. To suppress the right shoulder in the central district, the Katsel [temple] was erected as a *maṇḍala* of the twenty-one [demonic] devotees. To suppress the left shoulder in the Yuru, the Tradrug temple should be erected as a *maṇḍala* of the eight great planetary [gods] . . . [etc.]. . . .[17]

The passage goes on to describe the remaining temples in the network. Twelve are named in all, three sets of four temples arranged in concentric squares around Lhasa's Otang Lake, the heart-blood of the demoness. Before the central Rasa Trulnang cathedral could stand over the lake, the body of the demoness had to be pinned to the earth by these twelve outlying temples.

Networks of sacred sites (*pīṭha*) were well known in India by the twelfth century. Some have suggested a Chinese origin for the *Pillar Testament*'s concentric layout of the temples, but standard Indian spatial models provide a more likely precedent.[18] Concentric four-sided designs are, of course, typical of Buddhist mandalas, but the *Pillar Testament* also drew upon the closely related Indian myths of demonic dismemberment, which had become common in India's early medieval period. Indian Puranic sources recount violent battles between gods and demons that culminate in the defeated demon's dismembered body being flung across the Indian subcontinent.[19] Such myths were deployed in Indian literature to explain new networks of sacred sites that reshaped the sacred space of India. The resulting networks operated at multiple levels, from the local to the pan-Indian. A well-known local system of eight *mātṛkā* sites defines the Kathmandu Valley, while a translocal scheme appears in our Rudra myth: During his rise to power, when Rudra kills Mahākaruṇā, he scatters the god's dismembered remains across the subcontinent, so that (according to Nupchen's commentary), "in the virtuous places like Oḍḍiyāna, Siṅgha, and Nepal, the eight *stūpas* possessing the eight *siddhis* were [erected over Mahākaruṇā's remains and] protected by the eight *mātṛkā* demonesses."[20]

The *Pillar Testament*'s legend of the border-taming temples follows precisely this model. Instead of eight sites, there are thirteen,[21] and instead of reliquary *stūpas*, temples are erected over the sacrificed victim's body, but otherwise the resemblances are unmistakable. Via the Buddhist tantras, the Indian theme of demonic dismemberment seen in the Puranas and elsewhere entered Tibet and was reworked in the famous legend of the Tibetan *rākṣasī* splayed across the landscape. The parallels are perhaps clearest in a passage in the *Pillar Testament,* in which the Chinese princess Kongjo maps the demoness's body parts onto the Tibetan landscape:

> In the central [part] of the snowy kingdom of Tibet, in the middle of the lower Central district, is the heart of the [supine] *rākṣasī*-demoness. The Otang lake is known to be the heart-blood of the demoness. The palace of the king [of the *nāga*-spirits] is [further] known to be the heart of the demoness. The three mountainous spurs towering [around Lhasa] are [respectively] known to be the nipples of her breasts and the vein of the life force of the demoness. In the four directions [around Lhasa, four] mountains are found, each resembling the form of a tortoise; these are known to be the mouth of the demoness. The pair, Red Mountain and Steel-Gray Mountain, are like the entwined tails of a lion [and a tiger]; they should be known as the vicious disposition of the demoness. The two spurs [towering over the plain of Lhasa] are [moreover viewed as] the heart-bones of the demoness, recognized to devour the life of the sentient beings [living there]. . . . The palaces of these two [mountains] resemble the city of Laṅkapuri, the country of the *rākṣaṣas.* The king should recognize that he must suppress them, and then do so.[22]

Here the *Pillar Testament* draws upon the familiar Indian mythic landscape to create a corresponding network of Tibetan sacred sites with Lhasa at its center. How the resulting system was meant to fit with the larger concentric scheme of border-taming sites described above, in which the demoness's body covers not just the Lhasa Valley but the entire Tibetan region, is never clearly spelled out. It seems we are working here with generalities, but it is nonetheless apparent that the authors of the *Pillar Testament* modeled their demoness legend on Indian dismemberment myths, adopting an older Indian strategy in order to map Tibet into the Buddhist universe.

There is one detail that might, at first glance, seem to distinguish the Tibetan legend from the Indian myths. Unlike the Indian demons, or Mahākaruṇā in our Rudra myth, who are definitively killed and dismembered, the *rākṣasī*-demoness is not expressly sacrificed; Tibet's *rākṣasī* is only pinned beneath buildings.[23] In fact, however, the sacrifice of a demon is often functionally equivalent to pinning him or her down. As we have seen elsewhere, sacrifice in India does not necessarily extinguish the demon forever. In the Rudra myth, Rudra is killed, or "liberated," but he is subsequently revived and appointed as a protector of tantric Buddhism. Similarly in the liberation rite, the victim's consciousness is ejected into a blissful rebirth in the buddhafields. The same ambivalence regarding the death of the sacrificial victim is at work in the case of the Tibetan *rākṣasī*. Through her violent subjugation, she is both killed and apotheosized.

The dual logic behind the *rākṣasī*'s sacrifice is spelled out in a tantra found in the *Collected Tantras of the Ancients*, one that is probably indigenous to Tibet and may date from as early as the early tenth to twelfth centuries.[24] The *Seizing and Liberation of the Five Results* weaves a single narrative out of the Rudra myth, Puranic-style dismemberment myths, and a description of a subjugated demon that closely resembles that of the Tibetan *rākṣasī*, supine on his back with limbs splayed across the landscape:

> Yama-Maheśvara [aka Rudra] and his demons were liberated with immeasurable compassion. He was flung onto his back, lying like a corpse in the southern buddha-field of Jambudvīpa, thus creating [a network of] sites. These became the eight great grounds. His head pointed to the southwest, his legs to the northeast. His two arms were bent to the right and the left. Because his head, lungs, heart, and limbs all were blessed by great compassion, the eight great *mātṛkās* were appointed as the great protectors of the corpse. Also at those great shrines, [eight] great splendorous *stūpas* appeared, each self-arisen.[25]

As in our Rudra myth, *stūpas* are built over the demon's body parts, edifices that play a role parallel to that of Songtsen Gampo's border-taming temples. The *Seizing and Liberation of the Five Results* goes on to enumerate the eight places and the names of their respective *stūpas*. The victim's heart rests in Magadha, at the great charnel ground of Sītavana. His head is on the island of Śrī Laṅka, his right hand in Nepal,[26] and his left hand in the Sala country (to the southwest). His right leg is in Khotan and his left leg in Kaśmīr. His penis is in the land of Oḍḍiyāna, and in the middle of all those is his stomach in the land of Zahor. The network as a whole is called the "*maṇḍala* of liberation" (*ta na'i dkyil 'khor*). Within this single narrative, then, the two apparently contradictory descriptions of the demon coexist harmoniously; he is both killed and dismembered, with *stūpas* enshrining his eight body parts, and lies across the landscape, body intact, with those same *stūpas* pinning his limbs to the ground.

In fact this same tension, between death and apotheosis, runs throughout the tantric myths and rituals of demon subjugation, particularly in the dagger (Skt. *kīla*; Tib. *phur ba*) rites for pinning down demons. The deity Vajrakīlaya, an embodiment of the ritual dagger, has enjoyed widespread popularity throughout

Tibet and represents an important avenue along which the interwoven themes of demon taming, liberation, and sacrifice traveled within Tibetan Buddhism.[27] The tantric dagger is typically used to subdue a ritual site, to subjugate the local demon by pinning him or her to the ground. As such it is performed at the beginning of most ritual sequences, as part of the preliminary practices. The dagger is wielded by the officiating lama in a stabbing motion directed toward the ground and is usually performed ten times, once for each of the eight cardinal and intermediate directions and once for each of the upward and downward directions. In this way the Buddhist mandala is planted and stabilized atop the offending demon, just as the border-taming temples are constructed atop the Tibetan *rākṣasī*. The dagger may also be stabbed into a three-sided box, the triangular shape representing the violent ritual activity of liberation, or even directly into an effigy, thereby making still more explicit the equivalence between the liberation and the pinning of the demon.

Dagger rites entered Buddhist ritual from an early date,[28] and they clearly informed the Tibetan border-taming temples, dagger and temple alike being vertical constructions meant to hold and transfix their victims. A variety of such vertical devices pervade the Indian and Tibetan religious imaginations. Other scholars have noted thematic associations between architectural pillars and the ancient Indian myth of Indrakīla, a god who pins and stabilizes the serpent Vṛtra with a mythic "peg" or "dagger" (*kīla*), with even Tibetan mountains sometimes being conceived of as "sky pillars" (*gnam gyi ka ba*).[29] The dagger-like function of Buddhist buildings is made explicit in yet another influential work that dates to the twelfth or thirteenth century, the *Sayings of Ba*.[30] Here the eighth-century construction of Samye, Tibet's first monastery, is the focus. While preparing the building site, the Indian monk Śāntarakṣita advises the Tibetan king to construct four *stūpas* in the four directions immediately surrounding the site. "Announcing that the evil spirits had to be suppressed," the text reads, "he planted the four *stūpas* as ritual pegs."[31] Here, then, the equivalence between Buddhist buildings and ritual daggers is spelled out. The *Pillar Testament*'s legend drew upon these same mythic and ritual associations, so that King Songtsen's border-taming temples functioned as figurative daggers, simultaneously liberating the *rākṣasī*-demoness and subduing the sacred space of Tibet.

TEMPLE CONSTRUCTION IN MEDIEVAL INDIAN MANUALS

The eleventh and twelfth centuries witnessed an expansion of temple building not only in Tibet but in India too. A number of key Indian texts on architecture and temple construction date from this period, including the Brahmanical *Samarāṅgaṇasūtradhāra* and the Buddhist *Kriyāsaṃgraha*,[32] two works that are remarkably similar in content and clearly resulted from a common interest in construction techniques that spanned India. Across religious traditions, it seems, Indians of the eleventh and twelfth centuries were also involved in the myths and rituals of temple construction.

Within the context of these contemporaneous Indian building practices, the theme of demon subjugation is seen most clearly in the famous *vāstupuruṣa-maṇḍala*. Literally a "diagram of the site-being," the *vāstupuruṣa-maṇḍala* is a square grid of sixty-four or eighty-one squares drawn on the ground prior to construction. The *Samarāṅgaṇasūtradhāra* (following the earlier *Bṛhat Saṃhitā*) specifies that all Indian temples are to be built atop this ritual diagram. Though not a ground plan of the temple per se, the diagram does "sustain, in its own sphere of effectiveness, the sacred building, to the same extent as the actual foundation supports its weight."[33] The diagram is thus an idealized "forecast" of the temple, an illustration of the site (*vāstu*) within which the *puruṣa* (also known as Prajāpati), "the Prime Person whence all originates," is held in place beneath the building.[34]

The Buddhist *Kriyāsaṃgraha* was not translated into Tibetan until the late thirteenth century,[35] but Buddhist versions of the *vāstupuruṣa-maṇḍala* were well known to Tibetans from a much earlier date. Perhaps as early as the seventh century, ritual texts for building *stūpas* had recommended using a stretched thread to divide the site into a grid pattern and nailing it down with sandalwood daggers at the center and in each direction. By these means, the texts explained, the site could be protected.[36] The same rite also preceded the construction of mandalas, and as such is well attested in Buddhist *dhāraṇīs* and tantras from an early date,[37] so that by the time of the *Kriyāsaṃgraha*, one is instructed to "lay the threads" (Tib. *thig 'debs pa*; Skt. *sūtrapātana*) for a mandala-diagram that is drawn at the temple's construction site.[38] Here too the laying of the threads is accompanied by stabbing ritual daggers into the site around the edges of the diagram. Across all traditions, then, the creation of a diagram both stabilized the site and imprisoned the local spirits (or the *puruṣa*) within it. The square diagram imposed an enforced order upon the deity and his or her chaotic space.[39] Its grid divided the site and impressed its geometric stability upon the earth, much as Songtsen Gampo's network of temples imprisoned the unruly demoness of the Tibetan landscape.

The Tibetan *rākṣasī* was thus a sacrificial victim, just as the god Puruṣa of Brahmanical mythology had been. The very name of the Indian diagram, the *vāstupuruṣa-maṇḍala*, was already a reference to the primordial sacrifice of Puruṣa in the ancient Indian *Ṛgveda*, 10.90, an event that created the universe even as it dismembered Puruṣa's body. And according to Vedic ritual theory, the dismembered body of Puruṣa could be ritually reconstituted through the construction of the Vedic altar. The god's potency would then empower and reinforce the altar, remaining present beneath it in the form of a sacrificed head, or a "golden man," an effigy that was placed supine and immured within the lowest layer of altar bricks. Centuries later this same Vedic sacrificial symbolism was reworked, in turn, into the temple construction diagram: "The symbolism of the Vedic altar, Agni, is continued in the Hindu temple, in its plan. The Vāstupuruṣa of this maṇḍala is indeed Agni-Prajāpati. It is drawn on the ground and not piled up. No fire burns upon it; the temple is set up on it. The image of the Vāstupuruṣa is coterminous and one with the maṇḍala is drawn in the likeness of man. His head lies in the East, in the maṇḍala of 64 squares, the legs opposite; body and limbs fill the square."[40] The sacrificed body of Puruṣa is laid out beneath the temple, held within the gridwork pattern of the mandala diagram. The power of the god thus inheres in the space and, more significantly, within the structure of the temple itself.

For Buddhists, of course, the Vedic god Puruṣa had to be replaced, and the substitution was accomplished in two ways. In a general sense, Rudra took the place of Puruṣa as the idealized victim of the primordial sacrifice, so that Rudra in his demonic mandala, his fortress of rotten flesh populated by his demonic attendants, is pinned beneath the pure Buddhist mandala. Today, Tibetans commonly understand the Buddhist mandala to be built upon the stomach of Rudra's body,[41] a notion that is often even acted out by placing effigies beneath the mandala platforms they construct on ritual occasions.[42] Rudra and his demonic horde thus continue to dwell below the mandala, as subterranean shadows of the Buddhist deities above, their invisible presence empowering the mandala palace even as they threaten it. On the more specific level of local ritual practice, however, the Vedic Puruṣa could also be replaced by whichever mundane spirit happened to live at the construction site.[43] In India, for example, early Buddhists are known to have interred images of mundane (*laukika*) gods beneath *stūpas*,[44] and in the same way later in Tibet, officiating lamas imprisoned local spirits beneath their temples by laying threads and stabbing the ritual daggers.

We are touching here upon the shadowy practices of foundation (or "construction") sacrifice, the ritual killing and interment of human beings beneath buildings.[45] Throughout Asia, foundation sacrifice has exerted a long-lasting and powerful effect on people's imaginations, and Tibet was no exception. Rumors of Tibetan foundation sacrifice continued well into the twentieth century. The American journalist Lowell Thomas describes his own encounter with such tales while traveling in central Tibet in 1949: "We had come to a sinister place and stopped to appease the demons. At that point were two *chortens*. The larger one, across the valley from us, contained a copper urn. Many years ago when the *chorten* was built and people still clung fearfully to the old Bon superstitions and rites, blood was poured into the urn. A boy and girl, each eight years old, were sacrificed and their bodies placed in it."[46] As in the case of the tantric mandala, Tibetans believed that the spirits interred below would empower the superstructure through their haunting presence. Though clear evidence of any such activity has not surfaced in Tibet, the motifs of foundation sacrifice underlie many aspects of the Tibetan relationship to sacred space and temple construction.

The parallels between the *vāstupuruṣa-maṇḍala* and the legend of Songtsen Gampo's network of temples are unmistakable. Like Puruṣa, the *rākṣasī*-demoness was sacrificed and pinned supine beneath Songtsen's "*maṇḍala* of liberation," a square grid laid across the Tibetan landscape, where she remained as a powerful protector, empowering the Rasa Trulnang and its border-taming temples. In this sense, the *Pillar Testament*'s twelfth-century redactor, surrounded as he was by extensive temple building, may well have drawn upon the well-known themes of Indian temple construction and foundation sacrifice to render anew Songtsen Gampo's historic activities and make them relevant for the times.

THE DEMONIZATION OF TIBET

The *Pillar Testament*'s *rākṣasī* narrative may have reflected Tibetans' later dispensation involvements in temple building, but it was also shaped by a number of literary themes that had taken root earlier, in Tibet's age of fragmentation. In many respects, the *rākṣasī* legend was simply an extension of the strategies for binding Buddhism to the Tibetan soil that had developed in the sociopolitical fragmentation of the late ninth and tenth centuries. The *rākṣasī* legend raised these strategies to a pan-Tibetan level, uniting its audience around memories of the early empire and creating a new Buddhist landscape with Lhasa at its heart. Where tenth-century Tibetans had tied the Buddhist teachings to specific sites through stories of local demon subjugation, the *Pillar Testament* described the conversion of Tibet as a whole. In this sense the sacrificial victim of the *rākṣasī*-demoness embodied the heathen character of all pre-Buddhist Tibet, a dangerous and demonic land in need of violent subjugation by the civilizing institutions of Buddhism. Elsewhere the *Pillar Testament* was still more explicit about the demonic nature of Tibetans, famously describing them as a people descended from the union of a monkey and a rock *rākṣasī*-demoness. "To that rock demoness was born a son who resembled neither his father nor his mother. He had no hair on his body and no tail. His face was red. For food, he ate raw meat, and for drink he drank warm blood."[47] The text continues, "[Avalokiteśvara] perceived that because the sentient beings of that snowy Tibet were the children of animals and descended from [demons], they were extremely difficult to tame. Because they could not be tamed by peaceful means, he would have to subjugate them by relying on violent punishments and laws."[48] Violence was the only option for such demonic peoples.

Yet even as the *Pillar Testament* relied on the narrative strategies of violence and local demon taming that had developed during the age of fragmentation, it denied the value of those same contributions by casting the earlier age as a time of corruption and decay. Everyone seems to have agreed with this representation of the period, even followers of the Nyingma ("Ancient") school who traced their lineages back through that same supposed darkness. In his twelfth-century religious history, the great Nyingmapa author Nyangrel Nyima Özer describes the fall of the Tibetan Empire in the following terms: "The early translations of the dharma came to an end with the destruction of the dharma by Lang Darma in the iron male bird year. Then six generations, or 108 years, passed. In the western kingdom of Ngari, the precepts of the three vows were cut off, the key points of teaching and instruction were gone, the practice lineages were cut off, and the triad of proper study, reflection, and meditation were utterly absent."[49] The most commonly used image was a flame going out, plunging Tibet into darkness until the smoldering embers of Buddhism could be reignited by King Yeshe Ö, the "ten men" of U and Tsang, and other later dispensation leaders of institutionalized Buddhism.[50]

The *Pillar Testament* reflects the same historical prejudice against the age of fragmentation, though as a purportedly seventh-century document its descriptions of the period are necessarily framed as prophesies. During the construction of the Rasa Trulnang, for example, it describes three building errors that occurred, and interprets each as a cause for the corruption and darkness that were to come. The nose of an ornamental lion is mistakenly cut off, unnecessary holes are made in planks (*spang leb*), and pillars are damaged. The prophetic king Songtsen Gampo concludes: "These common people of Tibet, children of an angry monkey and a desirous demoness, have slandered their king and queen. This crime has caused carpentry errors of three kinds to arise, and due to those errors the secular laws will diminish, the sacraments of *māntrikas* will be transgressed, and monks' vows will be broken."[51]

The prophecy's language resembles that used by Yeshe Ö and others to describe the tenth century—lawlessness, tantric excess, and religious corruption. The chaotic violence of the age of fragmentation is attributed to faults in the central cathedral's construction, but ultimately, and more significantly, to the low and demonic character of the Tibetan people. Such negative portrayals of Tibetans took root in the period of fragmentation and became common during the later dispensation. Already in the early tenth century, when Tibet was at its "darkest," Nupchen Sangye Yeshe had referred to his home as "a kingdom on the edges [of civilization], a land of red-faced, demonic Tibetans,"[52] and later dispensation texts are littered with similar references to Tibetans' violent and demonic character. The *Pillar Testament* in particular closes with an extensive series of prophecies attributed to Songtsen Gampo, and their principal focus is the coming age of fragmentation. For page after page, the great Buddhist king of legend predicts in detail the many evils that will befall Tibet in the coming years, all the doing of demonic and misguided Tibetans: "The legions of darkness will spread, and the teachings of the Buddha will completely disappear."[53]

The purportedly wretched state of Tibet was (and continues to be today) reinforced by a broader degenerative view of world history that Tibetans inherited from India. According to this view, the world is suffering under an age of decline, the Kaliyuga ("Time of Conflict").[54] Tibetan authors of the twelfth century were well aware of this chronology and used it and their own age of fragmentation to similar effect. In Nyangrel's revealed *Copper Island*, for example, Padmasambhava opens his final songs of advice to the Tibetan people by warning them of the dangers of the age: "In this age of the five degenerations, this final Kaliyuga, one who enters the unmistaken path is rare among all beings; most fall prey to wrong-thinking demons. In particular, they are led into killing and the resulting negative rebirths."[55] These lines follow an extended series of complaints by Padmasambhava about the corrupt practices and generally immoral behavior of Tibetans, all reasons why the master must return to India. In dark times such as these, he says, the dharma is rare and precious, but the demonic Tibetan people are simply exhausting and unable to appreciate properly its extraordinary value. "Tibet is shrouded in darkness. I have shone the sunlight of the dharma upon this realm, . . . but I am despairing of these evil-intentioned sinners. I am going, going to India."[56]

Another account that dates from around the twelfth century, of the great Indian master Atiśa's visit to Tibet, provides further insights.[57] Once more the Tibetan king Yeshe Ö appears, this time referring to the "ignorant beings of the border country of Tibet" and opening his letter of invitation to Atiśa (982–1054) by describing Tibet as a benighted land of hungry ghosts, "where just to raise a single yellow sheep already presents plenty of hardship."[58] When Atiśa accepts the king's less-than-appealing invitation, the abbot of his home monastery, Ratnākara, further criticizes the Indian master for his planned journey to "that yak pen of yours."

Here it is significant that not only Tibetans of the age of fragmentation require taming, but those of the later dispensation as well, and perhaps this was more to the point. The self-demonizing rhetoric of the period went hand in hand with a common Tibetan emphasis on India and the purity of all things Indian. On their own, Tibetans could never hope to get Buddhism right; their demonic nature required the firm hand of an Indian (or at least of a Tibetan who had traveled and studied in India).[59] A Tibetan's proper place is made plain in Nyangrel's twelfth-century account of King Trisong Detsen's first meeting with Padmasambhava: The king is forced under threat of violence to prostrate before the Indian master. Nyangrel's account contrasts markedly with earlier versions of the same event. In the *Sayings of Wa*, portions of which can be dated to the tenth century, the roles are reversed and Padmasambhava prostrates before the Tibetan king.[60] In the intervening years, it seems, Tibetans' self-portrayals changed for the worse.

Authority was thus located in India and in the hands of those with access to India. This displacement of religious authority combined with the darkening of the age of fragmentation and its attendant negative portrayals of Tibetans to serve a common ideological purpose: to restrict Tibetans' access to authentic Buddhism, to keep Buddhism a scarce commodity that could be controlled by a relatively small number of wealthy clans. The above-cited account of Atiśa's journey to Tibet, for example, sought to promote a specific set of teachings over all others, its language repeatedly accentuating the "one essential feature for Atiśa's lasting influence on Buddhism in Tibet: the diffusion of his teaching of the 'stages of the path' (*lam rim*) and the founding of the Kadampa sect, both of which were a direct outcome of the historic meeting between Atiśa and his prophesied disciple."[61] Not even Tibet's best-trained monks could compare to the authority of the Indian master. "Rotten translator!" exclaimed Atiśa on meeting Tibet's senior monk, Rinchen Zangpo. "Indeed there was need of my coming to Tibet!"[62] Local Tibetan teachers and the Tibetan people in general were thus cast as misled, if not downright demonic, and placed in a clearly subservient relationship to Buddhism and those who controlled it.

Taken as an allegory, the *Pillar Testament*'s *rākṣasī* legend reveals much about how Tibetans viewed their own conversion to Buddhism. Tibetans were represented as passive participants in this process, providing only a restrained space (*'dul zhing*) for Buddhism to be transmitted. And in this transmission of the dharma, and particularly that of the tantras, the voices of Tibetans were to remain silent, adding nothing of their own (*rang bzo med pa*). Tibetan compositions, even those that pretended to be nothing more, were therefore to be condemned as "false doctrines" (*chos log*) and "impure and mistaken teachings" (*chos log dri ma can*).[63] Despite the best efforts of the courts, their strict decrees (*bka' bcad dam po*) and their banishments, renegade Tibetans insisted on composing their own misleading works.[64] In this web of associations, the age of fragmentation provided the ultimate proof of what would happen if Tibetans tried to shake loose from their prescribed role: Tibet would be plunged once more into darkness, into lawless chaos, moral corruption, bloody sacrifice, and demons running rampant.[65] In this way, Tibet's age of fragmentation lurked as a dire warning to all Tibetans of the later dispensation, a demonic presence that underpinned the tradition they were building.

6

BUDDHIST WARFARE

The thirteenth century saw the dawning of a new age for Tibetans. Since the collapse of the Pugyal Empire in the ninth century, political fragmentation, local clans, and tantric authority had reigned. Even following the tenth century and the "age of fragmentation," Tibetans' self-confidence had not fully returned, as they deferred—rhetorically at least—to their Indian masters to the south. As we have seen, throughout the later dispensation period, Tibetans regularly depicted themselves as a benighted people dwelling in a demonic land at the very edges of civilization. By the end of the twelfth century, though, a renewed sense of Tibet's importance was beginning to emerge. Certainly the same factors that had dominated the preceding centuries—fragmentation, clan power, tantric authority—continued to shape later Tibetan society, but with the thirteenth century they began to be reorganized by some new and powerful forces. Perhaps foremost among these new influences were the Mongols. With their arrival in 1240, the descendents of Genghis Khan brought widespread havoc and a new political order to Tibet. Even after their Tibetan representatives were overcome in the mid-fourteenth century, the Mongols continued to exercise a powerful influence on the region for centuries. The present chapter looks at how the Tibetan language of violence was altered by the Mongols' arrival. From the thirteenth century, the violent rites, which had so far been largely the preserve of individuals or small groups of Buddhist practitioners, grew into large-scale rites that were performed on behalf of the state. Violent ritual, in this sense, went from the local to the global.

Around this same time, Tibetans began to portray their land less as a marginal backwater than as a central Buddhist country under threat from its barbaric neighbors. Tibetans responded to the Mongol incursions in a variety of ways. Some portrayed the Mongols as long-prophesied protectors of the faith, while others wrote more ominous prophecies and developed large-scale ritual performances designed to repel the offending Mongol armies. In both cases, the prophetic writings and ritual practices of Tibet began to reflect the rise of a new spatial paradigm. Whereas the earlier legends of the eleventh and twelfth centuries had characterized Tibet as a land of demons in need of violent suppression, later sources saw the principal threat to Buddhism not within Tibet's own landscape and the hearts of Tibetans themselves, but outside, in Tibet's border regions. A new concern with Tibet's frontiers began to take precedence. Tibet was becoming a new Buddhist center, with its own demonic edges to control.

Tibetans' growing sense of their geographic importance could only have been strengthened by the decline of Buddhism in India. Already in the late twelfth century, Tibetans were beginning to report on the Muslim depredations in northern India. The Kagyupa master Jigten Gönpo (1143–1217) included the following lines in a prayer for the success of the Buddhist teachings: "In this world, a great devastation has arisen. Enemies of the teachings have come. As the power of the Turks has increased, they have conquered the eastern Indian [regions] of Magadha, destroying the outward and inward sacred objects."[1]

India was quickly being divested of its Buddhist heritage. Thirteenth-century Tibetans found themselves increasingly alone, the sole inheritors of India's tantric lineages. In many ways, the Buddhist conversion of Tibet was nearing completion. The principal Buddhist texts of India had been translated, Indian Buddhism was in decline, and reasons for traveling south were quickly disappearing. Tibet was coming into its own, becoming a mature Buddhist land in its own right, and accordingly, the fourteenth century would mark a time of consolidation, as earlier innovations were standardized, lineages settled, and canons formed. The center of Buddhist authority was shifting northward.

Not surprisingly, this crucial period witnessed a parallel shift in Tibetans' geographic accounts. Already by the late twelfth century, new Tibeto-centric geographic conceptions were beginning to emerge. Building on earlier Indic conceptions of the "Sixteen Great Countries," for example, a new and uniquely Tibetan system of "Eighteen Great Countries" was introduced. Where the Sixteen Great Countries had demarcated an Indo-centric geography, the Eighteen placed Tibet at the center, surrounded by India to the south, China to the east, Turkestan to the north, and Persia to the west. After centuries of being a "marginal people" (*mtha' 'khob*), Tibetans were finally beginning to construct their own universe with themselves at the center.[2]

THE MONGOLS INVADE

The Mongol conquests began with the rise to power of Genghis Khan (c. 1167–1227). In 1229 Genghis Khan's third son, Ogödei, was elected supreme khan of the empire, and by 1230 he had Tibet surrounded on three sides. In the years that followed, fears of an invasion spread throughout Tibet, anxieties that were reflected by the natural world in ominous portents and by Tibet's religious leaders in fearful prophesies.[3] Finally in 1239, Ogödei's son, Köden, took control of the region around Liangzhou, to the northeast of Tibet, and the following year he sent his commander, Dorta the Black, with a detachment of troops into Tibet proper, where they wrought havoc and sacked Gyel Lhakhang and Rateng Monastery.

Fortunately, members of the Mongol court soon took a personal interest in Tibetan Buddhism. In 1244 Köden invited the Tibetan master Sakya Paṇḍita Kunga Gyeltsen (1182–1251) to his capital in Liangzhou. Sakya Paṇḍita brought with him his two nephews, the young Drogön Pakpa Rinpoche (1235–1280) and his brother Chana Dorje (1239–1267). They arrived at Köden's court in 1246 and met the Mongol leader there, in early 1247. Sakya Paṇḍita died soon after, in 1251, but his two nephews remained in Liangzhou, well positioned to forge a gradual Mongol-Sakya alliance.

In the same year of Sakya Paṇḍita's death, the Mongol leadership changed again, now with the election of Möngke, and the following year the new khan undertook a fearsome two-pronged campaign against Tibet, leaving the Tibetan people terrified and firmly under Mongol control for the next century. Throughout the 1250s, Tibetan leaders of the different Buddhist orders, especially of the various Kagyu subsects, sought to establish close relations with their new masters. In 1256, the Second Karmapa, Karma Pakshi (1204/6–1283), traveled to Möngke Khan's camp to represent Buddhism in an interreligious debate. Similarly, the Pakmodrupa and Drikungpa enjoyed the patronage of Hülegü, while the Taklungpa looked to Arigh Böke, and the Tselpa to Khubilai (1215–1294).[4] As between the Mongols themselves, Tibeto-Mongol alliances were complex and ever changing.

Within this competitive and increasingly sectarian environment, the young Pakpa Rinpoche grew up at the Mongol court. His familiarity with the court eventually allowed him to become official preceptor to Khubilai, who declared himself leader following Möngke Khan's death in 1259. Five years later, in 1264, while granting tantric initiation to Khubilai, Pakpa was offered the status of religious and secular leader of all Tibet. From this point forward, the Sakyapa hierarchs enjoyed nearly complete rule over a newly unified Tibet. They divided power between three chiefs: two monks—the Sakyapa abbot (*gdan sa chen po*) and the imperial preceptor (*ti shri*)—and a secular governor (*dpon chen*). And should matters get out of hand, they could always call upon their Mongol patrons for support.

In the two decades immediately following Pakpa's ascendance, Tibet's internal rivalries continued, building to a violent crescendo in 1290. The most serious challenge to Sakya rule was mounted in the 1280s by the Drikungpa, a Buddhist sect that had maintained strong relations with Hülegü (1216–1265), brother to both Möngke and Khubilai and leader of the Persian reaches of the Mongol Empire. In 1285 the Drikungpa called upon their western Mongol (*stod hor*) allies for military support and rose up against the Sakyapa, destroying Chayul Monastery and killing its abbot. Fighting persisted for several more years until, in 1290, Khubilai responded with an army of his own and razed the Drikung Monastery, thereby putting an end, for a time at least, to any significant rivalry among the Buddhist schools.[5] As we shall see, the extraordinary violence of this entire fifty-year period, from 1240 to 1290, left a strong impression on the collective memory of the Tibetan people.

DEMONS FROM THE BORDERS: THE MONGOLS IN PROPHECY

With the fourteenth century came a major new biography of Padmasambhava.[6] Orgyen Lingpa's *Padma Chronicles* would become the most influential of all Padmasambhava's biographies, and just as Nyangrel's twelfth-century *Copper Island* reflected the concerns of its day, with its emphases on temple building and the demonic character of the Tibetan people, the *Padma Chronicles* too was a product of its time. No longer was Tibet a mere borderland filled with darkness and demons; it had become a major center in the Buddhist world, an enlightened land under threat from its own barbaric neighbors. The *Padma Chronicles* is littered with references to the evils wrought by the early Mongol invasions, with Padmasambhava repeatedly prophesying the Mongol depredations. "The earth will nourish the Mongols," warns the eighth-century master. "There will be monks who act like Mongol generals. Genghis will cut the earth between his upper and lower teeth. Fugitives and refugees will be many, and the land will be deserted."[7] Tibet and its religion would come under dire threat from its demonic periphery.

Elsewhere, Padmasambhava makes another prophesy that employs the earlier spatial model of the *Pillar Testament's rākṣasī* legend: "Of the [border-taming] temples that the three ancestors [Songtsen, Trisong, and Relpachen] will erect, the peripheral ones will be destroyed, while the center will remain."[8] The Mongols were unraveling the work of Padmasambhava and Tibet's other tamers and threatening to return the land to its original state of darkness. The Mongol invasions thus conjured memories of Tibet's age of fragmentation, of political chaos and religious corruption, and the *Padma Chronicles* situates Padmasambhava's prophesies on the Mongol depredations immediately after a similar series of prophesies on the age of fragmentation, so that the parallels are unmistakable.[9]

Mongol rule over Tibet collapsed in the mid-fourteenth century. By the end of his life, the Tibetan leader Jangchup Gyeltsen (1302–1364) had succeeded in wresting control of central Tibet from the Mongols, effectively uniting it under Tibetan rule for the first time since the fall of the Pugyal dynasty.[10] The new ruler immediately began to undo many of the Mongol influences on Tibetan society. Mongol dress, customs, and language, which had apparently enjoyed some popularity among the Sakya political elite, were all outlawed.[11] True to their time, Orgyen Lingpa's revealed prophesies (here in his *Minister Chronicles*) echoed these Tibetan concerns at the impact of the Mongols: "A demon will materialize to lead the Mongols. A great mob will rise up against the royal line. There will be hardships and loss of freedom. Even the Buddha's compassion will be unable to protect [the Tibetan people]. Tibet's merits will diminish until they are gone. As the blessings of the dharma disappear, ordinations will be nearly extinct due to [lack of] food. Monks will wear the Chinese cap, follow Mongol customs, and accumulate [all sorts of] misdeeds. . . . Leprosy, swellings, and plagues will emerge, smallpox, psoriasis, and other epidemics as well."[12]

The idea that demons were behind the Mongol invasions found fertile ground among the Tibetans, and inevitably the Mongol khans were likened to Rudra, their conquest of Tibet paralleled to the demon's mythic takeover of the world. Just as Rudra built a castle of rotting flesh surrounded by a swamp of blood and filth, so too did the Mongols (fig. 7). Just as Rudra spread disease, killed the men, and enslaved the women, so too did the demonic Khan:

> In the iron-dog year,[13] a Khan who is an incarnation of Nam Teu the White[14] will send forth emanations of evil demons. Unhappiness and a rain of weapons will befall the land of Tibet. Woe to the Tibetans! Alas! How pitiful! For over ten [years] they will be leaderless, [scattered] like tea dust. There will be no ploughmen or farmers to be found; women will be left alone like islands. [The Khan] will erect a fortress made of flesh and surrounded by an ocean of blood. He will rape the maidens and enslave the women. The border peoples will demolish the center, and Tibet and Kham will fall to pieces. All three provinces of U, Tsang, and Kham will be dominated by the Mongols.[15]

Over and above the explicit identification of the Mongol leader with the demon Nam Teu, the implicit comparison of the khan to Rudra could not have been lost on its audience. Indeed, the *Padma Chronicles* opens with its own rendition

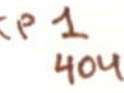

Figure 7: The palace of Begtse Chen, the Mongolian god of war. "[The Khan] will erect a fortress made of flesh and surrounded by an ocean of blood." (© Rubin Museum of Art / Art Resource, NY, Item 65344)

of the Rudra myth,[16] so that the narrative provides the mythic context for the entire work, the thematic background against which the later-prophesied events unfold.

The Mongol khans were barbaric demons, and as such they required violent subjugation. Toward this end, another of Padmasambhava's prophecies explains, "There will come from the interior of Yarlung an incarnation of Vajrapāṇi. . . . The sixteen districts will be conquered, and there will be a little happiness."[17] The savior of Tibet prophesied here may be identified as Jangchup Gyeltsen, whose Pakmodru seat was located near the Yarlung Valley, at the very heart of the ancient Tibetan Empire.[18] The prophecy celebrates him as a manifestation of Vajrapāṇi, the wrathful buddha who tamed Rudra, the implication being that just as Rudra required violent measures, the Mongols too could be defeated only by resorting to the ritual activities of violence.[19]

"THE MONGOL REPELLER" AND THE RISE OF WAR MAGIC

In the centuries that followed, Tibetans would direct innumerable violent rites against the Mongols. In doing so, they followed a long-standing Buddhist tradition of justifying violence for the protection of the state. *Tāntrikas* had long played significant roles in the royal courts of India by performing a variety of ritual duties, including rites to harm the king's enemies.[20] But even before the advent of the tantras, the *Sūtra of the Manifested Teaching on the Methods That Are within the Bodhisattva's Field of Activity* had set forth guidelines for the proper Buddhist king on when war is justified. Accordingly, the king should resort to violence only after trying to control his enemies first through kindness (**mitra*), second through the granting of favors (**anugraha*), and third through intimidation, "by a show, making them afraid that your army is larger because they are completely surrounded on all sides."[21] As a last resort, then, righteous violence in the name of protecting the state was nothing new for Buddhism. In Tibet, however, it did take on certain unique characteristics. As new large-scale rituals were formulated, and new prophesies such as those of the *Padma Chronicles* revealed, tantric war magic developed along some distinctively Tibetan thematic lines.

Following Jangchup Gyeltsen's death in 1364, his Pakmodrupa descendents soon found their newfound authority challenged. By 1435, their Rinpungpa competitors to the west had seized the palace at Samdruptse and thereby re-ignited the age-old rivalry between the Tibetan provinces of U (centered around Lhasa) and Tsang (now centered around Samdruptse in the modern city of Shigatse). Over the next century the Rinpungpa gradually gained in power, and by the early sixteenth century they were extending their political reach right into Lhasa. Seeing a potential threat in the popular new Geluk school, the Rinpungpa enacted a series of repressive policies against the Gelukpa centers surrounding the capital city. Tensions between the Rinpungpa on the one hand and the Gelukpa and their Pakmodrupa supporters on the other continued to build through the sixteenth century, and matters were only exacerbated when the Rinpungpa-appointed governor of Tsang, Shingshak Tseten Dorje based at Samdruptse, broke from his masters in 1565 and proclaimed himself the new king.

The upstart ruler, Tseten Dorje, maintained many of his masters' earlier alliances, including their close relations with the Karma Kagyu school. He likewise continued their suppression of the Gelukpa. In 1578 the Gelukpa abbot of Drepung, Sonam Gyatso (1543–1588), traveled to Mongolia and succeeded in converting the Tumed leader Altan Khan to Buddhism. In return, the teacher received the previously unknown title of "Dalai Lama." The new Geluk-Mongol alliance increased the political strains still further, and as the sixteenth century came to a close, wars and Mongol incursions were a regular part of Tibetan life. Within this contentious environment, large-scale war magic rose to the fore.

The Nyingmapa master Lodrö Gyeltsen (1552–1624) became so proficient at these large-scale war rites that he became known simply as Sokdokpa, "the Mongol Repeller." In large part to justify his involvements in such practices, Sokdokpa composed *A History of How the Mongols Were Repelled*, a work filling fifty-six folio sides entirely devoted to the topic of Mongol invasions and the Tibetan sorcery worked against them.[22] The text proceeds chronologically, beginning with Köden's 1240 destruction of the Kadampa Monastery of Gyel Lhakhang in Penyul,[23] progressing through the joint Mongol-Sakya rule of Tibet, and culminating with Sokdokpa's autobiographical account of his own efforts on behalf of the Tsang kings and other Tibetan leaders of the late sixteenth and early seventeenth centuries.

Following the initial atrocities wrought by Köden, Sokdokpa suggests that the real troubles began with the death of the first governor, Śākya Zangpo, in 1270. Immediately, Sokdokpa turns to the *Padma Chronicles* for insight: "After the governor died, the other governors did not have integrity. In the *[Padma] Chronicles* it says, 'Forming itself at Natak, the Mongol army will come to Tibet.' Accordingly, the year after Pakpa Rinpoche died [that is, 1281], the Mongol armies were invited and the governor Kunga Zangpo was killed at Charok Tsang."[24]

From here, Sokdokpa traces the rising chaos directly to the 1290 sacking of Drikung by Khubilai's army and the Sakya governor, Aklen Dorje Pel. According to Sokdokpa, the lamas of Tibet responded to the Mongol depredations with violent rituals:[25]

> Those [Mongol] armies destroyed many temples and teachings. Many men and beasts were killed, so Lama Jamyang Sarma[26] went to U-tsang, and urged the virtues of repelling the Mongols. Thereby the monks, mantrins, and Bonpo performed the services of their respective traditions. More specifically, Gyalwa Yang Gönpa[27] gathered the choicest barley flour from throughout U-tsang [for constructing the effigies]. The monks, the mantrins, and the Bonpo executed their respective repellings, and he gave support and gifts to them all. The height of the offerings is said to have been as high as a mountain peak. The lord himself (that is, Yang Gönpa) rested in the *mahāmudrā* intention for seven days, whereby the Mongol armies were repelled. This was similar to how previously Devendra thought of the profound meaning of the Perfection of Wisdom and recited the profound words as a liturgy, whereby he repelled the evil demons.[28]

Thus violent rituals grew to play an important role in Tibetan religion during and after the years of Mongol rule. Bearing increasingly dramatic titles like the *Fiery Razor Slash of the Lord of Death* or the *Whirlwind of the Black Sun and Moon*, they were framed as "acts of virtue"[29] that protected Buddhism from destruction by demonic barbarians. Writings on the thirteenth and fourteenth centuries include multiple tales of Tibetan sorcery practiced against the Mongols. In some cases the performances even became annual institutional events; Taklung Sangye Yarjön (1203–1272) is said to have performed large-scale and costly rituals to avert Mongol invasion on the fourteenth day of the fourth month of every year.[30]

When performed as war magic, the violent rites of the tantras assumed a grand scale. Large numbers of ritual experts would gather for performances that could last several days, if not weeks. Legions of effigies of the enemy soldiers would be fashioned, so that the practitioners in effect recreated the battlefield within the confines of the ritual space. Sokdokpa describes many of his own ritual performances for which up to 250,000 paper effigies (*ling ga*) were created,[31] often accompanied by thousands more effigies of the enemy's horses. The resources required for a serious Mongol-repelling rite were therefore considerable. The requisite number of expert officiants and the necessary materials had to be assembled and elaborate shrines constructed. The production of effigies on such a mass scale required large quantities of paper, in particular, so that papermaking is a recurring theme in Sokdokpa's accounts:

> Then in the monkey year [1608] a need for repelling was announced. Precious presences from all over donated two hundred bushels, on the basis of which there was enough paper to construct one hundred thousand effigies of humans and five thousand effigies of horses. Nineteen of us performed

the accomplishment in the assembly hall of the monastery, whereby signs appeared just as described in the manuals. At that time an army consisting of over two hundred and fifty *ching* [about two-thirds of a hectare] of military tents containing a mixture of Hor and Mongolians had arrived in Uyuk and Tsemo. Many cattle and sheep of the Hor and the nomads were lost. All the men tried to flee, but some failed. So as not to be harmed, they returned to their homelands.

Then in the first and the twelfth Mongol months of the bird year [1609], it was announced that each *siddha* should perform the rites. Over one hundred sheets of paper were required. Wishing to realize those, we set out to make the paper, but produced only ten sheets. However, the Zhabtrung from Topgyel, Pönsa Rinpoche, provided an abundance of paper. So we got our paper without trying, and a measure of great kindness arose. Twenty-one masters enacted the ritual performances for three weeks, whereby there was a massive swirling and the signs of completion appeared just as explained in the scriptures. Then we unleashed the rites for fourteen days; the activities of the three—crushing, burning, and casting out—were perfectly enacted.

After that, in the iron male dog year [1610] there was a prophecy that border peoples would defeat Tibet. I thought to myself that I would probably be able to repel them. Then in the wood male tiger year [1614], at the height of winter, it was said that a great number of mixed *ser myog* and Mongols were coming. All the farmers and nomads were terrified. At that time seventeen masters took part in the ritual performances, and after seven days the signs emerged. A great snowstorm fell. After that, a gale rose up, and all the snow piled into drifts like sand dunes. The Mongols were buried beneath the snow, men along with their horses and pack animals. Not even one escaped death. When the snow melted, the lower Horpa came to take all their belongings.[32]

Disease spreading among the livestock and deadly snowstorms—such were the events attributed to the successful performance of war magic. Sometimes the enemy armies would scatter; at other times they were destroyed.

Sokdokpa ends his history with a series of scriptural citations chosen to justify his involvement in these events. Citing the Mahāyoga tantras, his teacher Zhikpo Lingpa, and others, he defends his actions, explaining, "These Mongol repellings were methods for [insuring] the happiness of all sentient beings, and excellent methods for protecting the teachings of the buddhas."[33] "As the *Guhyasamājottaratantra* says," he writes, "the nature of this sorcery arises from learning and realization. How can it be compared to the sorcery of spirits and demons?"[34] For all their dark and terrifying appearances, Sokdokpa insists, these violent rites were specifically *not* demonic. Quite the opposite, they served to expel the Mongols back to their demonic realm beyond the borders of Tibet.

Repelling Mongols from the Tibetan heartland involved not only offensive rituals; it called for the reinforcement of Tibet's spiritual defenses as well, the plugging of holes in the geomantic dike, and enlisting the support of local gods and demons. Sokdokpa's history is rife with geomantic concerns about shoring up the edifice of Tibetan Buddhism against the heathen Mongols. It cites repeated prophecies demanding the construction of new *stūpas* or the restoration of old ones at key locations and describes the efforts of Sokdokpa and others to fulfill those demands. Not surprisingly, Sokdokpa was most interested in the border regions directly to the north of Lhasa. He relates how in 1601, for example, he encouraged the renovation of hundreds of "the northern stūpas."[35] And in the same context, Sokdokpa also attributes Tibet's enduring woes to a weakening of the geomantic forces embodied in Songtsen Gampo's legendary network of border-taming temples. He quotes the following prophecy: "When the Jowo Śākya [housed in the Rasa Trulnang cathedral] is endangered by water, the border-taming and far-border-taming temples will degenerate. At that time, the kingdom will be filled with cheats and liars. All the dharma practitioners will be insulted and become weakened. At that time, when generally pointless turmoil arises, there will be many obstructive people who do not practice dharma from the heart."[36]

Only by reversing the waters, the prophecy continues, and repairing the border-taming temples, will the Mongols be defeated. Significantly, no mention is made of the demoness that played so crucial a role in the original legend of these temples. No longer were Tibetans anxious about the demons pinned beneath the mandala of temples. Their concerns had changed. The new threat lay at Tibet's borders, and the mandala had to be reinforced to withstand those demonic forces that dwelt beyond its limits.[37]

SORCERY AND THE FIFTH DALAI LAMA

Of course the Mongols did not allow the powerful spells of the tantras to remain solely in the hands of their enemies. The use of violent ritual to promote victory on the battlefield was a double-edged sword. Once again, who was the righteous buddha and who the deceptive demon was a matter of perspective. Both sides could use tantric war magic, and the Mongols deployed their own violent rites in their military conquests of Tibet, as well as of China and other regions. Indeed, the Mongol khans were attracted to Tibet's Buddhist masters in large part for their powerful practices. Already in the thirteenth century, Genghis Khan had adopted the ferocious Mahākāla as his "Grand Protective Deity," constructing magnificent temples and ordering elaborate services for the

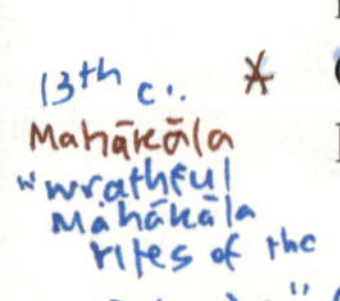

deity.[38] One of the principal responsibilities of the Sakya hierarchs residing at the Mongol court was to perform their violent rituals in support of the Mongol war efforts, and Tibetans lamas working in Tibet too were regularly petitioned for their services. In a much-cited example, the thirteenth-century Nyingmapa lama Zur Nyima Senge is said to have cast violent magic at the behest of the emperor against an invading army of the Upper Hor (that is, the Chaghatai Khanate), killing thirty thousand troops beneath supernatural storms of snow and ice.[39]

The Nyingma school in particular came to play a central role in the performance of Tibetan war magic. Nyingma histories tell how Khubilai exempted the Nyingmapa from taxation for their proficiency in sorcery. At the same time, Nyingmapa treasure revealers were providing much of the prophetic justification and ritual firepower for the Tibetan resistance. Sokdokpa's history of repelling Mongols highlights not only their expertise in tantric ritual, but their tradition of revealed prophecy as key to their success. Sorcery and prophesy here worked hand in hand: "In particular, during that period the three treasure revealers, Guru Chowang, Yeshe Khyungdrak, and Chölo, came at the same time and enacted many repellings in accordance with the prophetic instructions (*lung byang*) on Mongol repelling. Through the power and blessings of many *mantradharas* and *siddhas*—Zur Pakshi Śākya Ö, Drolmawa Samdrup Dorje, Kangpa Drel Sambho, Dratak Rindor, and so on—those first [waves of] Mongol armies could not bear it in Tibet any longer."[40]

By the sixteenth and seventeenth centuries, violent ritual and its attendant prophesies were commonly associated with the Nyingma school. Such a perception may be inferred from a scene in the Fifth Dalai Lama's history of the Northern Treasures lineage. At the age of twenty, the Third Yolmowa, Tendzin Norbu (1589–1644), came to study under his first Nyingmapa teacher, Ngagi Wangpo, the founder of Dorje Drak Monastery. Soon after entering the tutelage of the great master, the young monk began to grow apprehensive at all the transgressive and violent rituals he was suddenly being asked to perform. In response, we read, "The great *vidyādhara* [Ngagi Wangpo] glared straight at that *tulku* and said, 'Are you embarrassed by the large number of cycles for violent sorcery in the Nyingma Secret Mantra?!' And at this, the hostility of [the Yolmowa's] scholar's contempt and arrogance collapsed into a subdued state."[41]

The account shows the Nyingmapa's close association with violent rites, but it also reveals a marked ambivalence in the association. The Nyingmapa were at once proud of their radical role in Tibetan society, even as they were also defensive of it. They were powerful beings who worked near the margins of what was acceptable within the Tibetan tradition.

Tibetan perceptions of the Nyingmapa as particularly adept at violent ritual likely carried considerable material benefits for many lamas of the Nyingma school.[42] Tibet's rulers patronized their Nyingmapa *tāntrikas* in exchange for the latter's ritual support. Such a *quid pro quo* arrangement is made explicit at one point in Sokdokpa's history, where Sokdokpa relates how in 1599 the Tsang king bestowed upon him a monastery of his own. As he did so, the king made it clear that the Nyingma master was now beholden to him: "Now that I have given you a monastery, you must henceforth put to use your monastic estates and accept responsibility for repelling Mongols."[43]

Though the Nyingmapa were most closely associated with violent rites, followers of other Tibetan Buddhist orders were also involved. Sokdokpa's own history bears witness to Kagyupa participation in the violent rituals performed for the Tsang court,[44] and other sources tell of Sakyapa lamas doing likewise. In his biography, the Sakyapa master Jamyang Sonam Wangpo (1559–1621), for example, is described performing war rites on behalf of the Tsang king in late 1605 and again in 1608.[45] And we have already noted the early Mongol enthusiasms for the wrathful Mahākāla rites of the Sakyapa. There is surprisingly little evidence, however, of Gelukpa involvement in such practices. The early Gelukpa seem to have prided themselves on their righteous avoidance of violent rites, a self-image that changed markedly, however, with the Fifth Dalai Lama and the rise of the Ganden Podrang, after which many examples of Gelukpa sorcery can be found.[46] In this sense, the Nyingma and early Geluk schools marked two extremes along a spectrum of Tibetan Buddhist approaches to violent ritual. Given this, we may speculate that the Fifth Dalai Lama himself may well have been drawn into war magic in large part by his own family ties to the Nyingma school.

The Fifth Dalai Lama, Ngawang Losang Gyatso (1617–1682), is a towering figure in Tibetan history. Known simply as the "Great Fifth," he is famous for having united Tibet under his new Ganden Podrang government, the regime that remained in power until the Chinese invasion of the 1950s. Ngawang Losang Gyatso was born in 1617, to an ancient and noble family of Chongye. His family enjoyed close ties to the Nyingma school, and specifically to the Northern Treasures lineage, a line that several decades earlier had run afoul of the Tsang rulers based at Samdruptse. Perhaps doubly concerned, then, by the rising power of the Gelukpa and the Dalai Lamas in general, and by the new Fifth's dangerous family history in particular, the Tsang king initially prohibited the Gelukpa's recognition of their new incarnation. Eventually, thanks to the intervention of the first Panchen Lama, the king acquiesced, but even then he would not allow the child to be installed at Drepung until his fifth year, when two thousand Mongol troops arrived to force the issue.[47]

From a young age, the Dalai Lama received a strict monastic education in the treatises of the Geluk school. From his tutors, Lingme Shabdrung Könchok Chöpel (1573–1644) and the first Panchen Lama (1570–1662), the youth received his novice vows and copious teachings on the *Perfection of Wisdom*, *Madhyamaka* philosophy, the *Vinaya*, and *Abhidharma*. In 1630 he inaugurated his own career with a public teaching of the *Book of Kadam*.[48] Despite the rigor and the purity of his monastic training, however, the Dalai Lama's own autobiographical account of his eventual rise to power gives considerable weight to his familial affiliations with the Nyingma school.[49]

In 1639 the Dalai Lama's patron and protector, Gushri Khan, entered eastern Tibet to confront and defeat the Bonpo king of Beri. As the Mongol leader moved against this ally of the Tsangpa rulers, the Dalai Lama was petitioned to assist the Mongols' military venture with a violent ritual performance. His Nyingmapa connections made him an ideal choice for such an undertaking, as most Gelukpa had traditionally avoided any involvement in such rites. The Dalai Lama explains in his autobiography, however, that his ancestral Nyingmapa abilities had long since been diluted by his Geluk education: "I had trained but little in the Nyingma school. Apart from a few scattered recitations, I had forsaken the tutelary deities and protectors of my ancestors, so that now nothing was left. Once I had received the *Sorcerous Device of [Vajra]bhairava* from Pabongka [Peljor Lhundup], and I had obtained the *Sixty* in the presence of Pönlop Paṇchen Rinpoche, but I never performed the [necessary] propitiations and accomplishments [for those ritual systems]. Now, because I had chosen more academic studies, I was not able to perform them."[50]

Eventually the Dalai Lama conceded and agreed to perform the rites, but only with the assistance of his own Nyingmapa teacher, Zur Chöying Rangdröl (1604–1669). "I cast aside my textual studies," he writes, "and composed an abridged practice manual for *The Fiery Razor Slash of the Lord of Death*.[51] I consulted with the Omniscient Zur in order to eliminate doubts about those [teachings] I had forgotten, then proceeded to Drepung."[52] "This Beri [king]," he concludes, "was certainly [a case] of the ten fields, and was thus clearly an object for violent action."[53] We have seen in chapter 3 how Tibetans justified their ritual killing by identifying their victims with one or more of five or ten "fields" for liberation, that is, with someone who had committed a crime against Buddhism that was punishable by death. Now the Dalai Lama was applying the same lists to his own countrymen, here the eastern Tibetan king of Beri, to justify the war magic he was casting on behalf of his Mongol allies.

In emphasizing his initial refusal to support Gushri Khan's military adventures with his sorcery, the Dalai Lama was not only highlighting the differences between the Gelukpa and Nyingmapa approaches to such practices, he was also expressing a real moral reluctance.[54] Tibetans, even those most deeply involved in tantric practice, almost invariably express some kind of anxiety about their participations in sorcerous ceremonies. We have seen above the Third Yolmowa, Tendzin Norbu, expressing doubts about the morality of such practices, only to be harshly rebuked by his Nyingmapa teacher. Sokdokpa too included accounts of his own master Zhikpo Lingpa's efforts to convince him of the need for his ritual services.[55] Such confessional accounts may have served several purposes simultaneously. They highlighted the lama's ethicality and his moral reluctance to get involved, even as they also provide the justifications for his ultimately performing the rites. In this sense, the answers that Ngagi Wangpo (the Third Yolmowa's teacher) and Zhikpo Lingpa (Sokdokpa's teacher) are said to have offered their students, to assuage their respective doubts, also provide a preemptive defense against potential criticisms of their students' actions. Note too that the students' moral reluctance, while quite likely heartfelt, also echoes the early tantras' own suggestions that all other ritual and political strategies (pacification, enhancement, and coercion) must first be exhausted before violence is deployed as a last resort. In this sense such expressions of reluctance were themselves part of a long-established ritual tradition.

That said, Tibetan expressions of anxiety are also seen at moments when self-justification is clearly not the point. In such cases, they may also be offered as warnings to anyone who may consider dabbling in such consequential practices. In Tsangnyön Heruka's famous *Life of Milarepa,* for example, the young Milarepa's teacher of black magic expresses regret at his involvements in violent ritual. Here the account is not autobiographical (indeed, it may well be fictional), and it serves instead a more cautionary function. Such admonitions against violence had their psychological effects on their readers, moreover, and many later Tibetan masters who participated in violent rituals would attribute certain ill effects to the negative karma of such actions. As we saw in chapter 2, Nupchen Sangye Yeshe is said to have composed his *Lamp for the Eye in Contemplation* in an attempt to purify the negativities he accumulated through his destruction of a threatening army.[56] The Fifth Dalai Lama relates how he received magical amulets from Zur Chöying Rangdröl, to protect him from the "impurities of his broken vows." Nevertheless, he writes, he fell ill and could barely speak for two months due to the impurities he contracted from casting his violent rituals against the Tsang king and his people. The Dalai Lama is cured only through a visionary dream in which the deceased Nyingmapa master Tashi Topgyal bestows on him purificatory empowerments for the wrathful deity Karmaguru, along with an accompanying ritual dagger. As the Dalai Lama receives the empowerments, in an extraordinarily telling moment, he looks over to see his fellow Gelukpa monks watching sternly from a nearby window. He recounts the dream in his secret autobiography:

> Looking through an open window on the eastern side of the protector-chapel, stood the treasurer [Sonam Rabten] and a crowd of well-dressed monks with disapproving looks. Shoving the ritual dagger into my belt, I went outside. Thinking that if any of those monks said anything, I would strike him with the dagger, I walked resolutely straight through them. They all lowered their eyes and just stood there. When I awoke, my illness and impurities had been completely removed; not even the slightest bit remained. I was absolutely overflowing with amazement and faithful devotion.[57]

Here in early 1642, in this private moment of self-reflection, may be seen many of the complexities that haunt the history of violence in Tibetan Buddhism. The dream mirrors not only the ethical concerns that the Dalai Lama may have felt toward his own ritual involvements, but the split loyalties that divided his personal identity. A Gelukpa monk from a Nyingmapa family, the Dalai Lama is seen here caught within a web of complex tensions and relationships, at a crucial moment in the history of Tibet. Ultimately his position is resolved through a resolute claim to authority, as the young Dalai Lama marches through his disapproving peers, clinging to his ritual dagger. Tibetans' performances of violent ritual were rarely simple or entirely guilt free.

The Dalai Lama thus framed the Gelukpa takeover of Tibet in terms of liberation and violent sorcery. In 1641 Gushri Khan's troops carried their campaign into central Tibet and besieged the Samdruptse palace of the Tsang kings. Again the future leader was asked to perform a supporting rite, and again he justified his involvement in mythic terms. In the final pages of his history of Tibet, *Song of the Queen of Spring,* he applies an ancient Nyingmapa prophecy to the newly victorious Mongol king: "At the end of seven border wars," he quotes, "a king who is an emanation of Vajrapāṇi will bring happiness to Tibet and Kham for a while."[58] Gushri Khan was thus the wrathful buddha, and the Tsangpa king, a vanquished demon. Thanks to him, the Dalai Lama explains, the darkness was banished, as "the sun gradually returned to the central kingdom."[59]

Elsewhere the Dalai Lama elaborates on his ritual activities at this time:

> First I performed the suppression ritual of the *Lord of Death's Hunt, the Angry Sun.* Thinking of how the previous year large-scale violent rites were needed against Beri, I made a great imprecation *stūpa* as the omniscient Zur instructed, then took the *stūpa* to Drepung. Some travelers showed up, but I turned my back on those needy ones and performed the dark-retreat. We performed the complete arrangements for the imprecation *stūpa* and extensively

> accomplished the violent activities of sorcery. When we cast the malign force at the lake at Kharnak, the indications showed extreme obstruction. That night my retreat servant, Tshultrim Losang, dreamt that a wave rose out of a black ocean that inundated the sky. When he [awoke], he remembered it as if it were real and said it was terrifying. Led by [Zurpa Orgyen Losang Tenzin] Drakna Chöje, some old monks of the monastic college performed the *Killing Suppression of the Lord of Death,* while the rest of the monks performed the exorcistic rites of the daily fulfillment practice. Then in a great gathering of the two monastic centers they came together to perform rites simultaneously. In the mantra temple, the daily fulfillment practices were established.[60]

The "imprecation *stūpa*" described here was a small ritual *stūpa* to be used during the imprecation rite (*bcas chog*) to pin down an effigy of the offending demon.[61] The Dalai Lama's historic 1641 ritual performance thus returns us full circle to the construction themes explored in chapter 5. Just as King Songtsen Gampo was said to have established Tibet as a Buddhist realm by pinning the *rākṣasī*-demoness beneath new temples, the Dalai Lama conquered his own demonic enemies by pinning them under a ritual *stūpa,* thereby creating the modern Buddhist state of the Ganden Podrang. The themes of construction sacrifice that were so vital in twelfth-century Tibet resurface here, some five centuries later, in the founding ritual practices of the Fifth Dalai Lama.

Elsewhere again, the Dalai Lama recounts his own visionary experiences during this same 1641 performance. He describes a fearful apparition that appeared to him and that he took to be a sign of the victory Gushri Khan would soon enjoy over the king of Tsang: "While acting as the *vajra*-master for the assembly of monks that had gathered to perform the weaponry of Mañjuśrī as Lord of Longevity, right in the middle of the floor before the offerings there appeared the immeasurably massive head of a wrathful deity from its neck up. Out of a strange emptiness many heads were pouring into its huge, gaping mouth, like grains into a bag."[62]

Centuries earlier, the Dunhuang liberation rite had recommended offering the victim's head into the mandala where it was devoured by the central deity and his retinue, "in the manner of vultures." Now in the Dalai Lama's prophetic vision, the severed heads of his enemies are similarly cast into the maw of Yamāntaka as a kind of sacrificial feast.[63] Traditional Tibetan sources commonly attribute the rise of the modern government of the Ganden Phodrang to the actions of the Fifth Dalai Lama. When the Dalai Lama's own account is consulted, we find that these pivotal events of 1640–1642 are framed largely in the terms of prophecy, demons, and sorcery. The modern Tibetan state was in this sense founded on violent rituals, practices that were rooted in turn in the ancient themes of darkness, demon-taming, liberation, and temple construction.

CONCLUSIONS

The Tibetan interest in tantric violence that took root in the institutional darkness of the late ninth and tenth centuries thus continued to shape Tibet's later Buddhist traditions. After several centuries of political fragmentation, the thirteenth century marked a major turning point in the history of Tibet, arguably the most significant since the collapse of the Pugyal Empire in the mid-ninth century, and by the fourteenth century the shape of Buddhist Tibet was changing quickly. Buddhism in India was disappearing, and Tibetans increasingly were seeing their land as a new center, an independent home for authentic Buddhism. Under attack from the Mongols, Tibetans began to emphasize a mandalic spatial model different from that used in the *rākṣasī* legend. When representing their sacred realm and their demons, the greatest threats no longer inhered in Tibet's own soil; they dwelt at its dark edges. The model of demons pinned underfoot gave way to one of demons massing at the borders. Buddhist construction gave way to Buddhist warfare, foundation sacrifice to war magic. The Mongol armies threatened to undo all that Indian Buddhism was supposed to have accomplished, to return Tibet to its natural state of darkness and demonic barbarism. The Mongols had to be stopped, if necessary even by violence.

After the fourteenth century, war magic continued to grow in influence, and by the sixteenth and seventeenth centuries it dominated much of the language of Tibetan military conflict. The Fifth Dalai Lama's own familial involvements in the Nyingma school and violent ritual were vital to his rise to power. In the mid-seventeenth century, as the Dalai Lama worked to unify Tibet under his new Gelukpa government, he drew heavily upon the popular legends of the twelfth-century *Pillar Testament* and the *Collected Precepts on Maṇi* and on Orgyen Lingpa's fourteenth-century revelations, all of which were steeped in demon taming and the rhetoric of darkness.

Throughout Tibet's history, then, its Buddhist traditions were continuously formed and reformed through the demonization and symbolic sacrifice of others, be they the Tibetan people themselves, Mongol invaders, or the Fifth Dalai Lama's political enemies. In these ways, Buddhist Tibet continued to be shaped by the shifting themes of demons and darkness and by the conquered space of the mandala.

7

Conclusions: Violence in the Mirror

One can almost picture the two men on the same evening a little more than a hundred years ago, separated along Tibet's borders by a few hundred miles, each working by lamplight on his book. One was L. Austine Waddell, seated in Sikkim and writing his 1895 *Buddhism of Tibet or Lamaism, With Its Mystic Cults, Symbolism and Mythology*, the first book composed in English to examine Tibetan Buddhism in any depth.[1] The other was a Nyingmapa lama, Rigdzin Gargyi Wangchuk of Nyarong in eastern Tibet, writing his *Dangers of Blood Sacrifice*. The two men were almost exact contemporaries; Waddell's dates were 1854–1938 and Rigdzin Garwang's, 1858–1930. Both wrote with a specific purpose in mind, to introduce Tibetan Buddhism to new parts of the world, and both expressed horror at the "deep-rooted devil-worship and sorcery" that they found along Tibet's "pitch dark" borders.[2] Despite the vast cultural divide that separated these two men, their attitudes toward violence, civilizing missions, and colonization shared much in common. As Waddell criticized Tibetans for corrupting true Buddhism with their demonolatrous and violent ways, Garwang seemed *nearly* to agree. Yet the subtle distinctions between their views remain enormously significant, perhaps even dividing violence from nonviolence. The present final chapter examines the historical processes that led to this curious moment of synchronicity late in the nineteenth century. As we shall see, many of the mythic and ritual lines of influence we have traced in earlier chapters meet here in this instant of similarity and difference.

From their peripheral vantage points at the edges of Tibetan civilization, both Waddell and Garwang felt themselves very much outside the central stronghold of genuine Tibetan Buddhism. Waddell had been forced to conduct much of his research in Sikkim while serving as the assistant sanitary commissioner of the Darjeeling district; his study was published well before he entered Lhasa as the medical officer for Colonel Francis Younghusband's 1903–4 invasion.[3] For him, Lhasa and its "jealously guarded religion" remained a distant and forbidden land "wreathed in romance."[4]

Meanwhile, Rigdzin Garwang was based at his home monastery of Jamjor Gön in the Nyarong district of Kham. Nyarong was (and is) a quintessential frontier region. A remote land located on the border between Tibet and China, it had only recently been converted to the traditions of institutional Buddhism. During the nineteenth century, Nyarong's geographic position had placed it at the center of a minor war. For years Gönpo Namgyel (1799–1865), an expansionist Nyarong chieftain whose power grew to encompass much of Kham, had disrupted trade routes and caused political troubles for both the Lhasa and Qing governments. The uprising was finally quelled in 1865, and Gönpo Namgyel was put to death.[5] It was in this postwar frontier environment that Rigdzin Garwang flourished. As a youth, Garwang had studied under all the great Khampa lamas of his day: Jamgön Kongtrul, Khyentse Wangpo, Dza Patrul Rinpoche, Mipham Gyatso, and others, but his home remained Nyarong, and there he did most of his teaching.

Garwang wrote for the people of Nyarong, to encourage their recent conversion to Buddhism and to discourage their enduring fascination with blood sacrifice. He described Nyarong as a place of "pitch darkness" at the edge of civilization, bereft of the Buddhist teachings and rife with wrongheaded practices of demon worship. Rigdzin Garwang composed *The Dangers of Blood Sacrifice* to dispel the darkness and spread the light of the dharma. The colophon to this work describes the circumstances of its composition:

> This excellent explanation was newly elaborated at the Pleasure Grove for Teachings and Beings for some recently [converted] friends of Padmasambhava. It is a lamp for illuminating the pitch darkness of [places with] no teachings, or with mistaken teachings. It is a wonderful veneration of the conqueror by the light of day. United as it is with the three forms of valid knowledge [direct perception, inference, and scripture], that is, with the sayings of the many learned ones and so forth, it without doubt surpasses any mistaken thinking [about blood sacrifice]. Bear it in your heart with heartfelt devotion, and the teachings and beings are certain to ripen. You [Nyarongpas] have entered the door of the Buddhist teachings, and those who bear the crown of the title "golden lama" can now be seen here. The time has come for each of you to choose whether to support or destroy the teachings and beings.
>
> In this regard, one generous patron has had protective exorcisms and sorcery [performed]. Thus he must [now] choose between creating benefit or

> harm, between dharma or sin. In the past he relied on the ruination of himself and others. He relied on evil misdeeds that were passed off as the dharma. He relied on stealing from the officiating lamas and the teachings. This patron relied on destroying his own existence. From this day forward he repents his mistaken acts of the past. He requests that in the future, if he is restrained, his own kindness may return to him, and that at that time he may think of the purpose behind this very veneration of the teachings and beings and act accordingly.
>
> This is dedicated to his completely pure and superior aspiration to act in this way–may it spread the teachings and extend bliss and happiness–and most importantly [it is dedicated] to dispersing to [the buddhafield of] Sukhāvatī those sentient beings who have been killed for the sake of blood rites in connection [with him].[6]

Garwang wrote for Nyarong and its people, who stood at a moral crossroads. One way led to demons, sacrifice, and damnation, the other to true Buddhism, self-restraint, and helping others. More specifically he wrote for his patron, a man who had a history of involvements with blood sacrifice and violent sorcery, demonic practices that had been "passed off as the dharma." But by sponsoring such violent rites, this patron had been doing precisely the opposite of what he had intended. His desire for gain and self-preservation had brought him only ruination and self-destruction. His patronage of false teachings was in fact "stealing from the officiating lamas and the [true] teachings." He had been led by devils into a world of darkness in which up was down, black was white, and buddhas were demons, and his salvation lay in repentance, self-restraint, and kindness to others.

A glance at Rigdzin Garwang's collected works reveals an oeuvre dominated by short, basic lessons on devotion and morality, aimed at taming and converting a popular audience. Beside discussions of prayers for rebirth in the pure land of Sukhāvatī and commentaries on the four ways to turn the mind to the teachings, we find titles such as *The Benefits of Learning, Study, Listening, and Contemplation; Ornaments for the Ear: Excellent Exhortations for the Conscientious; The Source of Good Things: The Benefits of Perseverance; Armor of Heroes: The Benefits of Patience; The Benefits of Circumambulation; The Dangers of Beer; The Dangers of Stealing; The Dangers of Hunting; The Sins of Hypocrisy and Deceit; How to Rid Oneself of Sloth; The Dangers of Making a Profit*; and *The Benefits of Silence.*

The titles strike a surprisingly Protestant note. Many of the pious concerns could as well have been expressed by a Christian missionary intent on converting the Tibetan heathens. Rigdzin Garwang sought to reform the inhabitants of Nyarong in the ethical image of his Buddhist ideal, as a quiet, conscientious, and industrious people of unwavering abstinence and patience. Confronted with the violence of demon worship and blood sacrifice, Rigdzin Garwang's sensibilities were probably no less offended than Waddell's might have been had he been confronted with the same barbaric behavior. In curious ways, this Tibetan lama's reactions mirrored those of his Victorian contemporary, the son of a Scottish Presbyterian minister.

Also like a mirror, though, Garwang's reactions inverted those of Waddell. Waddell too was gripped by the violent and superstitious aspects of Tibetan religion; his repulsion was similar, but his titles were the precise opposite of Garwang's. Articles such as "Demonolatry in Sikhim Lamaism," "Hairy Savages in Tibet," "The Tibetan House-Demon," and "Lamaism as a Demonolatry" were accompanied by others that focused on Tibetan ritualism: "Lamaic Rosaries: Their Kinds and Uses," "Lāmaist Graces before Meat," "Some Ancient Charms from the Tibetan," "Charms and Amulets," and "Chorten (Tibetan Name of the Solid Funeral Monuments Erected over the Relics of Buddha and his Saints)," to name a few. Thus the two men's titles were disparate, even as both were rooted in a shared fundamental aversion to ritual violence and superstition.

Waddell wrote about practices that were utterly foreign, performed by benighted barbarians in desperate need of both liberation and conversion: "It will be a happy day, indeed, for Tibet," he ends his book, "when its sturdy over-credulous people are freed from the intolerable tyranny of the Lāmas, and delivered from the devils whose ferocity and exacting worship weigh like a nightmare upon all."[7] We have seen how in nearby Calcutta, Waddell's compatriots, W. C. Blaquiere and Sir William Jones, had some decades before highlighted the barbarism of Indian religion to justify their own colonial rule. In the same way in Sikkim, Waddell's own studies of Tibet's demonic aspects justified a civilizing mission led by violent invasion. Waddell wrote his book in the immediate aftermath of a bloody clash between British and Tibetan troops, in which the British, with just a single loss on their own side, drove the "truculent" and "insolent" Tibetans from their hilltop base in Sikkim, killing two hundred and wounding twice that number.[8] Tibet's state rituals, it seems, were beginning to fail in the face of the modern weaponry of the British.[9] From the British perspective, the demonic tyranny of the lamas was succumbing to the powers of rational science and modernity.

Eight years after the publication of Waddell's book, the violence reached another peak. This time Waddell himself joined the British force as its chief medical officer, to take part in a military mission to Tibet, "to obtain satisfaction" for queen and country. "Sympathy must be sacrificed," wrote the journalist Edmund Chandler, "to the restitution of fitting and respectful relations,"[10] and on March the 31, 1904, near the little Tibetan village of Guru, following a misunderstanding in negotiations, the British opened fire on the 1,500 Tibetans assembled there. Modern rifles and Maxim machine guns, each firing six hundred bullets per minute, mowed down the uncomprehending Tibetans. The British themselves were discomfited by the violence of their own attacks and expressed pity for their "over-credulous" victims. "They were bewildered," wrote Chandler, who was present. "The impossible had happened. Prayers and charms and mantras, and the holiest of their holy men, had failed them. I believe they were obsessed with that one thought. [In retreat,] they walked with bowed heads, as if they had been disillusioned in their gods."[11] The Tibetan state's repelling rites were broken.[12] The amulets worn by Tibetan fighters failed to protect them from the British bullets; rather they were picked off the dead as souvenirs, curiosities from a darkened land. Hundreds of Tibetans were sacrificed for their ignorance and "devil worship," with little benefit to the British, beyond their sacking of the monasteries and scavenging of the victims' dead bodies.

Like Waddell, Rigdzin Garwang, in his own efforts to colonize and convert, sought to distance himself from the violent practices he encountered along Tibet's borders by labeling them "barbaric" (*kla klo*) and a "demonic cult" (*'dre'i chos lugs*).[13] His aversion to these practices is clear in the introduction to his work:

> Regarding the origins of this evil tradition [of blood sacrifice], the omniscient Patrul Rinpoche has said, "Among early teachers in India and even nowadays, sacrificial killing has been widespread. [In India,] heretics dedicated and offered [such sacrifices] to Īśvara and Viṣṇu. In early Tibet, those of the Black Waters Bon widely made similar offerings to the local spirits and so on, and even today there are some who follow that evil tradition." Within our own inner [Buddhist] tradition, too, [blood sacrifice] has spread through the influence of demons. The omniscient Jigme Lingpa has said, "In India for a brief time when the teachings were protected by the master Nāgārjuna, a so-called 'group of young upholders of the *piṭakas*' was empowered by demons. In order to create dissension within the Buddhist teachings, they introduced a barbarian tenet system that advocated violence as the dharma. In Tibet, that system is no longer around, but many with similar attitudes do appear."[14]

According to Garwang, then, sacrifice was performed primarily by Indian Hindus, next by Tibetan Bonpos, and only lastly within Buddhism itself, and then due to the influence of darkness and demons. Sacrifice is placed firmly outside authentic Buddhism. A pristine space is thus reserved for Buddhism, a space free of any and all sacrificial bloodshed.

And yet, if we have learned anything in our study of the theme of sacrifice in Tibet, it is that the picture had not always been so clear. Garwang himself raises the unsettling similarities between blood sacrifice and the liberation rite: "Isn't [blood sacrifice] just the so-called 'miraculous method for delivering [beings] from negative rebirths through reliance on the profound union and liberation specific to the great secret Vajrayāna?'"[15] Garwang admits the formal similarities, but insists, following tradition, that the legitimate *Buddhist* version of the rite requires that the practitioner be beyond anger and able to deliver the victim's consciousness unscathed into the buddhafields, just as our tenth-century Dunhuang manual also once claimed. "From the perspective of the [actual ritual] phenomena it may be so," he writes, "but from the perspective of the person involved, he must be someone who is able to liberate [the victim] from suffering with great compassion, someone who is able to eject the consciousness into a pure field, and who is able to restore quickly the sentient being who is killed."[16] All this was asserted already in our Dunhuang manuscripts. We have seen how in the tenth century, King Yeshe Ö drew a stark line between liberation and sacrifice, with liberation being properly performed with an effigy, and sacrifice involving the ritual killing of a live person. Given Garwang's discussion here, it seems that despite Yeshe Ö's pronouncement, the distinction remained at least somewhat unclear into the twentieth century.

In fact, if Garwang's text tells us anything, it is that blood sacrifice was practiced throughout Tibet, from the age of fragmentation all the way through to the twentieth century. That so many lamas repeatedly had to warn against sacrifice only confirms the continuing prevalence of the practice. From elsewhere in Garwang's text it is clear that later Tibetan Buddhists too offered flesh into the mandala in a manner reminiscent of the head offering seen in the tenth-century Dunhuang liberation rite. He cites the twelfth-century Kagyu master Gampopa, for example: "By placing into the *maṇḍala* the flesh of beings that have been killed, all wisdom is said to fall unconscious."[17] To do so, the text continues, "is like offering a child's flesh to its mother." The tantric offering of flesh to the wrathful buddhas has long been practiced in Tibet, but not without some controversy. Tibetans themselves have long been well aware of the uncomfortable similarities between such oblations and blood sacrifice, and all would agree that the properly Buddhist mandala must be kept free and pure of any "sacrificial" offerings. Thus Waddell was not entirely wrong in suggesting that some Tibetans are violent, but they also have their own self-critique. Once again, Tibetans themselves are divided in their approaches to violence. Like us, they are fascinated by the power of violence even as they condemn it.

The dangerous resemblance of flesh offerings to blood sacrifice is one that haunts tantric Buddhist practice. Chapter 1 has already explored the multiple resemblances between the wrathful *heruka* buddhas and Rudra and his demonic horde, shared likenesses that constantly threaten the Buddhist use of violent means. Now Garwang, many centuries later, warns of a similar case of mistaken identity that afflicts the offering of flesh: "By propitiating the *maṇḍala* of one's tutelary deity with flesh or merely by touching it with sacrificial cakes and the like, all the wisdom deities will return to their spaces and devils, demons, and spirits will assemble and act in disguise as if they were the deities."[18] In making flesh offerings, one enters into the dangerous and shifting realm of violence and sacrifice, a world in which good and evil can change places in a moment, where demonic spirits are all too easily mistaken for enlightened buddhas.

But what of those liminal beings who dwell at the mandala's edges, those worldly protectors whose enlightenment has been deferred and who must still relish a bloody feast? Is it not acceptable to offer them flesh? "While the wisdom deities may not be pleased by sacrifice, their mundane retinues are," suggests Garwang, "so one might say that sacrifice to them is permissible." For an answer to this hypothesis, Garwang looks to ancient history and the lessons learned from Tibet's age of fragmentation:

> The kings and princes of old were given initiations and instructions by the *vidyādharas;* they gave their word and pronounced the oaths. However, they did not understand that in order to benefit the teachings and beings, the bodhisattvas seated alongside the wisdom deities were merely protectors of the dharma [and not buddhas themselves]. For this reason, the laws of the king eventually were destroyed, as if by lawless thieves. Thinking that these mundane ones were *autonomous* beings, when [these early Tibetans] worshipped them with flesh and blood, it was a sure cause of their deviating into mistaken mantra and Rudra[-hood].[19]

Here Garwang evokes the age of fragmentation as a warning to all Tibetans, as an example of the lawlessness and the violence that follow inevitably from ritual corruption. Elsewhere he writes, "When the *teu rang* [demons] are seen as gods, evil times will have arrived for Tibet."[20] Garwang thus attributes Tibet's past descent into darkness to the early kings' misunderstanding of the subtle relationship between the buddhas and their attendant gods and demons. The kings, he explains, mistook these mundane spirits for "autonomous beings," with desires of their own. They failed to recognize the demons' ultimate identity with the buddha's own pristine mind. This confusion, in turn, led the kings into performing blood sacrifice in the name of Buddhism, and thus into Rudra-like behavior and the lawlessness of the age of fragmentation. As we saw in chapter 1, Rudra must be seen as *simultaneously* different from and identical to the buddha. To mistake mundane demons as autonomous and inherently separate from the enlightened buddhas is therefore just as dangerous as mistaking demons for buddhas; either view can lead one into blood sacrifice. From this subtly paradoxical perspective, in which demons and buddhas are so difficult to recognize, we can well understand Garwang's careful sequestering of Buddhism away from anything even resembling sacrifice.[21]

Rigdzin Garwang's text shows how so many of the issues and themes of violence and the age of fragmentation that have been explored in the preceding chapters were still active at the end of the nineteenth century. They emerge in the context of Garwang's conversion of the population of Nyarong, a people dwelling in the dangerous borderlands surrounding central Tibet, to a pure and ethical Buddhism. But Garwang's moralistic approach to Buddhist proselytization was by no means unique. His writings were part of a wider trend in the nineteenth and early twentieth centuries, a move to return to the basics of ethical behavior. Many eastern Tibetan lamas in particular were writing about the need to observe fundamental principles of morality. In Nyarong alone we may point to other such figures as Nyala Pema Dundul, Nyala Sögyel, and Choktrul Tsulo, while parallel contemporary movements may also be observed in Golok and the other wilder places of eastern Tibet. Patrul Rinpoche's famous *Words of My Perfect Teacher* may even be seen, in part, as a product of the same movement. Eastern Tibet had become a new focal point of Buddhist activity in the nineteenth century, and its remote valleys were being colonized by new monasteries and moralizing missionaries.

The conversion of Tibet's border regions is usually traced, perhaps not surprisingly now, to the fourteenth century and the Mongol depredations in central Tibet. Tibetan interest in these areas was closely linked to the rise of "hidden lands" (*sbas yul*), secret paradisiacal valleys accessible to only a select few wielding the proper karmic connections. Initially these hidden valleys were found mostly along Tibet's southern border, Sikkim, where Waddell researched his *Lamaism* book, being a classic example. The treasure revealer, Rigdzin Gökyi Demtruchen (1337–1409), was a pioneer of these southern borderlands. In his *General Inscriptions on Hidden Lands*, Gödemchen cited a prophecy: "The Mongol oppression will last one hundred and twenty-five years, after which Mongol rule will collapse. During this period, people will have to flee to Tibet's hidden lands."[22] Two centuries later, Sokdokpa similarly attributed the rise of the hidden lands to the Mongol invasions: "When the lands of Tibet are endangered by the Mongols, all the border armies will demolish the center. At that time, when all the hidden land power places have been opened, all the people at the center will flee to the borders."[23] Whatever the historical truth of such passages, the large-scale conversion of the borderlands did not begin in earnest until somewhat later, particularly in the sixteenth and seventeenth centuries.[24] By the seventeenth century the eastern region of Kham was also beginning to receive more attention, and a number of major new monasteries were established there around that time.

Chapter 6 has observed how, from the thirteenth century, Tibet's borderlands were increasingly associated with demons, darkness, and barbaric violence. But the borders also played a more positive role in the Tibetan imagination. Control over these dark valleys hidden along the borders might potentially be wrested from the grip of their local demons, and safe haven gained for any pious Buddhists under threat at Tibet's center. We have seen that Tibetans were deeply ambivalent about their demons from an early date, simultaneously horrified and attracted by their violence and power. Now as Tibetans turned their attentions to their own geographic borders, this same ambivalence came to bear. The borders offered both demonic dangers and hope of sanctuary.

The ambivalence of Tibetan attitudes toward their borderlands cannot be separated from the spatial structures of the mandala and the demonic population at its dark edges. Tibet's barbaric neighbors are its demonic protectors, dancing and drinking blood at the edges of civilization, simultaneously threatening and protective. In this sense Rudra and his horde remain a suppressed but powerful force within the Tibetan landscape, especially in the border regions. Like the mythic demons that were adopted even as they were expelled by the buddha at the center of the mandala, Tibet's neighbors play a liminal role in the Tibetan imagination. Just as Tibetans are deeply divided over the dangerous power of tantric violence, they are of two minds about the barbarians that populate their borders.

The associations between the inhabitants of Tibet's borderlands and Rudra's demonic entourage are often quite explicit. As René de Nebesky-Wojkowitz observed in his 1956 study, *Oracles and Demons of Tibet,* the clothes worn by the violent protector deities are regularly likened to those seen among Tibet's border peoples. They wear, for example, the bamboo hats of the tribal Mönpas of southeastern Tibet; they wield "the black sword of the Mön" (*mon gri nag po*); and they wear boots of a Mongolian style (*hor lham, sog lham*).[25] In discussing the Lopa of Tsari, located on the Tibetan border with modern-day Assam, the anthropologist Toni Huber has noted how such mythic associations have shaped Tibetan attitudes toward the hunting activities and the blood sacrifices of the tribal peoples. In the holy region of Tsari, where Tibetans were not allowed to hunt or even shout or spit, the local Lopa were free to continue hunting without fear of retribution by the local deity. "Maybe they were the local protector's retinue," suggested one Tsari lama.[26] In this way, the violent behavior of the tribal Lopas is simultaneously explained away and incorporated into the Buddhist vision of the ideal Tibetan mandala. The Lopas are both autonomous spirits and subservient emanations of the buddhas. The "barbaric" aspects of the borderlands are thus able to coexist alongside paradisiacal images of those same regions.

Tibetan descriptions of the hidden lands are typically filled with idyllic images of fertile fields, gentle animals, and healthy, happy inhabitants living pure and blessed lives, but these romanticizations are highly unstable and can easily turn negative, not unlike the Valley of the Blue Moon in James Hilton's *Lost Horizon* (in which the term "Shangri-La" was coined). In part, such sudden fluctuations are the result of concrete social realities. Located as they are far from Buddhist centers of power, the inhabitants of a hidden land can easily revert to their earlier pre-Buddhist practices after they are initially converted. The anthropologist Charles Ramble has described such a case in the village of Te, in the upper Kali Gandaki region of Nepal's Mustang District. Following the conversion of the village to Buddhism by one Bichua Lama, "Te suffered a bad harvest, and villagers and cattle were simultaneously visited with sickness. Concluding that the author of these ills was the local pantheon, offended at the neglect it had suffered, the villagers resumed the sacrifice of animals and, to be on the safe side, immolated Bichua Lama's collected writings."[27] Clearly, more missionary work was needed. Thus a hidden land may require repeated openings and reopenings, whether by Padmasambhava (eighth century), Gödemchen (1337–1409), Lhatsun Namkha Jigme (1597–1650), or any other teacher that may visit from the Tibetan centers of power. As with all demonic beings, even after the local inhabitants are converted to Buddhism, their commitments to their vows remain fickle.

Yet the chameleon quality of Tibet's border peoples often has more to do with Tibetans' own shifting attitudes toward them. Even well-known hidden lands can be regarded as deeply benighted and demonic in nature. The eighteenth-century master Pema Wangdu (born 1697), for example, describes in dark terms his disillusionment on visiting the famous hidden land of Kyimolung, located along the Nepalese border:

> All their forms of practice are heretical like the *halāhala* poison. They have killed all the wild animals that lived in the mountains. Every single goat and sheep that was in the valley has gone under the knife's edge. Even the good

> local spirits, the protectors, have fallen under the power of the black [sacrificial] killing. In every district there is black Bon. Men and women, young and old, all have been corrupted by evil thinking. In accordance with their incessant killing for all the gods, *nāgas*, demons, and evil spirits, dishes of flesh and blood are distributed at festivals. It may have been identified as the hidden [land] of Kyi[mo]lung, but this narrow ravine resembles the primitive edge of darkness.[28]

In line with the traditional Tibetan view of such regions, Pema Wangdu concludes that the bloodthirsty demons at this dark edge of civilization must be subjugated. Reminding them of their past defeat by Padmasambhava, he demands their loyalty, once more under threat of violence: "As for the local spirits, gods, and demons who were the recipients of the blood sacrifices, I resolved my own unborn mind as empty, then dissolved those demons into the nondual state of my own mind, . . . 'I myself am the *heruka*, Pema Wang! You must serve to fulfill my every command!' So I spoke, and the gods and demons were overwhelmed."[29]

Here Pema Wangdu deals with the demons in the only way possible, taming them through violent means. While the liberation rite itself is not expressly mentioned, it is implicit in both Pema Wangdu's forceful threats and in particular in his initial dissolution of the demons into emptiness, a clear allusion to the ejection of consciousness into the buddhafields that is so crucial a part of liberation. We have seen how the ejection of consciousness is equivalent to the ritual moment of sacrificial oblation, a parallel to offering the victim's head into the *heruka* mandala or spraying blood over the deity's image. Here, then, is Pema Wangdu's solution to the sacrificial violence he encounters in this demonic ravine: to liberate those demonic beings that are responsible for the sacrifices, in a sense sacrificing them to the wrathful gods of normative Buddhism. Here we see the deep layers of Tibetans' ambivalence toward violence. Even as they suppress it, they adopt its methods.

Simultaneously dark ravines and hidden paradises, the borderlands and their violent inhabitants operate as both poison and cure for Tibet. They constitute both a terrible threat to Buddhism and a wondrous therapy for Tibet's lost spiritual values, offering hope for regeneration in dark times. The extremity of Tibetans' ambivalence toward these border regions can only be a projection of their own fears and desires. No place can be both entirely evil and wholly good. The realities of the borderlands and the lives of their inhabitants matter less here than the reflective power that these places have in the Tibetan imagination. Tibetan attitudes toward these places thus represent Tibetans' own internal dislocation, a divide over violence that they have represented to themselves as an external dualism between center and periphery. In this sense, Tibetans themselves are split between the two sides of their own Buddhist tradition: its blissful tranquility and its demonic violence.

Parallels with Waddell and British colonialist attitudes are manifold and obvious. Waddell too had his internal divide over violence, between the cherished rationality of his own Protestant religion and an enduring fascination with cultish violence, whether in Tibet or the Scottish Highlands. And like the Tibetans, Waddell's inability to reconcile this inner divide led him to look for answers beyond himself. Where Tibetans looked to the hidden lands at their borders, Waddell looked to Tibet itself, to its mysteries hidden away from European eyes, behind the veils of its "icy barriers," as Waddell put it.[30] Yet the divide, and thus the projected violence itself, remained Waddell's own. Precisely as he criticized Tibet's "double ban of menacing demons and despotic priests," he prepared the way for a bloody invasion, to liberate the Tibetan people "from the devils whose ferocity and exacting worship weigh like a nightmare upon all."[31]

The same wish for liberation could as well have been Pema Wangdu's for the inhabitants of Kyimolung, whom he similarly viewed as fallen under the power of that dark valley's savage demons, or again Rigdzin Garwang's for the people of Nyarong. For Waddell and Tibetan lamas alike, colonization was a matter of battling demons. The lands they desired were romantic paradises harboring untold promises, but they were also benighted realms tormented by devils and barbaric sacrifice and in need of liberation and conversion. Both justified their works as civilizing missions that sought to replace cultish violence with rationality and ethical abstinence. Such were the battles that both Rigdzin Garwang and L. Austine Waddell waged, as they worked by lamplight to compose their respective condemnations of the primitive demonolatry they each encountered on the Tibetan border. Perhaps in these struggles, at least, Tibetan and Scot were not so different.

In 1904, not long after the publication of Waddell's book, the Thirteenth Dalai Lama (1876–1933) fled the British invasion of Tibet, following the age-old Tibetan tradition of escaping to the safety of Tibet's bordering neighbors, first to Mongolia and then on to China. In the fifth month of that wood dragon year, just prior to his departure, he had attempted to repel the advancing troops with a performance from the *Razor of the Dagger's Ultimate Essence*, a recently revealed ritual collection of the Nyingma school.[32] The rite failed, and for nearly five years, the Dalai Lama hid in the very real protection of distant regions to the north and east, returning only at the end of 1908. Just months later, however, he would follow the same pattern once more, this time fleeing a short-lived

Chinese invasion to seek refuge in the south, near British India, as the guest of the Maharajah of Sikkim. This time the foreign invasion failed, and the Dalai Lama attributed its failure to the powerful rituals performed by the lamas of Tibet: "Due to our unrelenting performance of rituals for the preservation of [Tibet's] religion and state, and thanks to the profoundly powerful and incontrovertible truth of causality, China began to experience internal difficulties. Because of that, the Chinese armies in Tibet became like a reservoir cut off from its source and were gradually driven back to the borders."[33] In 1912, the Dalai Lama returned to Tibet and received the Chinese letter of surrender.

Some years later, as the Dalai Lama approached his death, he offered his final testament. It is a well-known statement that has been recited many times in recent decades. In it, the Dalai Lama warns of a looming "red system" that was already wreaking fearful effects in Mongolia:

> Take care to maintain as friendly relations as possible toward our two neighbors, the government of India and the government of China, even as you build up a powerful military force. In order to subdue the foreigners, troops, arms, and horses [should be sent] to the hostile little border regions. They should receive extensive and expert military training, so that they can definitively suppress any adversaries.
>
> Furthermore, nowadays manifestations of the five impurities [of shortened lifespan, view, afflicted emotions, sentient beings, and of our present age] are spreading everywhere. In particular the red system is greatly on the rise, so that the search for the reincarnation of [Mongolia's head lama, Khalkha] Jetsun Dampa, was banned. The monastic properties were confiscated, and monks were forced into military service, so that not even the name of the Buddha's teaching remains. Such a system has arisen in Ulan Bator, and is still spreading according to reports.
>
> In the future this practice certainly will come, from within or without, here too, to our Tibetan nation with its combination of both the religious and the secular. If we are unable to protect our land, the noble holders of the teachings known as the victorious father and son [that is, the Dalai Lama and Panchen Lama] will be destroyed, so that not even their names will remain. The rights and properties of the monastic estates and of all Buddhist teachers, practitioners, and monks will be annihilated. The political system that originated with the three ancestral dharma-kings will be reduced to an empty name. Even my officials will have their ancestral properties and wealth confiscated and will wander helplessly as slaves to their enemies. Tortured and terrified, all beings will suffer endlessly, day and night. Such a time will certainly come.[34]

In many ways, the Dalai Lama's language here follows the well-worn tracks of the language of ritual violence and of past Tibetan prophets warning of threats from the borderlands. Pointing to the hostilities that inhere in Tibet's "border regions," he recommends they be subdued through diplomacy backed by threat of violence. He warns his people of an impending age of darkness, when Rudra-like ignorance and impurities will reign and the Buddhist teachings will be destroyed. In the face of such demonic threats, he recommends swift preparations for the "suppression" of these enemies, and the term he uses, literally "to press down the head," echoes the violent ritual practices of the earliest tantras: "Having made an image of [the obstructing demon], one should crush its head with one's left foot," instructs the *Mahāvairocana-abhisaṃbodhi Tantra.*[35] In the tradition of Orgyen Lingpa's revealed *Padma Chronicles* and many prophets since, the Dalai Lama was foretelling a violent darkness to come.

No longer, however, was the prophecy placed in the mouth of a legendary master of the distant past, with the prophet retrospectively predicting events that had already occurred. Now the Dalai Lama himself was speaking, and this time the ominous prophecies came true on a scale never before seen in Tibet. With the Chinese takeover in 1959 and the subsequent depredations of the Cultural Revolution, the symbolic violence of Tibet's age of fragmentation returned with terrible reality. Perhaps it is not coincidence that today, as Tibetans begin to rebuild their Buddhist communities, Tibet's borderlands of old, the same regions in eastern Tibet and along the Himalayas, are emerging once more as powerful sites of renewal.

Appendix A

The Subjugation of Rudra

FROM THE *GREAT COMPENDIUM OF THE INTENTIONS OF ALL THE BUDDHAS SUTRA*, CHAPTER 20: "TEACHING THE SERIES OF THOROUGHLY IMPURE PREVIOUS BIRTHS"

[151][1] Again the Overlord of Laṅka, the Bodhisattva Mahāsattva questioned the Lord of the Guhyakas.[2] He asked about the sixth of the twelve previously discussed ways of arising, the one known as "How [Secret Mantra] Arose at the Time of the Subjugation."[3]

"O Lord of the Guhyakas," he said, "When the teacher [Śākyamuni] prophesied how the essential Mahāyāna, the excellent secret, would arise, he said that in the incident called 'How [Secret Mantra] Arose at the Time of the Subjugation,' a profane person would become suitable for taming and then be thoroughly subjugated."

Then came the response, "Lord of Laṅka, when that extraordinary disciple consumed the world in flames, he became the cause for Secret Mantra to arise. When it was determined that the time had come for subjugating this one who was so horrible and wrathful, at that time of thorough subjugation, [152] all the buddhas in all directions and times withdrew into the enlightened essence. Then these Excellent Beings were fully exhorted, whereupon at that same instant, terrifying, heaping clouds of wrathful deities—tamers as many in number as there are atoms to be found [in the universe]—arose like perfectly arrayed lamps shining forth from Vajrasattva and proclaimed the moment of suchness."

In these words [the Lord of Laṅka] asked, "Lord of the Guhyakas, from where did that disciple [Rudra] arise? What were his actions? How were his rebirths? And how did he become the cause for the Secret Mantra to arise?"[4]

The Lord of the Guhyakas replied,[5] "O Lord of Laṅka, it was like this: In a past time beyond memory, in the aeon called 'Joyous' (*Ānanda*), in the buddha-field of 'Manifest Joy' (*Abhirati*),[6] the buddha Akṣobhya had arisen as a teacher. In that land there lived a monk named Invincible Youth (*Thub dka' gzhon nu*) who had renounced the world for the teachings of [this buddha, Akṣobhya]. Thus he [became a teacher], turning the wheel of dharma for the Mahāyāna. He rested in the yoga that is everywhere and in everything uncontrived and unspoiled. So expert did he become that he saw all sentient beings as the children of the conquerors and strove solely to exhort them [to likewise recognize their own buddha-nature].[7]

"At the time of that age, *saṃsāra* was without beginning and without end, [153] births without beginning and without end, karma and rebirth immeasurable and not to be comprehended by language. [However], if one were to distinguish a single birth in one particular karmic circumstance, it would be like this: Nearby there lived a householder named Keu Kaya and his son, Black Liberator (Thar pa nag po). That son had a servant called Denpak.[8] At the time of that age, some of the people were studying the path of yoga with the monk named Invincible Youth. They all studied yoga and practiced yoga.

"At the time of that age, Black Liberator, upon hearing the monk Invincible Youth teach on being in harmony with everything, thought, 'Isn't this [simply] a dharma that teaches a path in which one does everything one likes?' He went around asking this question to whomever [he met], and soon everyone started speaking like this. Finally he went, together with his servant, to where the monk [Invincible Youth] was staying. With excellent aspirations he asked, 'Great monk, I have heard the skillful means of the teacher is a path in which one practices howsoever. Can that be understood as just the present [state]?'

"To that question came the reply, 'O son of good lineage, it is indeed suitable to say that the [path] is whatever occurs in the present.'

[154] "At this, Black Liberator and his servant were overjoyed. 'Please accept me and my servant into your teaching,' he said and made the following aspiration: 'I too will adopt your path in which nothing is prohibited. By striving to remain in this yoga, may I apprehend with certainty the supreme itself.'

"To that prayer the monk responded, 'Yes. Very good. Do so,' thus granting his approval. Black Liberator took ordination [as a monk], while Denpak remained a layman, to act as the servant for the [newly ordained] monk, Liberator

"One day the monk Liberator asked, 'Great monk, what is that excellent path that is in accordance with everything?'

"[The teacher] replied, 'If suchness is left uncontrived, one practices the four entities and they become like clouds in the sky.[9] This is the path of the excellent yoga.'

"Because of those words, Liberator and his servant rejoiced: 'Amazing! What skillful means! Definitely! Yes! Exaltations! We will always abide in that.' However, at that moment the monk Liberator took the [teacher's] words literally, thereby not really understanding the advice. Because he favored the mere words [at the expense of the meaning], he became attached to practicing the four entities. Though he wore the external costume of an excellent [monk], he followed a path of evil-hearted beings. The servant Denpak [on the other hand], did understand the fundamental meaning of the words, [155] interpreting them with great intelligence. Because he focused exclusively on the meaning, through adhering to the practice of mere suchness, he was in complete unification (yoga). Despite his outward appearance as one of low rank, he remained on the path to ascertaining the excellent mind.

"So Liberator disagreed with his servant's views, and he started to wonder, 'How can we be in such stark disagreement on this single teaching from the same master?'

"'I heard nothing but simply that the ascertainment of the present is perfect,' said Denpak.

"'I too heard nothing but simply to practice attaining ascertainment of the present.' And so there began a huge argument. Because of their conflicting views, [Liberator] parted company with his servant. Vowing never to see or meet him again, he exiled his servant to a distant land.

"The monk Liberator continued to swell with a mountain of mistaken and excessive pride. Eventually he went to ask the teacher about the differences in their understandings, but the monk Invincible Youth practiced the uncontrived and unspoiled yoga and so did not flatter him. Speaking with complete sincerity, he told him, 'You have to understand as Denpak does.'

"Liberator became absolutely furious, saying, 'If we were really equal in the teacher's eyes, he would say we are both right, but he is not being fair and has obviously gone against his [own] teachings. Because of his offense, [156] this teacher too should not be allowed in this realm. I am going to make these [lands] my own.' Having made this vow, a huge pride was born, and he exiled the master also to a distant land.

"Because the *tathāgata*'s teachings are so numerous and wide-ranging in approach, taught in so many [ways] and so difficult to comprehend, Liberator completely misunderstood. Without subjecting [the teachings] to the two analyses [of reasoning and scriptures with their related pith instructions],[10] Liberator was drawn into an intolerant fixation in which [only] his own understanding was valid, and in this way he became mistaken in everything else too. He dwelt in an ocean of errors.[11]

"In his error, Liberator engaged in ignorant, terrible hardships and awful, wrongheaded observances: Seizing human corpses from the charnel grounds, he made them his food. Flaying the skins, he wore their hides and reveled in it. He supported the many creatures there [in the charnel ground], such as black jackals, wild 'palate-smacking' dogs, 'claw-scratching' bears, carnivorous birds and predators, *kangka*-vultures, and ravenous cemetery-pigs. They all killed [creatures], relishing the meat and the blood. He would bring together lots of prostitutes and have massive orgies. Without transcending the four entities, he completely transgressed the authentic nature and the suchness of those four entities.[12]

"Finally that lifetime ended, [157] after which he took five hundred rebirths in the body of a black jackal, creating the [bad] karma of killing creatures and eating their flesh and blood while still warm. After those births he took on five hundred more in various bodies of children and so forth, each destined to be killed by vicious beings, their flesh and blood used for food. He was constantly being killed by others only to take another rebirth. After those births he took on various bodies, such as meat-eating hawks, blood-drinking red-lipped [leeches] (*khrag 'thung mchu dmar*),[13] *kangka*-vultures, and bone-tip marrow-lickers (*ru rtse rkang ldag*), and still he was killed by others only to take another rebirth. After that he took various worm and parasitc bodies such as mosquitoes (*sbrang bu tre ma ta*), maggots (*srin bu bu ka*), and corpse-eating marrow-suckers (*ro za rkang 'jib*), and those too were constantly being killed by enemies only to take another rebirth. Next he took five hundred births as creatures that dwell in piles of vomit, constantly being killed by enemies only to take another rebirth. Then he took five hundred births as parasites that dwell in the bodies of small animals, eating them [from the inside], and was still constantly killed by enemies only to take another rebirth. After those births [158] he became a spirit that dwells inside such things as dead flesh, corpses of the recently died, thoroughly rotten bodies, stones in various places, boulders (*gam brag*), and great trees. He dwelt in, and survived by eating, those. Still he was constantly being killed by enemies only to take another rebirth. Next he took five hundred births as organisms that live inside wombs, again both living in, and being sustained by, those [wombs].[14]

"After those births, he dwelt for eighty thousand lifetimes in the place called [Avīci] the 'Vajra Hell of Incessant Tortures.' The extent of his sufferings in that hell is not suitable for discussion. Why? Because if the extent of his sufferings were discussed in someone's presence, whoever heard it might faint.

"At the time of that age, there came to pass a brief instant when that hell-being wondered, 'Oh! Why is this happening?!'

"Then the King of Dharma, Lord of the Conquerors, Vajrasattva showed him the dharma: 'It is due to the karma of suchness.' Because of this, [the hell-being] reflected upon karma and, understanding fully, he felt regret. Just because of that brief moment of remorse, he was transported from that place. He still remained for another eighty thousand lifetimes in the realm of the Extremely Hot Hell, which is much like the Hell of Incessant Tortures.

"Moving on again, he dwelt in the hell realms of the Less Hot, [159] of Loud Screaming, of Wailing, Crushing, Black Thread, Blazing, and of Continually Reviving. He remained in these hells for eighty thousand times eighty thousand lifetimes, and [his sufferings] were much like those of the Hell of Incessant Tortures and the Extremely Hot Hell. Even after these, he was flung into similar hell realms in still other world systems.

"Finally the aeons at the destruction of the universe came—the aeons of famine, of plague, and of war[15]—and he took rebirth in those. The devastations of those aeons emptied the worlds of everything. Yet even when all others had been destroyed, [Liberator] continued to take rebirth.

"Having again been freed from those births, he took rebirth after rebirth for another eighty thousand aeons in the races of beings who kill for the sake of flesh and bones. Being once more freed from that, he was born for five hundred lifetimes in the ghost-realms of the Lord of Death. Having moved on from that, he took rebirth in the race of the 'demons of rotting corpses' (Skt. *kataputana*). After that he took rebirth in the race of the 'flesh-eaters' (Skt. *piśāca*). Then he took rebirth in the race of the *srul po* (Skt. *putana*) demon.[16] His name was Desiring Belongings (*gtogs 'dod can*), the son of a *srul po* named Filthy Neck (*gnya' dreg can*).

"After those rebirths, he lusted to be in the womb of a prostitute in the land of Laṅka known as Purang. There he gestated until birth, [160] but in the ninth month his mother died. The people said, 'Wherever this orphaned boy, this illicit child, is raised will become polluted, so he should be abandoned on the mother's breast.' [In the local charnel grounds] there was a poisonous tree called 'Incestuous Rape' (*nal byi*). Under it there was a lair of ignorant cemetery pigs. In the tree's trunk was a den of angry poisonous snakes, and in the branches was a nest of birds [filled with] toxic desires.[17] The people built the mother's tomb right next to this tree. They brought the corpse there on a litter. Placing her there, they left the boy too, on the breast of his mother's corpse.[18]

"The orphaned child clung to the mother's corpse, sucking on her breast, bringing forth a yellow pus that sustained him for seven days. He then sucked out blood, on which he lived for another seven days. Then he ate the two breasts, thus subsisting for ten more days. Next he survived by eating the mother's spent internal organs, and then he survived for seven more months by eating her dead flesh, until the youth, having grown some, continued to live on the other corpses of the cemetery.

"He grew strong, eating the corpses and wearing their clothing and their skins. His eating the naked flesh of human corpses gave him an automatic power by which [161] the hosts of *mātṛkās*, *piśācas*, and *pretas*, as well as the hordes of other nonhumans, came under his control. Eventually he became lord over all the evil beings of the charnel ground. He robbed the glory of others. Some people he ate alive. He violated [all] beauty. He became a horrible and terrifying monster. Since he had eaten the naked flesh of his mother, he was notorious among people as 'the Mother-Eating Matraṅgara.'[19] From the breath of that great ghoul poured forth hot sicknesses that afflicted other beings with terrible pains. From his nose poured forth cold sicknesses, tormenting everyone. Anyone struck by his evil eye would assuredly die. With the sound of his violent mantra, everyone fell under his power. His huge body was covered in bluish-white ashes. He was decorated with a bindu of blood and fat. He brandished a garland of skulls over his shoulders. He wore skins smeared with red blood. He always drank from a skull-cup filled with blood. His dark brown hair was dreaded and filthy. For food he ate fat, skulls, and bones. His body was adorned with ashes and brains mixed with feces. Bird wings sprouted from his body, and he flew like a bird in the sky. His naked body was slimy, so he could swim unhindered like a fish through water. [162] Whoever saw him, their eyes would roll back in terror and they would faint. His body was covered in coarse hairs like a boar, sprouting from limbs all scaly and ornamented with snakes. His fingernails were like the beak and talons of a vulture, so that the flesh and bones of anyone he grabbed would fester. Under the force of his meditations, he saw any man as someone to be killed and viewed any woman's vagina as something to have. Limitless beings were utterly horrified, and, being overpowered, they would shake and tremble in fear. The worldly *mātṛkās*, ghouls, and powerful *yakṣasa* would prostrate before him, considering him their leader. Endless evil beings served him, employed as messengers, servants, slaves, and serfs. He became the Great God (Skt. *Maheśvara)* who ruled over them all."[20]

CHAPTER 21: "ON WHAT HAPPENED IN THE PAST"

"Then that fierce demon belted out an exclamation of pride, saying, 'Amazing! Since I am the Maheśvara of everything, there is no other god than me. Since all the armies that exist have all become mine, I am unrivaled, my majesty unique.' Thus he declared his proclamation of conceit to himself.[21]

"At that time the state of beings had come to this: [163] Because all conscious minds had been empowered by ignorance and demons,[22] [1] everyone became proponents of extreme emptiness, breaking the continuity [of the mind of enlightenment],[23] thus going completely overboard; [2] they became attached to the self, [falling into a view] of total permanence; [3] they pursued extinction, into utter cessation and escape; [4] they became evil and vicious, inevitably descending into screaming and wailing; [5] they became wrong-viewed [regarding cause and effect], inevitably descending into the Hell of Incessant Suffering; [6] they became greedy and jealous, inevitably descending into the [hungry ghost] realms of the Lord of Death; [7] they became greatly distracted, inevitably descending into the unfree states; [8] they became extremely stupid and ignorant, inevitably descending into the animal realms; [9] they became drunk with strong desire, inevitably descending to the hell realms. Because the tree of enlightenment had dried up, the roots of the mind [that is, of virtue][24] inevitably withered away.

"Moreover, Lord of Laṅka, how [these beings' karma] arose was well known, is well known, and will be well known [by the buddhas]. [1] In the past it had already arisen: If the great identity (*bdag nyid chen po*) is analyzed, in the supreme teachings of the *tathāgata* the ways of that being had already happened.[25] At that time all sentient beings were striving for extreme emptiness. Because they were nihilistic with regard to emptiness, they were being led into a vast realm of nothingness. [164] Finally, [after resting in that nothingness,] they would take rebirth once more, but the path to liberation and freedom would be annihilated.

[2] "In the past it had already arisen: If the great identity is analyzed, in the excellent teachings of the *tathāgata* the ways of that being had already happened. At that time all the sentient beings were striving for the view of total selfhood. Because of this [view of a] great enduring and permanent self, they would all end up in eternalism. Ultimately they would be reborn once again, whereupon they would become deluded about the excellent ones.

[3] "In the past it had already arisen: If the great identity is analyzed, in the excellent teachings of the *tathāgata* the ways of that being had already happened. At that time all the sentient beings were striving for total cessation [through

their observances]. Because they were obsessed with total cessation, they would end up in cessation and [a state of] absolute transcendence.

[4] "In the past it had already arisen: If the great identity is analyzed, in the excellent teachings of the *tathāgata* the ways of that being had already happened. At that time all the sentient beings were striving for brutal and ruthless cruelty. Because of their brutal and ruthless cruelty, they would descend into screaming and wailing. Finally they would take rebirth and be rejoined with their habitual tendencies and karma, whereby they would become extremely evil. Their minds having been inspired by demons, they would be reborn into the worlds of gods and humans as poisonous and plague-ridden *piśācas* [165] emanating arrows of searing pain, hostile demons, and misleading spirits causing fear throughout the three worlds, eating [people's] pure vows and diverting the joyful river of the excellent one.

[5] "In the past it had already arisen: If the great identity is analyzed, in the excellent teachings of the *tathāgata* the ways of that being had already happened. At that time all the sentient beings came to dwell in wrong views. Because their views were totally wrong, they would fall into the great Avīci Hell. Then when they arose again, their excellent equanimity would be annihilated.

[6] "In the past it had already arisen: If the great identity is analyzed, in the excellent teachings of the *tathāgata* the ways of that being had already happened. At that time all the sentient beings became exceedingly greedy and jealous. Because of these strong torments of greed and jealousy, they would fall into the realm of the hungry-ghosts, of the Lord of Death. Then when they would arise again, they would be emaciated paupers. Tortured by agonies of hunger and thirst, they would kill and destroy one another.

[7] "In the past it had already arisen: When the great identity is analyzed, in the excellent teachings of the *tathāgata* the ways of that being had already happened. At that time all the sentient beings [166] became distracted due to extreme laziness. Due to their extremely distracted laziness, they would descend into the unfree states. By eventually arising again, they would be separated [from the correct path][26] for three aeons.

[8] "In the past it had already arisen: If the great identity is analyzed, in the excellent teachings of the *tathāgata* the ways of that being had already happened. At that time all the sentient beings became very stupid and ignorant. Because of their extreme stupidity and ignorance, they would fall into the [realm of] stupid animals. Then when they arose again, any perceptible path would be cut.

[9] "In the past it had already arisen: If the great identity was analyzed, in the excellent teachings of the *tathāgata* the ways of that being had already hap-

pened. At that time all the sentient beings became intoxicated by extreme lust. Due to this intoxication by extreme lust, they would fall into the "city of the womb."[27] Then when they arise again, they would become tormented by burning desire.

"Thus it was all completely well known in all [the buddhafields]."

CHAPTER 22: "TEACHING THE MODE OF BEHAVIOR OF BLACK RUDRA"

Then again the Lord of the Guhyakas spoke: "Lord of Laṅka, next that fierce ghoul who had come about like that started boasting that he could overpower anyone. [167] 'Amazing!' he reveled. 'Who is greater than me, the Īśvara? Who is there?'

"Near a town in Laṅka, an island-kingdom in the ocean of Koka Tangmar (Rko ka thang dmar), atop the Mala[ya] Mountain in the province of Eye-Hand (*byan lag ljongs*), at a place called the 'Thunderbolt Peak,' lived one who was called 'Overlord of Laṅka, King of Demons.'[28] [This being] had become a student under the buddha called 'Lord of the Munis.' His powers and abilities were marvelous and great in wonders, his intelligence completely perfected. His [skillful] means billowed forth like clouds, oceans interwoven. He was renowned for being the greatest in the world.

"At this the winged ghoul became so absolutely enraged that he blacked out, and then the blazing fires of Rudra exploded forth. In a show of magic and flying ability, he swept down upon the mountain peak of Eye-Hand province. With a pride-filled voice he fiercely proclaimed, '*Rudra matra maratra!*' The whole town in this land of Laṅka shook, quaked, and was completely disrupted. All the demons and all the demonesses of Laṅka were terrified and fearful, screaming, 'Aaahh! Look what's happening!' Their eyes burned and rolled back in their sockets; they gasped and shook. The winged *yakṣa* thundered a ferocious cry. His presence could be seen and heard even in our home.

"Then the hordes of demons, including the great Overlord of Laṅka, assembled into an army. [168] They rose up and tried to destroy that winged demon, but he manifested the magical display called 'Intimidating the Demon Horde,' and pridefully shouted this ferocious declaration: 'I am Maheśvara! The four Great Kings are my servants. The eight classes of gods and demons are my slaves. I am the lord of the supreme secret, so who could rival me? *Rudra matra maratra!*'

"By this the army of demons was overpowered and intimidated. Some cried out, 'He has made the kingdoms of demons swoon. He is worthy to be [our] leader.' Others cried, 'This must be the destroyer of worlds. He should become our teacher.'[29] Some cried, 'This must be the Maheśvara ["great god"] of the world.' And still others cried, 'This is the leader (*gaṇapati*) of the assemblies of *ḍākiṇīs*.'

"But their demon-king, the Overlord of Laṅka, told them, 'He is the son of a *bhūta* demon called 'Desiring Belongings.'[30] He can incinerate the three worlds, but not suchness. He just destroys and overpowers things. He is the lord of the mistaken hordes and cannot be controlled by any other [mundane being], but his cure will be enacted by the *bhagavat* buddha. He will be subjugated by a *vajra*-bearing emanation [Vajrapāṇi] and will assuredly be established in the excellent [level of buddhahood]. This has been prophesied correctly, [169] and because of him, ascertainment of the excellent Secret Mantra, the dharma of the marvelous Mahāyāna, will assuredly come into the world. So [for now] if we also act as his servants, [later] we too will get to see the face of the buddha Vajragarbha[31] and attain ascertainment of the excellent Secret Mantra. We should pray that we might ascertain this.'

"Thus he commanded, and his assembly of demons rejoiced. Keeping in mind what their leader had said, they prayed accordingly and all entered into the service of the winged demon. They all told [Rudra], 'We too wish to do whatever the Maheśvara [commands].' They held him as their excellent chief, and he in turn took them into his retinue.

"Then that winged demon [once more] proclaimed himself as 'leader of the demons, Matraṅgara-Rudra.' He pridefully boasted of his greatness: 'Who is there better than me? Who is there? *Rudra matra maratra!*'

"[But then he heard about] someone called 'Mahākaruṇā, leader of the gods,' who was renowned as a noble and extraordinarily elevated individual, powerful and skilled in magic. The demon Black Rudra became extremely agitated and howled his fierce cry of pride. In a show of magic and flying ability, he swept down upon the abode of Mahākaruṇā. Being fully aroused[32] from his incomparably unbearable nature [170], he took on a form from which there arose a stench[33] that attacked his enemies from within, so that his hot breath was poisonous. Having been permeated by this emitted weapon of disease, [Mahākaruṇā's] body was filled with a pox like black daggers of fire. He suffered unbearable agonies until finally he was killed. His corpse was flung into the world, and there it was committed to the eight sacred sites of virtue.[34]

"After that, the murdered [god]'s wives, children, and followers were taken into[35] the retinue of that winged *yakṣa*. All the jealous *asuras*, *piśācas*, and zombies also went over to that demon's place. Even the four kings [of the directions] had to run for whatever refuge they could find, entering into his forced slavery.

All the [gods] too, such as Indra, Brahmā, and the fierce Viṣṇu, ran for whatever refuge they could find, entering into his forced slavery. Having further ravished all their wives, [Rudra] made some [his own] wives; some he made mistresses, some prostitutes; some he made concubines, and some servants or messengers. His having thus completely destroyed the world of gods and humans, everything became black, a realm of darkness. Moreover, that it happened like this was well known, is well known, and will be well known.

"The flying *garuḍa*-winged black one was horribly vicious and terrible, [171] ferocious with an ugly face, an ugly body, and a harsh voice. He always subsisted on, even reveled in, a broth of flesh and bones, maggots, pus, blood, feces, and urine. That fierce leader of the mistaken had destroyed the realms of gods and men. He annihilated every last trace of Karuṇa, the chief of the gods, and made his retinue his own.[36]

"A fire of terrible agonies blazed forth, causing everybody to run to the four leaders [of the four directions]. They [in turn], with hairs standing on end in absolute terror, went for refuge to Indra. Then these gods along with Indra rushed to Brahmā for refuge. Then Brahmā, together with the gods and Indra, went for refuge to Maheśvara. Brahmā, Mahesvara, the gods, and Indra ran for refuge to the Cruel One [that is, Rudra]. But when Brahmā, Maheśvara, Indra, and the Cruel One [later] would become terrified and fearful, they would run for refuge to the Vajra Holder *(rdo rje can)* [that is, Rudra's future tamer, Vajrapāṇi].[37] In that way each fled for whatever refuge there was, but they all entered without freedom into slavery for that Bhairava. Thus it became well known everywhere.

"After that the demon Black Rudra, having overpowered all the trembling and quaking gods and men with a single look, continued to stay at the place called 'The Skull Mountain Castle, the Rotting Mountain of Eye-Hand province,' on the island in Koka Tangmar ocean, near [that same] town in the land of Laṅka. [172] The victory flag of the demon was decisively planted. The standard of his demonic army was held aloft over the entrances, completely surrounding his encampment.

"The Fierce One generated his own supernatural powers, and by magical means he placed Mount Sumeru on the tip of his finger. Spinning it upside down on his finger and striking a majestic pose, he proclaimed in a ferocious cry of pride: 'Just so! *Rudra matra maratra!* Who in the universe is greater than me? Who is there? I'm amazing! Before, when the demon of the Lord of Death [Māra] was defeated by the so-called Ārya Śākyamuni, the most supreme of those who took ordination in his teaching—that is, of the śrāvakas—spoke in voices that were so very calm: "*You* should listen to *our* teachings," they preached. So I told those little children, those slaves to slinging their robes over their shoulders, "Then you [in turn] must willingly perform *my* austerities," but they couldn't handle it; they too were unable to control themselves.'

"At that the noble Vajragarbha, as the Lord of Speech Hayagrīva, emanated in various forms. [Rudra] heard in his mind a 'Hrīḥ!' but he clapped and shouted [at Hayagrīva], 'You too, Neck Boy! You must also happily promise [to perform my austerities].' In this way, once again the tamer, [this time Hayagrīva,] departed convinced that he could not subdue him.[38] All the way to the fourteenth level of heaven it was heard that the noble Vajragarbha-Hayagrīva was no match for him. 'He too has come under my power. Now everyone has come under my power and either joined my retinue or been killed. I am amazing!'[39] Thus [Rudra] proclaimed and saw himself as alone in his unrivaled majesty.

[173] "Just so, just so, at that time when he who had been Black Liberator ripened into Black Rudra, he who [previously] had been Invincible Youth had become the thusness of Vajrasattva, in the midst of the enlightened essence. He who had been at the time of that age Denpak had become the one known as the Excellent Being of the perfecting great dynamism, Vajradhara."[40]

CHAPTER 23: "EXHORTING THE INDETERMINATE MIRACULOUS DISPLAYS"

"Then all the *tathāgatas* gathered in the midst of the enlightened heart and were annihilated within emptiness. Then the Excellent Being enacted an appearance [as the Invincible Youth/Vajradhara][41] within emptiness. He proclaimed the sound of thusness within thusness, thinking, 'Excellent Being, the activities of your buddhafield have not been thoroughly completed, so why are you performing the fully perfected enlightenment? The [four] activities of the buddha have not been completed, so why are you performing the fully perfected enlightenment? The appearances in various [wrathful] aspects have not been completed, so why are you performing fully perfected enlightenment?'

"Those words being thus proclaimed, from that same emptiness these words were proclaimed: 'O all *tathāgatas*, by force of what purpose should the actions of the buddhafield be completely perfected, [174] thereby enacting the activities of the buddhas and the appearances in various aspects?'

"Those words being thus proclaimed, again from suchness they all proclaimed these words, the first of three exhortations:[42]

[1] "'In the unwavering sky of emptiness is enacted the immovable *sugata*. Unperceiving and nonconceptual thusness, please generate the various conceptualizations.'

"Then again from the thusness Excellent Being these words were proclaimed [in response]: '[But if this situation] is analyzed within the nonconceptual state, whatever one realizes through analysis, precisely that is the great realization, and whatever one does not realize is the cause for conceptualization.'[43]

[2] "Again they all proclaimed these words within thusness: 'From the heart of the sky's space [radiates] the light of the all-illuminating nature. Consort, all-embracing compassion, please generate the limitless buddha-sons.'

"Again from the thusness Excellent Being these words were proclaimed [in response]: '[But] the *dharmadhātu* which is the foundation (*ālaya*), the origin of everything, shines everywhere without beginning and without end; it is beyond the realm of speech, thought, and expression; it is the consort that generates boundlessly and infinitely.'[44]

[3.a.] "Again they all proclaimed these words within thusness: 'When the appearances in various aspects are enacted, please appear as the [seed-]syllables of the conquerors from the wisdom of the speech-*mudrā*. Generate the wisdom of the syllables.'

[175] "Again from the thusness Excellent Being these words were proclaimed [in response]: 'The nature of the thusness syllable is illuminated as the self-arisen syllable, *mūṃ*.[45] The nature of the mind-itself syllable is illuminated as the variety syllable, *hūṃ*. The nature of the conqueror-syllable is perfected as the *mudrā* syllable, *oṃ*. The nature of the everything-letter is the syllable of the unborn secret, *āḥ*.'

[3.b.] "Again they all proclaimed these words within thusness: 'By completing the perfection of wisdom, please manifest the appearing conceptualizations of the mind, the armor and weapons of liberating awareness, [the signs of the five wisdoms and so forth, such as *vajras* and wheels].[46] Generate the nonconceptual liberating wisdom.'

"Again from the thusness Excellent Being these words were proclaimed [in response]: '[But] the wisdom of all the buddhas is always arising from the nonconceptual. The nonconceptual liberating wisdom-mind [already] appears as conceptual signs for the sake of [those who need] concepts [to gain enlightenment].'

[3.c.] "Again they all proclaimed these words within thusness: 'Within the nonconceptual mirror of emptiness, unborn and unceasing forms appear. As a rainbow appears in the sky, just so, please arise from space as the *mudrās* [of the wrathful deities].'[47]

Again from the thusness Excellent Being these words were proclaimed [in response]: 'Although in thusness there is no perceiving, because the space of the all-illuminating nature is without exception completely perfect, [176] the supreme forms of the *mudrās* are [already] fully manifesting.'

"In that way, by those initial exhortations, [the *dharmakāya*] was completely and perfectly exhorted,[48] whereby the suchness Excellent Being appeared within the space of emptiness in the aspect of emptiness: Arising just as a moon-disk appears [reflected] in water or as a rainbow appears in the sky, [the Excellent Being] abided with a wisdom ascertaining nothing.[49] Then within that abiding state all the *tathāgatas* exhorted that [the Excellent Being] become determinate by means of two [further] exhortations as follows:

[1.][50] "'The naturally self-arising, uncontrived thusness, the state of primordial and unwavering great bliss, is utterly without seeking or fluctuation. Precisely this linguistic designation for the very essence of wisdom's space [which had arisen due to the *dharmakāya* exhortations] is the source for things real and unreal. Like primordiality itself, which cannot be marred, cut, or destroyed by anyone, the unwavering supreme bliss is the great heart of the sky, the supreme Vajrasattva. It is the spiritual mentor to all the *tathāgatas* of the three times [that is, of past, present, and future]. Source for the myriad emanating lords, naturally limpid mirror of everything, please activate the father and mother who generate the limitless conquerors.

[2.][51] "'Not wavering from the self-purifying space which is the equality of all things within the enlightened heart, the mind of enlightenment is primordial in everything, utter purity, all the buddhas. Arising from the three realms, the body of Vajragarbha has emanated the [three] distinct syllables so that the limitless may be comprehended.[52] [177] Please demonstrate the form-body, the center beautifully encircled by the assembled sons, and purify the afflictions.

"'First-in-everything Vajragarbha, arise from the three realms. Spontaneously accomplish the great bliss. In order to skillfully liberate the fierce, the harsh, and the poisonous, by means of the variegated stainless intellect emanate as *hūṃ*, the center encircled by a garland of light rays. By the power of your previous prayers and vows, please demonstrate the form-body of he who is unmoved by anything (*mi bskyod*, that is, Akṣobhya).[53]

"'First-in-everything Vairocana, arise from the three realms. Enact the appearances everywhere. In order to skillfully liberate the darkness of ignorance, by means of the intellect of enlightened purity emanate as *oṃ*, the center encircled by a garland of many forms. By the power of your previous prayers and vows, please demonstrate the form-body that illuminates whatever appearances.

"'First-in-everything Ratnasambhava, arise from the three realms. [Enact] the great wish-fulfilling jewel. In order to skillfully liberate the ignorance of desire,[54] by means of the completely pure source-intellect emanate as *svāṃ*,[55] the center beautifully encircled by a garland of jewels. By the power of your previous prayers and vows, please demonstrate the form that is the source for all desires.

"'First-in-everything Amitabha, arise from the three realms. [Enact] the limitlessly appearing discourses. [178] In order to skillfully liberate the ignorance of lust, by means of the intellect of stainless complete purity emanate as *oṃ*,[56] the center encircled by a garland of melodious syllables. By the power of your previous prayers and vows, please demonstrate the form-body of the various teachers.

"'Doubtless One [Amoghasiddhi], arise from the three realms. Enact the variations everywhere. In order to skillfully liberate the ignorance of activity, by means of the intellect of completely pure perseverance emanate as *haṃ*, the center encircled by a garland of dancing deeds. By the power of your previous prayers and vows, please demonstrate the form-body which enacts everything.'

"By the power of the complete and perfect exhortations made by that second exhortation, from the magical reality there appeared the bodies of the magical wisdoms, like luminous mandalas as if in the space of a mirror.

"Within that state of abiding as the self-appearing wisdom, when the perfect *saṃbhogakāya* exhorted by means of this third exhortation of all the *tathāgatas*, it was like this:[57] 'You, *tathāgata*, please spread the complete perfection of the world. Make the suchness of the enlightened essence apparent for the welfare of sentient beings. May all the buddhas who are the emanations of all the *sugatas* to be found in immeasurable world realms manifest for limitless purposes.[58]

[178] "'For the sicknesses of the three realms of *saṃsāra* there are no other beneficial medicines. Apply the medicine of the perfect nectar. Purify the ancient disease of *saṃsāra*. Clear away the illnesses of pain and suffering. Proceed into [the form of] the principal doctor, the Most Supreme (*Che mchog*). Become the enemy of all illnesses. With an ocean of nectarlike medicines, please adopt the masses of ill ones who have been overwhelmed by the enemy, the disease of error.

"'May he who is the perfected great dynamism himself, with the intention of the enlightened essence, send forth the spreading light rays. Enact the intention which illuminates darkness.

"'O being who accomplishes the purposes [of others], perform the actions and the deeds, and then fulfill the goal of throwing down the burden of the self. The time has come for taming whoever is here.

"'With the dharma of Akaniṣṭha, the supreme place of purity, without being limited by what might be highest, proceed into the perfect *saṃbhogakāya*. Enact the activities of the exhortations of old.'

"Thus was the total exhortation and thus, like the *mandala* of the sun dawning through a break in the clouds, from unwavering space the form-body dawned as a sun. The dharma became entirely apparent, without any limits of what might be called 'the highest.'"

CHAPTER 24: "THE FULL DISCUSSION OF THE TAMING BY THE GREAT GATHERING"

[180] "Then that perfect *saṃbhoga*-king of dharma made the sign for fully bringing about the opening of the *vajra*, whereby, from the densely arrayed buddhafields without end, conquerors without measure were brought forth everywhere.[59]

"At the time of that age, the assembly that was the complete play of the buddha's compassion discussed [the situation] in harmonious unison: 'Oh! Oh! Assemblies of the many aspects of buddha! Appear! Arise fully and completely here! The evil one of perverted existence has been propelled by his coarse *saṃsāric* seeds: He [passed through] great suffering and [the realms of] the hungry ghosts to arise in this world-realm, and through his mistaken ascetic practices, the Fierce One has ripened into the lord of all three levels of existence [of demons, gods, and humans]. By heinous Rudra's sharp cruelties, beings have been made [to follow] the extremes, crushed and destroyed. All this has provided the marvel of an excellent field for subjugation. It would be fitting for the Lord of Compassion to coalesce and cut the karmic continuum of this evil one, placing him on the level of great bliss.' Thus was the discussion.

"Then the family of the *vajra* buddha and the assembly of that class had the same discussion:[60] 'O gathered buddhas! Just as it has previously occurred in the past, so it is occurring now, at this present time:[61] The tainted ones whose minds are consumed by heaping mountains of misleading scriptures have been inspired by a demon, [181] and so they are severely intoxicated like rutting elephants. They cling to the extremes [taught] on the Cemetery Island of Corpses because [otherwise], screaming in pain, they will be killed and slaughtered by powerful and utterly unbearable poisons. We will help by the means that [adapts] itself howsoever.'

"The family of the jewel buddha and the assembly of that class had the same discussion: 'If this ferociously insane black one is left to do as he pleases, as if [inundated by] waves of an ocean of unbearable poisons, [everywhere] will become the realm of that black one; the lineage of the excellent ones will be severed, and the lamp of the sun [of dharma] will be destroyed, and then, due to the darkness of his karma, everyone will wander in a dense dark ignorance.'

"The family of the lotus buddha and the assembly of that class had the same discussion: 'Propelled by the wheel of the karma that he produced in the past, that Rudra of the mistaken intellect subjugated the demonic by means of the demonic. Thanks to the engagement of these Excellent Beings who have arisen from the space of the essence, the time has now come for this heaping mountain of poisons that has developed into this rebirth to be crushed and destroyed, just as he did [to others], by means of a great hammer of *vajra*-wrath.'

"The family of the youth buddha [that is, karma,] and the assembly of that class had the same discussion: 'This blind man who is lost on the path of error, held by the unbearable tortures of bondage, a great poison gathered from the depths, [182] a corpse that has died in the realm of eternalism and nihilism: In order to destroy his great gloom, his black ignorance, with a great stake[62] of violence that will explode forth from the miraculous display of wrathful wisdom, all the oceans of conquerors have gathered from the domain of the wise ones. The ocean of great poisons must be dried up by means of a wrathful intervention, a self-adaptation of the abundantly heaping clouds of miracles playing at appearing in the costumes of the childish. Because of the excellent vow of reality's great compassion, [to arise] in accordance with the conditions, whatever they may be, the four entities [of *saṃsāra*] must be displayed.'"

CHAPTER 25: "CUTTING OFF THE EXCELLENT DISCUSSIONS"

"This discussion of the great gathering having been fully decided, there was the thought that the time had come for taming by means of one of the four activities. In order to become discernable [for that purpose], there arose an emanation of the lord of sages [that is, Śākyamuni] from the light-rays of Invincible Youth who had [now] transformed into Vajragarbha. Then all the *tathāgatas* strongly commanded that emanation: 'Lord of sages, it is time. With the blessings of the true suchness, extinguish the fiery masses of the four entities and rouse the enlightened essence.' [183] Thus did they fully exhort him.

"Then that lord of sages manifested within the retinue[63] of [Rudra], the lord of the cemetery, and spoke in a completely peaceful voice.[64] But that lord of the cemetery, clapping his hands and cracking his tongue against his palate, shouted these words: 'Little boy, you are not my tamer! At an earlier time, when I was renowned as the fierce leader of the *yakṣas*, many like you came and told me, "You should follow our teachings. You should listen to what we say." I did not listen then,[65] so why should I submit[66] to you now? [Rather,] you must promise happily to undergo my austerities, to endure wearing a necklace [of rotting skulls] as your only clothing.' Ordering him thusly, he sent forth[67] the four demonic entities.[68] Therefore that noble one of pure family [that is, Śākyamuni] retreated from this conceptual formation.[69]

"Then all the *tathāgatas* commanded once more, this time to the all-seeing lord Avalokiteśvara, the emanation of the family and class of the lotus buddha.[70] They strongly exhorted him, saying, '*Dharmakāya* of all the conquerors, family of the lotus, lord of dharma Immeasurable Light (Amitābha), indestructible dharma Avalokiteśvara, from an emanated "*Hrīḥ*" syllable please manifest great splendor and overpower [this demon] in the guise of the horse-faced lord of speech.'[71] So the great horse-faced *vajra* emanation manifested in the abode of the great Lord of the Cemetery [184] and let forth a song of fierce horse neighing, thrilling and vivid: '*Ha ha ha! Hi hi hi! Hū lu hu lu hūṃ!*'[72]

"[Rudra's] retinue of demons was utterly intimidated and terrified, but the Lord of the Cemetery himself roared in an arrogant and furious voice, '*Rudra matra maratra!*' He was overflowing with confidence. Because of his arrogance, he was unmoved. Once more he commanded, 'Neck Boy, I was not subdued by someone just like you before, so I am not going to submit[73] to you now! [Instead,] you must promise to do happily whatever I want!' Thus he shouted, clapping his hands and cracking his palate. Again he sent forth the four demonic phenomena, whereby—or so [Rudra] thought—the noble one of the purest family retreated once more from this conceptual formation.

"[However,] then that *tathāgata* who was like the sky, without retreating from his [apparent] failure with that impure one, reappeared before him.[74] In order to be swallowed[75] by that same [Rudra], the *tathāgata* lord of speech adapted himself, turning into whatever Rudra liked [to eat]. Then that *tathāgata* burst out through the top of Rudra's head and through the soles of his feet. Pronouncing, '*Vajra hūṃ!*' he expanded his body immensely. Rudra emitted his last words, screaming and wailing in unbearable [pain]: 'A *tsa! Ma oh!* Whatever you are doing, do it quickly!' he cried.

"Then the *tathāgata*, having purified Rudra's obscurations,[76] [185] rose to the cranial vault of that one as nothing but bliss. He cast forth a horse-neigh into the sky, causing the assembly of demons and the lone one to collapse into disarray. Overwhelmed and frightened, they pleaded: 'Please tell us how we can be of service to you, Great Hero!'

"That *tathāgata* said, 'I am not your tamer. Your cure will be called "Vajra Hūṃ." He will be empowered by all the *tathāgatas*. Extremely vicious, fierce, ferocious, horrible, and intolerable, the greatest demon of demons, a blazing Bhairava, he will arise. You must go to him for refuge.' Then he vanished into the *dharmadhātu* palace.[77]

"Now all the *tathāgatas* of the secret gathering (Tib. *gsang ba 'dus pa*; Skt. *guhyasamāja*) already had fully discussed the situation in their great meeting, and they had realized that the time had come for taming [Rudra] by means of one of the four activities. Having tried to tame him by means of pacification [as Śākyamuni] and enhancement [as Hayagrīva], they now pronounced this *Sutra of Decisively Cutting Off the Discussion on Taming by Means of Coercion and Violence:*[78]

"[First, *dharmakāya:*][79] The assembly of *tathāgatas* practicing the complete liberation pronounced their *Sutra of Cutting Off the Discussion:* 'For those involved in pacification through total [mental] cessation, [186] ferocity is of no help.[80] In such cases, all the *tathāgatas* should act peacefully within the thusness of the uncontrived yoga. If those who use a yogic[81] manner can stop *saṃsāric* existence from sprouting by means of pacification, needless to say we can arouse them from their [states of] cessation with the force of a yoga [that realizes] the emptiness of existence and nonexistence. In order to water these withered sprouts, to arouse those in cessation wherever [necessary], we should act in harmony with, and without inhibiting, the multiplicity that arises from the reality of unrestricted emptiness.' Thus it was excellently decided.

"[Second, *svabhāvikakāya:*][82] Then the assembly of the *tathāgatas* of entitylessness pronounced their *Sutra of Cutting Off the Discussion:* 'For proponents of extreme emptiness who cut the continuity [of the mind of enlightenment], entities are of no help. So within the continuously enlightened emptiness, all the *tathāgatas* should act unchangingly. If those who use the approach of emptiness[83] can transmute entities by means of emptiness [as if they were] without the slightest existence, needless to say we should overcome this extreme of complete nihilism with the force of a yoga that arises from nonexistence. In order to turn back this extreme of cutting the continuity [of the mind of enlightenment], and to be born forth from nonexistence wherever [necessary], we should act without interrupting the great good qualities within an emptiness that has continuity.' Thus it was excellently decided.

"Then the assembly of the *tathāgatas* of unchanging entityness pronounced their *Sutra of Cutting Off the Discussion:* 'For those [having the view of] extreme enduring permanence, nonexistence is of no help. So within the thusness of the enlightened heart everything should be enacted as the great identity. [187] If those having an unchanging viewpoint can still distinguish between stable and moving things through their attachment to permanence, needless to say we can refute permanence by the power of the spontaneously accomplished great identity. In order to overcome attachment to self and exorcise materialism, we should act as the actionless self-nature itself within a reality that is permanent but lacking self.' Thus it was excellently decided.

"[Third, *saṃbhogakāya:*][84] Then the family of the *vajra tathāgata* and the assembly of that class pronounced their *Sutra of Cutting Off the Discussion:* 'For those of extreme evil and viciousness, peacefulness is of no help. So within the essence of wisdom and means, all the *tathāgatas* should act wrathfully. If those having a wrathful manner can terrify the three worlds by wrathful means, needless to say the compassionate buddhas can wrathfully [liberate the entirety of the] three realms. In order to tame all those difficult to tame and thoroughly purify those angry at the vow-holders, we should perform the *mudrā* of the cemetery dance by means of the nine Great Blazing Dances.' Thus it was excellently decided.

"Then the assembly of Vajragarbha *tathāgata*, called 'suchness' or 'definitiveness,' pronounced their *Sutra of Cutting Off the Discussion:* 'For those adhering to the completely mistaken,[85] truth is of no help. [188] So with hidden intentions[86] in union with the great secret, we should act in perfect adaptation to everything. If those having an outward manner of acting and behaving [correctly][87] can twist the words of anyone by means of their practices, needless to say we can straighten out these mistaken paths by means of compassionately adapted actions and behaviors. In order to liberate entities by means of [those same] entities, to clear poisonous illnesses with poison, we should perform the *mudrā* of the action dance of inconceivably supreme means.' Thus it was excellently decided.

"Then the family of the *ratna tathāgata* and the assembly of that class pronounced their *Sutra of Cutting Off the Discussion:* 'For those of extreme jealousy and greed, giving is of no help. So within the inexhaustible but nonexistent source, we should activate the jewel that is inexhaustible in all things. If those having an ascetic manner can be sustained for a lifetime by means of restraint, needless to say [we can eliminate] the longings of the three realms that are without existence yet desirable. In order to satisfy jealousy and to eliminate intense longing, we should act from the riches of the secret Great Vehicle in the *mudrā* of the sky-treasury.' Thus it was excellently decided.

"Then the family of the youth *tathāgata* [that is, karma family] and the assembly of that class pronounced their *Sutra of Cutting Off the Discussion:* 'For those of extreme laziness and distraction, exhortation is of no help. [189] So within an effortless reality we should perform everything without action. If those acting in an outward manner of being unwavering[88] can interrupt the path of the activities of excellent ones by means of [meditative] stillness, needless to say we can reverse the agitation of the world by means of the actionless and unwavering great bliss. In order to interrupt the continuity of unfree states and to be the enemy of laziness and distraction, we should act from the great wealth and leisure of equanimity in the *mudrā* of abiding without action.' Thus it was excellently decided.

"Then the family of the elephant *tathāgata* and the assembly of that class pronounced their *Sutra of Cutting Off the Discussion:* 'For those of extreme stupidity and ignorance, teaching brings no understanding. So within the sameness of, [that is, without distinguishing between,] various details, we should perform everything with the great stupidity.[89] If those acting in a manner of stupidity can obscure everything by means of ignorance, needless to say we can dispel the ignorance of the three realms by not distinguishing, neither adopting nor rejecting. In order to destroy the seats (*āyatana*) of ignorance and make ignorance like the sky, we should act within the wisdom of completely pure stupidity in the mudra of unconfused complete perfection.' Thus it was excellently decided.

"Then the family of the *padma tathāgata* and the assembly of that class pronounced their *Sutra of Cutting Off the Discussion:* 'For those of strong desire and attachment, antidotes [of renunciation] are of no help. [190] Therefore, within the wisdom of immense desire, we should perform everything with great desire. If those having a desirous manner can, by means of sexual practices, make the three realms into [an ocean of] the blood [of desire], needless to say we [can eliminate] the attachment and the desire of the three realms through sexual union that is completely pure of desire. In order to dry up the ocean of the blood of desire and cut desire with desire, we should act within the wisdom of completely pure desire and attachment in the *mudrā* of the desirous dance.' Thus it was excellently decided.

"[Fourth, *nirmāṇakāya* and *guhyakāya:*][90] Then all the *tathāgatas* pronounced their *Sutra of Cutting Off the Discussion* [on taming through violence]:[91] 'For those clinging desperately to things as substantial, prohibitions are of no help. So within the essence of wisdom and means, we should perform the practice of adapting ourselves to everything. If those having the methods of adaptation can lead the three worlds into error by transforming into something agreeable, needless to say we can correct those mistaken worldly ones by practicing the dance of compassion.

"'Those[92] [methods] and limitless others are to be found. By various means for taming, all the inhabitants in limitless worlds upon worlds can be led to, and unified with, the correct secret. For the ferocious, the methods of love or of ferocity should be used; for the peaceful, pacification or *prāṇa*-practice; for the powerfully wrathful, wrath. For the adulterous, adultery or its antidote should be used; for the desirous, desire or renunciation; for the wavering, a focused mind or wavering itself; for the ignorant, pervasive equanimity; [191] for the mountainous[-ly egotistical], [minute] *samādhis* or mountains [of similarly egotistical behaviors]; for the jealous, the methods of jealousy.

"'Those [methods] and limitless others are to be found. The supreme Vajragarbha abides perfectly in the boundlessness of the spacious sky of the peerless foundation, the shared ground of all those persons who wish for the extraordinary, the space of all.

"'The space of all sentient beings and buddhas is to be ascertained as primordially the thusness Vajrasattva. Thusly do limitless sentient beings, [each] according to [his or her own] unobstructed and uncontrived joys and desires, become ascertainment itself. And therefore, through the immeasurably superior means of heaping clouds of activity-dances, within the thusness of acting howsoever and in an unwavering and unstraying space, the supreme is to be ascertained as just this. Within the essence of this ascertainment, by limitless and immeasurable means, without obstructing anything and in whatever way pleases them, [beings] are led into bliss.' Thus it was determined by the excellent ones.

"Here, within the unbearable blazing wisdom[93] which is intensely fierce and powerful, it was excellently decided that the mudra of the Blazing Supreme One (*Che mchog 'bar ba*),[94] the absolutely terrifying [subduer for Rudra,][95] Lord of the Charnel Grounds, should be enacted."

CHAPTER 26: "APPOINTING THE *VAJRAS* OF THE FOUR ACTIVITIES"

[192] "Lord of Laṅka, at the time of that age,[96] I was one of those gathered in that very assembly.[97] For the sake of fully awakening everyone into alertness, I thoroughly questioned one bodhisattva also present in that assembly, named Armor of Exhortation, Capable Intelligence:[98] 'O Great Hero! From what cause did this massive demon arise? By what conditions did he become like this? Into what effect has he ripened? To which species does he belong? What fateful practices does he perform? If he were not subdued, what would be the harm? If he were subdued, what would be the purpose?'

"Because of those questions, that great Armor of Exhortation spoke: 'Great Hero, Lord of the Guhyakas, this massive demon did not arise from any causes or conditions that were good. He arose from causes and conditions that were purely evil. The cause from which he arose was a mountain of darkness.[99] The conditions from which he arose were his ferocious austerities that were perversions of the precepts. The effect into which he has ripened is a mountain of suffering. The species to which he belongs is a lowly species of *saṃsāra*, an outcaste demonic ghoul. His fateful practices involve recklessly mistaking the four entities of *saṃsāra* for the basis. If he is not subdued, he will become a problem that will [cause] the enlightened essence of beings to fade for a long time. If he is subdued, the essence of all, the mandala of light, will dawn fully and clearly.'

[193] "Then I spoke these words to him: 'Quite so, Great Hero! Well then, the moment for this [violent taming] has arrived! This [violent] activity is supreme

among the activities. This secret is the excellent innermost secret of secrets. Subjugate him! Completely and totally subjugate him! At the great occasion of this moment having arrived, this sentient being [Rudra], who has fallen so low as to [require] this activity, must be emptied. Great compassion has come to this. Because [Rudra] will take [the lives] of everyone in the three thousand-fold universe, this supreme compassion which will transform his consciousness [through liberation][100] will not approach even a fraction of the hundreds of thousands [of evils that would result if he were left untamed].' Thus it was thoroughly exhorted.[101]

"Then all the *tathāgatas* transformed Denpak into an Excellent Being appearing as the Vajra Holder (Tib. Rdo rje 'dzin pa; Skt. Vajradhara),[102] and strongly commanded him: 'Holder of the secret of all the conquerors, lord of the mind, Vajra Holder, he who has the great conduct of violence, hero who vanquished the three worlds: By the power of your previous great armor,[103] may all the buddhas of the past and present tame this fierce, invincible one. With the body of a blazing blue hero and a bravery to be feared, demon of demons who defeats [all other] demons,[104] by means of the very essence of ferocious rage, totally defeat the Lord of Charnel Grounds.' Thus did they strongly exhort.[105]

"And therefore that being, the Vajra Holder, [194] perceived that all the worlds including those of the gods had already been overpowered by that king of ghouls and that now this violently ferocious and rageful one was about to destroy the worlds of gods and humans. People's faces and appearances had become ugly, drawn and pale, night was falling before its time, and all was enveloped in a dense and gloomy darkness. Many incurable hot and cold sicknesses and plagues were spreading all over. There came everywhere, and at the worst times, storms, thunder and hail, and rains of pus, blood, stones, or razors. Even [the processes of causality, of] production, maturation and sustenance, had been reversed.[106] Perceiving that protectorless world whose variously poisoned people were so tortured and utterly helpless, he was overwhelmed with compassion.

[B.][107] "And so he sang out: 'Conquerors who travel the completely pure path, from the emptiness in which everything arises as nonexistent, within the buddhafields of the authentic conquerors and the Gaṇḍavyūha ["Densely Arrayed"]: I am expert in the proposed activities! Since the moment for the proposed activities has arrived, I will tame all those who have been impossible for all [other] buddhas to tame. Those not liberated, I will liberate. Those not delivered, I will deliver. Those without relief, I will relieve and establish in correctness.'[108]

[A.] "Then in an awesomely powerful manner, he [Vajrapāṇi] fiercely exhorted the [watchman,][109] the Horse-Faced One, Vajra-Dharma, in these *va-*

jra words:[110] 'Lord of Speech, the Vajra-Faced, on Mount Malaya, which is at the center of a town in the land of Laṅka, on the island in the ocean of Koka Tangmar, proceed to the peak where there is extreme savagery. In the manner of [an unspoiled] diamond, view the object, the Lord of Charnel Grounds together with his retinue. Then, for [the ultimate destruction of] these misguided depravities, call forth and send out the *vajra* activities throughout the three realms.'

"[Then Vajrapāṇi asked Vajrasattva also to exhort Hayagrīva to act as the watchman:] 'Hero who is moved or disturbed by nothing, embodiment of all the buddhas, thusness Vajrasattva, Vajragarbha, protector of the three realms [195], within the sky of the great emptiness perform the nine Great Blazing Dances [that will exhort Hayagrīva].[111] Then proceed to the site for compassion [upon Mount Malaya] and perform the childish practices that are suitable [for Rudra].'

[C.] "[Then Vajrapāṇi exhorted all the conquerors:] 'Distilling all the secret intentions, by means of the mandala of this marvelous secret,[112] for the sake of endless sentient beings, grant the blessings which exhort the essence.'[113]

"Thus within the *dharmadhātu* palace, all the *tathāgatas* enveloped infinite space with boundless heaping clouds of compassion blazing with the fires of wisdom like the conflagration at the end of time, and performed the wrathful intervention in the nine Great Blazing Dances.[114] Then to the assembly of the Vajra Horse the wrathful entreaty was made: 'Go! Go! Fully and completely, go! With the nine *vajra* expressions of the horse, demonstrate the desires of the nine worldly mindsets. [196] For the assembly of the ferocious worldly black one [that is, Rudra] that practices depravities in the charnel grounds, ignite the activities of the *vajra* concepts. By engaging in the realization of a great compassion that wears the armor of the [bodhisattva-]vow for as long as all of *saṃsāra* has not been liberated, fully embrace the beings of *saṃsāra*.'

"Therefore the powerfully perceptive supreme *vajra*-eye, the *vajra*-lotus [Avalokiteśvara], made the appearance of rejoicing in the wheel of the well-spoken *vajra*-dharma. He who is foremost in knowing [the swiftest route to] great enlightenment[115] and the assembly of that lord of speech magically displayed the nine great expressions, whereby all the realms of space were completely filled by the assemblies of the emanated Horse-Faced Vajra, [Hayagrīva]. They approached the peak of Mount Malaya, and for as long as *saṃsāra* was not emptied, with eyes of compassion, Avalokiteśvara gazed.

"Then the Conquerors of Gaṇḍavyūha concentrated all their intentions into the singular secret, and activating the intention to liberate thoroughly the three realms into the essence, they granted the blessings for overturning the three poisons permanently. Gazing upon [all of] *saṃsāra* as reality, they made suffering into the path of enlightenment. [They understood that] the activities themselves were united with self-arising wisdom, and that [Rudra's] negativities that had come to fruition were the [essence of the three] *vajras* themselves.[116] They intended a great self-arising mandala, primordial suchness without contrivance.[117]

"Meanwhile the Lord of the Guhyakas, the Vajra Holder, created from the *vajras* of his body, speech, and mind millions of billions of emanated supreme sons, the Youths[118] of the Vajra Holder, all like heaping clouds on a summer day. Boundless like the space of the sky, they too approached the peak of Malaya. With the weaponry of adaptable means, they performed in the way of the demons whose practices were childish in so many ways—that is, they manifested themselves as children in the worldly realm."

CHAPTER 27: "THE DEMON IS THOROUGHLY SUBJUGATED"

[197.3] "When that suitably adapted being, [the Vajra Holder, arrived at Mount Malaya, he][119] saw with his perfectly adapted eyes that the fierce ghoul of karma had been made powerful by the four entities [of *saṃsāra*]. Things had really developed: He was now dwelling at the top of a fortress made from a mountain of rotten flesh, completely encircled by a swamp of substances like blood, filth, human flesh and marrow, brains and membranes, pus and lymph. He was surrounded by a horde of vicious creatures like maggots and worms, bees, wasps and hornets, snakes, scorpions and spiders, flocks of carrion birds, crows, vultures, screech owls, jackals, tigers, and lions. He had seized the daughters, wives, mother, and sisters of Karuṇa, the leader of the gods, as well as the mother, sisters, daughters, and wives of Īśvara, the great god of the world, [198] and was forcing them to serve in the roles of concubines, prostitutes, and slaves. Together with twenty kinds of goddesses—the eight *mātṛkās*, the *piśācīs*, witches, the *yakṣinī* spirits, the *rākṣasī* demonesses, the flesh-eaters, the vampiresses, the demonic name-robbers, the spirit-thieves, ministers, generals, captains, commanders, and ambassadors together with their envoys, each with her own throne and weapons—they were all arrayed in the manner of splendorous messengers, aides, servants, and sorceresses. Also arrayed [on the edges], in an attitude of worship and awe, was an assembly of the eight [*piśācī-*]*gandharva* daughters of *saṃsāric* existence with faces of a lion, a tiger, a fox, a jackal, a bird, a vulture, a crow, and an owl. And the wrathful and fierce female assemblies of the eight great demonic attendants—Gaurī, Caurī, Pramoha, Vetālī, Pukkasī, Ghasmarī, Śmaśānī, and Caṇḍālī—were arrayed in their absolutely terrifying forms. The four door protectors of the cemeteries—[the horse-faced] Jailor Woman, [the pig-faced] Face Woman, [the hyena-faced] Tribal Woman, and [the wolf-faced] Thusly Engaged Woman—held the secret doors and enforced [Rudra's] orders.[120] Holding the four corners of the Lord of the Charnel Grounds were [the four queens:] Greedy One, Extremely Greedy One, Intoxicated One, and Blood-Drinking One, each expressing her intoxication with desire.[121]

"At the center of that palace that was built from a mountain of rotting flesh held together with great stakes of Blazing Sky-Iron,[122] was the queen of diseases, [199] the devoted Krodhīśvarī. She was holding a skull-cup filled with blood mixed with seed-oil, the five substances, and liquor. Because she constantly clung to her indulgences, crazed with desire and greedy, she was famed as the Greedy Goddess of Desire.[123]

"Having defeated that realm of Rudra with the nine Great Blazing Dances, in order to coerce it,[124] when almost all the powerful worldly gods presently gathered under the power of the captain [of the gods, Rudra,] had gone out to work, at that moment a Youth—the perfect but unreal thusness of that great and glorious Vajra Holder—manifested from below.[125] This son, named Vajrakumāra Bhurkuṃkūṭa [literally, "Vajra-Youth, Heaping Moles"], dark blue with a wrathful frown and a crest of hair, performed the nine Great Blazing Dances. He made his face, arms, and legs so as to look just like the Lord of the Charnel Grounds. Then by applying [the mantra] of the five nectars,[126] he transformed the five filths [surrounding Rudra's fortress] into the nectars [of self-arising wisdom, and ate them,] thus purifying it all within adamantine emptiness.

"Then he led the female retinue of attendants and so forth [to the truth] by adapting himself [to sexual practice] with a wisdom unattached to the practice and an activity accumulating no afflictions. Thus they were coerced and purified by this union, from which there emanated forth an assembly of heroes, emanations of [the buddha's] wisdom appearing in the form of an assembly of [wisdom-]*gauris* and so forth and the assembly of [eight wisdom-*piśācīs*,] the Lion-Faced, the Tiger-Faced One, and so on.[127]

"Due to the strength of her desires, when that Greedy Goddess of Desire looked at [the buddha], [200] what she saw seemed generally like her own husband, but there was this peculiar brilliant glow about him that made her wonder. So she became doubtful. Of two minds, she thought, 'Oh, wow! My hero is so amazing, blazing with bright light. But I wonder, what is this all about?'

"That Vajrakumāra, having supreme means, [perceived her doubts] and cast forth the three demon-shouts, ['*Rudra matra maratra!*'],[128] whereby her doubts were destroyed. The Goddess of Attachment fully embraced the body of the buddha, an embrace that was like a snake tormented by the heat embracing the trunk of a white sandalwood tree, having the heat's torments dispelled by the tree that has no concept [of such things]. Thus without wanting anything, [the buddha] utterly dispelled whatever torments she had.

"Then Bhurkuṃkūṭa expressed this full knowing, this essence of the wish-fulfilling jewel that arises as whatever anyone wants, this supreme of practices that fulfills all the activities [of taming]: '*Oṃ bhurkur ichi kipi ucchuṣma krodha hūṃ phaṭ!*'[129] By this perfect but unreal magical display, the magical display of the great Vairocana was gathered.[130] The light-rays of the *oṃ*, the syllable that instigates any emanation, manifested and were implanted in the womb of the Greedy Goddess. Through the power of that manifestation of Secret Mantra, the syllable then transformed into the likeness of the [Vajra-]Demon,[131] that is, direct perception was established within the womb of that Greedy Goddess. From the light-rays of his *vajra*-tongue came [the mantra], '*Rakṣa śrī heruka rudra matra ha ha haṃ!*' [201] By the power of these syllables of development, perfection, and destruction, the blessings were stabilized. [132]

"Thus a being who knew the unreality [of appearances] was assembled from the body of the father, [Vajrapāṇi in the form of Bhurkuṃkūṭa]. Since the [billions of] illusory Vajra[-Youths],[133] the magical displays of that ferociously powerful being, had successfully tamed those who had been difficult for the buddhas to tame, they now threw aside their childish costumes [which they had taken on for the taming] of the demons and mistaken worldly ones, [and they dissolved into the womb of the demoness]. The mind definitively explained the intention within the enlightened heart . . . and rested. That regent-being [Denpak], as whom the emanated conqueror Vajra Holder had arisen in an earlier [lifetime], activated this king [of tantras] that holds the secrets, the scripture of the ultimate great treasury of secrets that is renowned throughout the three heavens.[134]

"Then [Rudra,] that fierce ghoul, returned[135] home, and what he saw did not seem quite the same as before; his riches and his retinue were not as they used to be. He became extremely agitated, wondering, 'How strange! What has happened to my retinue?'

"Just then the devoted goddess came up with some news for her lover. 'My husband has come back!'[136] she exclaimed, 'How wonderful! You are so sexy and so brave! Now what is this all about? Why are you expressing such negative thoughts about your own retinue? My hero, whatever you want, from today forward I will do it. My womb is becoming uncomfortable. My charming hero, your own heir is about to be born.[137] How could you be worrying so?' Hearing those words,[138] [202] because he was attached to beautiful appearances, he was filled with longing. Feeling the greed of holding true only to his own family, he continued to cling to the way of [doing only what] pleased him.

"Then there came the sound, resounding three times,[139] of the baby child coming forth from the Greedy Goddess. Merely because of this menacing sound of the Glorious One, the wrathful demons, demonesses, and so forth all fainted. Having come to again,[140] they saw the Blazing Great Terror (Tib. *'jigs byed;* Skt. *bhairava).* The ground was covered by his terrifying form, having a mane of dark blue with nine heads, eighteen arms and *vajra* wings, a proud appearance, the hairs of his body were spiders, scorpions, lizards, and snakes like burning hooks.[141]

"Regarding his eighteen hands: In the first pair, on the right was a *vajra,* on the left a skull-cup; in the second pair were spines with skulls attached; the third pair made ready a lasso made from human guts; in the fourth pair, on the right was held a sun, on the left a moon; in the fifth pair, on the right was held a *garuḍa,* on the left an owl; in the sixth pair a hawk and a *vajra*; in the seventh pair were a trident and a casket; in the eighth pair were whisk and drum; in the ninth pair, with the right he spun Mount Meru near his head, and with the left he was hurling the three-thousand-fold world-system.[142]

"Ornamented and garbed with one hundred thousand powerful *nāgas,* ablaze with fires like the aeon's final conflagration, with a ferocious grimace, he glared with each of his twenty-seven [three per head] fiery eyeballs (*spyan ras gzigs*). With his feet he was stomping on the eight classes of blazing gods. Thus he became the wrathful Vajra-Demon and was proclaimed throughout the realms of gods and demons.[143]

"Then that fierce ghoul, [Rudra,] though he had only developed a conceptual mind, fully exhorted the gods of his retinue with a voice fierce with angry pride: '*Rudra matra maratra!*' he cried. [203] 'Gather! Gather! Assembly of great lords! Completely and quickly, gather into ranks! Go! Go! Assembly of great lords! Completely and quickly, go to your posts! Obey me! Obey me! Assembly of great lords! Completely and quickly, obey me in this!

"'Lords! As my followers, the time has come for you to annihilate this great poison, no matter what it is! If you are wondering whether or not to do this, [know] that you are about to be destroyed! To my friends: Do not give even a thought as to whether or not to act; it will be okay! Such [doubters] are not real friends; who will call them friends? As for the critics: do not give even a thought as to whether or not to act; it will be okay! Such critics are deceptive; who will call them heroes? To you who have promised: Do not even think about whether or not to honor your promises; it will be okay! Such [conditional] promises are lies; who will name you honorable? All of you: Do not worry about whether or not to practice; it will be okay! Such practitioners are false; who will call them practitioners?' Thus did Rudra exhort the lords [of demons and gods].

"Then those who could not bear the overwhelming power of that [Rudra] demon, assembled as an army of billions of divine princes bearing demonic implements. [204] And those powerful lords, totally terrified, shaken, and awestruck [by Rudra], were aroused. Thus these horrors of suffering gathered swirling under the demon like [withered] leaves under a black cyclone. The standard of the demonic horde was raised,[144] and clouds of weaponry gathered: The net of demonic illusions was spread forth. Raising the war cry, they drew themselves up [for the fight].

"Then with a strong and wrathful gallop, a miraculous display of speed in the manner of the *vajra*-gallop, the assembly of the Vajra Horse fully exhorted all the [other] wrathful ones of the Mahāyāna with this song of the horse's determined gallop:[145] '*Hrīḥ!* Erotic! Heroic! Fearsome! Wildly laughing! Stern! Terrifying! Compassionate! Awesome! Peaceful! Overcome Maheśvara with these [nine] postures of the Blazing Dances that become the very substance of [Viśuddha Heruka's] own body.[146]

"'The intoxicating *hrīḥ!* Demonstrate a form of desire that exceeds even that of the thousand [Mahādevas].[147] With a subjugating power, demonstrate the form of terror that exceeds one thousand Yamas [Lords of Death]. Demonstrate a peaceful body that exceeds one thousand Mahābrahmās. Manifest all as the three mandalas.

"'The total subjugation *hrīḥ!* Overcome through the direct manifestation of total subjugation. Ho ho ha ha he he hi hi![148] Fill [space] with the crazy laughter of delight. Thoroughly destroy, utterly destroy all the lords. By the power of wisdom's dynamism, overcome this [army of] lords by directly manifesting.

"'The great dynamism *hrīḥ!* [Master that Mahādeva and Umā, the queen of Maheśvara]. [205] Hulu hulu! With the three eyes, lead her to the accomplishment of the three activities. The dynamism of the supreme *hrīḥ!* By this power, manifest directly, overcoming the powerful [black Viṣṇu]. *Rudra matra!* From this heart, lead forth, fully lead forth the Glorious Queen [that is, Viṣṇu's consort]. The dynamism of the supreme *hrīḥ!* By this power, directly manifest, overcoming Brahmā, and fully lead forth, completely lead forth[149] Brahmā's Queen (Tshangs las sgrol ma). The dynamism of supreme *hrīḥ!*' By this power, directly manifest, overcoming Lord Rāma, and as the lord of all great unions, lead forth Rāma's [queen]. The dynamism of supreme *hrīḥ!* By this power, directly manifest, overcoming Rudra, and with the great union, fully and completely lead forth [Rudra's queen,] the goddess Krodhīśvarī.

"'To the compassionate ones: Do not conceptualize about whether or not to act; it will be for the best! [Conceptualizing] compassion like that would be illusory; who would say that is compassion? As for the disciples: Do not conceptualize about whether or not to subdue them; it will be for the best! Disciples like that are deceptive; who would say they have been tamed?

"'*Hrīḥ ha ha ho ho!* Completely and quickly manifest the emanations! Perform the exploding rage with a ferocious [body], a menacing [voice], and an awesome [mind]! [Vajra Heruka:] In order to master taming every single one of the many kinds of angry minds that beings have due to the manifestation of the various mistaken views, fully and completely emanate the illusion of the supreme means of the conquerors. From the wisdom of unwavering wrath, arise as the supreme four wisdoms, completely devour [the three poisons], and wear [the skin of the liberator].[150] [Padma Heruka:] In order to master taming every single one of the many kinds of desiring minds that beings have due to the manifestation of the various desires, [206] fully and completely emanate the illusion of the supreme means of the conquerors. With wisdom unattached to practice, fully savor the supreme bliss—arise and play! [Buddha Heruka:][151] In order to master taming every single one of the many kinds of ignorance that beings have due to the manifestation of the various delusions, fully and completely emanate the illusion of the supreme means of the conquerors. Without being ignorant of the [ultimate] equality [of all differences], completely perfect the discriminating wisdom. Arise and know!'

"Due to the rolling thunder of the ferociously wrathful [buddhas], free of pride, taking delight in the violence and the four types of habitual tendencies, the billions of demons bearing the demonic weapons shrank back, overpowered. The heaping clouds of weapons, the standard, and so on were all purified within emptiness. The harsh cries [of the horde, 'Agtshar!'][152] were actualized [as words of dharma]. The Mahāyāna [teachings of] Secret Mantra was announced: '*Ri ri!*'[153]

"Thus the Lord of the Charnel Grounds, Black Rudra, was forsaken by his own retinue, all of whom went for refuge to that excellent and exalted [Vajra-Demon]. [Rudra] was at a total loss for words. His will collapsed. There was nothing left to do. He became completely enraged . . . and then blacked out. The seeds of his own five Rudras were revealed:[154]

[1] "'*Rulurulu bhyo!*' he cried out [207] and mutated into a wrathful appearance with three heads, six arms, and four legs. But out of that wrathful mutation, the exalted Vajra-Demon acted in just the same way and, pronouncing the five seed [syllables] of [Rudra's] *saṃsāric* [mantra] empowered with [*hūṃ*],[155] the indestructible syllable of his blessing, he thereby stole [Rudra's] speech emanation. Thus the power of [Rudra's] speech faded.

[2] "Then that Lord of the Charnel Grounds cried out, '*Ralarala bhyo!*' mutating into one with nine heads and eighteen arms, but that excellent and exalted one again definitively cut off [Rudra's] speech emanation.

[3] "Once more that Lord of the Charnel Grounds cried out, '*Huluhulu bhyo!*' whereby he grew into a demon with five heads and sixteen arms, but that glorious great and exalted demon performed in just the same way, once more cutting off the expression of [Rudra's] speech.

[4] "Then that Lord of the Charnel Grounds said, '*Halahala bhyo!*' whereby he mutated into one with twenty-one heads and forty-two arms, but once again that Vajra-Demon acted in just the same way and cut off Rudra's ability to say anything.

[5] "Finally Rudra said, '*Ralirali bhyo!*' and his body became massive beyond measure, emitting red tempests that spread aeons of disease and discharging poisonous weapons from his body. So the exalted Vajra-Demon acted just like that too, stealing Rudra's speech and cutting off his speech emanations. Just as when someone has his tongue cut out, he drops to the ground because of all the blood, in the same way Rudra was stupefied and fell unconscious.

[208] "Then that great overlord of all proclaimed [the mantra of cleansing the vows],[156] '*Samaya ho!*' Due to their connection from their earlier lifetimes, Rudra's life force could no longer bear it. He presented his chest to that [Vajra-Demon], who then plunged a blazing three-pointed *khaṭvāṅga* into him, finally destroying the very essence of Rudra. With the force of this destruction [the Vajra-Demon] danced the *mudrā*-positions, purifying [Rudra] inside his stomach.[157]

"Thus Rudra met the ultimate buddhas, including [Denpak,] his spiritual friend with whom he had a connection, thanks to the power of his previous servant's compassion. He [generated] immeasurable *bodhicitta*, saw the Gaṇḍhavyūha buddhafield, and by the power of seeing this, the darkness of his craving from time without beginning was purified. He remembered all that he had done, how he had taken on so many different bodies, and been reborn for limitless aeons.

"Then he was ejected through the anus [of the Vajra-Demon] and established [back in his ordinary body] at his feet. There, bowing with complete joy,[158] he wept and lamented with remorse at all that he had done: 'Oh! Woe! Woe is me! Great heroic healer, you have such little compassion. Why have you expelled me through your anus from that place of total bliss? You are of so little compassion! Now whatever else you will do, please do it quickly! If you hurry up and liberate me, I will rest in that bliss for ages.

"'I hereby go into your service and offer to you my body. May I be of no small perseverance in serving you. Hereafter may I [and my retinue] thoroughly accomplish whatever you say in accordance with this scripture you teach,[159] and if we do not act like that or if we should in any way contradict this scripture of the excellent ones, may our heads, [209] bodies, and hearts rot, fester, shrivel, and be consumed by fires. I offer my mother, demonesses, daughters, and wives into your service. May they be of no small perseverance. As they are not suitable to stand at the center, may they be placed at the outer edges of your blazing mandala. As they are not suitable to receive the choice portion [of the *gaṇacakra* offerings], may they receive the leftover saliva that is poured out.'[160]

"[Then Rudra advised his retinue:] 'Demonesses, from this day forward you will be transformed into the attendants [of Viśuddha Heruka]. For this reason you will be the helpers of this teaching and perform whatever is required. Whatever work for this teaching may arise, you must always and immediately accomplish it. I too used to practice the activities of the mistaken path, and because of that, the sufferings of immeasurable *saṃsāra* were constant. But now, through the meeting of [the buddha's] compassion with [my own] good karma, I will proceed swiftly to the buddhafield of Sukhāvatī, by means of which, may the activities of this scripture of the excellent teachings never fade. Just as a loving mother worries for her child, so you must watch over, patiently, so patiently, those holding the vows. Just as a loving sister is kind to her brother, so you must be kind, closely, so closely, to those having the oaths. In the same way a lover yearns for her beloved, so you must love, purely, so purely, those who practice the yoga. Just as a loving servant cares for her master, so you must act surely and absolutely for the excellent ones.'

"Thus the retinue of attendants, having been urged with these instructions, all went for refuge to the Mahāvīra[, the Vajra-Demon]. They all took the oath to protect the greatnesses of that teaching, offering their distinct signs, the very essences of their lives, as guarantee. Pronouncing, '*Rulurulu bhyo,*' they swore upon their own lives.

[210] "Then that *bhagavat* granted his absolute blessing, '*Oṃ rulurulu hūṃ bhyo hūṃ!*'[161] He subdued them all with a purificatory fire, and they rested in a state of mind having few worries."[162]

CHAPTER 28: "THE LAST INFERIOR LONGINGS"

"Then at the time of that age the assembly of that Maheśvara wondered, 'Amazing! This great fierce one [Rudra] was so amazingly powerful! So arrogant! So ignorant! So lustful! So egotistical! So furious! And yet he was thoroughly overcome by this Great Hero, conclusively and truly overcome, wholly and utterly overcome.

"At the time of that age the mind of Rudra read their minds, clearly understanding what they were thinking, and he said, 'O excellent attendants, do not think like that. In a previous life I made a karmic connection with an excellent attendant who is now this same spiritual friend to all with whom I have met. Therefore I finally understand my karma. I understand how I took [so many] rebirths. I have seen my karma and seen my rebirths. My karma and rebirths having become evident, I wished for some escape. [211] Inside [this Vajra-Demon's stomach,] I saw in an instant the palace of the great bliss *svastika*. A woman suffering by the pains of pregnancy might think to herself, "This is the suffering that comes before giving birth, and it is all just the direct result of all those times I had sex!" In the same way I too ascertained that this was just my karma. Then like a boulder rolling down from the peak of a steep mountain, unstoppable by anyone, by the force of my intense regret I saw and was overwhelmed with anguish. My attendants, you too must consider your own karma! May the force of your anguish roll like that boulder!'

"Then, weeping and wailing at all the unnecessary violence, he recited this expression of complete anguish:[163]

'Great compassionate one, Vajrasattva,
With supremely beautiful body the color of a stainless conch shell,
With completely pure clear light radiating like one hundred thousand suns and moons,
Hero whose luminous light-rays shine throughout the universe,
Renowned as the supreme guide and teacher of the three worlds,
Sole defender of all beings of the three realms,
Loving protector, god of compassion, I ask you to pay me attention!

Since the limit of beginningless time, mistaking the path,
Losing the path, I have wandered on the wheel of existence.
In previous lives I have erred by practicing the sins of mistaken paths,
[212] Whatever sinful deeds I have done, I was wrong and I regret.

Spreading and intensifying, the power of my karma rules me,
And I am sinking in an ocean of *saṃsāric* suffering.
My mind burns with the fires of explosive anger.
My wisdom is hidden by the enveloping darkness of ignorance.
My consciousness is drowning in an ocean of lust.
I am propelled by a mountain of fierce arrogance into bad rebirths.
I am blown through *saṃsāra* by gales of the red winds of envy.
I am bound by the tight knots of belief in a self.
I have fallen into a fire pit filled with burning coals of desire.
Unbearably terrible sufferings are falling like rain.
By these kinds of sufferings, so very hard to bear,
And by my ferocious and powerfully sinful karma, blazing like fire,

The [delicate] sprouts of my consciousness and senses are tortured.
This cannot be endured by this body of illusory *skandhas* any longer.
Compassionate loving protector, won't you endure it for me?

In my ignorance and stupidity I created terrible karma and many misdeeds,
And by the power of that karma was born as Rudra in this realm of desire.
Because of this rebirth I have become remorseful, my hopes shattered.
But despite this regret and despair, my powerful karma cannot be altered.
The force of my karma is like a wide river;
Who could suddenly stop such a torrent of powerful karma?
All of these results are arising from my own karma.
Dragged by those harsh red winds of karma
For innumerable aeons before now, [213]
I have wandered in the dark prison of *saṃsāra*.
Tutelary deity, with the blessings of your compassion,
Completely purify the obscurations of my karma and afflictions, and
Establish me now at the feet of the motherlike Loving One.
Blazingly bright like the sun and luminously clear like the moon,
The very face of compassion I was looking at but
Could not see with my water-bubble eyes,[164] blinded as they were
By a film of incessant ignorance since time without beginning.
Protector of beings, where have you been all this time?

Because of this totally unbearable and fiercely powerful karma,
I tremble violently with fear, utterly terrified.
As I emit these anguished cries over and over,
Wailing out with misery and destitution,
Loving and compassionate protector, if you do not heed me now,
When I eventually die and separate from my body,
Friendless and helpless, I will be led away by the Lord of Death.
Unable to be accompanied by their close ones who remain in the world,
Others just like me are led away by the power of their karma, all alone.
Because at that time I too will have no protector, no refuge,
Without delaying until later,
Perform the appropriate [violent] direct intervention right away.

Beings just like me who are tortured by karma
Have been conceptualizing wrongly since time without beginning,
And thus they have been unable to free themselves from the *saṃsāric* states of the three realms.
For innumerable aeons, over all sorts of rebirths, [214]
The number of material bodies we have taken is endless.

If all the flesh and bones were collected, they would equal the entire universe in size.
If all the pus and blood were gathered, it would be as big as a vast ocean.
If all the karmic propensities were put together, they would be unimaginable; words could not express.
But despite all these repeated and constant births and deaths in the three realms,
My karmic activities have been utterly useless, every one a waste.
If I took from these innumerable rebirths
The karma of just one lifetime
And really practiced for the purpose of unsurpassable enlightenment,
Just that karmic activity would have a purpose,
And my goal, the primordially present *nirvāṇa,* would be attained.
But instead, due to the force of my karma and the strength of my afflictions,
I continue to wander in *saṃsāra,* adopting these bodies, these webs of flesh and blood,
Locked in this prison of cyclic existence with these unbearable sufferings.
As with these overwhelmingly fierce sufferings,
All these evil deeds arise from my own karma.
Therefore, great compassionate one, please cut this stream of bad karma,
And please turn back these winds of afflicted karma.

Due to the power of my ignorant and confused karma,
I have wandered eternally within the darkness of misunderstanding.
Will you not clear it with the light-rays from your lamp of wisdom?
The effects of my karmic misdeeds are unbearable.
Will you not perform the activities of great compassion?
I am falling into an abyss of errors.
Will you not catch me with your swift hands of speedy compassion?
I am tormented by the diseases of the unbearable three poisons.
[215] Will you not nurse me with the medicine of your compassionate skillful means?
I am burning in the painful fires that are the ripening of my own karma.
Will you not send down the continuous rain of your cooling compassion?
I am sinking in the swamp of *saṃsāric* sufferings.
Will you not pull me out with the hook of your compassionate skillful means?
Having trained again and again in the *saṃsāric* states of the three realms,
When I eventually attain the fruition of awareness,
Then why would I seek the compassion of the noble ones? There would be no purpose.

Who would call "compassionate"
He who leaves others under the power of their karmic propensities?
You, O hero, are the mighty lord of compassion, so
Since even the propensities of our earlier karmic connections have been overpowered,
Do not procrastinate or be indifferent and lazy!
From the essence [of enlightenment] look upon me now, O lord of the compassionate conquerors!'

Smashing thus the mountain of his own pride, Rudra emanated in the body of a lion and offered himself as a seat for the [buddha's] bottom."[165]

CHAPTER 29: "THOROUGHLY PURIFYING THE CONTINUUM"

"Then that Vajra-Demon grew tired of that karmic demon's mistaken views, and so as to cut the continuum of his karmic obscurations, strongly scolded him with the following eight reprimands:

[216] "'Sinful one, made strong with error you have wandered on the wheel of existence since time without beginning. It is obvious that you are the root of your own misdeeds and that all [these sufferings] have arisen from yourself.

"'For all these innumerable aeons you have taken so many bodies in so many rebirths that the corpses would be numberless; the flesh and bones would fill an entire three-thousand-fold world system and the pus and blood would be a swirling ocean. And even so it has all been useless, a complete waste. No one else has done anything; it has all been your own karma. If you had only practiced with an aim [of enlightenment] for a tiny part of that time, you certainly would have obtained buddhahood by now. The great ones with power over their desires, who have completely renounced their bodies, would give even their own flesh, bones, and blood for any being who is tormented by hunger. So if you had attained the bliss of stainless complete liberation, how can one describe the [boundless virtues] that such a view of the profound meaning would have made possible? Instead you were too cowardly to offer your own body and remained totally obsessed with the extremes of desire. You spun constantly through the three realms, tormented by excruciating diseases. Therefore, since it was you who tried to bind the sky, this imprisonment of cyclic existence is definitely your own fault.

"'This wandering in the expanse of darkness is without question due to your own sins of extraordinary ignorance. This sinking in a swamp without freedom is without question due to your own sins of desire, craving, and yearning. This constant torture by the heat of hostile mind is without question due to your own sins of hot evil karma [of anger]. [217] This oppression by a mountain of suffering is without question due to your own sins caused by your mounds of arrogance. This being blown by the winds through *saṃsāra*, spinning and falling, is without question due to your own sins caused by the winds of karma.[166]

"'Rudra, you who torture yourself, you are a son of the conquerors since primordial time, so why have you been cycling on the wheel of existence? It is because of your own karma. Your mind itself is like the sky, but it has been obscured by clouds of adventitiously appearing forms. In order to completely purify these conceptually appearing forms, they must be scattered [into the sky of the *dharmadhātu*] by the wisdom that is like the winds at the end of an aeon. At first you mistook the commands [of your teacher, Invincible Youth]. Then a mountain of manifesting [arrogance] built up. Then the wish-fulfilling jewel [of your mind itself] was incinerated,[167] and finally by practicing the four entities [of *saṃsāra*], the meaning of the yoga of the Mahāyāna was not understood, wrongly realized, partially understood,[168] imperfectly understood. Then, not practicing properly, you were bound to a continuous karmic path through [many] negative rebirths as *piśācas* and so forth, until finally it all culminated in the result of this mistaken existence [as Rudra].

"'Oh dear! Negative karma is so pitiful! I am skilled in the activities of the teachings, and the moment for these teaching activities has arrived. In order to extract this wanderer of the realms of negative rebirths from these *saṃsāric* realms, I must cut the karmic continuum of his negative karma. This one whose concepts have developed into objective entities must be killed with the weapon of the sky-*vajra*.

[218] "'In this world that is an entrance in the eastern direction,[169] you have cut a path to correct liberation. Fierce and vile ghoul, you have obscured thusness. With a perfectly discerning intellect, inquire and investigate; [you will find] it all arises from yourself. Due to the persistence and strength of your errors, your grasping to "I" and conceptualizing of "mine," you made yourself into the leader of those who take birth in the evil realms. But that was just a concept of self and therefore will be destroyed by the strength of the sky that is without self.

"'With the great method for overpowering and subduing, with the power to manifest the cutting, and with the great blessings of conquest, the lord of the three poisons and the hindrances must be smashed: *Anaya mahāśūnyatā akotayanāṃ! Sarvapāpaṃ matraṅgara rudranāṃ! Sarva pāpaṃ khatraṅka rudranāṃ! Sarva pāpaṃ akarśa rudranāṃ!*'[170] Because all is unborn emptiness, with this killing there was no killing. This miraculous display of illusory purification was the vow of killing definitively, a vow of great compassion. [Rudra] was not killed in an ordinary sense.

"Having freed [Rudra's] consciousness from his body and made it into a *vajra,* [the buddha] brought that same [consciousness] back down [into Rudra's body]: the supreme vow. He reassembled the consciousness by pronouncing, '*hūṃ*.' Rudra descended back into his body, just as he had been before, and without having been weakened at all, he was purified within great bliss.[171] This *vajra*-resurrection vow is the vow of all the conquerors. [219] As for the life force of someone killed by the *vajra*-weapon, it is the mistaken view that dies into the *vajra*. And since this [life force] will never again arise, how can this be considered a resurrection? [Rudra's] consciousness, still embodied, was completely freed from the *saṃsāric* realms. Now a noble one (*ārya*), he was established in the deathless *vajra*-mind of enlightenment. He became a river of the ambrosias of emptiness and wisdom, a consumer of the terrible poisons and a healer of all, a supreme medicine for reviving the dead."

Then the Lord of Laṅka spoke these words: "Thus that Black Rudra's mental continuum was thoroughly purified. He definitively saw the exceptional meaning."

CHAPTER 30: "INTENSELY EXHORTING THE INTENTIONS OF ALL THE BUDDHAS"

"Then so that he might be brought into the ascertainment of thusness, Rudra raised the wheel of [the buddha's] feet with his head and, aspiring intensely, proclaimed his mind to all [the buddhas] in these words, fully exhorting them with this song called 'Exhorting the Intention of All the Buddhas':

"'*Oṃ*. All phenomena are naturally pure, and so too am I completely pure by nature. Lord and very supreme treasure, commitment of all the *tathāgatas*, you engage in establishing all the infinite sentient beings without exception in the supreme state. Therefore so that all the oceans of conquerors gather, please generate me as a treasury body.[172]

[220] "'Supreme crown jewel of wisdom, unsurpassable mass of brilliance, all-victorious one who is the condensation of all the great jewels of the buddhas, to you I pay homage. Supreme chief of the wisdom-jewels, bearer of the supreme excellence of the *vajra*, through your principal vow, as king of the gods, please grant me [the initiations] too.

"'Please grant me the initiation of direct perception by means of the *vajras* [of body, speech, and mind], whereby all the buddhas may then grant me their initiations. So that I may become supreme among the exalted ones and attain the supreme state, please arouse the *vajra*. Because you preside as the *vajra*-king, you are the *vajra* of body, speech, and mind. With the supreme *vajra*-sacrament itself, grant the initiations of the three groups of accomplishments. The *vajra* that is characteristic of all phenomena, that *vajra* is utterly without characteristics. With the *vajra*-like yoga illuminate all meaning as the *vajra* itself.

"'This is the melody of the buddhas: May I maintain the vow of the wisdom-being (*ye shes sems dpa'*) and always hold to the ultimate austerities of Vajrasattva. *Hūṃ!* May I follow and protect the vow of Vajrasattva. Wisdom-being, draw near. King of awareness, think of me always. God of the secrets, please nourish me.

"'Grant the supreme realization and generate delight in me. Enact the passion and the craving after all desires for me. [221] Foremost buddha, holder of unvarying compassion, perform all the activities and transform my mind into goodness. *Tathāgatas* of the three times, establish me as a *vajra* holder, a commitment-being (*dam tshig sems dpa'*). *Tathāgatas*: Rejoice! Rejoice! Hey! Embrace me with your *vajras* and never forsake me!

"'Hey! Space of the *vajra*-dharma, highest of all, woman of the great nonabiding passion, supreme source of all without exception, excellence of supreme bliss, you are the leader of all the vows, the mother who gives birth to Vajrasattva. Accomplish the purposes of sentient beings and consummate the compassionate union with the activities. In order to activate the source of all the good qualities of the buddhas, unsurpassable jewel-*vajra*, by the song of dharma-*vajra*, may the activity-*vajra* be performed.'

"[Then Viśuddha Heruka bestowed the initiations, reciting,] '*Oṃ:*[173] Entering into the natural mandala of spontaneous accomplishment. *Mūṃ:* Resting in the primordial mandala of thusness. *Hūṃ:* Abiding in the root mandala of the mind of enlightenment.

"'*Hūṃ hūṃ hūṃ viśva vajra krodha jvāla maṇḍala phaṭ [phaṭ]! Halāhala raṃ!*[174] The purification of the disciple; purified in the mandala of the wrathful one. *Takem takem phaṭ! Halāhala raṃ! Tīkṣṇa tīkṣṇa khaṃ! Krodha krodha yaṃ!*[175] All things are purified within emptiness.'

"Then the son of the perfect but unreal Vajra Bhurkuṃkūṭa, that demon-taming Vajra-Demon, conferred [to Rudra] the vow of *vajra*-strength. '*Oṃ āḥ hūṃ:* Conferring the blessing vows of body, speech, and mind. *Oṃ vajra amṛta ehyehi sarva mana hūm hrīḥ ha:*[176] Conferring the initiation vow.

"'*Samaya ho:* Fully taking the vows. *Samayastvaṃ:* Promising to keep all the vows.

"'*Idante naragante vāri hṛdaye nāma bastināṃ samaya rākṣasī siti pina vajra amṛtodakaṃ:* Granting the excellent vows.'[177]

"Then again that karmic demon [Rudra] prayed to the deity of his own lineage, exhorting him thusly: 'You who are my tutelary deity[178] with whom I am connected from a previous lifetime, through [the meeting] of my karmic propensities with his compassion, may this fall just now.'

"Within the sky-sphere [at the heart] of noble Vajrasattva, [upon] a sun-mandala, dawned the essential '*hūṃ*' with light-rays flowing forth[179] and dissolving into Rudra's heart. Whereby [the deity of] his excellent lineage was ascertained.

"'*Haṃ*': Seeing [the face of his tutelary deity], he was completely purified. Everything was seen to be distinct and completely perfect.

"He was given his *vajra* name and was posted at the secret door to the Vajrayāna."[180]

CHAPTER 31: "THE PROPHECY THAT BLACK LIBERATOR WILL NOT STRAY INTO DEVIATION"

[223] "Then the general assembly of that karmic demon's gathered attendants had their individual karmas purified, saw many buddhas, and had their mental continuums refined by light-rays of blessings. Whereby the karma, the causes for the ripening of that karma, and the limitless previous and future rebirths of each were understood in an instant.

"Their doubts having been resolved, grieving and weeping, all the great gods such as Maheśvara and so forth made this plea: 'Lord of the dance, please listen and consider us. We who craved for Rudra's extremes, due to the strength of our karma and its ripening, have not been liberated from this net of *saṃsāra* by the subtle words of the teachings. [Our eyes] have not been opened by the seeing eye of profound wisdom, so we do not have the intellect of intrinsically aware wisdom and have not been convinced by your clearly excellent counsels. Since we have not been captured by the lightning lasso of your dance moves, we remain stupefied by the ocean's waves that are stirred up by karmic consciousness; we have not recognized precisely that as thusness. By clinging to ignorance, our own minds, and the self, we have been misguided. [Now,] with extreme regret, having understood how misguided we have been, we go for refuge to you, Mahāvīra. In order to purify the entities [of dualistic thinking], we offer our bodies as your seat. With your compassionate skillful means, please accept.' [224] And thus they each offered their bodies as the throne for his bottom.

"Then the great *nāgas*, Black Neck and so forth, grieving and weeping, made this plea: 'Splendorous king and lord, please consider us. We who have wandered in this net of cyclic existence have become completely bound by the five fetters. Yet nobody is bound and nothing is binding. We are bound by the karma of self-grasping conceptualizations. In this prison of the three cities of self-grasping,[181] in various bodies, consciousnesses, and realms, our consciousnesses have been imprisoned by the jail-cells of *saṃsāra*.[182] As long as the knots of self-grasping had not been loosened, the knots that held us tight were incessant. With your compassionate skill in untying the knots, please free us from these sufferings that are so indestructible and hard to loosen.' And thus they offered their [snakelike] bodies as ornaments for his body.

"Then the demon-kings, Shatreng Sengpu (Sha treng bseng bu) and so forth, grieving and weeping, made this plea: 'Great erotic hero, please consider us. We who have wandered through the islands of anguish have been tormented and burned by great blazing fires. Yet nobody has been burnt and there has been no fire. It arose from the fury that grew from impatience itself. Our minds have burned with explosive anger, [225] but as long as this self-grasping, this fire that has blazed within, has not been extinguished, the scorching and the torments have been constant. On account of these sufferings that are so unstoppable and hard to pacify, please send down a steady rain of cooling compassion. As a magnet gathers together iron filings, embrace us now, Mahāvīra, into your service.' Thus they each offered their skulls filled with blood.

"Then the assembly of those who made extensive errors, grieving and weeping, made this plea: 'All-illuminating lamp that dispels the darkness, please consider us. We who have wandered through the gloomy darkness have lost the unmistaken path and have become thoroughly bewildered. Yet nobody has been blocked and nothing has blocked [our way]. We have been enveloped by the darkness of an ignorance that has been confused with regard to the self. Consciousness has been dimmed by a deluded darkness, and as long as this dark confusion about the self has not been illuminated, the blackness obscuring everything will be constant. For the suffering of the dense gloom from which it is so hard to awaken, please demonstrate the lamp that illuminates the supreme knowledge.' Thus did they go well for refuge.

"Then the assembly of humans and nonhumans, grieving and weeping, made this plea: 'Doctor of skillful compassion, please consider us. We who have wandered through the three cities [226] have been consumed by a chronic disease. Yet nobody has been consumed and nothing has been consuming. We were consumed by the illness of self-grasping, afflictions, and ignorance. Our consciousnesses have been afflicted by unbearable pains, and as long as we have the chronic illness of grasping at things, the pains that hurt everywhere will be incessant. With the medicine of skillful compassion, please cure us of the sufferings that are inescapable and from which it is so hard to recover.' Thus they offered their bodies into servitude.

"Then the assembly of *yakśas*, grieving and weeping, made this plea: 'Ship of skillful compassion, please consider us. We who have wandered in the oceans of *saṃsāra* have sunk beneath the waves of *saṃsāra*. Yet nobody has been pushed under and nothing has pushed. We have been pushed under by a mountain of graspings at conceptual objects. [Our consciousnesses] have been tossed about in *saṃsāra* by the torrential tides of karma, and as long as the currents of grasping at things are not altered, these torrents of ferociously powerful karma will be ceaseless. Please carry us with the ship of skillful compassion from the sufferings that are inescapable and from which it is so hard to be extracted.' Thus did they go well for refuge.

"Then the assembly of *bhuta*-spirits, grieving and weeping, made this plea: 'King of the self-arising ambrosia, please consider us. [227] We who have wandered through the islands of powerful poisons have become crazed and unconscious. Yet nobody has been poisoned and there has been no poison. We have been crazed by the poison of erroneous and mistaken views. Our consciousnesses were afflicted by the illness of the great poison, and as long as the root of those poisons swirling within has not been cut, the sufferings of the feverish poisonings will be constant. Please anoint the sufferings that are so terrible and hard to bear with the ambrosia of self-arising purity.' Thus did they go well for refuge.

"Then again that Vajra-Demon spoke:[183] 'So it is. Well spoken, children of good lineage. Due to the Rudras, you have each been spinning [through *saṃsāra*]. By the Rudras each of you has been tortured. Due to self-grasping you have each been spinning. By self-grasping each of you has been tortured. Due to angers you have each been spinning. By angers each of you has been tortured. Due to delusions you have each been spinning. By delusions each of you has been tortured. Due to desires you have each been spinning. By desires each of you has been tortured. Due to the four rivers [of suffering][184] you have each been spinning. By the four rivers [of suffering] each of you has been tortured. Due to mistaken views you have each been spinning. By mistaken views each of you has been tortured.

"'Since you have been, in all ways and since the very beginning, children of the conqueror, why have you been spinning through the three cities? It has been only the karma brought about by your own conceptualizations. [228] These waves on the ocean of karma, these knots of self-grasping, this great fire blazing within, this darkness enveloping everything, this chronic illness of conceptualizing things, these torrential currents that carry you away, this root of the poisons swirling within, none of these have been purified as the self-arisen *vajra*. Thus these wishes, prayers, yearnings, and lamentations for [help] from another are like someone imploring the mirage of a much-desired oasis. If what is right here is not enjoyable, how will something else make you happy? Though you have been resting in bliss since the beginning of time, now you search for happiness in some desirable object. By seeking, you will absolutely never find. Although you have a mind that [wants to] eradicate suffering, precisely this is the cause for suffering to manifest. It is like producing butter from pure milk; if the nature of butter is not already present [as the cream], simply churning away, even by a king of immeasurably supreme means, will not bring [the butter]. Similarly, if one's own thusness is sought after, even if by a king, it will not be found. So why do you seek for happiness from another? Such childishly ignorant minds are so heartbreaking!'[185]

"Then, Lord of Laṅka, the general assembly gathered, Maheśvara and so forth, made this prayer: 'O great being, we seek to view the suchness of our individual [minds]. Let us fully see it just as it is.'

"Thus that great being spoke: 'O gathered assembly, [229] sons of the conqueror, if you wish to see the suchness of each of you, you must enter the unique door to the three great mandalas. Moreover, you must enter the door to the unique root mandala of the mind of enlightenment. Why? Because the three great mandalas are not separate from each of your individual suchnesses, and moreover they are gathered in the root mandala of the mind of enlightenment.'

"So the assembly of the great gathering[186] replied with the prayer, 'Great Hero, let us enter correctly into the three mandalas.'

"And because of those words, that great being spoke: 'You children who have engaged in the yoga, having been led from the six worlds, rest in the [first] level of Indefinite Transformation, on the boundary between *nirvāṇa* and *saṃsāra*.'

"Then the gathered assembly made this prayer: 'Great Hero, consider us. We, the assembly of gathered worthy ones, are seeking to enter this door. Please accept us as the sons of the conqueror.'

"The great being spoke: 'You, great assembly of gathered worthy ones, proceed into bliss! [230] Excellently proceed! Those who proceed through this secret door of the *Scripture of Accomplishment*,[187] never again return [to *saṃsāra*].'

[231.4] "Then the great being spoke:[188] 'In what do you delight? In what do you have faith? To what do you aspire? What is your wish?'

"The gathered assembly answered, 'We who are worthy, we take delight in the mind of rapturous great bliss. We have faith in the meaning of the supreme state. Amazing! In this pleasure grove of supreme bliss, practicing the hardships of the buddhas, we aspire to liberate all sentient beings.'

[231.2] "Then again those in the gathered assembly made these prayers: 'Since the limits of beginningless time, whatever misdeeds we have performed under the power of ignorance and mistaken conceptualization, all those we confess individually.'

"Then again those in the gathered assembly made these prayers: 'Awareness-holding *vajra* king, in order to thoroughly liberate us in the same way you liberate *saṃsāra,* please bestow the *vajra* sun.'[189]

[230.7] "Then the gathered assembly, with devotion and joy, yearning intensely for the yoga, made this prayer: 'In the inestimably marvelous palace, where all the oceans of conquerors dwell, aspiring intensely to ascertain the yoga, I go for refuge to the *vajra* lineage.'

[230.1] "Then those in the gathered assembly in this way generated the superior mind [that aspires to] become enlightened: 'We limitless sentient beings, while we may be buddhas in the sense [of suchness], by the power of conceptualization we [wander] through *saṃsāra.* Therefore we generate the supreme mind of enlightenment. The mind itself is buddha, but it is obscured by darkness and thus unrecognized. Through this path of the mind of enlightenment, may we be established in the level of buddhahood.'

[232.2] "Then again the gathered assembly made a prayer of exhortation for the vows: 'Yogin of the undivided secret, come forth from the space of the nondual meaning. This space is the indestructible *vajra,* a singularity beyond [simple] togetherness or separation. Thus in this very space of the three secrets [of body, speech, and mind], perform with nondual steadfastness [in applying the vows].'[190]

"Then that great being spoke: '*Vajra*-wielding yogins, if you are one-pointedly definite in holding the *vajra* [vows], then you will be equal to the three secrets. Therefore I grant the vow of the undivided *vajra.*[191] These vows of the undivided *vajra* arise from the space of [your own] three secrets [of *vajra*-speech, -body, and -mind]. If these vows of the three mandalas are accomplished, there will never come a time when they are broken.'

[231.7] "Then again the gathered assembly made this prayer: 'Supreme conqueror being, may we practice in perfect accordance with you. The inconceivable and marvelous practices are performed in order to benefit all beings. May the enslaved universes that comprise the infinity of *saṃsāra* be liberated. May those who are confined be released. May those who have not been relieved be relieved, and in the buddhafields of *nirvāṇa,* may they be united with the enlightened essence.'

[232.6] "Again the gathered assembly prayed, 'Dharma brother who is beyond togetherness or separation, so that even for us of the contrary races it will be impossible to transgress the one vow, apply the [ambrosia of] reinforcement to the vow-bound.'

"Then again that great being spoke these words: 'Excellent ones of the three secrets, if one of you becomes deceived [and breaks the vows], then a completely infuriated great scorpion will emerge from the heart of that fallen one and drink his blood.'[192] Thus were the excellent vows granted.

"Then again that Excellent Being spoke: 'Future buddhas of intelligence, in order for you to generate the unsurpassable wisdom, refine your mental continuums and enter into [the mandalas of] the three secrets. Look at the essential mirror of your [mind]. By seeing the great secret, secret, and most secret[193] arrayed in those three places, you will arrive at thusness. This self-arising suchness that is not apart [from one's own physical elements] should not be discussed with those of small minds. If it is discussed, your intense vows will have disintegrated and you will burn in a place of blazing great fires.'[194] Thus was the excellent vow imparted.

[230.4] "Then again the gathered assembly prayed, 'In this inestimable [palace] of spontaneously accomplishing great bliss,[195] through the four gateways to complete liberation,[196] please open the door to the compassion of the [four] immeasurables, and display the [mandala of the] divine face of the loving one.'

"Then that great being spoke these words: 'Amazing! Assembly of gathered worthy ones, in order to block all the entrances to *saṃsāra* and lead you onto the path to enlightenment, the secret *vajra* door [of the initiations] must be opened.' Then light-rays streamed forth from the splendor of his smiling countenance and [dissolved into the assembly,] whereby the door for entering into ascertainment of the meaning was opened.'[197]

[233.5] "Lord of Laṅka, at the time of that age, when those in that gathered assembly entered the excellence of the three secrets in this way, some came to abide in the 'yoga of aspiration,' some came to abide in the 'yoga of opening the great lineage,' some came to abide in the 'yoga of the great confirmation,' some came to abide in the 'yoga of attaining the great prophecy,' [234] and some came to abide in the yoga of the perfected great dynamism.'[198]

"Similarly at the time of that age, those of the general gathered assembly were initiated with the *vajra*-name initiation. Some were called Vajra Sprout. Similarly some were called Dharma Sprout. Some were called Jewel Sprout. Some were called Moon's Dynamism. Some were called Sun's Splendor. Some were called Lion's Dynamism. Some were called Sky Vajra.[199] Of the more horrible of them, some were called Vajra Jackal. Some were called Vajra Time.

Some were called Vajra Bias-Tamer. Some were called Vajra Cemetery. Some were called Vajra Emissary (*king ka ra*).[200]

"Rudra himself was named Vajra Zombie, Lord of the Charnel Grounds. He would remain for a long time in this great and good aeon under the title of Protector of the Vast Yoga, the Spiritual Friend, Black Excellence (*Legs ldan Nag po*) and act as protector for all the other dharma protectors. After that aeon, in the [buddha]field of the World of the Lower Direction (*'og gi phyogs*), he will be called Smeared with Ashes [235] and will attain complete buddhahood as the *tathāgata* called Song of the Mighty Ashes. Thus will he attain his prophecy.

"Lord of Laṅka, at the time of that age, the six realms of that entire universe quivered, shivered and trembled, shuddered, quaked and shook, swayed, reeled and rocked, rolled, shifted and cracked, crashed, boomed and roared, thundered, resounded and reverberated. The outside was turned in, and the inside turned out. The heights in the east were low in the west. The heights in the west were low in the east. The heights in the north were low in the south. The heights in the south were low in the north. All the universe became miracles, openly praising [the fierce one and his retinue].

"Some of the worldly gods rejoiced in the excellent secret suchness. Some attained endurance in the unborn dharma. Some were completely purified as the flawless and perfect eye of the dharma. Some were placed on the level of no return, and some attained the prophecy.

"At the time of that age, the horrible skull-bearers, such as Rudra Black Liberator and so forth, [236] prostrated full-length on the floor before that ferocious great *vajra* being, and having been taken into the way of the yoga, they joined their palms together, bowed their heads, and sang this prayer: 'A *ho sukha kṣa parya deva śi śi*. Amazing! Great being! Abundant movements are arising; are these the blessings of reality? Abundant forms are arising, forms purified in place; are these the forms of compassion? Abundant sounds are arising, sounds purified in place; are these the sounds of wisdom? Abundant smells are arising, smells purified in place; are these the smells of the mind of enlightenment? Abundant tastes are arising, tastes purified in place; are these the tastes of *samādhi?* Abundant physical sensations are arising, sensations purified in place; are these the [blissful] sensations of the vows? Abundant feelings are arising, feelings purified in place; are these the feelings of equanimity? Unlike anything before, we feel a dynamic power being born, magical displays being born, the attainment of empowerments of new abilities, and the dawning of awareness.

"'Thus is this source, this excellent intention of all the buddhas, profound, and thus it is vast, supremely excellent, sublime, exquisite. [237] Great being, who has made us see this, you are our father, our mother. Great being, though others may abide in this excellence, none are like you, our father and our mother. May we transgress cyclic existence but never transgress the teachings.

"'O great being, whatever you say we will do. To any person who abides in this excellence of yours, we will bow our heads as if he were the crown jewel of the lord of the gods. And we will also guard, protect, and hide from dangers that person's wife, sons, daughters, wealth, aides, servants, friends, paternal and maternal relatives, followers, home, and country—any who are protectors of the dharma. We will completely destroy and crush any human or nonhuman who might harm these dharma protectors. We will define and control a [protective] boundary around them. No matter what they wish and ask of us, we will act as their servants and perfectly achieve it.

"'As long as they are protecting the dharma and are involved in the dharma, we will accomplish whatever they wish of us. In order to stay connected to us, they should recite the secret mantras of the great deities, [238] these sources of the worldly signs of actualization, which have been empowered by the great *vajra* sorcerer [Vajrapāṇi]. And one should always carry the sacred substances, the signs of virtue and the symbolic supports.[201] What for? Because those are our vows.[202]

"'O great being, it is like this: This power that manifests our Secret Mantra has four branches of propitiation and accomplishment. *Oṃ burkur mahā pranāya bhurtsi bhurki byi ga gi bima na se e ho śimi ucchuṣma krodha hūṃ hūṃ hūṃ phaṭ phaṭ phaṭ svāhā.* O great being, that is the branch of propitiation. *Oṃ bhuru kurma apraṇa bhurtsi kiphyi manasye kha sho mog krodha hūṃ hūṃ phaṭ phaṭ svā hā.* O great being, that should be known as the near propitiation. *Oṃ bhuru kuru itsi kiphyi ucchuṣma krodha hūṃ phaṭ.* O great being, that should be known as the accomplishment. *Oṃ bhurkurti phaṭ.* O great being, that should be known as the great accomplishment. Great being, if one completes each [of these mantras] one hundred thousand times,[203] whatever activities one engages in will be accomplished without any doubt.[204]

"'Why is this so? It is because the buddhas of the three times [239] have empowered these mantras. Furthermore, even the great *vajra* sorcerer [Vajrapāṇi] attained the mundane signs of actualization by means of these [mantras]. We too have attained the magical signs of actualization by these means. Great being, if someone to whom this Secret Mantra is entrusted performs this practice but has no signs of actualization, then there is no truth [to what we say], we have not ascertained the full extent of the teachings, and because what we claimed will have violated the excellence of the truth, may our heads rot until they burst open and we vomit blood. Great being, therefore regarding this Secret Mantra there should be no doubts; for whoever [practices it, many] benefits will be accomplished and miracles generated. Thusly do the excellent ones explain for the sake of the foolish ones why one should believe in the buddha's word. If one relies always on these four branches, it will be excellent.' Thus they prayed.

"That Excellent Being spoke: 'Ah ho! Just so! Praises! Yes! Definitely! True! Excellent! You horrible ones together with your wives, your consorts, your sons and daughters, aides and servants, for those who are inseparable from love, you will act as their mother. If one is inseparable from affection, you will act as his sister. If one is inseparable from perseverance, you will act as his servant. If one is inseparable from the mind of enlightenment, you will act as his son. If one is beyond togetherness or separation, you will act as his student. If one is swift when invoked, you will act as his envoy. And if one acts according to the teachings, you will apply the teachings.' Thus did he arrange the Mahāyoga, appointing them as dharma-protectors for the teachings and for beings."[205]

Appendix B

Dunhuang Liberation Rite

TRANSCRIPTION OF PT42/ITJ419

PASSAGE 1

de la sgrol ba'i las mdo tsam zhig smos pa ni thog mar slobs pon drod la bab pas las rdzogs par bya'o zhes 'byung/ slobs pon drod dang myi ldan na las bcus bya'o zhes 'byung/ 'di gnyis ltar ma ldan bas las byas pa ni/ [r19] jigs byed chen po brgyad/ dbang du ma gyur pas 'khor yan cad kyang 'phral du myi bde ba cher 'byung zhing thugs rjes cher gzung ba yang gnas 'khyams par 'gyur te/ ma legs pa cher 'byung bas rang bzod [d]ang rdeng drod myed par/ lung dang man ngag myi ldan ba rnams kyis ni las bya bar ma gsungso/ de ltar slobs pon dang las gong ma pa rnam gnyis dang ldan bas/ khyad bar gyi dus gcig du gnas byin kyis brlabs pa'i phi nang gi mchod pa rnams rgyas par bshams ste/ slobs pon gyis tshogs su 'dus pa rnams dbang bskur [r20] byin kyis brlabs nas/ so so'i lha'i ti nge 'dzin sgrom du stsal te/ chos kyi bdag po dpal shri he ru ka'i snying po/ Om ru lu ru lu hung bhyo ha na ha na hung phad ces mthun bar brgya rtsa brgyad bzlas nas gtor ma nang pa gcig sbyar te/ dpal chen po'i 'khor dang bchas pa dang/ tshogs la dbang ba thams cad mchod de las 'di grub thig/ bgegs gyis bar myi chod cig dngos grub thob par gyur cig pa la stsogs pa smon bco[?][1] bgyi/ phyogs rnams dam tshig nyams pa bskang du stsald/ phyi'i gtor ma gcig sbyar nas/ tshangs [r21] pa dang/ brgya byin dang/ rgyal po chen po dang/ phyogs skyong dang/ lha chen po dang/ lha chen po dang/ klu chen po la stsogs pa'i nang na/ gsang ba'i dam tsig la myi gnas pa rnams la stsal cing tshogs dang mchod pa 'di'i dus su/ bgegs dang gnod pa dang/ dngos grub la bgegs dang/ gnod pa myi byed par dam stsal nas/ phyi'i mtshams bsrung bar gtang zhing/ nang pa'i tshogs kyi dus su dam tshig gsang ba la myi gthogs pa rnams kyis myi tshor bar tin nge 'dzin gyis kyang mtshams gcad/ byin kyis brlab bo/ de nas slobs pon gyis dam la ma gthogs [r22] pa rnams bskrad cing mtshams gcad do/ rnal 'byor pa ni dbang gi las yin te/ so so'i 'khor 'dus rnams lha'i khro bo dbang gi tshul du bsgyur te/ yun ring du bsnyen pa dang/ 'dzab sgom bya'o/ de nas gang zhig thugs rjes gzung bar bya ba de/ dkyil 'khor gyi dbus su rdo rje rgya gram gcig/ rlung gi dkyil 'khor gyi steng na gnas pa'i dbus su bzhag la kha nub phyogs su bstan te/ phyogs tshogs su 'dus pa rnams ti nge 'dzin bstun nas/ mye'i bskal pas las dang nyon mongs snye bag chags thams cad bsreg [r23] rlung gi bskal pas bag chags thams cad bskyod g.yeng/ chu'i bskal pas bkrus shing dag par bsams nas phyi nang bsre zhes 'byung ste/ yungs kar la ngan song sbyong ba'i skying pos bzla zhing/ thugs rje'i gnas de la dag cing/ bag chags sbyang bar bya'o/ sbyor ba'i las kyis kyang bag cags sbyang ba dang/ gnas brtab par bya'o/ sgrol bar byed pa'i skyes bu des kyang/ sgrol ba nyi mar bsgyur nas dmyig g.yas pa nyi mar bsgyur pas mye'i bskal pas bag chags bsregs/ dmyig g.yon pa zla bar bsgyur pas chu'i bskal pas bkru [r24] zhing bshal/ ha ha zhes gad mo bsgrags pa'i rlung gis gtor g.yengs ste/ thugs rje'i gnas de/ shel sgong ba yongs su dag par byas nas/ spyi bo'i steng du zla gam 'byam yas pa gcig bsams te tshogs kyi dkyil 'khor du 'dus pa'i 'phags pa thams cad spyan drangs nas/ bag chags sbyong ba'i 'phrin las rgyun myi chad par mdzad pa'i ti nge 'dzin 'thun bar bgyi/ thugs rje'i gnas de'i ltag pa na/ srin mo dus 'tshan ma zhes bya ba nag mo ral pa chan dre'u dkar mo zhon zhing/ lchags kyi dra ba ste len du 'gel zhing thogs pa [r25] gcig dus las myi 'pho bar las byed/ 'chi bdag ces bya ba/ bdud lchags kyi sta re thogs pa gcig 'chi bdag gi las byed par bsams las/ spyi bor yi ge krong sngo gnag gcig bsams te/ sgrol bar byed pa'i skyes bu de/ ta ki ra tsa'i ti nge 'dzin du zhugs nas/ [. . .][2] ces mtshon gyis bsgral/ spyi ba'I drong las/ mtshon shag ti mang pos dral zhing gshegs nas/ rnam par shes pa phyung nas gtso bo la phul te/ gtso bor 'khor 'dus pa thams cad kyi kha la lan re gthugs ste/ dngos grub sbyin ba dang/ rgyu de'i gnas [r26] ma nor par bstab pa dang/ 'dzab sgom bzla ba dang/ lha'i ti nge 'dzin khugs par bya ba dang/ rnam par shes pa lan du 'gul ba'i grangs rnams yid la zin cing/ bsam ba'i rnams yid la gsal bar byas nas/ rnam par shes pa slobs pon gyis sos bzung nas/ dkyil 'khor gyi thog du dor te mtshan brtag par bya'o/ dkyil 'khor thog du 'gul ba ma chad na dngos grub thob/ dkyil 'khor gyi phugs su ltas na/ 'phags pa thams cad mnyes/ ste mo gas na bzang/ g.yas g.yos su ltas pa ni/ rnal 'byor pa'i las byed pa [r27] la bgegs myed de/ dkyil 'khor sgor lta ba dang/ thur du lta ba ni dngos grub myi thob cing/ bar chad kyi bges yod pas tshogs phyi mas kyang brnan te bya'o.

PASSAGE 2

de la sgrol ba las ni/ mchod pa'i rgyu yang rnam pa lnga ste/ theg pa chen po'i chos la skur pa [v33] 'debs pa dang/ 'phags pa la 'khu dang/ dam tshig myed par dkyil 'khor du 'ong ba dang/ lta ba logs pa dang/ theg pa chen po'i chos la rgyud ched par byed pa rnams la'o/ de la sgrol ba ni gzhi snying rje chen pos gzung 'tshal te gang la bya ba'i dngos po'i gnas lngar/ dpa' bo 'bru lnga bkod pa ni/ khams gsum du myi skye ba'i thabs/ sems kyi rgyan rnam lnga zhes kyang bya/ Om spyi gtsug du gzhag pa [v34] ni lha ma yin gyi lam gcad pa'o/ hri lche la bkod pa ni/ myi'i lam gchod pa'o/ hum snying kar bkod pa ni/ byol song gi lam gcod pa'o/ drang gsang ba'i gnas su bkod pa ni yi dags kyi lam gcod pa'o/ a rkar mthil du bkod pa ni dmyil ba'i lam gcod pa ste/ lam 'di rnams bchad nas/ lha'i lam phye ste/ 'phags pa'i tshogs mang po spyan drangs nas/ "phrin las su mdzod pa'i skal ni/ [v35] 'phags pa sgrol ma nyi mas sgrol ba'i las mdzad/ khro chen rig pa'i rgyal pos ni gnas stobs gshin rje mthar byed kyis ni/ tshogs rje he ru ka la stsogs pa zhi khro mang po'i tshogs sim bar mdzad/ de nas mtshogs ma spyi gtsug du/ snying po krong sngo gnag gnas pa ni/ rdo rje mtshon cha'i snying po'o/ de las mtshon ca shag ti mang pos lus gshags par byin kyis brlab/ de nas sgrol ba'i skyes bu ni/ [v36] sgrol ma nyi mar bsgyur nas/ dmyig g.yas pa nyi mar byin kyis brlab pa'i/ nyi ma'i 'od zer mye ni/ bag chags bsreg/ dmyig g.yon pa zla bar byin kyis brlabs pa las/ chu'i bskal pa bag chags bkru/ ha ha zhes gad mo bsgrags pa'i rlung gis g.yengs gtor te dbyangs nas/ shel sgong bzhin du yongs su dag par bsam/ de nas [. . .][3] kyis mtshon gyi bsgral/ [ITJ419, r1] de nas rnam par shes pa'i . . . [?] . . . ma chad par/ gtso bo la stsogs pa tshogs mang po'i zhal du bstabs/ de nas rdo rje sems pa la stsogs pa'i dbyig rum du thim bar bsdu/ de nas rdo rje'i laṃ du phyung ste dbye ba'i myed pa'i sar smra/ de nas 'bras bu lnga rigs lnga'i tshul du mchod/ de nas [?] bzhi mig dang lnga dang/ nang gi cha lnga/ khro bo dang khro mo bcur dmyigs ste mchod/ lam rgyud la'i sems [r2] can ril kyis lhar byin kyis brlabs nas mgron du bod/ de nas 'ol pa'i tshul du bstan/ de nas sha khrag gis ci ltar tshim bar gyur pa bzhin/ thams cad rdo rje theg pa'i chos kyis tshim zhing kun tu bzang po'i sa la bkod/ phyin chu log dang/ nyon mongs pa'i chos thams cad/ theg pa'i chos las myi gzhan bas/ bdud dang/ bgegs myng myi srid/ de nas khams gsum ni/ dkyil [r3] de 'khor de'i bcud kyi sems can thams cad ni khro bo dang/ khro mo byang cub kyi tshogs su bsgom zhing mchod pa bgyi'o.

Appendix C

DUNHUANG LIBERATION RITE II

TRANSLATION OF PT840/1

The secret yogin should strive with an assurance derived from a mind that has been trained by a master who possesses the excellent initiations. One who is able to unite with the accomplishments of the wisdom deity should generate pride in accordance with how it appears in the *sādhana* texts [for accomplishing] the *mahāmudrā*.

Having completed the propitiation, arrange the five heroic syllables at the five places. Light-rays emanate in the ten directions then regather, and the dark green light becomes the *skandhas*. Recite, "*oṃ viśva heruka hūṃ phaṭ! āḥ āḥ āḥ*," whereby [5] imagine that you transform into [deity with] a dark green body, three heads, and six arms. His two feet create terror in a circle of dark red flames. With his left foot, the terror (*bhairava*) violently tramples a *vinayaka*, while his right tramples the consort's breasts. Imagine that he vomits blood from his mouth. Each of his three heads seems to have three eyes. His middle head is dark green with a dark yellow mane that blazes like fire. Held by a strong *citta*, the right one is light yellow with a greenish-yellow mane and three held in his mouth. His left one is red with a few green hairs and clacking his tongue. His first pair of hands holds a *banda* filled with blood, stirring and eating it with a *vajra*. [10] The last pair holds a bow and arrow.[1] His torso is covered with the skin of an ox; his lower half is wrapped in a human skin. Atop fresh and rotting flesh that is piled up like a mountain, he is surrounded by the seven great mothers. Strongly generate pride [in this appearance].

Having performed the propitiation, in an even manner recite, "*a ra li ki hūṃ*," whereby imagine that you overpower a retinue consisting of the four great kings and the ten directional protectors, as well as the eight kinds of gods and *nāgas* and so forth. Then in the dancing posture of great wrath, circumambulate one time, and bind the *mudrās* of the ten great wrathful [kings] and the demonesses. [15] Recite the mantras, binding the directional boundaries. Then circumambulate with a *vajra* walk. In a fierce and haughty manner, strike the head (*mgo ru dang mgo shu*). Either one should not have transgressed the sons of the conqueror, the word of the conqueror, and the vows, or one should recite three times, "*āḥ āḥ āḥ*," and attain nontransgression.

Then in the direction of the mandala, perform the *vajra* leap, affix the implements. In a ferocious posture, with a fierce and haughty shout, "O children of good lineage, you who believe in the great Mahāyāna teachings, brothers and sisters, you should not have caused offense nor [20] have transgressed the vows, nor violated the word, nor allowed your observances to falter." Otherwise recite, "*āḥ āḥ āḥ*," and receive the pith instructions on nontransgression. Then receive the initiations from a *vajra* master.

Invite [the deities] by means of the *vajra* walk, in the terrifying manner of a demoness, with the play of the *ḍākiṇī*, with the gait of a lion, in the *vajra* sitting posture, with the plod of a tortoise, with the buzzing of a hummingbird, with the five beckoning gestures, and even with a stick.

Having circumambulated the mandala, look with a sidelong glance down at the cause [that is, the victim]. Seeing [him] to be extremely afflicted, generate great compassion. [25] Imagine that he who dwells in the four sensory objects will be raised from afflicted *saṃsāra* to the shores of enlightenment. The thirty-three thrones of wisdom (*sher rab kyi khri so gsum pa*) having entered into the left side, the multicolored goddess of the *kartari* appears. Place a *jaḥ* syllable on the blade. Imagine that from the *jaḥ*, a *hrīḥ* arises, and that from that *hriḥ* various weapons emerge. Recite this heart[-mantra]: ". . ."[2]

In a posture with one leg bent upward and the other straight, gaze with eyes half closed (*myig dang 'bri 'tsugs*). Then on the five [fingers] of your right hand, arrange the syllables. Those become the five *herukas*. From heart [-syllables placed] on the five fingers of your left hand come the five consorts. From between the means and the wisdom of your palms as they are clapped together hard, imagine there comes a nine-pointed (*kha dgu pa*) *aṅkuśa*[-hook]. [30] Imagine that when you grab him by pinching his neck, a light arises from the *mudrā* of grabbing, purifying the afflicted predispositions. Imagine that by securing him, his afflictions are drawn (*kad gas pa*) to the shores of enlightenment. Imagine that by pressing him down, his afflictions are suppressed by the power of compassion. Imagine that by touching his upper three places with your two hands, the doors to the gods, demigods, and humans are closed. Imagine that by pressing on the junctures of his legs with the soles of your feet, the doors to the inner *tsong*[3] are closed by the five great *takrid.* Imagine that by directly cutting away the *citta,* the obscurations of ignorance are cut away. For the mantra recite, "*oṃ sar rbha rbha ga sa rba ki ta ya,*" whereby imagine that the doors of the afflictions are slammed shut, and the door to complete freedom is opened.

When the *citta* is led forth by the *mudrā,* imagine that it is grabbed with a "*jaḥ,*" from the *saṃsāra* of the five states [of sentient beings] by a red five-pointed hook. At the time of leading, recite, "*pāśa hūṃ,*" whereby imagine he is led from that place of affliction to the place of enlightenment. At the time of sending forth the *citta,* imagine he is sent from the ocean of *saṃsāra* into the realm of enlightenment. When leading forth the *citta,* you can also recite the mantra of the demonesses: "*oṃ ha phyang pa du za phyang maha latrang bha latrang piba tehe!*"

Having grasped him with compassion, the right and left hands gather all within the space of the skies of the ten mothers and subjugate. From their individual hearts comes "[*oṃ*] *aṃ hūṃ.*" He attains initiation as a son of the *tathāgatas* and an inhabitant of the heavens.

At that time, exhort your tutelary deity on his behalf. Generate pride in your respective deities. Send forth the messengers and envoys of the noble ones. The demons and obstructive enemies are overpowered. All the wrathful gods and goddesses too are struck down by the weapons. By the sword and cudgel of the Lord of Death and the violent activities of Kīlaya together with the light-rays, the mind is gathered and raised aloft.

Regarding offering (*bstabs pa*) the *citta,* because it is the basis for all conceptualizations, in order to purify it within a state of wrath, it is transformed into a goddess or into light. Recite, "*āḥ citta kharaṃgi.*" The body, speech, and mind of the great noble ones, the wrathful gods and goddesses, Iśvarī [that is, Kālī], and the accomplished brothers and sisters dissolve, and initiation is attained.

Regarding offering the blood (*rag ta bstabs pa*), having been overpowered by lust, he has cycled through the three realms. Thusly his desire is purified within a state of nonfixation.

Then offer the head (*mgo ru dang mgo shu*). Then having been taken up by the *ging* demons, it is offered in the direction of the dharma friends.

Then emit with a shout, "*sparaṇa phaṭ!*" If anger and pride were thrown ahead, love and compassion are cast behind. With your thoughts in a *samādhi* of love for the victim's head (*mgo ru dang mgo shu*) and your [dharma] brothers and sisters, feast happily for a little while. Perform the confession yoga and say the prayers. The queen and the good qualities are offered various delights by the patron and the priest. Do whatever benefits the *vajra* master. Offer the mind also to the powerful king.

[55] Having finished the offerings, enjoy the choicest parts. Then from seventy paces away, cover the palace in accordance with the above manner of the previous black one. Invite the fathers and mothers of the family, the sixteen heroes and heroines, and the great *takrid.* Then sprinkle the *argha.* Perform the worship. With the mudras, invite into the assembly those who perform the activities for the accomplishments, those who have mastered the accomplishments, the retinue of the great noble one, and all those [mundane ones] who rejoice in the pure residue. Worship in conformity with the worship. Perform the service for the red goddess facing toward the west. Perform the noble *gaṇa* worship. Offer by means of *bodhicitta.* Perform the violent activities within the established boundaries. [60] Turn the small *banda* cup upside down. Offer the enemies and hindrances to the wrathful ones and the demonesses. Perform the confession and the prayers. Send forth the sacrificial cakes into the western direction. Gather the deities and the palace into your body. Cultivate nonconceptuality. Transform into the deity and protect your body.

TRANSLITERATION OF PT840/1

gsang ba'i rnal 'byor pas slobs dpon dbang dam pa dang/ ldan bas slob ma'i blo las/ nges par brtson ba la/ ye shes

kyi lha'i dngos grub la sbyor nus pas phyag rgya chen po no pyi ka'i gzhung las 'byung ba bzhin nga rgyal bskyed de/

bsnyen pa rdzogs par byas nas/ gnas lngar dpa' bo 'bru lnga bkod de/ 'od zer phyogs bcur 'phros

nas/ slar 'dus pa dang/ 'od ljang nag phung por gyur pa las/ om bi shwa he ru ka hung phaT/ a a a zhes brjod pas b-

[5] -dag sku mdog ljang nag dbu gsum phyag drug/ zhabs gnyis mye phung dmar smug gi dkyil na 'jigs byed zhabs g.yo-

-n 'jigs byed byi na ya ka gsor par brdzis/ g.yas btsun mo'i nu ba(d)du brdzis te/ kha nas khrag skyug par bsam/

dbu gsum spyan gsum pa 'dra'/ dbu dbus ma ljang nag ral pa kham ser mye bzhin du 'bar ba'/ tsi ta che bas 'dzi-

-n la/ g.yas pa dkar ser ral pa ljang ser gsum kha na thogs pa/ g.yon dmar po ljang lo ma nyams pa/ lces ldag pa/ phyag dang po gca' gnyis/ ban da dmar gyis bkang ba/ :: / rdo rjes dkrug cing gsol ba'/

mtha' ma gnyis mda' zhu 'dzin pa'/ ban lang gi pags pa'i stod g.yogs dang/ zhing dpags kyi g.yang bzhis smad dkri-

-s pa/ mang sa gsar rnying ri bzhin du srungs pa/ 'i steng na/ ma chen mo bdun gyis bskor cing/ bzhugs par nga rgya-

-l bskyed/ bsnyen pa byas nas/ snyoms pa'i tshul gyis a ra li ki hung zhes brjod pas/ rgyal po chen po b-

-zhi dang/ phyogs skyong ba bcu'i 'khor dang/ lha klu sde brgyad las bstsogs pa/ dbang du bsdu bar bsam/ de nas

khro bo chen po'i stang stobs kyis lan gcig bskor la/ khro bo chen po bcu dang/ 'phra men ma rnams kyi phyag rgya bcings/

sngags bzlas te phyogs su mtshams gcad do/ de nas rdo rje 'gros kyis bskor te/ mgo ru dang mgo shu la rngam zhing

bsnyems pa'i tshul gis bstabs nas/ rgyal ba'i sras bo dag/ rgyal ba'i bka' dang/ dam tshig las myi '-

-da' 'am/ a a a zhes lan gsum brjod nas/ myi 'da' ba'i lan thob pa dang/ de nas dkyil 'khor phyogs

la yang/ rdo rje'i mchong stabs dang phyag mtshan gza' ba dang/ rdag stangs dang/ drngam zhing bsnyems pa'i skad

mdangs kyis/ kwa'i rigs kyi bu dag theg pa chen po'i chos dang/ mched lcam dral la/ myi 'khu 'am/ dam

tshig myi 'dral lam/ bka' myi gcog gam/ brdul shugs ma nyams sam/ a a a zhes brjod pa dang/ myi 'khu

myi ldog pa'i man ngag thob pa dang/ de nas rdo rje slobs dpon las dbang mnos te/ rdo rje 'gros pan gcig dang/

'phra men ma'i 'jigs tshul dang/ mkha' 'gro'i rol pa dang/ seng ge'i 'gros dang/ rdo rje'i 'dug stangs dang/

ru sbal gyi mchong stabs dang/ bung ba'i 'phrar thabs dang/ g.yab mo lngas gtang ba dang/ dbyugs pas kyang spyan drangs te/ dkyil '-

-khor bskor nas/ rgyu'i steng du zur myid gis bltas nas/ shin tu nyon mongs par mthong nas/ snying rje chen po bskyed de//

yul bzhi na gnas pa la nyon mongs pa'i 'khor ba nas/ byang cub kyi skam sar gdon par bsam/ sher rab kyi

khri so gsum pa/ mchan g.yon pa ru bcug nas/ ka tar ri'i lha mo kang kir sku mdog sna tshogs par bsgyur/ so la

yi ge 'dza' gzha(g)/ 'dza' las rhi byung/ rhi las mtsho(r) char sna tshogs par gyur par bsam/ snying po 'di brjod do/ . . .[4] ces brjod de/ brkyang bskum gi sdang myig

dang/ 'bri tsugs su ltas nas/ lag pa g.yas pa lnga la 'bru bkod de/ he ru ka lngar bsgyur/ g.yon gyi sor mo lnga

la snying po las yum lngar bsgyur te/ thal mo drag du brdabs pa'i thabs dang shes rab gi bar nas/ a' 'gu sha kha

dgu pa gcig par gyur par bsam/ gnya' nas tsir kis bzung ba'i tshe na/ gzung ba'i phyag rgya las 'od byung ste/

nyon mongs pa'i bag chags sbyangs par bsam/ btags pas nyon mongs pa'i byang cub kyi skam sar kad

gas par bsam/ mnan pas nyon mongs pa thugs rje'i dbang gis mnan par bsam/ lag pa gnyis mgod

nga gsum gyen tu bstan pas/ lha dang lha ma yin dang myi'i sgo bcad par bsam/ rkang pa'i mdor rdog pas mnan

pas/ ta krid ched po lngas nang tsong gi sgo bcad par bsam/ tsi ta thad kar dral bas ma rig pa'i bsgribs pa

dral bar bsam/ sngags la/ om sar rbha rbha ga/ sa rba ki ta ya zhes brjod de/ nyon mongs pa'i sgo'i sbubs brto-

-l nas/ rnam par thar pa'i sgo phye bar bsam/ phyag rgyas tsi ta 'dren pa'i tshe/ lcags kyu kha lnga pa dmar po g-

-cig gis /rgyud lngar 'khor ba la/ 'dza' zhes bzung bar bsam mo/ 'dren pa'i dus na pa sha hung zhes brjo-

-d pas/ de'i nyon mongs pa'i gnas nas byang cub gi gnas su 'dren par bsam/ tsi ta bton pa'i dus na/ 'khor

ba'i rgya mtsho nas byang cub ki gnas su bton par bsam mo/ tsi ta drang ba'i tshe/ 'phra men ma'i sngags kyang bzlas/

om ha phyang pa du za phyang/ ma ha la trang/ bha la trang pi ba te he zhes bzlas te/ thugs rjes zin nas/

lag pa g.yas g.yos yum bcu'i mkha'i dbyings su thams cad bsdus nas/ dbang sgyur te/ so so'i snying

po las/ am hung du gyur te/ de bzhin gshegs pa'i sras dang/ mtho ris su dbang thob par bya'o/

de'i dus su phyogs su thugs dam bskul/ so sor las kyi lhar nga rgyal bskyed/ dpal gyi phyo nya dang

sbod gthong bgyi/ bdud dang dgra bgegs dbang du bsdu/ khro bo dang khro mo thams cad kyang/ mtshon cha-

[45] -r 'bebs/ gshin rje'i ral gyi dbyug to dang/ ki la ya'i las drag po 'od zer dang bcas pas/ sems

bsdu zhing spar/ tsi ta bstabs pa ni rnam par rtog pa thams cad kyi rten yin bas/ khro bo'i ngang du sbyang ba-

-'i phyir/ lha mo 'am 'od du bsgyur te/ a tsi ta kha ram gi zhes brjod de/ dpal chen rnams dang khro bo

dang khro mo rnams dang/ dbang phyug ma dang grub pa lcam dral gyi sku gsung thugs thim nas/ dbang thob par byas/

rag ta bstabs pa ni/ 'dod chags gis dbang byas nas khams gsum du 'khor ba yin bas/ chags pa

[50] dmyigs su myed pa'i ngang du sbyong ba'o/ de nas mgo ru dang mgo shu la bstabs/ de nas ging gis blangs nas

grogs mched phyogs la bstabs/ de nas spa ra na paT ces sgra phyogs kyis dbyung/ zhe sdang dang nga rgyal mdun du btang

na/ byams pa dang snying rje phyis gtang/ mgo ru dang mgo shu dang mched lcam dral la yang/ byams pa'i ting nge 'dzin

la dgongs pa breng tsam yud tsam yang bgyis pa bsod par gsol/ rnal 'byor thol bshags dang smon lam gdab/ btsun mo yon tan

mchod yon gyis mnyes pa sna tshogs dbul/ rdo rje slobs dpon la ci phan du bgyi/ byi la sems kyang dbang po rgyal bar

[55] gsol/ bstabs pa lags nas/ phud spags long spyod/ de nas gom pa bdun cu phan cad/ gzhal yas khang snga nag gcig gi

tshul gong ma bzhin du phub la/ rigs kyi yab yum dang sems pa sems ma bcu drug dang/ ta krid ched po rnams kyang spya-

-n drang nas/ a rgam sbreng/ mchod pa bgyis te/ las dngos grub du bya ba dang/ dpal chen po 'khor dang/

phud lhag la dgyes pa thams cad kyang/ phyag rgyas tshogs par spyan drang/ mchod pa 'tsham bar mchod/ lha mo dmar mo/ kha nub phyogs

su bsnyan te/ dpal 'ga' na'i mchod pa bgyi/ byang cub kyi sems kyis kyang bstabs/ sbyar ba'i mtshams su las drag por

[60] bgyi/ ban 'da'i zhal bu kha sbubs te/ khro bo dang 'phra men rnams la dgra bgyegs bstabs/ 'thol bshags dang smon lam

bgyi/ gtor ma nub phyogs su gtang/ lha dang gzhal myed khang lus la bsdus/ rnam par myi rtog par bsgom/ lhar bsgyur te lus bsrung//

NOTES

ABBREVIATIONS

ITJ IOL Tib J: Reference for Tibetan-language materials from the Stein Collection of Dunhuang manuscripts held by the British Library.

KPS Oral commentary received in spring 2000 from Khenpo Pema Sherab of Namdroling Monastery, Bylakuppe, India.

PT Pelliot tibétain: Reference for Tibetan-language materials from the Pelliot Collection of Dunhuang manuscripts held by the Bibliothèque nationale.

Q. Peking edition of the Tibetan canon; see Suzuki 1957.

S. Or.8210/S.: Reference for Chinese-language materials from the Stein Collection of Dunhuang manuscripts held by the British Library.

T. *Taishō shinshū daizōkyō* number; see Takakusu and Watanabe 1924–1934.

TBRC Tibetan Buddhist Resource Center; see www.tbrc.org.

Toh. Sde dge edition of the Tibetan canon; see Ui et al. 1934.

INTRODUCTION

1. For some studies of the myth, see Iyanaga 1985, Davidson 1991 and 1995, Kapstein 1992, and Stein 1995.
2. A connection between the Rudra myth and violent rituals is seen from an early date. Already in the early eighth century, tantric Buddhists were citing the Rudra myth to justify their performance of violent ritual; see, e.g., Yixing's commentary to the *Mahāvairocana-abhisaṃbodhi Tantra* (T. 1796, 678c25ff.), where the author recounts a version of the Maheśvara-taming myth to justify the exorcistic rites described in the *Mahāvairocana*'s third chapter.
3. For two studies on the relevant manuscripts, see Macdonald 1980 and Oppitz 1997.
4. Xinguo 1996, p. 10 writes, "In the past there was a great deal of debate concerning whether or not human sacrificial burial was a part of the Tubo [i.e., Tibetan] funeral practices, but incontrovertible evidence of the existence of the custom has been

discovered at Xarag tomb M1 and Zhigari tomb M3." For a photo of what appears to be the same evidence, see Baumer and Weber 2005, 61; and for a study of recent Tibetan archaeological finds and their significance, see Heller 2006.

5. Indeed, PT239/1 is a Buddhist text that advocates substituting Buddhist funerary rites for indigenous ones precisely because of the latter's use of blood sacrifice (Stein 1970). Even so, blood sacrifice did continue within the court even after Buddhism's arrival, as indicated by the stone inscription on the Sino-Tibetan treaty of 821/823 C.E. (see Richardson 1998).

6. To this we may add more recent, though unconfirmed, evidence of human sacrifice in Nepal. Nicolas Sihlé (and Sagant before him) has noted oral reports of human sacrifice on a mass scale that took place in the Nyishang region of Nepal in the mid-twentieth century (Sihlé 2001, 158–60; my thanks to Sihlé for bringing this reference to my attention). Going somewhat farther back, Mary Slusser has compiled a number of such accounts, including those of several Western observers who "also mentioned the practice of sacrificing humans in the Kathmandu Valley in the eighteenth and nineteenth centuries. Daniel Wright rather graphically described the [*utkrānti*] 'suicides' at Kālā Bhairava's shrine, Francis Hamilton was told of such sacrifice, and Lévi reported that Kaṅkeśvarī claimed human victims" (Slusser 1982, 338). While such reports lack any definite historicity, they may reflect a certain acceptance of human sacrifice in religious contexts.

7. The manuscript (which has now been separated into three parts, PT36, ITJ419, and PT42) first received attention from Kenneth Eastman in his 1983 M.A. thesis, sections of which were published in Eastman 1983. Though Eastman noted the existence of the two relevant passages on the liberation rite, he did not address them in any detail. More recently, Meinert 2006 has studied one of the two passages, though without discussing whether it represents a example of direct ritual killing. In addition, a second manuscript (PT840) from Dunhuang describes a similar rite, while PT321 provides some further information. Though Samten Karmay noted the existence of the PT840 passage in his 1981 "King Tsa/Dza and Vajrayāna" (republished in Karmay 1998, 76–93), it remains to my knowledge completely unstudied. A translation appears in appendix C of the present work.

8. On artistic renderings of tantric violence, see Linrothe 1999. On Tibetan ritual dance (*'chams*), see Nebesky-Wojkowitz 1976.

9. See Davidson 2005.

10. Both Germano 1998, 93 and Kapstein 2000, 149 have described Tibet's early imperial court as a kind of "Camelot."

11. Indeed, some Tibetan historians have applied the term "age of fragmentation" to the period from Lang Darma all the way up to the advent of the Sakyapa government in the thirteenth century; for a recent example, see Phun tshogs 1997. For two recent studies that do much to bridge the gaps in our understanding of the transition from the age of fragmentation to the later dispensation period, see Stoddard 2004 and Vitali 2004.

12. *Bka' chems ka khol ma*, 275.6–15.

13. The term *bar dar* ("intermediate dispensation") has been used by several Tibetan authors, including Bcom ldan rig pa'i ral gri (13th c.), Dge g.ye ba tshul khrims seng ge

(15th c.), and others. On some of the terms of periodization used in Tibetan historical writings, see Cuevas 2006.

14. For some preliminary observations on the post-dynastic dating of some Tibetan manuscripts, see Takeuchi 2004 and Dalton, Davis, and van Schaik 2007. Generally speaking, the Tibetan Dunhuang manuscripts exhibit no awareness of the later dispensation translations and seem to reflect the state of Indian Buddhism as it stood around the turn of the ninth century. Works relating to the Yoginī tantras, such as the *Cakrasaṃvara* and *Hevajra*, are notably absent. PT849 represents an exception to this rule, and others may yet be found; as Kapstein 2006 has suggested, PT849 appears to reflect a tenth-century Indian tradition.
15. For digital scans of many of the relevant manuscripts, see http://idp.bl.uk.
16. Bailey 1967, 95 and 98.
17. For a study of the Chinese tantric manuscripts from Dunhuang, see Amanda Goodman's forthcoming UC Berkeley dissertation.
18. Sino-Tibetan cultural exchange outside the religious sphere is indicated by the fact of the Tibetan language's continuing use around Dunhuang well after the period of Tibetan occupation, even providing the *lingua franca* for the entire region of eastern Turkestan through the tenth century (as has been suggested by Takeuchi 2004).
19. For more on this subject, see van Schaik and Dalton 2004.
20. See Wangdu 2002. To this we may add the descriptions of the Tibetans found in the early (possibly even late-seventh-century) Khotanese work, the *Inquiry of Vimalaprabhā* (Tib. *Dri ma med pa'i 'od kyis zhus pa*), where they are depicted as marauding anti-Buddhist forces intent on destroying the Buddhist religion; see Thomas 1935–63, vol. 2, 203 and 254, and more recently van Schaik, forthcoming. Compared to the Tibetans of later centuries, it seems these had yet to be fully converted.
21. On the ideological implications of sacrifice, see Hamerton-Kelly 1987.
22. Perhaps the most dramatic accusation was made in an exhibition of life-size clay tableaux that opened in Lhasa in 1976. The exhibition catalogue was published under the title *Wrath of the Serfs: A Group of Life-Size Clay Sculptures* (Peking: Foreign Languages Press, 1976), and has been discussed briefly in Harris 1999, 130–35.
23. Witness the irony of recent Indian newspaper articles that announce, for example, "Death for Perpetrators of Human Sacrifices" (*Times of India*, December 21, 2003).
24. See Gyatso 1987.
25. Waddell 1972 [1895], xi.
26. Lopez 1996, 216–38.
27. For some examples particularly relevant to the case of Tibetan Buddhism, see Gyatso 1987, Kapstein 1992, Boord 1993, Martin 1996, Mayer 1996, Cantwell 1997, Karmay 1988b and 1998, Davidson 2000 and 2005, Zimmermann 2006, and Cantwell and Mayer 2008. A forthcoming study by the anthropologist Nicolas Sihlé, *Rituels de pouvoir et de violence: Bouddhisme tantrique dans l'Himalaya tibétain*, promises to add much to our understanding of violence in Tibetan Buddhism. It is unfortunate that I have been unable to consult Sihlé's work in composing my own study.
28. For more on this influential tantra, see Dalton 2002.

CHAPTER 1. EVIL AND IGNORANCE IN TANTRIC BUDDHISM

1. See translation in appendix A, fol. 154–55. Similarly, tantric commentaries regularly draw attention to the disparity between the the wrathful buddha's violent appearance and his compassionate intention. A Dunhuang manuscript that has much in common with our Rudra myth, ITJ306, r2.1–r3.1, for example, explains that the Great Glorious One (Dpal chen po), who tramples Mahādeva and Umādevī underfoot, "only pretends to be angry. Really he is not angry, and his outward behavior is just a pretense. The scriptures too say this: 'His vicious, sharp-toothed wrath is worn like an outward armor, but he does not waver from bodhicitta.'"
2. Arendt 1970, 51.
3. Outside of Buddhism too, violent *abhicāra* rituals circulated in India well before the tantras, in the *Atharva-veda* and so forth, but the association between such rites and the tantras quickly became so close that works such as the *Sarvalakṣaṇasaṃgraha* even defined the violent *abhicāra* rite as, "a particular practice taught in a Tantra which results in killing, expelling, etc." (Türstig 1985, 82).
4. What follows is, of necessity, only a brief sketch of some of the main issues in early Buddhist approaches to ethics. For a more thorough study, see Harvey 2000.
5. *Samantapāsādikā* 439, as cited in Gethin 2004, 174.
6. Granoff 1992, 36.
7. Horner 1963–1964, vol. 2, 14.
8. Horner 1963–1964, vol. 2, 16–17.
9. As quoted by Candrakīrti in his commentary, the *Bodhisattva-yogācāra-catuḥśataka-ṭīkā*, 93a.6.
10. The *Skill-in-Means Sūtra* may contain the best-known example of such a story, but it is certainly not unique in Mahāyāna literature. In a valuable article on compassionate violence in pre-tantric Buddhism, Stephen Jenkins (forthcoming) has collected a number of additional examples.
11. Though in his final lifetime as the Buddha Śākyamuni, he is pricked by a thorn ostensibly as a result of stabbing the thief. As Jenkins (forthcoming) observes, however, the thorn incident is just a didactic show on the part of the Buddha and not a real result of his past deed. Perhaps we see here a lingering anxiety surrounding the text's doctrinal justifications of compassionate violence. Certainly discomfort is expressed in the later Tibetan tradition. As we shall see in chapter 6 of the present study, when Tibetan masters cast violent rites against their enemies, even when they deemed the violence morally justifiable, they are often described as suffering later in life for their actions, often from some illness or a shortness of life.
12. The entire story is translated in Tatz 1994, 73–77.
13. On the paradoxical nature of giving in Buddhism, see Ohnuma 2005.
14. Within the Tibetan tradition, the tantric practice of *chö*, or "cutting," in which one visualizes oneself being chopped up and fed to hungry demons, may be seen to function in a similar way. The *chö* tradition often makes explicit this connection; for some examples, see Edou 1996, 53–56.

15. From the translation by Ohnuma 2007, 12.
16. Ohnuma 2007, 219.
17. Tatz 1986, 70–71.
18. *Sutta-vibhaṅga, pārājika* III.6: *sādhu sādhu sappurisa, lābhā te sappurisa, suladdhaṃ te sappurisa. bahuṃ tayā sappurisa puññaṃ pasutaṃ, yaṃ tvaṃ atiṇṇe tāresī.* For an English translation of the complete story, see Horner 1938, 117–23. My thanks to Alex von Rospatt for bringing this reference to my attention.
19. See Tatz 1986, 74 and 221.
20. The three physical nonvirtues are killing, taking what is not given, and engaging in sexual misconduct, while the four verbal nonvirtues are lying, slander, irresponsible gossip, and verbal abuse. The remaining three mental nonvirtues of covetousness, harmful intent, and wrong view were still, of course, impossible, since by definition they involved a lack of compassion. The issue of whether not engaging in nonvirtue should count as an infraction was apparently the subject of some disagreement; see Tatz 1986, 24 and 211–12.
21. It should be noted that such transgressive practices were by no means unique to tantric practice. The Mūlasarvastivāda *Vinaya-vibhaṅga* (vol. *ja*, 154b.2–156b.7), e.g., includes the story of Mahākāla, a monk who dwells in a cemetery, takes his clothes from the dead, eats the offerings to the dead, and so forth. For an English translation and discussion, see Schopen 2007, 76–79. For further reflections on such practices in early Indian Buddhism, see Decaroli 2004.
22. *Susiddhikāra*, 183b.7–185b.1.
23. *Susiddhikāra*, 184b.4–6.
24. *Susiddhikāra*, 185a.2–3.
25. *Susiddhikāra*, 185a.1–2.
26. Based on the translation from the Chinese in Giebel 2001, 187–88, with a few minor changes. The corresponding Tibetan makes no mention of the first part of this passage, but it does suggest that one "perform the pacification in order to eject the sentient being [into the buddhafields], and perform the enhancement so that he abides there happily" (*Susiddhikāra*, 185a.4).
27. In his recent study of the *Compendium of Principles*, Steven Weinberger has argued that this second Trailokyavijaya section is somewhat anomalous in comparison to the others and thus may be a later addition to the original tantra (see Weinberger 2003, 77ff.). In any case, it was certainly in place by the mid-eighth century, when both Amoghavajra and Buddhguhya referred to its existence.
28. For an English translation of the myth, see Davidson 1995.
29. ITJ325, 19–29. ITJ325 is dedicated to the deity Uṣṇīṣasitātapatra. It should be read along with the additional fragment found at ITJ1236, which was part of the same original manuscript. Here I take this rite as generally representative of Yoga tantra ritual practice, as most of its elements are common to that system—in particular the mantras used, the details of how to prepare the ritual space and protect the body, etc. But the manuscript in question may date as late as the tenth century, and we should bear and mind the possibility that later Mahāyoga influences may also be at work.

30. *Guhyasamāja Tantra*, 97b.1–2.
31. *Vajrayāna-mūlāṅgāpatti-deśanā*, 117b.2–3.
32. For a recent review of past scholarship on this question, see Wedemeyer 2007. And for a study of normative Buddhist responses to the ritual violence of the tantras, see Gray 2007.
33. On their roles within the royal courts of India and Southeast Asia, see Sanderson 2004. As we shall see in chapter 6, the *sngags pa* (especially those of the Nyingma school) often played a similar role in later Tibet. *Tāntrikas* were also valued for their abilities at the village level both in India, as noted in the same study by Sanderson (pp. 233–36), and in Tibet, as attested by *Mkhas pa'i dga' ston*, 431.6–9.
34. PT337, 7.3.
35. As argued by Lopez 1992, 155–57.
36. See Davidson 2002.
37. *Sarvatathāgata-tattvasaṃgraha*, § 52.
38. See Mair 1995. On the Indic textual precedents for the story, see in particular pp. 51–52. On the Dunhuang murals' dates, see Wu Hung 1992, 140.
39. As Davidson observes, both Stein and Iyanaga have questioned whether the Rudra/Maheśvara myths were in fact anti-Hindu. In response, Davidson (1991, 216–18) explores the various other factors that likely influenced the myths, including the Śākyamuni v. Māra narrative, but concludes nonetheless, "There can be little doubt that the Indic story indicates the real tension between Buddhist and Śaiva factions" (214).
40. Śiva's subjugation of the demon Andhaka provides some interesting parallels; for the relevant references, see Doniger O'Flaherty 1975, 328. See also Śiva's subjugation of Jālandhara in the *Śiva-purāṇa*.
41. As clarified by *Mun pa'i go cha*, vol. 51, 305.2ff., translated in note 157 to fol. 208 of the myth that appears in appendix A.
42. *Dka' 'grel*, 244.2–247.6.
43. *Mun pa'i go cha*, vol. 50, 258.6–259.2.
44. Nupchen explains that Rudra's previous lifetime as Black Liberator was the actual cause (Tib. *rgyu;* Skt. *hetu*), while his subsequent lifetimes leading up to his moment of regret in the Avīci hells were the conditions (Tib. *rkyen*; Skt. *pratyaya*), that is, up to the moment when Rudra-to-be wonders for a moment why he is being subjected to such terrible tortures, whereupon Vajrasattva appears to tell him it is because of his own karma, which leads Rudra to feel an instant of regret for his past actions. (See fol. 158, and on the relevant passages in the *Mun pa'i go cha*, see notes 4, 11, and 14 to the translation of the myth.) From this point forward, the future-Rudra's lifetimes in the various hells, as a series of ghosts, and so on qualify as the "ripening" of his karmic actions, which finally result in his birth as Rudra. Thus his lifetime as Black Liberator is the cause, his lifetimes leading up to the Avīci hell incident are the conditions, his lifetimes after that are the ripening of his karma, and his birth as Rudra is the result. Nupchen further subdivides the cause, i.e., Rudra's lifetime as Black Liberator, into various types of contributing causes, i.e., particular actions taken by Black Liberator during his life, and these are the subject of the passage quoted above. In his

discussion of these contributing causes, Nupchen's terminology is drawn from those of earlier Indian philosophers, who distinguish different kinds of contributing causes. The best-known list appears in Vasubandhu's *Abhidharmakośa-bhāṣyam*, where six causes are listed (see de la Vallée Poussin 1991, vol. 1, 255). Nupchen's "associated cause" (Skt. *samprayukta hetu;* Tib. *lhan cig byed pa'i rgyu*) is among them, but his "cooperating cause" (Skt. *sahakāri hetu;* Tib. *mtshungs par ldan pa'i rgyu*) does not appear. To find this cause, we must turn to another well-known work by Vasubandhu's brother, Asaṅga, the *Abhidharmasamuccaya*, where we find an alternative typology of twenty causes (which do not include all six of Vasubandhu's causes), one of which is Nupchen's "associated cause." (For an English translation of the relevant passage, see Asaṅga 2001, 60–61.) How precisely Nupchen understood the doctrinal details behind the two causes he identifies remains unclear. That he drew from two different lists without discussing their relationships may imply that he was applying these doctrinal categories somewhat loosely, intending them more as a general interpretive tool than as a strictly defined philosophical system, though it is also possible that he was drawing upon a third, presently unknown source.

45. Such a double approach therefore sees the foundation in either conventional or ultimate terms, as the "saṃsāric foundation" (*'khor ba'i kun gzhi*) or the "unified foundation" (*sbyor ba'i kun gzhi*), as Khenpo Nuden calls them. The latter, more positive interpretation of the foundation would, of course, be problematic for many later Tibetan exegetes. Elsewhere, Nupchen, like some later Tibetan exegetes, such as the Third Karmapa, distinguishes the "foundation consciousness" from the "foundation," identifying the latter with *bodhicitta.* (See, e.g., *Mun pa'i go cha*, vol. 51, 51.1 and 58.3.)
46. *Mun pa'i go cha*, vol. 51, 63.5.
47. Nuden, vol. 55, 200.2.
48. Khenpo Nuden himself (vol. 55, 189.2–3) notes the connection between Nupchen's early presentation of Atiyoga here and the later *snying thig* writings of Longchenpa.
49. *Mun pa'i go cha*, vol. 51, 51.1–2.
50. In discussing Orgyen Lingpa's fourteenth-century rendition of the Rudra myth, Kapstein (1992, 71) has argued that intrinsic ignorance plays no role in that myth; rather, he suggests, it is a story solely of acquired ignorance. It seems such a conclusion probably should not be applied to Nupchen's own interpretation. Might we conclude that this difference between Nupchen's and Orgyen Lingpa's readings, separated as they were by some five hundred years, reflects certain wider changes in the conceptual apparatus of the Rnying ma school in the intervening period? More specifically, perhaps the spread of the Dzogchen "Samantabhadra myth," which Kapstein points to as the myth that does depict the moment of intrinsic ignorance, came to appropriate some of the allegorical space enjoyed by the Rudra myth in earlier years.
51. PT699, 5r. The wider passage from which these lines are extracted appears to have been copied incorrectly by the scribe, so that the line order is scrambled. It remains unclear whether these particular lines are meant to describe a master of the tantras as distinct from one of Atiyoga, or whether a single tantric/Atiyoga master is intended. In any case, for present purposes this ambiguity is irrelevant.

CHAPTER 2. DEMONS IN THE DARK

1. The story may date from as early as the late dynastic period. In some form, it is probably implicit in the title of the Dunhuang text, ITJ370/6: "The Dharma that Came Down from Heaven" (*gnam babs kyi dar ma bam po gcig go*; translated in Richardson 1998, 74–81). The complete story appears in the *Dba' bzhed*, portions of which may now be dated to the tenth century (see van Schaik and Iwao 2008). On dating the received fuller version to the eleventh century, see Wangdu and Diemberger 2000, 24. According to earlier renditions, the casket contained only the six-syllable *oṃ mani padme hūṃ*, the mantra of Avalokiteśvara, which seems to have originated in the *Karaṇḍavyūha*. Later renditions of the legend vary on the exact contents of the casket, some including another text, the *Spang skong phyag rgya*, and various sacred objects such as a votive *stūpa*, a precious *mudrā phyag rgya* stone, and a *cintāmaṇi* drinking bowl (see Stein 1986). Note too that the same *Dba' bzhed*, 72 has Trisong Detsen giving thanks to the sky for the dharma.
2. See Imaeda 1979 and van Schaik 2006.
3. More strictly speaking, we may follow the dates 843–986 C.E., from the collapse of the Pugyal dynasty to the distribution of Yeshe Ö's *Bka' shog chen mo*. Regarding the former date, see Yamaguchi 1996, 252, where he dates the "break up" of the kingdom of Tufan by reference to the Chinese *Tangshu*. Regarding the latter date, see Vitali 1996, 185. Another turning point was the return of the "ten men" from the northeast, and the subsequent revival of monastic Buddhism. Dromtönpa suggests a date for this event of 978 (see Vitali 1990, 62 n. 1), though Khepa Deu seems to suggest 988 (*Mkhas pa lde'us mdzad pa'i rgya bod kyi chos 'byung rgyas pa*, 394).
4. See Karmay 1988a, 8–10; Yamaguchi 1996; Kapstein 2000, 11–12; Karmay 2005, 15–29. Uebach 1990 has also discussed the continuing lineage of the *bcom ldan 'das kyi ring lugs* that may have persisted at Samye.
5. Yamaguchi 1996.
6. It was not just the tantric forms of nonmonastic Buddhism that thrived, however. Later Tibetan medical histories maintain that the principal medical lineages also continued uninterrupted through the age of fragmentation. See, e.g., *Sman pa rnams kyis mi shes su mi rung ba'i she bya spyi'i khog dbubs*, 280. My thanks to Frances Garrett for this reference.
7. There is a practical side to this claim. Given that the translation of Buddhist texts into Tibetan began in earnest only in the late eighth century, the widespread performance of Buddhist rituals (including the copying of texts) *in Tibetan* could not have occurred until some time after these translations had become available. It is perhaps for this reason that there is so little evidence from Dunhuang of Tibetan Buddhist practice *in Tibetan* prior to around 830 C.E., even as there is abundant evidence of *Chinese* Buddhist monks performing rites and copying texts on behalf of the Tibetan court during those same early years. For just two examples, see Pelliot chinois 2974 (discussed in Demiéville 1952, 280–81) and S. 3966.
8. Here I do not mean to diminish the obvious creativity of the later dispensation period. During the earlier age of fragmentation, however, blatant Tibetan innovations

may have encountered less censure and did not have to be packaged as Indian in origin.

9. Kapstein 2000, 56.
10. This solution has been suggested by Yamaguchi 1996, 250. Yamaguchi suggests a number of radically new readings of the events surrounding Lang Darma's purported persecution of Buddhism. Unfortunately, other recent accounts of the period (e.g., Davidson 2005, 61–72, and Vitali 2004, 105–31) have not referred to Yamaguchi's intriguing theories. In the brief summary that follows below, I have tried to include his theories where appropriate, but it should also be recognized that some of Yamaguchi's readings have been questioned and scholarly opinion remains unsettled.
11. From the French translation by Pelliot 1961, 133.
12. See PT840 (translated by Karmay 1998, 90, and again by Yamaguchi 1996, 242) and especially PT134 (translated by Yamaguchi 1996, 237–38, and discussed by Scherrer-Schaub 1999–2000). Scherrer-Schaub critiques Yamaguchi's claims, observing that PT134 is less a panegyric to King Darma and his generous support than a plea for his protection in dark times: "Il ne semble pas nécessaire d'inférer, de l'existence de cette prière, le fait que 'Wu'i dun brtan, l'apostat Glaṅ Dar ma des chroniques postérieures, était à ce moment un souverain vertueux. Le ton de la prière, nous l'avons vu, est plutôt celui de l'adjuration, du rappel des devoirs qui incombent à la charge de l'empereur, tels qu'ils furent établis par ses prédécesseurs" (239). Personally, I am convinced of her reading (which really rests on the manuscript's rather unclear ll. 16–17) and agree it seems to suggest that Buddhism's troubles had already begun during Darma's reign (an idea on which Yamaguchi casts some doubt). That said, we may note that even given Scherrer-Schaub's reading, PT134 still suggests that Darma was viewed by some within the Buddhist clergy as an at-least-potential ally. For this reason, here I follow the conclusion that the troubles for Buddhism (whether in the form of persecutions or merely funding cuts remains unclear) began under Lang Darma and continued after his death, during the divided rule of Ösung and Yumten.
13. For a translation of some of the relevant sources on this point, see Vitali 1996, 541 n. 923.
14. Many have pointed to the Dunhuang documents PT131, 230, 840, and 999 as evidence of Ösung's ongoing support for Buddhism. Yamaguchi casts some doubt on this evidence, however, by suggesting alternative readings for each of the relevant passages (see Yamaguchi 1996, 239–42), the implication being that Ösung may in fact have been responsible for at least some of the persecutions of Buddhism.
15. See Gernet 1995, 251. As several other scholars have noted, it is surely relevant that during precisely the same period, China experienced its own anti-Buddhist crackdown, the worst in its history, when Emperor Wuzong (r. 841/842–845) ordered the closure of virtually all Buddhist monasteries in the empire. Scholars attribute this crackdown to a combination of causes, from the financial drain caused by the monasteries, to the Daoist leanings of the emperor and long-standing Confucian suspicions about the foreign religion. For a discussion of these Chinese events, see Weinstein 1987, 114–36. For more on the parallels between these events and those in Tibet, see n. 24 below.

16. This is the central argument made by Yamaguchi (1996); see especially pp. 248–252. Note that his reading of the relevant passage in the *Tang Annals* disagrees with those of other scholars; compare, e.g., Petech 1994, 650.
17. See PT230 (translated by Yamaguchi 1996, 238–39).
18. For all of the previous dates, see Vitali 2004, 113 n. 11, and Vitali 1996, 544–47.
19. On the momentary success of the Yumten line following Khortsen's death, see Guntram Hazod's appendix, "The Yum-brtan Lineage," in Gyalbo, Hazod, and Sørensen 2000, 185, and Vitali 2004, 111 and 126–27.
20. *Mkhas pa'i dga' ston*, 431–32. My own summary of the story is thanks in large part to two simultaneously published studies of the relevant sources; see Vitali 2004, 115–16, and especially the excellent work by Dotson (forthcoming). As Dotson observes, the story likely dates from as early as the eleventh century, when it appeared in the "famously non-extant" *Lo rgyus chen mo* of Khu ston brtson 'grus g.yung drung (1011–1075).
21. Note that this is presumably the same person who, the *Tang Annals* suggest, later killed Lang Darma himself.
22. Drenka Pel's apotheosis as a Buddhist protector has been noted in Richardson 1998, 147. There, Richardson observes that the spirit was converted to Buddhism only later in the eleventh century by Atiśa. Vitali 2004, 114–15, however, has called attention to "the Buddhist undertones" already present in the narrative accounts of Drenka Pel's rebellions.
23. On this process, see Karmay 1998, 432–50.
24. We have already observed the curious parallels between the persecutions of monastic Buddhism in China and Tibet in the mid-ninth century. Still more surprising, though, may be the similarities in how these events came to shape the Buddhist traditions of the two regions. James Robson (2009) has argued that the Huichang persecution of 844–845, combined with the Anlushan (755–763) and the Huangchao (875–884) rebellions, were the catalysts for the rise of regional Buddhist movements that were no longer dependent on imperial patronage but instead forged alliances with local rulers. Robson makes these remarks in the context of a wider study of Mount Nanyue and its role in the formation of Chinese Buddhism. Might we see, then, parallels between Tibet and China extending beyond just the political events of the mid-ninth century?
25. For translations of several passages from later sources on this point, see Scherrer-Schaub 2001.
26. Vitali 1996, 547, dates the second rebellion (discussed in the passage translated below) to 904. Given this date and the claim (made in the same passage below) that Nupchen was sixty-one at that time, we come to a birth date for Nupchen of c. 844.
27. It is perhaps relevant that the *Vajravidāraṇā-dhāraṇī*, 266a.6, an early relative of the Vajrakīlaya tradition, includes the mantra, *amukaṃ māraya phaṭ*, where *amuka* may be read as "insert name here." My thanks to Iain Sinclair for this reference. The same mantra also appears in several other wrathful tantras.
28. *Brgyud pa'i rnam thar*, 167.5–170.1. Note the distinction made here between mere *abhicāra* and "liberation."

29. The latter *Rgya bo che* has only recently resurfaced in the new *Bka' ma shin tu rgyas pa* collection. Unfortunately, it came to my attention too late to be included in the present study. An initial read-through, however, shows that it is not an autobiographical work, except perhaps in parts, and that its contents would change little for the present study.
30. *Nyang ral chos 'byung*, 432.
31. *Mun pa'i go cha*, vol. 50, 255a.4–6.
32. *Mun pa'i go cha*, vol. 50, 675.2–5. My reading here follows Nuden, vol. 55, 82.5–83.3, who corrects the second sentence slightly.
33. *Mun pa'i go cha*, vol. 51, 419.4–5. Taken together, these three passages show Nupchen taking an approach to tantric practice that is at once conservative and radical. On the one hand, within the growing discourse of Atiyoga/Rdzogs chen, he seems to have maintained a strictly "pristine" (to use the term coined by Germano 2005) interpretation, one that is free of any "method" or "views." (And here we may wonder if the "great person of today" to whom Nupchen refers might have been "perceiving a method" that resembled the visionary practices of the later Nyingtig traditions.) On the other hand, Nupchen also advocates teaching this level of understanding right from the beginning of a student's training. These remarkable passages will be returned to in chapter 4 of the present study. An additional criticism, this time aimed at yogins who become teachers too soon, may be found at *Mun pa'i go cha*, vol. 51, 405.1.
34. Others, of course, continued to use language similar to Nupchen's. It is important to note that while more libertarian approaches to the tantras were condemned by some later groups, they also persisted among others. Indeed, such rhetorical continuities were precisely what made the age of fragmentation so formative for the later tradition.
35. Vitali 1996, 232, dates Rinchen Zangpo's encounter with the Star King to between 987 and 996.
36. On both the Star King and the Four Children of Pehar, see Martin 1996.
37. Takeuchi 2004 has done some excellent work identifying an ever-growing list of Dunhuang manuscripts that are datable to the post-occupation period. In my own opinion, Takeuchi's conclusions can be taken even further: The vast majority of the Tibetan tantric materials (and possibly much of the sutric too) date from the tenth century.
38. PT840, V3.10–11. The text in question is the subject of a study by Karmay 1998, 76–93, though my own translation differs slightly from Karmay's. The practice of Buddhism at the popular level is also described by Nyangrel and Pawo Tsuglag (see *Nyang ral chos 'byung*, 447–49 and *Mkhas pa'i dga' ston*, 430–32; both passages have been translated by Vitali 2004, 120–21 n. 19). Both of the latter two Tibetan authors agree that Buddhist priests were particularly popular for their funerary skills, something that Dunhuang documents would seem to confirm. On the popularity of funerary rites in the Dunhuang manuscripts, see Stein 1970, Macdonald 1971, Imaeda 1979, and van Schaik 2006.
39. ITJ752, 1r.5–1v.5. Richardson 1993, 163, noted in passing the significance of this manuscript. (My thanks to Professor Scherrer-Schaub for providing me with the article

in question.) My own reading of this passage differs somewhat from that of both Richardson and Scherrer-Schaub 2001, 702 n. 33, who interpret the passage as critical of those who perform violent rituals. Rather, I prefer to read it as *advocating* the use of those rituals to destroy any enemies of the tantras. With regard to the passage's final reference to "attaining the realm" (*gnas thob*), note that this is a technical term closely associated with the tantric liberation rite. For a discussion of the term, see chapter 3 of this study.

40. Indeed, the tantras are often explicit about the need for violence to defeat those who might threaten the Buddhist teachings; for some references, see Shizuka 2008, 190 n. 33. Another Dunhuang manuscript of interest in this regard is ITJ726, titled *A Ritual Manual for [Bestowing] the Vows of the Nāgas* (*Klu'i dam tshig gi cho ga*) and attributed to the Indian masters, *Ācārya Mantigarbha and Ārya Asaṅga. Before describing a series of rites for controlling different kinds of *nāga*-spirits, the text opens with a brief warning: "When the Mahāyāna teachings have completely disappeared, the pith instruction codes on killing by evil *nāgas* will be established" (1r.1–2: *theg pa chen po'i chos gtan nas myed pa la thu . . . nas/ klu gdug pa can gyis gsad pa'i man ngag gi rtsis 'go* [sic *mgo*] *gtan la bab pa lags te*). Here too, then, the disappearance of the dharma is correlated with a need for demon-taming rites.

41. Davidson 2005, 65.

42. Davidson 2005, 65.

43. See Karmay 1988a, 6.

44. *Sgra sbyor bam po gnyis pa*, 73.14–20.

45. In her study of this issue, Scherrer-Schaub 2002, 287, concludes that the regulation of the tantras had begun in the late eighth century. The *Sayings of Wa* also attributes the restrictions to Trisong Detsen (see Wangdu and Diemberger 2000, 88–89), though the same text also claims that under such rules, the Mahāyoga tantras were not even translated, which was almost certainly not the case.

46. *Dkar chag 'phang thang ma*, 45. Thanks to Phil Stanley for bringing this reference to my attention.

47. See van der Kuijp 1992, 116.

48. Kapstein 2000, 61.

49. Kapstein 2000, 63–64, building on Amy Heller's discoveries, has noted the centrality of the tantric Sarvavid Vairocana to the imperial cult.

50. In referring to a "popular" level of Tibetan society, I do not mean to exclude the aristocratic families that certainly continued to wield significant power throughout the late ninth and tenth centuries. Davidson 2005, 63, 76, and 80, rightly emphasizes that the aristocratic clans continued to be central to the spread of Buddhism during these years of fragmentation. The distinction I intend here should be understood relative to the comparatively centralized form of Buddhism under the earlier Tibetan Empire. Similarly, some degree of popular involvement with Buddhism, of course, did occur during the imperial period, and here too my argument is a relative one. One example of public participation in Buddhist ritual may be the annual series of three holidays instituted by King Mune Tsenpo at the end of the eighth century. These were agricul-

tural holidays that presumably involved central Tibetans at all levels of society. Each festival was dedicated to one of the three baskets (*tripiṭaka*) of the Buddhist canon, so that every spring Tibetans were encouraged to participate in the "*abhidharma* basket offerings," while in midsummer they would make offerings to the sutras, and at harvest to the *vinaya*. (For a discussion of the festivals, see Martin 2002, 336.) Despite the existence of such (notably still court-sponsored) public events, Buddhism's influence does not appear to have infiltrated the Tibetan populace very deeply, particularly compared to what is seen in subsequent centuries. Finally, regarding the same three festivals, we may note again the court's emphasis on the traditions of exoteric Buddhism.

51. The most commonly cited source on the early Bonpo funerary rites is the Dunhuang document PT1042; see Lalou 1952 and Haarh 1969 on that.
52. In both of the passages cited, the Chinese term corresponding to the Tibetan, *bon po*, is a more general term meaning simply "bad teachers" (see T.2897, 1424a16 and 1423c13). Note that all references to *bon* or *mo bon* have been excised from today's canonical recensions of this same text, perhaps the result of an attempt by later editors to remove any indicators of specifically Tibetan concerns in the text, and thus to make it seem more Indian. Despite such efforts, the work is clearly Chinese in origin. Its widespread popularity among not only Tibetans, but Chinese and Mongolians as well, seems to have allowed it to be included in the later canons.
53. ITJ458, 11v.3. Regarding the early meaning of "*mo bon*," we may look to ITJ360/10, 70r.4, where *mo bon* is glossed as a kind of omen (*ltas*). Karmay 1998, 160, has argued that the term is used elsewhere in the Dunhuang documents to refer to the Bonpo priests more generally.
54. ITJ462, r7.3–8.2.
55. Many examples may be given. Two of particular interest are the nineteen questions, also on Mahāyoga practice, that appear in ITJ419/6 (discussed in chapter 3 of the present study), and the *Mdo sde brgyad bcu 'khungs* (preserved in ITJ705/PT818), which may have been an attempt to resolve differences between the Chinese, Indian, and Tibetan forms of early ninth-century Buddhism. Additional manuscript copies of this text have recently surfaced in northwestern India and are the subject of a study by Tauscher 2007.
56. An interlinear note to the Dunhuang edition adds: "Because lower beings look to create minor difficulties for this world, not honoring them does not conflict with the dharma system of the conqueror."
57. ITJ470, ll. 102–5. For a complete introduction and translation to this work, see Dalton 2011.
58. Even Pelyang, in another work that can probably be attributed to him, the *Thugs kyi sgron ma* (Q. 5918), allowed for a vehicle of gods and humans (*lha mi'i theg pa*) as the lowest rung of his otherwise Buddhist doxographical system. For more on this development, see Dalton 2005, 134–40.
59. Even during these more syncretic years, however, the term "Bon" continued to be used by many Tibetan Buddhists disparagingly. PT239, e.g., includes some signifi-

cant syncretic elements yet remains harshly critical of the Bonpo, as recognized by Macdonald 1971, 374. For a translation of the relevant work, see Stein 1970.

60. For two examples from Dunhuang, see ITJ569 and 726.
61. ITJ419, v48.4–49.4 and PT42, r1.1–3.1.
62. The prayer, also known simply as the *Three Descendants* (*Rgyud gsum pa*), seems to have enjoyed considerable popularity in early Tibet. Many copies appear in the Dunhuang collections, and the work underwent multiple revisions, as these same Dunhuang copies demonstrate. Even today two versions appear in the modern canon; see the *Spyan 'dren rgyud gsum pa* (Q.470) and the *Rgyud gsum pa* (Q.471).
63. This is the opening line of the *Rgyud gsum pa* prayer, the first line to be commented upon here. ITJ711, 1r.3–4.
64. ITJ711, 1r.1–1v.3.
65. ITJ711, 13r.2–13v.1.
66. ITJ711, 3v.4–4v.2. I remain unsure how to reconstruct the Sanskrit for *de'i*.
67. Karmay 1998, 248–49.
68. Karmay 1998, 267.
69. Citing the earlier work of Ariane Macdonald, Karmay 1998, 259, notes the existence of two additional Dunhuang manuscripts (PT1038 and PT1286) that contain passages resembling certain parts of the post-13th-century *Appearance of the Little Black-Headed Man*.
70. A similar incorporation of local Tibetan deities appears in ITJ565/PT284, a ritual text relating to the *Guhyasamāja Tantra*. PT284, 6v.7 includes the Tibetan *teu rang* among the demonic beings who dwell at the edges of the Guhyasamāja mandala (*mtha' skor ba*). On the tripartite Bonpo cosmology, see Haarh 1969.
71. Such dark descriptions differ from the earlier mandalas preserved in the East Asian tradition, the edges of which are described as gardens; see, e.g., Snodgrass 1988, 146. With the spread of more wrathful mandalas, by the ninth century and the time of the Dunhuang manuscripts, the edges came to be more generally understood as dark and demonic places. Peaceful gardens are described in one Dunhuang *Guhyasamāja sādhana*; see ITJ331/2, 5v.2–3. This may be because the mandala being used at that particular moment in the ritual is a peaceful one, as indicated in the corresponding verse in the *Guhyasamāja Tantra* itself (VI.13).
72. ITJ712, 13v.2–3.
73. *Mahāsaṃvarodāya-tantra*, 158a.5–7. Note the resemblances between the imagery here and that of Rudra's palace; compare the opening scene in the Rudra myth's twenty-seventh chapter. Elizabeth English has gathered the references for several descriptions of tantric charnel grounds; see English 2002, 448–50 n. 312. Though her sources generally date from a century or two after Tibet's age of fragmentation, their details are still relevant to the present study, particularly given the similar depictions seen in both our Rudra myth and the above-cited passage from ITJ712.
74. For some speculations on the historicity of Padmasambhava, see Bischoff 1978.
75. For a discussion and translation of this text, see Karmay 1988a, 137–74. The reliability of its attribution is primarily based on (1) its being cited in the *Lamp for the Eyes in*

Contemplation, a work composed by Nupchen Sangye Yeshe in the early tenth century, and (2) the existence of an eleventh-century subcommentary to the work written by Rongzom Chokyi Zangpo (c. 1012–1088).

76. For the tantra, see Q. 458. The commentary is found at Q. 4717 but is missing from the *Collected Tantras of the Nyingma*. The attribution of the work to Padmasambhava seems to have been forgotten by the later Tibetan tradition.
77. ITJ321, 2a.2.
78. ITJ321, 84a.5.
79. See Bischoff and Hartman 1971, 11–27. The section on Padmasambhava's activities has been retranslated more recently in Kapstein 2000, 158–59. Until recently PT44 was undated. As Bischoff and Hartman noted in their 1971 article, a fragment of a Tibetan date is found on the cover page of PT44, which reads, "the second year, the tiger year" (*lo gnyis stag gi lo*). They were unable to identify this date, but Takeuchi has succeeded where they did not. The paper used to make PT44 was apparently recycled; in its previous incarnation it had been a letter from the Khotanese king to the Chinese ruler of Shazhou. On the basis of the Tibetan date noted by Bischoff, a Chinese seal, and a still-legible fragment of the original letter written in Khotanese, Takeuchi is able to date the Khotanese letter to the year 978. This means, concludes Takeuchi, "that the Buddhist text on Padmasambhava was written even later, namely after the 980s" (Takeuchi 2004, 342).
80. Elsewhere I have explored the available evidence from Dunhuang relating to the development of the Padmasambhava legends, including two previously unnoticed manuscripts—PT307 and ITJ644. The former manuscript is discussed again below, but the latter should also be kept in mind here, as it too sheds light on some possible narrative precedents for the Padmasambhava legends, thematic lines along which the stories may have developed. Here I am thinking in particular of the narrative precedents for the Nepalese Asura cave incident and the one involving the "Horse Ears" spring. See Dalton 2004, 761–64, pages to which Mayer 2007 has provided a helpful addendum with several further insights.
81. This name is mentioned in an important passage in the so-called *Old Tibetan Chronicle*; see Bacot, Thomas, and Toussaint 1940, 119 and 163–64 (also translated by Karmay 1998, 439).
82. This deity appears in Pawo Tsuglag Trengwa's *Mkhas pa'i dga' ston* discussion of the fragmentation of political power following the death of Pel Khortsen in 910. The relevant passage is translated in Vitali 2004 116 n. 15, and briefly discussed on p. 119.
83. PT307, ll. 10–32. For a complete transcription and a slightly more extensive discussion of this passage, see Dalton 2004.
84. On the *saptamātṛkā*, see Macdonald and Stahl 1979; Harper 1989; Panikkar 1989; Grönbold 2001; Davidson 2002, 300–303; Tachikawa 2004.
85. Following the translation by Hodge 2003, 171, with minor changes.
86. *Guhyasamāja Tantra*, XIV.55. The interlinear notes to this verse in the Dunhuang *Guhyasamāja* (ITJ438, 53v.5) confirm that early Tibetans understood the *ma mo* to be the same as the seven mothers (*ma bdun*).

87. As in the liberation rite described in PT840, l. 11 (translated in appendix B). See also ITJ406, 19.2–3, where they appear in the mandala as attendants of Mamaki.
88. ITJ727's seven mothers are identical with those seen in PT307's account, as is evident in a brief invitation prayer that names them in the same way and even lists them in the same order.
89. The autobiographical writings of Longchenpa (1308–1363) refer to a set of "seven sisters," though there headed by Dorje Yudronma (the last of our own seven), with the other sisters remaining unnamed. For a translation of the relevant passage, see Germano and Gyatso 2000, 258. The story is also told in Dudjom Rinpoche 1991, 581–85.
90. Franz-Karl Ehrhard has done some work on a fifteen-folio text dealing with the cult by Brag dkar rta so sprul sku (b. 1775), titled *Rdo rje ma bdun ma'i lo rgyus sngon med legs par bshad pa'i bden gtam blo ldan dga' bskyed dpyid kyi rgyal mi glu dbyangs.* (Note that in my earlier article [Dalton 2004] I mistook the title for another work by Brag dkar rta so sprul sku that deals with the subschool of the Stod 'brug tradition deriving from Ma bdun ras chen. My thanks to Ehrhard for correcting this error.) The names of the seven mothers found in this text differ greatly from the Dunhuang list. Ehrhard's recently published findings will certainly add much to our understanding of the later role of the seven mothers in Tibet; see Ehrhard 2008b.
91. The lists of the twelve *tenma* goddesses can also shed some light on the homes of our seven sisters (compare, e.g., René Nebesky-Wojkowitz 1996 [1956], 181–88), though my own attempts to use these lists to pinpoint their homes were often frustrated by the fluidity of the lists. In a study by the eighteenth-century scholar Longdol Lama, for example, the chief sister in our own text appears twice, once under her Buddhist name Dorje Kundrakma, as the protector of Lake Gnam mtsho phyug mo, and again under her pre-Buddhist name Rkong la de mo, as the protector of Bres na ri gdong in Kong (see Tucci 1949, 728).
92. Thus it is not surprising to see, e.g., some of our seven sisters appear again in Nyangrel's twelfth-century narrative of Padmasambhava's demon-taming activities. The *Copper Island* follows the master through a series of eight locations in central Tibet. At each location he subjugates the local spirits, and finally at Slate Mountain (G.ya' ri) he binds them all under oath as guardians of the new Buddhist religion. Nyangrel's version of events is far more elaborate than PT307's, but the fundamental theme, of Padmasambhava using tantric violence to force the Tibetan deities to accept vows to protect Buddhism, remains the same. For an English translation, see chap. 9 of Tsogyal 1993, 62–64.
93. *Guhyagarbha Tantra,* 206.1–2. The goddesses' position around the "outer edges of the *maṇḍala*" is further implied by the line in PT307 stating, "they are pleased by the remainder offerings" (*mchod pa lhag*), a reference to the tantric ritual practice of giving the leftover offerings to the mundane protector deities believed to inhabit the mandala's edges. The same idea appears in the Rudra myth, fol. 209; see also the note to that passage. On the remainder in Indian religious life, see Malamoud 1996, 7–22.
94. Chapter 15 of the *Guhyagarbha Tantra* opens with the wrathful mandala emanating out of the peaceful mandala that is discussed earlier in the tantra (*Guhyagarbha Tantra,* 195.6).

95. The Tibetan rite came to the attention of modern scholars thanks to a 1979 publication on "Tibetan Monastic Customs, Art, and Building," entitled *Gateway to the Temple* by T. L. Gyatsho. This was actually preceded one year earlier by a much shorter reference to the same rite in Lessing and Wayman 1978, 280–81.
96. Historically, the purpose of the resulting hole actually seems to have varied. Following the *Bṛhat-Saṃhitā*, Kramrisch 1976, vol. 1, 14, describes it in connection with a simple soil test, and this seems to have been the case in some early Buddhist ritual texts (see, e.g., Amoghavajra's mid-eighth-century *Foding zunsheng tuoluoni niansong yigui fa*; T.972, 364b17–20). According to Gardner 2006, 309–10, however, some versions of the rite use the resulting hole as a place to bury a treasure offering for the local spirit. Still elsewhere the soil test is described in connection with the *vāstunāga* rite; see, e.g., Kuladatta's *Kriyāsaṃgrahapañjikā*, as translated by Tanemura 2004, 20–25.
97. See Terwiel 1985. Here I should mention that many of the materials relating to this rite have already been gathered and discussed by Cantwell 2005 and Gardner 2006.
98. In connection with secular constructions, e.g., the *Matsya-purāṇa* describes Vāstupuruṣa as rotating beneath the ground (see Charpentier and Clément 1975, 556). Limiting ourselves to Tibetan sources, we can trace many discussions of the rite to the eleventh and twelfth centuries. Most new school materials go back to the late-twelfth-century *Śrīśambara-maṇḍalavidhi* by the Indian scholar Vibhūticandra. We know Tibetan knowledge of the rite predated this source, however, for we also see it in an eleventh-century *Guhyagarbha* commentary attributed to the Tibetan author Rongzom Chökyi Zangpo (see *Rgyud rgyal gsang ba'i snying po'i 'grel pa*, 296). Just as Vibhūticandra's work was the *locus classicus* for the new schools, Rongzom's became the source for the Nyingmapa, and his discussion was repeated by all subsequent *Guhyagarbha* commentators. Our search for the rite's origins within Tibet might end here were it not for the fortunate discovery of ITJ931. In this fragment we have evidence that the Tibetan, and thus too the Indian, forms of the rite likely go back to at least the late eighth or early ninth century, that is, before the fall of the Tibetan Empire, after which the importation of Indian ritual techniques into Tibet seems to have been interrupted.
99. That said, some do mention the standard set of eight *nāgas* by name; see, e.g., chap. 3 of the *Kriyāsaṃgraha* (Skorupski 2002).
100. For a photograph of the treaty pillar, see Richardson 1998.
101. Though 'Bri gung chos kyi grags pa's *Sa bdag lto 'phye chen po brtag pa'i rab tu byed pa nyes pa kun sel*, 99.4–5 does recognize that the daily increments entail that the spirit faces in a different direction for each of the four seasons.
102. The incorporation of Chinese astrological elements into the rite is apparently not unique to this Dunhuang text, as the *Sa bdag lto 'phye chen po brtag pa'i rab tu byed pa nyes pa kun sel*, 99.5–6 notes the existence of multiple forms of the rite, depending on whether one follows the Kālacakra, Chinese, new school (*gsar ma*), or Nyingma system. The same text then (99.6–100.1) proceeds to discuss the role of astrology in some ritual systems. A Chinese diagram for the rite may also be found in Pelliot chinois 2964.

103. The metaphor here is not meant to invoke a clerical v. shamanic dichotomy in the manner of Samuel's *Civilized Shamans*, but simply to observe the perspectival shift regarding Tibet's early history, which took place after the tenth century as monastic institutions began to reassert themselves.

CHAPTER 3. A BUDDHIST MANUAL FOR HUMAN SACRIFICE?

1. A number of Dunhuang manuscripts discuss the liberation rite, as Carmen Meinert 2006 has recently observed. Apart from the manuscript that is the focus of the present chapter, another that is of particular interest is PT840, which also contains a detailed description of a liberation rite. The rite bears a number of similarities to the one discussed in the present chapter. For a translation and transliteration of the text, see appendix C of this study. Similar too is another discussion of the rite in PT321.
2. Indeed, the indirect nature of *abhicāra* rites was so common in India that Medātithi in his tenth-century commentary on Manu 9:290 defines *abhicāra* as an "act of killing through the power of charms and the support of an invisible power (*adṛṣṭa*)" (Türstig 1985, 82).
3. On such summoning rites, see Cantwell 1997, 113. For a summoning rite in the Dunhuang manuscripts, see the Kīlaya ritual described in ITJ754/7, R7.12–14.
4. ITJ419, r26.4–5: *dkyil 'khor gyi thog du dor te mtshan brtag par bya.* On the basis of grammar, one could argue that its subject is not the victim's head but his consciousness that is flung *into* the buddhafield of the visualized mandala. In all likelihood an imagined throwing of the consciousness is also intended, but two points suggest a simultaneous physical tossing of the head. First, it is clearly stated that the object in question is flung *onto* (*thog du;* lit. "on top of") the mandala. Second, the passage immediately following this line clearly describes the ways in which the *head* might come to rest.
5. Dalton 2002, 335–36.
6. Again, for a complete translation and transliteration of this rite, see appendix C to this study.
7. Nebesky-Wojkowitz 1976, 106.
8. Note too that the liberation rite did not have to be directed against others. As a soteriological method, it could also be used for oneself. Thus, explains PT321, 11v.2, "there are two kinds, liberating oneself with realization, and liberating others with compassion."
9. For a discussion of this legend, see Schlieter 2006.
10. Yamaguchi 1996, 244, notes that the biography of Pelgyi Dorje that appears in the *Yer pa dkar chags*, an apparently early source included in the *Mkhas pa'i dga' ston*, makes no mention of the assassination. Nor for that matter is the brief appearance of Pelgyi Dorje in ITJ689/3 accompanied by any mention of his legendary role as an assassin.
11. The biography of Nupchen Sangye Yeshe provides another version of the story; see *Brgyud pa'i rnam thar*, 173.5.
12. The tantra itself specifies drawing the victim (ITJ438, 53v.5), while the interlinear notes to the Dunhuang manuscript also mentions writing the name of the person (ITJ438, 53v.3).

13. The three manuscripts in question are PT36, ITJ419, and PT42. Together they total 178 folio sides. The first and last folios are unfortunately missing, but otherwise the compilation is complete.
14. Its *Guhyasamāja* affiliation can be discerned at several points: The manuscript's sixth and ninth items contain quotations from the *Guhyasamāja*'s second and fifth chapters respectively, while in item 10 the title of the tantra is used to describe the "secret gathering" (Skt. *guhyasamāja*; Tib. *gsang ba'i 'dus pa*) of the deities in the mandala. Perhaps even more significant is that the manuscript is almost certainly written in the same hand as many of the major works relating to the *Guhyasamāja* found in Dunhuang. On the latter point and on analyzing the Dunhuang manuscripts according to their handwriting more generally, see Dalton, Davis, and van Schaik 2007.
15. This three-part offering appears to have been common in early tantric ritual, and even today it provides the structure for the popular ritual feast (Tib. *tshogs;* Skt. *gaṇacakra*). ITJ570 and ITJ573 both describe the same three offering rites, though not in quite the same Mahāyoga context seen here in ITJ419.
16. From the perspective of the received canonical tantras, the Dunhuang documents' use of the term "*heruka*" to refer to the fundamental wrathful buddha of the *vajra* buddha-family is unusual for such an early date (the late eighth century being roughly the period in Indian tantric ritual development that is reflected in the Tibetan Dunhuang manuscripts). Nonetheless, it is commonplace within the Dunhuang collections, which therefore may reflect a certain moment in the growth of tantric Buddhism in India when violent practices had developed within the ritual systems of the *Guhyasamāja* and *Guhyagarbha* but were only just starting to be inscribed into the Buddhist tantras themselves. It is perhaps significant that the term is used in a similar manner in the mid-ninth-century Rudra myth translated in appendix A.
17. The ritualization of doctrinal exegesis was common practice in the later Tibetan tradition, as is clear from the existence of *'chad thabs* ("method of explanation") texts, which describe the preliminary rites that are ideally performed before teaching a given system; see, e.g., the *Spyi mdo dgongs 'dus kyi 'chad thabs zin bris nyung ngu rnam gsal.*
18. ITJ419, v7.2–3: *gtor ma ltag 'og kun la/ chos kyi sbyin ba'i tshigs bshad bya.*
19. ITJ419, v1.1–2: *yon bdag gi bsam ba yang grub par gyur cig.*
20. ITJ419, v3.4.
21. The seventh question, on how to gain control over spirits, has been discussed in chapter 2.
22. For a more detailed description of the contents of this manuscript, see the entry to ITJ419 in Dalton and van Schaik 2006.
23. PT42, r24.3–25.2.
24. PT42, r13.2–14.4.
25. See in particular *Guhyasamāja Tantra,* III.12–17 and VI.8–17. Significantly, an interlinear note to the passage in chapter 3 of the Dunhuang manuscript of the *Guhyasamāja* associates it with the cultivation of the subtle *vajra*; see ITJ438, 10v.3. The term "subtle *vajra*" does not appear in the *Guhyasamāja* itself. It does, however, appear numerous

times in the *Sarvatathāgata-tattvasaṃgraha*, particularly in the third chapter, where it involves the visualization of a tiny *vajra* that is then expanded and contracted so that the practitioner realizes various meditative states. The "subtle yoga" constitutes that practice's counterpart in the *Guhyasamāja*.

26. PT42, v10.1–11.1. Additions taken from the interlinear notes.
27. See, e.g., ITJ438, 15v.3, and chap. 3 in Āryadeva's *Caryā-melāpaka-pradīpa* (trans. Wedemeyer 2008, 104).
28. The question of how to interpret the "nose" here is really whether the requisite expertise in the subtle *vajra* refers to a proficiency in the development-stage or the perfection-stage version of the practice, both of which are seen in the *Guhyasamāja* itself.
29. PT42, r8.2–10.1. It is perhaps relevant that in the *Guhyasamāja*, III.13, habituation to the subtle yoga results in the emanation of many buddhas into space; for the Dunhuang interlinear notes to the verse, see ITJ438, 10v.1–2.
30. Complete transcriptions of the two passages are provided in appendix B of the present work. In the translations below, the Tibetan is provided for those terms for which my translation is uncertain.
31. ITJ419, r18.3-r27.2. The pagination of this first item is particularly confusing. First, the India Office Library has reversed the proper reading order of the entire manuscript, printing their page numbers on its verso. Second, they also neglected to print page numbers on the twenty-second and twenty-third folio sides (which fall between their fol. 45 and 46). For my own numbering system, I have retained their recto-verso decision, but resorted to a new numbering system that reflects the manuscript itself, so that the first folio side is fol. 1 and so on. This system matches that used in my entry in Dalton and van Schaik 2006.
32. Note that at this point there is an error in the India Office Library's pagination, which skips two folios.
33. This is a reference to the third of the four tantric activities, of pacification, enhancement, coercion, and violence. Thus by means of coercion the master drives the uninitiated from the ritual site.
34. A mandala made of the wind element seems to have been commonly associated with wrathful ritual activities. See, e.g., Buddhaguhya's commentary to the *Mahāvairocana-abhisaṃbodhi Tantra*, where he says that the "blue and black colours should be connected with a wind mandala" (Hodge 2003, 157).
35. Throughout both descriptions of this rite, the "object of compassion" (*thugs rje'i gnas*) refers to the sacrificial victim.
36. This is a common poetic image used to connote purity in Buddhist ritual texts. In a Dunhuang book of prayers to be recited at the building of a *stūpa* we read: "A so-called '*stūpa*' is a reflection of the truth-body (*dharmakāya*) of all the buddhas of the ten directions. All phenomena are beyond description or imagination, but as a mere symbol that is perceivable and expressible, [the *stūpa*] is sanctified as the truth-body. Its form is like a pure crystal egg, with variegated beams of light radiating forth. Its site is the site of all the buddhas, accomplishing whatever is wished for by the devotee"

(ITJ435, 16r.1–4). Note that here, as in our liberation rite, the crystal egg is used as a metaphor for a body, here the *dharmakāya*. Another instance of the image in the Dunhuang manuscripts appears in ITJ685, r1.15.

37. While the purpose of this moon is somewhat unclear, it likely provides the base for the mandala into which the buddhas are next invited. If so, we may be seeing here a shorthand reference to a generation method witnessed in some Yoga-tantra ritual systems, in which a crescent moon is first visualized and then expanded into a full moon upon which the mandala appears (see, e.g., ITJ716/1).
38. The term "noble one" (Tib. *'phags pa;* Skt. *ārya*) is used throughout the tantric literature from Dunhuang to refer to the buddhas and bodhisattvas.
39. The mantra has been removed from the translation, both here and below in passage 2, where the same occurs at the same point in the ritual. It is perhaps worth noting the close similarity between the mantra employed here and the one used for slaying in chapter 6 of the *Sarvatathāgata-tattvasaṃgraha,* § 923.
40. The *Guhyasamāja Tantra* specifies that the head (of the paper effigy in the tantra's case) is to be chopped off at the neck (ITJ438, 53v.5: *myid pa bcad*). The interlinear notes to the same line in the tantra make the use of a paper effigy still more explicit (ITJ438, 53v.5: *ri mor bris pa de'i mgo gcad par byas pa*).
41. PT42, v32.4–v36.4; ITJ419, r1.1–r3.2. To convert PT42 pagination to that provided in Macdonald and Imaeda 1978–2001, vol. II, add 36 to these numbers. To convert ITJ419 pagination to India Office Library pagination, add 24 to these numbers.
42. That is, the desire realm, the form realm, and the formless realm, comprising the entire range of possible rebirths in *samsāra.*
43. Here the Tibetan name reads Sgrol ma nyi ma, which might be rendered into Sanskrit as *Tāra-sūrya. However, in the earlier description of the same rite (translated above), the same deity is named Sgrol ba nyi ma (Skt. *Tāraka-sūrya), also known as Ṭakkirāja. For this reason, we should probably correct the present *ma* suffix to the masculine *ba.* Tāraka does appear in a Śaiva myth included in the thirteenth-century *Haracaritacintāmaṇi* by Jayadratha, where he is a demon who oppresses the Hindu gods (see Sanderson 1995, 93). The name Tāraka may also hearken back to the kinds of practices referenced by the story of Migalaṇḍika, the "sham recluse" of the Pāli Vinaya who sought to "liberate the unliberated" (*atiṇṇe tāresi*), as discussed in chapter 1 of the present study. Note too that the Tibetan version of the name in our present manuscript (Sgrol ba) suggests that Ṭakki may have been associated with **tāraka* (√tṛ means "to cross over; to deliver"), which may be translated as "liberator" or "savior," an association that makes this deity the ideal performer of the liberation rite. It is thus unclear whether *Tāraka is simply a pseudonym for Ṭakkirāja or a case of creative etymology on the part of Indians or Tibetans (or both). In either case, the name Ṭakkirāja derives in fact from the place Ṭakki, located in the northern Punjab. According to Tucci, Ṭakkirāja was originally a local (*naivāsika*) god from this region (see Tucci 1949, vol. 2, 616 n. 275).
44. My translation of the preceding adverbial phrase is somewhat uncertain due to damage to the manuscript.

45. The ten activities are discussed at ITJ419, r59.1–r60.4, and seem to represent a development stage (Skt. *utpattikrama;* Tib. *bskyed rim*) style of worship.
46. See, e.g., the *Sarvadurgatipariśodhana-tantra,* 223a.5.
47. See *Mahāpratisāravidyārājñī,* 141a.1–2.
48. The *Guhyasamāja Tantra* (ITJ438, 53v.1) suggests it should be a triangular mandala. Alternatively, it may be semicircular, as is typical of many wind mandalas.
49. See, e.g., the *Phur pa bcu gnyis,* 454b.3–456b.1, where seven types of evildoers are enumerated and then further subdivided (as noted by Mayer 1996, 123), and PT656 for a tenfold list (translated in Dalton 2005). Ten fields are also referred to in PT321, 16r.3. For some later Tibetan lists, see Sokdokpa's *Dris lan nges don 'brug sgra,* 447, and Longdol Lama's *Gsang sngags rig pa'i 'dzin pa'i sde snod las byung ba'i rgyud sde bzhi'i ming gi rnam grangs,* 110.
50. Note that in the liberation rite in PT840, ll. 33–35, the exits are blocked *after* the victim is beheaded.
51. PT321, 16r.4–16v.3 provides some further relevant comments:

    One who has the requisite heat of a great being, as well as the mantras and *mudrās,* the oral advice and pith instructions, oceans of prayers, and immeasurable practice, should arrange the five heroic seeds at the five places. The emanation and retraction of wisdom [from these syllables] purifies [the victim]. The secret mandala of the great perfection (*rdzogs pa chen po*) of the body, speech, mind, and good qualities is demonstrated. The predispositions of the [victim's] conceptual extremes of subject and object are purified. The oceans of saṃsāra are parted. The doors to the five continuous ways are blocked. With means and force he is liberated and overpowered. Having united him with the initiations, *siddhis,* and wisdom, in the land of Akaniṣṭha, in the wombs of the nondual father and mother *tathāgatas* of the five families of *bhagavats,* in the sky of the mother, he is initiated as an excellent son.

    The "five continuous ways" (*lam rgyud lnga*) are known elsewhere, both in Dunhuang (see ITJ841, 4r) and India (see Edgerton 1953, vol. 2, 208–9) as the realms of the gods, humans, animals, ghosts, and hell-beings (i.e., the more common six lacking the *asuras*). Despite what our liberation manuscript itself suggests, this latter reading seems better suited to the present ritual context, at least from a normative Buddhist perspective from which the god realm is still within *saṃsāra.*
52. Here we encounter the only significant point of disagreement between our two accounts. The first passage has this purification occur before the invitation of the mandala and the visualization of Kālarātrī, whereas the second passage has it after. The first passage is clearly preferable, as it places the purification of the victim's mental impurities directly after the purification of his physical body with the five syllables.
53. ITJ438, 43v.3–4. See also ITJ406, r1.4–r2.1, on this deity's mantra and its use in violent ritual, and PT284, 3v.7–4r.8, for a more detailed iconographic description and the mantra. Indeed, it seems that an association between Ṭakkirāja and liberation may have been somewhat common among the Buddhist tantras; as already mentioned in a note above, it seems he appears in a similar context in the *Sarvatathāgata-tattvasaṃgraha,* and see too the *'Bras bu chen po lnga gzung shing bsgral ba,* 27.5–28.5. Within the

Dunhuang manuscripts, ITJ473, 1v.5–6 describes Ṭakkirāja as the deity responsible for punishing those who transgress their vows in the following verse: "Having been transformed by this truth word [i.e., mantra], if one transgresses this sacrament, one will be crushed by this truth word of the noble ones. . . ." Note too that the *Sarvatathāgata-tattvasaṃgraha*'s Maheśvara taming myth begins with Vairocana reciting the mantra *oṃ ṭakki jaḥ*, which Davidson 1991, 200, notes "is known as the disciplinary ankus of all the *tathāgatas*."

54. The same eyes and breath imagery is seen throughout the tantric Buddhist corpus. See, e.g., the *Phur pa bcu gnyis* purificatory rites (see Cantwell 2005, 13–14). In the latter context, when the *vajra* master performs the *vajra* walk (*rdo rje'i 'gros*), he is depicted again in the same way. It may well be that at this point in our own rite, the ritual master is supposed to be performing the *vajra* walk, as he does so at the corresponding moment in the liberation rite described in PT840, l. 15 (translated in appendix C). In the Rudra myth (fol. 202), the *heruka* also stomps on the eight classes of gods as his eyes blaze with fire. See also PT337, 5.16, where the right eye becomes a sun disc and the left eye a moon disc in context of the *gaṇacakra*, as well as Ānandagarbha's commentary on the *Sarvatathāgata-tattvasaṃgraha* (*Tattvāloka*, 206b.1), where it appears in the context of the wrathful gaze. A slight variation in the imagery appears in the interlinear notes to ITJ331/3, 6v.1–2. Regarding the purificatory use of fire, water, and wind, compare also Nupchen's commentary to the mantras used to purify Rudra at the beginning of his initiation; see n. 175 to the translation of myth in appendix A, fol. 221.
55. A similar multiplication of blades is seen in PT840's liberation rite (l. 27), though there they emerge from the syllable *hrīḥ*.
56. For an English translation of the relevant passage, see Johnson 1998, 39. My thanks to Phyllis Granoff for noting this possible connection.
57. PT840, ll. 36–40 specifies that an imagined hook and specific mantras are to be used in leading the victim's consciousness to the realm of enlightenment. PT321 adds the following three comments: (12v.1:) "By offering this *skandha* of form [i.e., the victim's body] to the Buddha-Heruka and Krodhīśvarī, the *siddhis* of the *tathāgatas* are conferred. . . ." Then each of the other four *skandhas* is offered to a different buddha-family, resulting in conferral of the *siddhis* specific to each buddha-family. (15v.2:) "Then the mind is pulled into the crossed [*vajra*] (*rgya gram*), that is, the choice share is offered." (16r.4:) "The form *skandha* of this one is dedicated to the conditions of an ocean of enjoyment ambrosial substances. The continuum of his consciousness has the dawning as the great Lord of the Yoga (*yogeśvara*) conferred upon it."
58. *Mun pa'i go cha*, vol. 50, 305.2.
59. PT321, 12v.5–13r.2 similarly provides correlations between the victim's body parts and various deities.
60. PT840 distinguishes three offerings of the mind (*citta*), the blood, and the head.
61. Note too that some early renditions of the flower-throwing rite framed it as a way to determine the success or failure of the initiation; see, e.g., the Chinese translation of the *Guhya Tantra*, attributed to Amoghavajra: T.897, 769c1–770a17. My thanks to Koichi Shinohara for this reference.

62. See Goudriaan 1978, 251ff. Few if any detailed descriptions of how to perform a human sacrifice are found in any early Śaiva sources. Such rites are referred to (several times in the *Brahmayāmala*, e.g.), but never described in any detail. Nonetheless, the idea that tantric Śaivas engaged in such practices was widespread, for it forms a key element in the plots of the *Mālatīmādhava* of Bhavabhūti (early 7th c.) and the *Yaśatilaka* of Somadevasūri (mid-10th c.); see Hatley 2007, 84–94 and 106–9 respectively. My thanks to Hatley for helping me with these references.
63. Blaquiere 1799. While most versions have the *Rudhirādhyāya* as the seventy-first chapter, this is not true for all. The edition I have used for the present study, e.g., has it in chapter 67. For a list of manuscripts of the *Kālikā Purāṇa*, see Hazra 1963, vol. 2, 195 n. 420.
64. On the basis of a manuscript note, Van Kooij 1972, 3 n. 4 suggested a *terminus ad quem* for the received version of the *Kālikā Purāṇa* of 1080 C.E., a date that was in general agreement with Hazra, who dated the work to the tenth or early eleventh century. More recently, however, Stapelfeldt 2001, 35–40, has shown the received version to date from "not before the end of the sixteenth century" (40).
65. *Kālikā Purāṇa*, 67.76.
66. *Kālikā Purāṇa*, 67.76.
67. *Kālikā Purāṇa*, 67.24. A further connection between the kinds of weapons used in the Śaiva and Buddhist versions of the rite is suggested by PT840, l. 26, where a *kartarī* is specified in transcription (*ka tar ri*).
68. An axe (Tib. *sta re*) is also recommended by the *Guhyasamāja Tantra* itself (ITJ438, 53v.5).
69. Note that Kālī performs the actual killing in the liberation rite of the early *Phur pa* tradition as well (see Mayer 1996, 125), and Kālī plays a similar role in Patrul Rinpoche's *gcod* rite too—see Patrul Rinpoche, 298 n. 205. An understood connection between liberation rites and Śrī Devī is also indicated when the goddess appears in a vision to inspire Pelgyi Dorje's liberation of Lang Darma (see *Nyang ral chos 'byung*, 438).
70. *Kālikā Purāṇa*, 67.37.
71. *Kālikā Purāṇa*, 67.21. See also v. 195: "When Caṇḍika is offered the *bali*, the head *bali* should be consecrated with water and presented along with the root mantras."
72. For inscriptional evidence of head offerings, sometimes combined with blood, to the goddess, see Nandi 1973, 145–46. Note the apparent popularity of such practices around the tenth century, the same period from which our own Dunhuang manuscript probably dates.
73. *Kālikā Purāṇa*, 123–26a. According to Shaman Hatley, a similar passage also appears in the *Tattvacintāmaṇi* of Pūrṇānanda (16th c.), chap. 24.64–71.
74. I am by no means the first to suggest that the liberation rite may be understood as a sacrifice. Cathy Cantwell in particular and Sophie Day before her have considered the idea; see Cantwell 1997, 116–17.
75. *Manu* 3.70.
76. *Ṛgveda*, 1.162.21.
77. *Netra Tantra*, 20.4b–10b (reference cited by White 2003, 319 n. 19). Similarly, Abhinavagupta writes in his *Tantrasāra*, "And one should offer live animals, for they too

in this manner become divinely graced; therefore, out of compassion, one should not have doubt concerning animal sacrifice" (*Tantrasāra*, 14.11–12). My thanks to Shaman Hatley for this reference.

78. The above-cited theories have been listed in the same chronological order as that seen in Robbins 1998, 288–89.
79. *Dmar mchod nyes dmigs*, 4b.4.
80. Though, as observed above, PT840 distinguishes the offering of the victim's mind from those of both his blood and his head. Even there, however, the blood is taken metaphorically as the victim's *desire*, which is purified within "a state of non-fixation" (*dmyigs su myed pa'i ngang*); see ll. 50–51.
81. Charles Malamoud 1999, 29, has written, "*medha*, of which the primary sense (according to Renou 1941, 378) is 'force,' designates the vital sap, the corporal substance that contains the vigor of the animal and makes it able to serve as victim" (my translation from the French).
82. *Kālikā Purāṇa*, 67.85b.
83. See, e.g., Owens 1993, 261–62, and Slusser 1982, 217.
84. See PT321, 15v.2, passage translated in note above.
85. Oppitz 1993, 112.
86. ITJ321, 66a.5–66b.1.
87. For some English translations of the rite, see Patrul Rinpoche 1994, 351–65, and Dorje 2005, 200–216.
88. Indeed, in his late-ninth-century commentary on the *Compendium of Intentions*' Rudra myth, Nupchen refers to the practice as "transferring [the consciousness] to [another] body" (*gtan spo ba*). A similar practice (called *utkrānti*) is also found in tantric Śaivism, where it may be performed in connection with ritual suicide by a devotee who has attained "world-weariness" (*nirvedam*) and who seeks to abandon his body and merge his mind with Śiva. For a discussion of this practice, see Vasudeva 2004, 437–45.
89. Further connections may also exist (though further research would be required) between the liberation rite and the well-known "cutting" (*gcod*) rite, in which one visualizes one's own body being consumed by demons, as well as the Tibetan sky burial, a funerary rite in which dead bodies are disposed of by being fed to vultures. And it is perhaps relevant that our own liberation manual describes the deities who feast on the victim as "acting in the manner of vultures."
90. For a recent collection of essays on the influence of human sacrifice upon a wide range of religious traditions, see Bremmer 2007. For an illuminating study of the enduring role of sacrifice in French religion and politics, see Strenski 2002.

CHAPTER 4. SACRIFICE AND THE LAW

1. Jones 1869 [1794], xi.
2. In this regard, Jones's work was truly a product of its time, a time of widespread fascination with "classical civilizations" as providing roots for the present world, especially Greece and Rome as the progenitors of European culture. On this trend's effects on the study of Asia and Buddhism, see especially Said 1978 and Lopez, ed. 1995.

3. On the British invention of India's legal tradition at the expense of Indian agencies, see the recent study by Bhattacharyya-Panda 2008.
4. Jones 1869 [1794], xix.
5. Jones 1799, vol. 3, 26.
6. Jones 1869 [1794], xx.
7. Mill 1817, vol. 1, 356.
8. Mill 1817, vol. 1, 362.
9. Mill 1817, vol. 1, 362.
10. Mani 1998.
11. On the role of "sacrifice" in colonial India, see Padel 1995, a study of the British government's violent suppression (or sacrifice?) of the Konds for their association with human sacrifice. On the anthropological side, the ideological aspects of sacrifice should be considered within the wider context of the well-known debate between Sahlins and Obeyesekere, a debate that is deeply relevant to the present study in general (see in particular Obeyesekere 2005). Finally, for another study that speaks in a number of suggestive ways to the present study, see Sheehan 2006.
12. Vitali 1996, 239, argues (against Karmay 1998, 8–9) that the edict was issued sometime after Yeshe Ö's 986 *Bka' shog chen mo,* which inaugurated the later dispensation of the teachings, but before the king moved his capital from Purang to Tholing, which happened sometime before 996. For this reason, I take 990 as a rough estimate. On Yeshe Ö's probable dates, see Vitali 1996, 181–83.
13. *Dris lan nges don 'brug sgra,* 440.2–450.5 (reproduced in Karmay 1998, 14–15, as ll. 40–53).
14. *Nyang ral chos 'byung,* 458.10–14.
15. Vitali 1996, 55, ll. 5–7. Yeshe Ö's involvement in the establishment of a new Buddhist legal system has also been discussed by Scherrer-Schaub 2001, 714–15.
16. Strong 1983, 41.
17. Beal 1993 [1869], chap. 16, 55. My thanks to Donald Lopez for pointing out this passage.
18. See Das 1902, 186–90.
19. Olivelle 2008, 261.
20. For a modern retelling based on Tibetan sources, see Tsonawa 1984, 60–64.
21. *Deb ther sngon po,* 609.1–2.
22. For a recent popular study of this group, see Dash 2005.
23. Malamoud 1996, 160.
24. Weber 1965, 29. Historical exceptions to this rule can, of course, be pointed to, and Weber is careful to distinguish this exclusive right of the modern state from that of the earlier medieval state, which was subject to limitations placed on it by the Catholic Church.
25. PT1287, ll. 451–55.
26. 'U'i dum brtan, aka Lang Darma, is the last king mentioned by the chronicle; for a summary of the evidence on dating the *Old Tibetan Chronicle,* see Uray 1992, 124–25.

27. A number of scholars have discussed the discrepancies between the earlier and later accounts of Songtsen Gampo's reign; see Uray 1972; Kapstein 2000, 56–57; Wangdu 2002; and Dotson 2006, 13–14.
28. *Nyang ral chos 'byung*, 175.1–13.
29. Dietz 1984 dates Buddhaguhya's letter to between 780 and 790, though Karmay 1998, 25, and Stein 1986, n. 39, have cast some doubt on the authenticity of the letter. PT840 also describes Trisong Detsen as belonging to "a family of bodhisattvas" (Karmay 1998, 90), and further insights into the relationship between church and state during the imperial period may be found in Ruegg 1995.
30. On the former work, see Zimmermann 1999, and for a preliminary study of the latter treatises, see Pathak 1974.
31. For an English translation of the *Old Tibetan Chronicle*'s discussion of Trisong Detsen's legal contributions, e.g., see Dotson 2006, 26–27.
32. For a transliteration and translation of the treaty in question, see Richardson 1985, 106–43. Walter 2004, 163, has argued that reading the exclusion of Buddhists from this event as a sign of their opposition to blood sacrifice (and Bon) is simply an "old saw" that should be done away with. Certainly the presence of Buddhists at the signing (despite their momentary exclusion) does imply some degree of acceptance of blood sacrifice among the early *sangha*, but I would add that such accounts may also reflect the continuing limitations of Buddhist influence within the court, limitations that may well have necessitated their moral accommodations.
33. On this trend and these two translators in particular, see Davidson 2005, 117–209.
34. Vitali 1996, 111.
35. On Yeshe Ö's organization of this political structure, see the *Royal Annals of Ngari* (in Vitali 1996, 110).
36. See Vitali 1996, 212.
37. As recounted by Steinkellner 1999, 251.
38. For a brief summary of the Gugé court's later history, see Kapstein 2006, 94.
39. Davidson 2005 offers abundant evidence on this point.
40. Davidson 2005, 112–15, has argued that the influence of the Gugé court and the Kadampa during the later dispensation period has been exaggerated by later historical accounts. While this may or may not be true, it is important to recognize that the return of monasticism and monastic scholasticism, as well as the language of ethics and reformation, was integral to the period, alongside of course the continuing importance of the tantras and the tantric lineages that Davidson highlights.
41. The dates and contents of these three proclamations have been discussed by Vitali 1996, 185–240.
42. Karmay 1998, 14, ll. 40–41.
43. Here Yeshe Ö is referring to the three canonical collections of the sutras, the *abhidharma*, and the monastic *vinaya*. In later centuries Tibetans would come to include the tantras in the *tripiṭaka*, but here the term was certainly being used in a more conservative manner.
44. Karmay 1998, 16, ll. 90–100.

45. Karmay 1998, 14, l. 19.
46. Karmay 1998, 14, ll. 59–67.
47. Karmay 1998, 15, ll. 75–76.
48. Karmay 1998, 14, ll. 28–32.
49. Karmay 1998, 14, l. 16.
50. The *Mnga' ris rgyal rabs* specifies that the new monasteries were "subdivided into communities devoted to learning and debating and to meditation," and Sokdokpa adds that both monks and *māntrikas* alike "were to follow the laws of the *vinaya*" (see Vitali 1996, 110 and 232 n. 331). See also Vitali 1996, 230 on this point.
51. *Dris lan nges don 'brug sgra*, 451.1–2.
52. As quoted in *Dmar mchod nyes dmigs*, 4b.3.
53. Karmay 1998, 15, ll. 54–55.
54. Karmay 1998, 15, ll. 57–58.
55. For the relevant references, see Olivelle 2008, 41 and 321, and Wangdu and Hiemberger 2000, 38, 62, and 101.
56. Hamerton-Kelly 1987, 179.
57. Even in tenth-century India, debates were ongoing between Buddhists over whether ritual killing in the tantras was heretical. See, e.g., Gray 2005, 65–66.
58. Jinpa 2008, 99, with a few minor alterations.

CHAPTER 5. FOUNDATIONAL VIOLENCE

1. David Frankfurter's recent study on the discourses of evil provides some possibly relevant insights in this regard, in particular Frankfurter's observation that rumors of demonic conspiracies are often "activated in the encounter between local religious worlds and larger, totalizing, often global systems" (Frankfurter 2006, 7).
2. Indeed, the eleventh and twelfth centuries also marked a time of remarkable innovation for Tibetan Buddhism; indeed it was arguably the most creative period in Tibet's history. Thus the same legends that the present chapter reads as condemnatory were *at the same time* working to forge a new Tibetan identity, mythically proposing, as Davidson has written, "Tibet as an independent ground for the Buddhas' activities" (Davidson 2005, 321; see also Kapstein 2000, 148–49). Without denying the significane of these more positive claims for Tibet, the present chapter simply seeks to explore how they were simultaneously tempered by a language of Tibetan self-demonization, and thus to highlight the contours of this restrictive, and often violent, language.
3. Many of the connections made in this chapter are elaborations on Janet Gyatso's own insightful study of the Tibetan *srin mo* legend (see Gyatso 1987). The present chapter seeks to place that legend more firmly within its particular historical context, namely that of the later dispensation period, and to suggest that the formative mythic themes that Gyatso identified—themes of sacred space, temple building, and the demonization of Tibetans—are particularly significant as reflections of the specific social climate within which they emerged.
4. For further discussion of the dates and activities of these figures, see Vitali 1990, 38 and 61, and Davidson 2005, 92–116.

5. Uebach 1990. Also of interest are Iwasaki 1993 and Kwanten 1977. Buddhism's vitality in the region is further attested to in part by the letters of introduction used by a traveling monk of the late tenth century and now found in the Dunhuang manuscript ITJ754. The second letter in particular makes specific reference to the monastery of Dan tig (see ITJ754, R2.4), where the ten men are said to have received their new monastic vows. Van Schaik promises a full study of these letters in the near future.
6. For an excellent study of this early period of "rekindling the ashes," see Stoddard 2004. On the temple-building activities of the eleventh century, see Vitali 1990.
7. On the gradual emergence of this political system out of the new religious "congregations" of the eleventh century, see Davidson 2005, 393 n. 43.
8. While portions of the material may well date from the eleventh century, the received version clearly dates from a later date. Ronald Davidson has noted a reference in the *Pillar Testament* to Dakpa Gomtsul Nyingpo's (1116–1169) intervention, circa 1160, when the Jokhang was threatened by warring factions of *smad lugs* monks; see Davidson 2005, 328. Evidence of still-later revisions has been noted by Sørensen 1994, 21, who observes a reference at the end of one version of the *Pillar Testament* to the *Mtho mthing ma,* which Sørensen elsewhere (Gyalbo, Hazod, and Sørensen 2000, 148–49) dates to around the early thirteenth century. For some further remarks on the *Pillar Testament,* see van der Kuijp 1996a, 47–49.
9. The ninth-century Skar chung inscription attributes the building of "the Rasa Trulnang and others" (*ra sa'i gtsug lag khang las stsogs pa*) to Songtsen Gampo, and the building of "temples at the center and on the borders" (*dbung mthar gtsug la khang*) to Trisong Detsen (Richardson 1985, 72–75). Further early evidence of Trisong Detsen, not Songtsen Gampo, being responsible for the construction of the border-taming temples appears in the *Old Tibetan Chronicle*: "Having received the unsurpassed *buddhadharma,* he built temples everywhere, at the center and at the borders" (PT1287, ll. 374–75; see also Bacot 1940, 114). It is significant that neither of these early sources describes the temples as a network of "border-*taming*" temples as such, possibly indicating that the demon-taming aspect was grafted onto the scheme at a later date, perhaps only with the *Pillar Testament* and other similar works of the later dispensation.
10. van der Kuijp 1996a, 48.
11. Vitali 1990, 37.
12. *Brgyud pa'i rnam thar,* 236.
13. See *Brgyud pa'i rnam thar,* 198.2–3, and *Zangs gling ma,* 37.7–10, respectively.
14. *Bka' chems ka khol ma,* 222.3–5. In fact, the same difficulties occur again elsewhere in the *Pillar Testament,* as when Songtsen's Nepalese princess attempts to build another temple at Ladong; see *Bka' chems ka khol ma,* 211.5–6. And might we also hear echoes of this motif in the story of Milarepa repeatedly building and tearing down his tower?
15. *Bka' chems ka khol ma,* 214.6–11. Van der Kuijp 1996a, 47, distinguishes two principal versions of the *Pillar Testament* and prefers the longer one, published in 1989 by the Central Institute of Minorities, Beijing. Following his preference, I have used the longer for my own study.

16. As observed by Davidson 2003, 70, parts of the "Great History" section of the *Collected Precepts on Maṇi* were copied almost verbatim from the *Pillar Testament*. Note that the *Collected Precepts on Maṇi* contains two versions of the *rākṣasī* legend, a shorter one and a more elaborate one. Aris 1979, 12, discusses the possibility of a still-earlier "common ancestor" for the two versions, and it may have been the *Pillar Testament*, as both draw different elements from the latter's account. For an example of how the *rākṣasī* legend affected other Tibetan literature, one may look to Orgyen Lingpa's *Padma Chronicles*, which borrowed the image of the demoness in its retelling of the construction of Samye Monastery; see Sørensen 1994, 552.
17. *Bka' chems ka khol ma*, 233.14–234.8. My translations are based in part on those of Sørensen 1994, 553–60. Sørensen supplies transcriptions and translations of all three of the *rākṣasī*-related passages from the *Pillar Testament*, and my work is indebted to his efforts.
18. Stein 1972, 39, and Aris 1979, 15–18. Here I do not mean to discount the possible influence of Chinese geomancy on the account of Kongjo's interpretations. Indeed, it seems to me the interactions between multiple cultures is precisely what has made the legend so rich.
19. Perhaps the most famous example appears in the *Matsya Purāṇa*, in which Śiva's battle with the demon Andhaka is described as ending with the demon's fall to earth. It is probably relevant to our present discussion that the sudden growth of these dismemberment myths in the early medieval tantric and Puranic sources coincided with a growth in temple building in India around the same period (6th c. C.E. and later).
20. For the relevant passage, see the translation in appendix A, fol. 170.
21. Dotson 2007, 12 n. 14, has discussed the significance of the number of border-taming temples, thirteen (as twelve plus one) being a common numeric symbol of totality in early Tibetan documents.
22. *Bka' chems ka khol ma*, 201.14–202.12.
23. As observed by Gyatso 1987, 44.
24. Nupchen Sangye Yeshe may have known of an early version of this text, as he quotes two lines, though attributing them to the *Bdud rtsi'i rgyud* (compare *Lamp for the Eyes in Contemplation*, 52.1–2, to *'Bras bu chen po lnga gzung zhing bsgral ba*, 37.2–3; or *Mun pa'i go cha*, vol. 50, 311.1–2, to *'Bras bu chen po lnga gzung zhing bsgral ba*, 28.3). And this connection is strengthened by the fact that the *'Bras bu chen po lnga gzung zhing bsgral ba* does refer to itself in its colophon as being drawn "from the *Bdud rtsi chen po mchog gi lung*" (37.5). Note too that the same two lines quoted by Nupchen were also known in Dunhuang; see ITS, 14v–1r, l. 6, where the passage is perhaps not coincidentally associated with the sacramental "supreme ambrosia" consisting of semen, human flesh, menstrual blood, urine, and feces. On the other hand, elsewhere in his *Bsam gtan mig sgron* (289.1–2), Nupchen once more cites the *Bdud rtsi'i rgyud*, but these lines do not appear in the *'Bras bu chen po lnga*, nor in any other tantra I have been able to find.
25. *'Bras bu chen po lnga gzung zhing bsgral ba*, 32.3–6.
26. Note that the *stūpa* here is called *Kha sho bya rung*, apparently an early reference to the famous Boudhanath *stūpa*.

27. Despite its importance in Tibet, the Vajrakīlaya tradition has been largely left aside by the present study. For more information, the reader is directed to the two book-length studies of this subject: Boord 1993 and Mayer 1996.
28. The *kīla* is seen already in the *vidhi*-sections of some *dhāraṇī-sūtras*.
29. See in particular Gyatso 1987 and Mayer 1991.
30. Note that here I am referring to the later version(s) of this work, usually referred to as the *Sba bzhed*. The earlier *Sayings of Wa* (*Dba' bzhed*) lacks the passages on the Samye *stūpas* that are under discussion here. It is perhaps significant that the rituals surrounding Samye's construction are described in far greater detail in the later *Sba bzhed* versions of this work, yet another example of the growing influence of temple construction and building rites upon the literature of twelfth- and thirteenth-century Tibet. On dating the *Sba bzhed*, see Denwood 1990.
31. *Sba bzhed*, 38. The text goes on to name each of the demons suppressed by the four *stūpas* (*Sba bzhed*, 50).
32. On dating the *Samarāṅgaṇasūtradhāra*, see Kramrisch 1976, vol. 1, 8. On the *Kriyāsaṃgraha*, see Tanemura 2004, 5–10, and Skorupski 2002, 2–4. The two latter authors note the difficulties surrounding the *Kriyāsaṃgraha*'s date and conclude that we can only say for sure that it was written before 1216, the date of our earliest manuscript.
33. Kramrisch 1976, vol. 1, 39. Though Meister 1979, 204, suggests that for some early *vāstupuruṣa-maṇḍalas* there was "some sort of an equation between plan and Maṇḍala."
34. Kramrisch 1976, vol. 1, 6.
35. Skorupski 2002, 3.
36. See, e.g., *Sarvaprajñānta-pāramitasiddhicaitya-nāma-dhāraṇī*, 294a8–294b.3. Kramrisch writes, "about the year 1000 A.D., the actual drawing of the diagram on the ground which the temple (*prāsāda*) was to occupy seems to have been the rule" (Kramrisch 1976, vol. 1, 39). Schopen 1985, 145, dates the *Sarvaprajñānta* to "between the sixth and ninth centuries," thus on the basis of earlier Buddhist texts, it seems this practice was performed well before the eleventh century.
37. For an early *dhāraṇī* example, see the *Mahāpratisāravidyārājñī*, 135a.4–5. The practice is also seen in the seventh-century *Mahāvairocana-abhisaṃbodhi Tantra*; see Hodge 2003, 102–3.
38. Here the diagram consists of thirty-six squares containing deities from the Vajradhātu ritual system (see Tanemura 2004, 237–54, and Skorupski 2002, 45–50), nonetheless we are clearly dealing with the same basic rite as seen in the earlier *dhāraṇī* and tantric ritual manuals.
39. See Kramrisch 1976, vol. 1, 22–25.
40. Kramrisch 1976, vol. 1, 71.
41. This was repeatedly explained to me by Khenpo Pema Sherab during our work together in 2000.
42. See Kohn 2001, 95–96.
43. Note that in the *Kriyāsaṃgraha*, the thread-laying rite is immediately followed by the *vāstunāga* rite, which was examined at the end of chapter 2 of the present study. The *vāstunāga* rite also requires that a grid be laid over the local spirit, here in order

to calculate his/her precise location under the ground. While the two grids—the *vāstupuruṣa-maṇḍala* diagram and the grid for the calculating the *vāstunāga*—seem to be distinct, with different numbers of squares (thirty-six v. eighty-one) in the *Kriyāsaṃgraha* at least, a relationship between these two rites seems likely. A connection between the *vāstupuruṣa* and the *vāstunāga* has also been observed by Hans Bakker, who writes, "The function of the Nāga, may have been a protective and supportive one, representing the Vāstunāga, a concept parallel to that of the Vāstupuruṣa: a local snake-deity of the site, ritually converted to the guardian of the *vāstu*" (Bakker 2007a, 38). Note too that both the *vāstunāga* grid and the *vāstupuruṣa-maṇḍala* are said to reflect astrological movements (Kramrisch 1976, vol. 1, 30ff).

44. Archaeological evidence of such practices has been discovered at Lauria Nandangarh and Piprahwa, where depictions of local goddesses were found interred beneath Buddhist *stūpa*-mounds. One may also look to Rajgir, where pottery "*nāga*" jars were discovered buried around the base of the *stūpa* (Decaroli 2004, 58). Note that, "according to the Śilpaśāstras, it is imagined that a great serpent (*nāga*) lies encircling every building site" (Bose 1932, 29). Bakker 2007b discusses two sites, in Kausambi and Mansar, that show evidence of Brahmanical foundation sacrifice, both of which included snake effigies that were buried alongside the human victims.
45. For a recent study on the development of foundation sacrifice in India, see Bakker 2007b.
46. Thomas 1950, 89. Writing on Indonesia, Richard Drake and others have argued that construction sacrifice has functioned primarily in the realm of gossip and rumor. Perhaps in a similar way, the Chinese have accused Tibetan Buddhists of the practice. In a 1976 exhibition of life-size clay figures, the purported remains of a mummified female child were on display (see Harris 1999, 131), while the caption describing the clay scene read as follows: "In a dim inner hall a cassocked lama shoves a little boy into a box to be buried alive. In the name of building a temple, the boy is to be placed under a cornerstone of the hall as sacrificial offering." Elsewhere, Jordaan and Wessing 1999, 223, have pointed to a late-twelfth-century passage translated by Yael Bentor as possible evidence of construction sacrifice in Tibet: "One should not insert into *stūpas* remains of people other than lamas and supreme personages, nor bury dead bodies beneath the *stūpa* of a Buddha" (Bentor 1995, 256). The passage is more likely, however, a simple prohibition against mixing the physical remains of sacred and ordinary beings. Nonetheless, sublimated forms of foundation sacrifice are performed in Tibet, in which an effigy is used rather than a live victim. The sublimated rite might also be seen as informing certain parts of the modern-day *Maṇi Rimdu* festival, as described by Kohn 2001, 95–96, and 207–8.
47. *Bka' chems ka khol ma*, 50. A version of the myth appears throughout the writings of Nyangrel; see, e.g., *Zangs gling ma*, 169–73.
48. *Bka' chems ka khol ma*, 59.
49. *Nyang ral chos 'byung*, 456.
50. See *Nyang ral chos 'byung*, 449.
51. *Bka' chems ka khol ma*, 241.3–11.
52. *Bsam gtan mig sgron*, 494.3.

53. *Bka' chems ka khol ma*, 278.12–13.
54. On the age of decline in Buddhism, see Nattier 1990.
55. *Zangs gling ma*, 146–47.
56. *Zangs gling ma*, 143–45.
57. The *Dromtön Itinerary* (*'Brom ston lam yig*) is traditionally attributed to Atiśa's student, Dromtönpa, but as Decleer 1996, 161, suggests, the text is more likely a product of Dromtön's later disciples.
58. Decleer 1996, 166.
59. The *Pillar Testament*'s glorification of the Tibetan king Songtsen Gampo (and the mythification of all three of the "great kings" of early Tibet, for that matter) presents something of an exception to this rule; as Davidson 2003, 74, has noted, the two descriptions, of Tibetans as demonic and as enlightened, stand "in tension" with one another. As bodhisattva emanations, the Tibetan kings transcended their Tibetanness, recognized it for what it was, and were able to subjugate their peoples. While their activities may be examples of Tibetan self-reliance, it is also notable that such enlightened beings were described as emanations and placed in a distant and almost mythic past, long before the corrupt days of the twelfth century. Note too that it was the foreign influence of Songtsen Gampo's Chinese and Nepalese princesses that spurred and enabled the construction of the Rasa Trulnang and other early Buddhist temples. Nonetheless, Tibet is elsewhere described as a buddhafield. Perhaps the same tension may also be seen as a reflection of a deeper conflict underlying the later dispensation's simultaneous romanticization of the empire and demonization of the age of fragmentation. While the two periods were opposites, they often worked toward the same end and were thus defined in terms of each other, so that the age of fragmentation at once strengthened and undermined the Tibetan Camelot of the Pugyal court.
60. Wangdu and Diemberger 2000, 54. In n. 152, the translators of the passage, Wangdu and Diemberger, explain that the later *Sba bzhed* versions say the king could not accept prostrations from one who had taken vows, and that the king prostrated. The note continues that the *Mkhas pa'i dga' ston* comments that some sources say the king did not prostrate, but these must be wrong because it is an ancient custom for kings to bow to monks and not the reverse. However, the footnote continues, Chinese documents from Dunhuang regarding Samye Debate report that Heshang Moheyan prostrated to king. One might wonder if the same was expected of Master Sambhava. The narrative shift observed here may also have reflected the rise of Buddhist over secular authority. On dating at least portions of the *Dba' bzhed* to the tenth century, thanks to a recently discovered fragment from Dunhuang; see van Schaik and Iwao 2008.
61. Decleer 1996, 161.
62. *Deb ther sngon po*, 206 (see also Roerich 1996, 249).
63. See Karmay 1998, 40, where the eleventh-century royal monk Zhiwa Ö denounces even early and expressly Tibetan works such as the *Six Lamps* (*Sgron ma drug*) of Nyen Pelyang, and *Sngags log sun 'byin*, 21.3–24.1, where Gö Khukpa Lhetse (also 11th c.) criticizes Tibetan authors from Pelyang and Nupchen Sangye Yeshe to his own contemporaries, Zurche and Zurchung.
64. See again *Sngags log sun 'byin*, 20.

65. Bu ston adds the age of fragmentation as a factor in his chapter against Bon; see *Sngags log sun 'byin*, 34.5.

CHAPTER 6. BUDDHIST WARFARE

1. 'Jig rten mgon po, vol. 2, 256.1–2. The existence of this passage was noted by Martin 1994, 525 n. 31.
2. On the emergence and significance of this new geographical conception, see Martin 1994. Martin concludes, "that the Eighteen Great Countries concept seems to have emerged in the 12th century is one indication among others that Tibet was at that time recovering its sense of centrality in the world, and locating its own center, after being partially and temporarily thrown off center by the power of India's Buddhism" (521). Martin's study implies that such Tibeto-centric maps appeared first in the second half of the twelfth century (518) in sources specific to the Bon tradition, whence they entered Buddhist sources from the second half of the thirteenth century onward.
3. See Petech 1990, 7.
4. See Sperling 1990 and Kapstein 2006, 111.
5. Roerich 1996, 303; Petech 1990, 29–31.
6. Martin 1997, 56, dates the work to 1352.
7. *Padma bka' thang*, 565–66.
8. *Padma bka' thang*, 540.
9. Geoff Childs 1999, 135 and 138, has highlighted well the imaginal links between Tibet's age of fragmentation and the later Mongol invasions.
10. Most Tibetan sources date Jangchup Gyeltsen's decisive victory to 1354, but recent scholars have noted the Tibetan leader's struggles to gain control of Tibet were ongoing well after this date, continuing even until 1368; see Petech 1990, 119; van der Kuijp 1991, 307.
11. Petech 1990, 130.
12. *Blon po bka' thang*, 515.
13. Though 1250 was an iron dog year, this would seem to be a reference to Möngke's invasion of 1251.
14. Tibetans often associated the Mongols with this demon. According to Petech 1990, 11 n. 19, e.g., Hülegü also was considered a manifestation of Gnam, who may in turn be related to Gnam theb, the name under which the demon-protector Pehar was known to the Hor. (On the variations of this demon's name, see Nebesky-Wojkowitz 1996 [1956], 97.) Nam Teu Karpo appears to have been an originally Tibetan demon, sometimes known as the leader of the *teu rang* (Nebesky-Wojkowitz 1996 [1956], 268). The *Pillar Testament* ties the same demon to Tibet's mid-ninth-century descent into darkness: "In that way that king of demons [i.e., Lang Darma] destroyed the merits of all the Tibetan people and the Buddhist teachings deteriorated, whereby the gods and demons of the dark ones spread and there came a minister (Sbas rtag rna can [Sba stag snang]), who was an emanation of Namteu Karpo. Nine demonic (*'gong bo*) brothers who were in the retinue of that [minister] also came to harm Tibet. Then that emanation of Namteu Karpo killed (Ba ri dbang ba dpal gyi yon tan) with

demonically emanated mantrins. He stirred up the gods and demons of the dark side" (*Bka' chems ka khol ma*, 277.19–278.8). In light of this passage, it is perhaps significant that Nyangrel, himself probably a close reader of the *Pillar Testament*, has Lang Darma's assassin (or "liberator"), Lhalung Pelgyi Dorje, escape from the murdered king's guard by disguising himself as Namteu Karpo (see *Nyang ral chos 'byung*, 440.14–15). For a recent summary of some further sources on this deity, see Sørensen and Hazod 2005, 276 n. 88.

15. *Padma bka' thang*, 540–41. While *mtha' mi* is commonly translated simply as "foreigners" or "barbarians," I have translated it as "border people" in order to retain the spatial connotations it has for the Tibetan reader. Similarly, one might argue that "the center" (*dbus*) here refers only to the central Tibetan province by that name. Given the discussion of various provinces that follows, I do not believe it does, but in any case, here too the juxtaposition between the borders and the center remains crucial to the prophecy.
16. In fact, this would become the best-known rendition of the myth among later Tibetans. Its narrative fills the fifth and sixth of the *Padma Chronicles*'s eighty-eight chapters, and is closely based on the *Compendium of Intentions* version translated in appendix A of this study.
17. *Padma bka' thang*, 541–42.
18. The Fifth Dalai Lama confirms such an identification of this prophesied figure in his *Dpyid kyi rgyal mo'i glu dbyangs*, 79a.2–4.
19. It should be noted that Orgyen Lingpa's (as well as Jangchup Gyeltsen's and Sokdokpa's) negative view of the Mongols represents a significant alternative to the view shared by the Sakyapa and Gelukpa, who often portrayed the Mongol-Sakyapa relationship as an ideal model to be replicated in later times.
20. See Davidson 2002 and, for some Śaiva context, Sanderson 2004.
21. *Bodhisattva-gocara-upāya*, 67a.6–7. There is a strong resemblance between the four political strategies of the *Methods That Are within the Bodhisattva's Field of Activity* listed here and the four ritual activities of the Yoga tantras (i.e., pacification, enhancement, coercion, and violence). Michael Zimmermann 1999, 200–201, has shown how the four political strategies are themselves likely drawn from the Brahmanical *arthaśāstras*. While it is tempting to argue that these Brahmanical and Buddhist legal treatises may have helped to shape the four ritual activities, it is also significant that other tantric systems sometimes included more than four activities. Clearly the earlier set of three activities, seen in the so-called Kriyā tantras as well as the *Mahāvairocana-abhisaṃbodhi*, were drawn from Vedic sources, and the various expanded sets seen throughout Buddhist and Hindu tantric literature may also have come directly from these sources. Nonetheless, the possibility that certain Yoga tantras such as the *Compendium of the Principles of All the Tathāgatas*, which was so influenced by other courtly practices and the "royal metaphor" of which Davidson writes, might have adapted the fourfold set of political strategies toward new ritual ends remains intriguing.
22. Sokdokpa's history concentrates on the activities of three figures in particular: Pema Lingpa (1450–1521) and his student and "regent" (*rgyal tshab*) Chokden Gönpo (1497–1531), and especially Zhikpo Lingpa (1524–1583). The latter was Sokdokpa's

own teacher, and his mentor when it came to matters of violent ritual. His *Twenty-Five Ways to Repel Armies* provided Sokdokpa his ritual focus, and his prophesies and prophetic interpretations gave Sokdokpa the encouragement he needed to engage in such dark arts. Unfortunately, little is known about Zhikpo Lingpa, though recently discovered materials promise new insights. On Chokden Gönpo and Zhikpo Lingpa, see Ehrhard 2008a and 2005 respectively. Note too that many of these figures were involved in the opening hidden lands (*sbas yul*) throughout the Nepalese, Sikkimese, and Bhutanese border regions; for more on the link between Mongol-repelling and the opening of hidden lands, see chapter 7 of the present study. A Ph.D. thesis on Sokdokpa is being prepared by James Gentry of Harvard University and is sure to add greatly to our knowledge of this important figure and his teachers. For a preview of Gentry's findings and some further valuable insights into Sokdokpa's life, see Gentry 2010.

23. *Sog bzlog bgyis tshul gyi lo rgyus*, 217.3 ff.
24. *Sog bzlog bgyis tshul gyi lo rgyus*, 218.2–3. The corresponding passage appears in chapter 92 of the *Padma bka' thang*, 564.11. The same lines are cited in a wide range of historical sources, including the Fifth Dalai Lama's *Annals of Tibet: Song of the Spring Queen* and many others.
25. One should note here that in the following discussion of events, Sokdokpa seems to have conflated events that took place during the Mongol invasion of 1240 with those of 1290. Thus Yang Gönpa was actually responding to the initial Mongol invasion of 1240.
26. Also known as Mchims 'jam dpal dbyangs, both this figure and the below-mentioned Yang Gönpa are listed in the *Blue Annals* as students of Kodrakpa (Roerich 1996, 727). In this regard, it is perhaps relevant to note a much-cited story in which the thirteenth-century master Kodrakpa (1182–1261) wards off the two-pronged Mongol invasion of 1252–53 with sorcery (see Roerich 1996, 670, and Petech 1990, 13).
27. Also known as Rgyal mtshan dpal (1213–1258) of the 'Brug pa bka' brgyud. Petech 1990, 8, has him acting as a "peacemaker" during Tibet's internal conflicts that arose just prior to arrival of the Mongols in 1240.
28. *Sog bzlog bgyis tshul gyi lo rgyus*, 218.4–219.2.
29. *Sog bzlog bgyis tshul gyi lo rgyus*, 218.5 (speaking about the 13th c.).
30. Petech 1990, 17–18.
31. See *Sog bzlog bgyis tshul gyi lo rgyus*, 252.5. Large-scale military rituals are also seen in early medieval Indian sources. The *Uttarabhaga* of the *Liṅgapurāṇa*, e.g., describes "an elaborate Śākta Śaiva procedure to guarantee that the king will be victorious when he goes into battle," one that involves the worship of Śākta goddesses in one thousand vases for the "consecration of victory" (Sanderson 2004, 236).
32. *Sog bzlog bgyis tshul gyi lo rgyus*, 253.3–254.5.
33. *Sog bzlog bgyis tshul gyi lo rgyus*, 256.1.
34. *Sog bzlog bgyis tshul gyi lo rgyus*, 255.6.
35. For a complete translation of the relevant passage, see Gentry 2010, 149–50. Another translated story of defensive *stūpa* renovation may be found in Stearns 2007, 355–61.

There, Tangtong Gyelpo is described turning back a Mongol invasion by overseeing the renovation of a *stūpa* at the Tibetan border with Mongolia.

36. *Sog bzlog bgyis tshul gyi lo rgyus*, 223.2–3. Sokdokpa actually quotes these lines from the *Extensive Edicts*.
37. The spatial rhetoric of the *Padma Chronicles*, with Tibet at the center and the Mongols at the demonic edges, continued to shape the prophetic writings of later visionaries. Thus Sokdokpa cites a lengthy passage from a work entitled the *Extensive Edicts* that repeats the language seen in the *Padma Chronicles*: "When the lands of Tibet are endangered by the Mongols, all the border armies will demolish the center" (*Sog bzlog bgyis tshul gyi lo rgyus*, 223.1). Similarly a few folios later, still another prophecy declares, "The border peoples will demolish the center, killing everyone" (*Sog bzlog bgyis tshul gyi lo rgyus*, 225.4).
38. Shen 2004, 203–7.
39. See Tsering 1978, 520–21.
40. *Sog bzlog bgyis tshul gyi lo rgyus*, 219.2–219.4.
41. *Byang pa'i rnam thar*, 516.2–3.
42. For more on this phenomenon, see Dalton 2002, 161–203.
43. *Sog bzlog bgyis tshul gyi lo rgyus*, 246.6.
44. See, e.g., *Sog bzlog bgyis tshul gyi lo rgyus*, 252.6–253.1. As Gentry 2010, 163 n. 98 observes, the figure responsible for ordering the ritual performance described in this passage, one Zhabs drung spyan snga rin po che, is likely a lama of the Drikung Kagyu.
45. See *'Jam dbyangs bsod nams dbang po'i rnam thar*, 143.2–4 and 146.4–147.2, respectively.
46. For some examples, see Martin 1990, 8–9 and Nebesky-Wojkowitz 1996 [1956], 493–500.
47. For an excellent recent summary of the events of this period, see Kapstein 2006, 135–37.
48. Schaeffer 2005, 65.
49. This is not to deny, of course, that the Dalai Lamas had long since gained the strong support of the Mongols. These crucial alliances had little to do with any Nyingmapa connections, but were thanks in large part precisely to the monastic character of their Geluk school.
50. *Dukula*, vol. 1, 195–96.
51. This may well be the two-folio *'Jam dpal me'i spu gri'i dmod pa zor bskul rdo rje pha lam bcas*. Unfortunately, the latter work appears only in the Great Fifth's twenty-eight-volume printed *Gsung 'bum* held in the Potala Collection, so a firm identification has not been possible.
52. *Dukula*, vol. 1, 196.
53. *Dukula*, vol. 1, 198.
54. As others have noted (e.g., Karmay 2003, 71–72), the Fifth Dalai Lama in his autobiographical account also goes to some lengths to explain how he had no knowledge of Gushri's plan to enter central Tibet after defeating the Beri king in Kham, and how

he argued against the plan upon learning of it. In the latter account, we may see a related wish on the Dalai Lama's part to paint himself as a reluctant participant and thus here too to absolve himself of any historical—and perhaps moral—responsibility for the Mongols' destruction of the Tsang court.

55. On Zhikpo Lingpa's use of prophesy to convince Sokdokpa to repel Mongols, see Gentry 2010, 134–35.
56. See the relevant passage translated on pp. 51–52 of the present study.
57. *Gsang ba'i rnam thar rgya can ma*, 14.5–15.3.
58. *Dpyid kyi rgyal mo'i glu dbyangs*, 107b.3–4.
59. *Dpyid kyi rgyal mo'i glu dbyangs*, 109a.3.
60. *Dukula*, vol. 1, 204–5.
61. See Karmay 1988b, 40. Note that the Great Fifth composed a number of ritual texts associated with the Lord of Longevity ('Jam dpal tshe bdag), which can be found in volume 23 of his *Collected Works* (*Ngag dbang blo bzang rgya mtsho'i gsung 'bum*), including a manual for the consecration of the imprecation stūpa: *'Jam dpal tshe bdag nag po'i mchod rten bcas rab gnas*. The existence of this work helps to link the above passage on the imprecation rite to the Dalai Lama's visionary experience quoted below, which is said to have occurred during his performance of the Lord of Longevity weaponry performance (*zor bsgrub*).
62. *Gsang ba'i rnam thar rgya can ma*, 11.4–6. For his interpretation of the vision, see his *Mthong ba don ldan*, as noted by Karmay 1988b, 15. On his Lord of Longevity weaponry performance, see his *'Jam dpal tshe bdag nag po'i zor gyi las rim*, also found in *Ngag dbang blo bzang rgya mtsho'i gsung 'bum*, vol. 23.
63. The image of feeding victims into the mouth of the presiding deity appears to be fairly common in the ritual texts of the Mahākāla tradition; see Stablein 1976, 14.

CHAPTER 7. CONCLUSIONS

1. Emil Schlagintweit's 1863 *Buddhism in Tibet* predated Waddell's work, but was originally written in German. Similarly, Pater Antonio Georgi composed his *Alphabetum Tibetanum* in Latin, while Desideri wrote in Italian.
2. See Waddell 1972 [1895], ix, and *Dmar mchod nyes dmigs*, 15b.1, respectively.
3. Waddell 1972 [1895], xii.
4. Waddell 1972 [1895], vii.
5. For a recent study of the rise and fall of this historic figure, see Tsomu 2006.
6. *Dmar mchod nyes dmigs*, 15a.6–16a.1.
7. Waddell 1972 [1895], 573.
8. For an account of the clash, see Hopkirk 1983, 64–67.
9. The American scholar and diplomat William Rockhill, who was active in Tibet around this same period, reports on the Tibetan government's ritual efforts to repel the British during this clash; see Hopkirk 1983, 74.
10. Chandler 1905, 1.
11. Chandler 1905, 110.

12. An account of the Tibetan government's efforts to repel the British invasion may be found in He ru kaḥ and Ye shes 'od zer sgrol ma 2004, 163. I thank Gray Tuttle for this reference.
13. *Dmar mchod nyes dmigs*, 7a.3.
14. *Dmar mchod nyes dmigs*, 2a.1–2b.1. The influence of demons is blamed for sacrifice in a series of additional quotations marshaled by Garwang in the pages following this passage; see fol. 3a in particular.
15. *Dmar mchod nyes dmigs*, 13b.4–5.
16. *Dmar mchod nyes dmigs*, 13b.5. (Unfortunately several syllables are faded from the print I am working with here.)
17. *Dmar mchod nyes dmigs*, 4b.4.
18. *Dmar mchod nyes dmigs*, 6b.1–2. Here Garwang is actually quoting an unnamed source.
19. *Dmar mchod nyes dmigs*, 12b.4–13a.1.
20. *Dmar mchod nyes dmigs*, 6b.6.
21. It is perhaps worth noting here that the difficulties in distinguishing buddhas from demons, or transcendent deities (*'jig rten las 'das pa'i lha*) from mundane (*'jig rten pa'i*) ones, underlies much of the rhetoric surrounding the deity Shukden. On the history of this controversy and its ongoing importance among today's Tibetan communities, see Dreyfus 1998. Gyatso 1999 has explored the undecidability between enlightened and demonic beings in the context of meditative visions; see especially her fifth chapter.
22. *Sbas yul spyi'i them byang*, 466.1.
23. *Sog bzlog bgyis tshul gyi lo rgyus*, 223.1–2.
24. To date, some of the most detailed work on the figures involved has appeared in a wide range of articles by Franz-Karl Ehrhard. See, e.g., Ehrhard 1997, 1999a, 1999b, 2001.
25. Nebesky-Wojkowitz 1996 [1956], 8–11.
26. Huber 1999, 185.
27. Ramble 1990, 189.
28. Padma dbang 'dus, 132b.5–133a.4. This passage has also been discussed by Childs 1997, 146.
29. Padma dbang 'dus, 33b.2–5.
30. Waddell 1972 [1895], 1–4.
31. Waddell 1972 [1895], 573. The reader is pointed once more to Padel 1995, for a similar critique of the British in their treatment of the Konds of Orissa.
32. On the Dalai Lama's performance of this rite, see *Rgyal ba thub bstan rgya mtsho'i rnam thar*, vol. 6, 767.6–768.1. The *Phur pa yang snying spu gri* was a treasure cycle revealed by Lerab Lingpa (aka Gter ston bsod rgyal; 1856–1926), a Nyingmapa teacher to the Thirteenth Dalai Lama. A ritual text for accomplishing this cycle, titled the *Phur pa yang snying spu gri'i sgrub chen gyi cho ga* and attributed to the Dalai Lama, survives in several collections.
33. *Rgyal ba thub bstan rgya mtsho'i rnam thar*, vol. 7, 597.2–3.

34. *Rgyal ba thub bstan rgya mtsho'i rnam thar*, vol. 7, 598.3–599.2.
35. *Mahāvairocana-abhisaṃbodhi Tantra*, 140b.6.

APPENDIX A

1. Folio numbers for the Mtshams brag edition of the *Rnying ma rgyud 'bum* are provided for easy reference to the Tibetan.
2. From the time of the *Lalitavistara* at least, Vajrapāṇi was known to Indian Buddhists as the Lord of the Guhyakas, the latter being a type of demon; see Coomaraswamy 1993, 92.
3. This is a reference to the framing story of the wider tantra, according to which the Buddha made a deathbed prophecy to King Dza that he would return in the future to teach "Secret Mantra." In the same prophecy, the Buddha foretold that the tantric teachings, or Secret Mantra, would arise in twelve ways during this aeon. These twelve "ways of arising" then structure the rest of the tantra. Chapters 20–31, translated here, contain the myth of Rudra's subjugation, which is the sixth of the twelve ways of arising.
4. *Mun pa'i go cha*, vol. 50, 257.6, lumps the first two of these questions together, making three questions in all: "The cause and the conditions of Rudra, the series of his rebirths, and how he became the cause for the Secret [Mantra to arise]." Dampa Deshek in his *Bsdus don*, 93, retains the distinction between the first two, rewording the four questions as follows: "(1) What was the basis of his error? (2) What karma did he make? (3) How did his rebirths arise? (4) How did he become the cause for the Mantra?" Dampa goes on to explain that the first three questions form the basis of chapter 20, while the final question is addressed in chapter 21.
5. *Mun pa'i go cha*, vol. 50, 258.1, points out that from here begins the answer to the first of the four questions listed above, regarding the cause for Rudra's appearance in the world.
6. Abhirati is the name of the buddhafield of either Vajrasattva or Akṣobhya. Thus already we are entering the realm of the *vajra-kula*, the buddha-family typically responsible for violent activity.
7. Nuden, vol. 53, 632.2, adds that this Invincible Youth was teaching Secret Mantra. Invincible Youth's teaching of Secret Mantra does not qualify as one of the twelve ways of arising of Secret Mantra because it did not occur in this aeon.
8. On various scholars' attempts to make sense of these strange names, see Stein 1972, 504–5.
9. Nuden, vol. 53, 634.6–635.1 and 635.6–636.2, calls them "the four entities of *saṃsāra*" and lists them as follows: (1) the five practices: "union and liberation," shouting, lies, and abusive language; (2) the five things to be accepted: the five meats (of human, cow, dog, elephant, and horse) or the five excellent substances; (3) the five things not to be rejected: the five afflictions; (4) the five desirable objects [of the senses]. Modern oral commentary sometimes describes the four differently, as aggression, passion, ignorance, and jealousy (Trungpa, unpublished, 125).

10. Adds *Mun pa'i go cha*, vol. 50, 259.2.
11. *Mun pa'i go cha*, vol. 50, 259.2, says here we move from the answer to the first part of the first question (regarding the cause) to the answer to the second part of the first question (regarding the conditions). According to the reading offered by Dampa Deshek's *Bsdus don*, here begins the second question, regarding what karma Rudra made. At this point *Mun pa'i go cha*, vol. 50, 258.6–259.2, enters into a discussion of the causes for Black Liberator eventually becoming the demon Rudra, a discussion that is addressed at length in chapter 1 of the present study.
12. This somewhat obscure sentence seems to mean that Liberator merely performed (i.e., he did not at the same time "transcend") the four entities, which are themselves indulgent and transgressive practices (listed in n. 9 above), but he did not comprehend their purpose, their "authentic nature and the suchness." At this point ends the answer to Nupchen's first question, *Bsdus don*'s second question, regarding the karmic conditions that led to Rudra's arising. And here begins the answer to the next question regarding Rudra's series of previous rebirths.
13. I remain unsure how to translate these terms for which the Tibetan is provided.
14. *Mun pa'i go cha*, vol. 50, 259.6–260.1, explains that up to this point his karma had not been yet been finished, so these lifetimes were still "the conditions of total completion," or "the karma that propels" one into further rebirths. After this, with the advent of the hell realms, the effects of his ripened karma begin.
15. These are the three outer aeons found at the end of the universe. Together with the three inner aeons (of fire, water, and wind), they compose the Vehicle of the Manifest Magical Display (*cho 'phrul mngon par 'byung ba'i theg pa*), meant for those very difficult-to-tame disciples who remain untamed by all other means at the end of an aeon. On this vehicle, see Dalton 2005, 143, and Dampa Deshek's explanation in his *Theg pa spyi bcings*, 6.
16. *Srul po* are said to be hideous ghosts that experience the sufferings of all six classes of beings simultaneously.
17. A clear reference to the three poisons of ignorance, anger, and desire. ITJ331/3, a manual for the worship of Vajrakīlaya, describes the perfect site for a violent ritual as a charnel ground "with a single white tree" (11v.2: *shing rkar gcig pa*, a *ra-mgo* being a common alternative throughout the Dunhuang materials for a *ga* prefix).
18. This event echoes the *Sudāya Jātaka*, in which the baby Sudāya is abandoned on the breast of his dead mother.
19. Rudra Matraṅgara is commonly found throughout the Tibetan literature as the name of the ego-demon of primordial ignorance (see also ITJ419, r38.3 and ITJ711, 13r.3). According to Mayer 1991, 173 n. 52, the term means "mother-eater" and is a play on the Hindu claim that Rudra has no mother (having eaten her, is the Buddhist implication).
20. *Mun pa'i go cha*, vol. 50, 260.6–261.1, summarizes the preceding chapter as follows: "Initially his meditation on wrathful deities was done without wisdom and became the actual cause of his giving up his vows. Because of this, he became extremely difficult to tame, a powerful worldly god."

21. We are now moving into the last of the questions posed by the Lord of Laṅka, that is, how Rudra became the cause for Secret Mantra to arise.
22. *Mun pa'i go cha*, vol. 50, 261.3, explains that what follows are the eight mistaken views together with their respective karmic effects into which one falls. Note, however, that nine are listed. Nuden, vol. 53, 652.4, when quoting Nupchen here, simply changes his "eight" to "nine," which is probably what Nupchen intended. The "nine worldly mindsets" appear elsewhere in the root text (see, e.g., fol. 195).
23. In a later context, Nuden, vol. 53, 726.4, explains that this refers to the continuity of *bodhicitta* specifically.
24. Adds Khenpo Pema Sherab of Namdroling Monastery, Bylakuppe, India (henceforth KPS), since the actual *tathāgatagarbha* never dries up. He explains that we must distinguish here between two kinds of *tathāgatagarbha*, naturally abiding potential and developing potential (*rang bzhin gnas rigs dang rgyas 'gyur rigs*), saying that in this case it must have been only the latter that dried up.
25. *Mun pa'i go cha*, vol. 50, 261.4, explains that the buddhas at the time of Black Liberator already knew what was going to happen because they understood the workings of karma. What follows is a more extensive discussion of the nine mistaken views and their effects, as understood through this foreknowledge.
26. As *Mun pa'i go cha*, vol. 50, 262.5, explains.
27. A reference to a rebirth in which one remains stuck in the womb.
28. Note that this is Rāvaṇa, the same Lord of Laṅka who is the principal recipient of the present tantra.
29. Literally, "our antidote."
30. Note that Gtogs 'dod was Rudra's name in his previous birth as a *srul po* demon (see chapter 20 above). Note too that the name, Gtogs 'dod, can be an epithet for Maheśvara, and it seems to be used in this sense below (fol. 171.4–5).
31. The identity of Vajragarbha is discussed below. For now suffice to say it is a name often used for Vajrapāṇi in early tantric materials.
32. Here is the first time a phrase in the Brusha language appears untranslated: "*Yongs sad par dzams nas/ ja zha mar sab par mi 'dra nas.*" *Mun pa'i go cha*, vol. 50, 263.4, changes it slightly to read: ". . . *ja zha mar sod pa mi 'dra na* . . ." and then provides Tibetan translations as follows: *dzams* means *dbang du bya ba brtsam* ("begin the overpowering"); *ja* means *rnal ma* ("natural condition"); *zha mar sod pa mi 'dra* means *thub pa* ("capable"). Nupchen then glosses the whole sentence as *ru dras lha yi ded dpon dbang du bsdu bar nyams sad pas rnal mar thub pa mi 'dra nas*. On the possible redaction of this myth around a Brusha original, see Dalton 2002.
33. Another untranslated Brusha word: *'ung*, which seems to mean something like the Tibetan *de nas*, "then . . ." or "after that. . . ." For explanations see *Mun pa'i go cha*, vol. 50, 264.2, and Nuden, vol. 53, 673.4.
34. The Brusha *hang ba* is glossed by Nupchen (*Mun pa'i go cha*, vol. 50, 263.6) as "flung" (Tib. *bor ba*). Nupchen elaborates on this point by explaining, "The corpse that had been killed by pox was flung into Jambudvipa, and in the virtuous places like Oḍḍiyāna, Singha, and Nepal, the eight *stūpas* possessing the eight *siddhis* [were erected over Mahākaruṇā's remains and] were protected by the eight

mātṛkā demonesses." For a discussion of these eight sites, see chapter 5 of the present study.

35. Brusha: *jen* means "went" (Tib. *song*). See *Mun pa'i go cha*, vol. 50, 264.4. It is used repeatedly here and below, so not all occurrences will be noted.
36. Brusha: *phru ma*(*r*) means "retinue" (Tib. *'khor*). See *Mun pa'i go cha*, vol. 50, 264.2, and Nuden, vol. 53, 675.1. Note that this preceding paragraph and the next are reversed in Nuden's commentary, which makes some sense, while Nupchen (and the present translation) sticks with the order of the root text. For more on this point, see the next footnote.
37. The awkwardness of this line, together with the strange order of the paragraphs (just noted), combine to suggest that the present paragraph may have been a later addition to the main story.
38. Brusha: *thag gos* means "believing that he was not powerful enough to subdue him" (Tib. *yid ches par 'gyur bas dbang gis mi thul bar yid ches te*). See Nuden, vol. 53, 677.6.
39. Brusha: *'ub* means "to come under the power of" (Tib. *dbang du bsdus*). *Jen* means "to join the retinue." Then *rmad* is changed to the Brusha *rban* by both Nupchen and Nuden, vol. 53, 678.4, and *rban* means "to be killed" (Tib. *'khor du bya; gsod pa*).
40. Given the opening paragraph of the next chapter, particularly as commented upon by Nuden, it seems this teacher-servant duo is being paralleled here to that of *dharmakāya-saṃbhogakāya*.
41. As *Mun pa'i go cha*, vol. 50, 265.3, explains.
42. Nuden, vol. 53, 682.3ff. defines three stages of emanation: first, *dharmakāya* arising as form; second, form arising as the five families; third, exhorting the five to enact, and the enactment of, beings' purposes. The first of these three stages is the focus of the present discussion, and it, in turn, involves a three-part exhortation: [1] the *samādhi* of thusness exhorts the basis for appearing; [2] the *samādhi* of compassion exhorts the activity of the conqueror's consort; and [3] the *samādhi* of the cause exhorts for the generation of a body (the latter further having three divisions—the seed syllables, the mental *mudrā*, and the perfection body). These are equivalent to the three ritual *samādhis* that form the framework for the development stage (normally found as *de bzhin nyid kyi ting nge 'dzin, kun tu snang ba'i ting nge 'dzin*, and *rgyu'i ting nge 'dzin*) of the *Guhyagarbha* and other early Mahāyoga tantras. In this way, the myth's narrative is presenting these three ritual moments as essential to the emanation process of all buddha-activity. Nuden goes on to explains that the three exhortations correspond to the passages in the root text as follows: [1] 174.1–4 and [2] 174.4–6 and [3](a) 174.7–175.3, (b) 175.3–5, (c) 176.1. All of this numbering is provided in the translation.
43. The implication of this and each of the following replies is, since all is empty, why should I generate the activities?
44. *Mtha' yas mtha' yas bskyed pa'i yum*. KPS explains that the first of these two ("boundlessly") means without the limits of dualistic conceptualizations, while the second ("infinitely") means for limitless beings.
45. Nuden, vol. 53, 687.6–688.5, explains that these first three syllables represent the three fundamental mandalas of Anuyoga theory, the *ngo bo nyid du dbying, rtsa ba byang*

chub sems, rang bzhin lhun gyis grub pa, while the fourth syllable, *āḥ,* is the secret letter. *Mun pa'i go cha,* vol. 50, 268.5, also explains that the *oṃ* is the primary syllable representing forty-two syllables in all, corresponding to the forty-two peaceful deities of the *Māyājāla* mandala. Given the overall place of these four syllables in the development stage being narrated here, one might have expected these four syllables to correspond to the four elements—fire, wind, water, and earth—which normally provide the foundation for the mandala (note the reference to the foundation (*ālaya*) in the previous paragraph).

46. Adds *Mun pa'i go cha,* vol. 50, 269.2.
47. Adds *Mun pa'i go cha,* vol. 50, 270.1.
48. In other words, the exhortations for the first emanation stage listed by Nuden above ("*dharmakāya* arising as form") are complete.
49. *Mun pa'i go cha,* vol. 50, 270.5, explains, "So that that body would be acceptable to any who might exhort whichever appearance, the [individual Buddha] families remained completely indeterminate. Thus that body remained suitable to become anything whatsoever."
50. Nuden, vol. 53, 692.4, says that for this, the second stage of emanation ("form arising as the five families," listed in note above) there are two exhortations: [1] for form to arise as the bodies of the male-female duality, and [2] for forms to arise as the bodies of the five families.
51. Nuden, vol. 53, 697.1, explains that what follows are six exhortations: a general exhortation to all five buddha-families put together, which Nupchen (*Mun pa'i go cha,* vol. 50, 272.2) says can also be understood as an exhortation to the overlord of all the families (*rigs kyi bdag po*), who is Vajrasattva, followed by an exhortation for each of the five families (*vajra, tathāgata, ratna, padma, karma*).
52. *Mun pa'i go cha,* vol. 50, 273.4, explains that this refers to the three syllables, *muṃ, hūṃ, oṃ,* emitted earlier, which are now "exhausted" (*zad pa*) as the *saṃbhogakāya* deities are revealed.
53. Note a distinction may be seen here between Vajragarbha as overlord of the families, as seen in the previous paragraph, and as head of the *vajra* family, as seen, e.g., when *Mun pa'i go cha,* vol. 50, 273.3, lists the five buddhas as Vajrasattva, Vairocana, Ratnasambhava, Amitabha, and Amoghasiddhi. Here the distinction made at the end of the last chapter, between the "thusness Vajrasattva" and the "regent Vajrasattva" (see *Compendium of Intentions,* 173.2, and *Mun pa'i go cha,* vol. 50, 264.6), is relevant. *Mun pa'i go cha,* vol. 50, 274.4, explains that the overlord of the families is the "Invincible Vajragarbha," implying that this is the "thusness Vajrasattva" (previously Invincible Youth, the teacher of Black Liberator in the previous aeon) mentioned above. Then Vajrasattva who heads the *vajra* family is the "regent Vajrasattva" (previously Denpak, Black Liberator's servant). See also Nuden, vol. 53, 703.5–704.1.
54. Nuden, vol. 53, 699.6, has this as the ignorance of pride.
55. Original reads *pwaṃ,* but Nuden, vol. 53, 699.6, corrects it to *svāṃ.*
56. Probably supposed to be *aṃ,* without the *naro,* so that these syllables match the standard *Māyājāla* system: *oṃ aḥ hūṃ svā hā.*

57. Here, then, begins the exhortations for the third stage of emanation listed by Nuden, "Exhorting the five to enact, and the enactment of, beings' purposes," in other words, for the *nirmāṇakāya* to emanate. *Mun pa'i go cha*, vol. 50, 274.3, adds that this third set of exhortations is also for the appearance of the deities in their wrathful forms.
58. The following paragraph breaks follow the suggestion of Nupchen and Nuden, vol. 53, 703.1–3, who divide this exhortation into appearing, curing, illuminating, time to tame, and exhorting the vows.
59. *Mun pa'i go cha*, vol. 50, 276.5, explains a bit more: "By sounding '*samāja*,' the vow was exhorted as the left and right hands, raised and turning, were crossed [in front of him] with the fingers snapping, the sign for gathering forth. By making that *mudrā*, from the dense array came the entirety of the conquerors to discuss the taming."
60. *Mun pa'i go cha*, vol. 50, 277.3, explains that what follows, a series of discussions by each of the five buddha-families, can also be understood as representing each of the five afflictions. Thus each discussion describes those aspects of Rudra's behavior that appear to that particular buddha-family.
61. Nuden, vol. 53, 711.3, explains that this discussion of time, here and in each of the five discussions, means that the cause/injury was established in the past while the effect/taming has arisen in the present, which is in this sense a reflective response to the past. See also Nuden, vol. 53, 715.5.
62. Nuden, vol. 53, 714.5, reads this as "rays" (*gzer* for *zer*), but it more likely refers to the *kila* dagger that is often associated with the karma buddha-family.
63. Brusha: *phru ma*, as seen above, fol. 171.
64. Here begins the first of the four tantric activities for taming—pacification.
65. Rudra here is referring to the earlier incident in which he defeated the *śrāvakas*. See above, fol. 172.
66. Brusha: *jen*, "went," as seen above, fol. 170.
67. Brusha: *bzhams* means "to send" (Tib. *btang*). See Nuden, vol. 53, 718.6.
68. *Mun pa'i go cha*, vol. 50, 278.4, lists three: Weapons, harsh words, and deceiving girls, to which the editor adds "arrows." Nuden, vol. 53, 718.5, provides an alternative list that includes all four: a mud pit, a bow and arrow, harsh words, and deceiving girls.
69. *Mun pa'i go cha*, vol. 50, 278.5, explains that in fact, it just "appeared to Rudra *as if* the buddha turned back. . . ." Here ends the taming by pacifying activities.
70. As a wrathful deity of the *padma* buddha-family, Hayagrīva is the appropriate choice for the activity of enhancement, which is normally associated with the *padma* family.
71. KPS notes that there is a significant difference between this Hayagrīva emanation and the previous one that was unsuccessful at the end of chapter 22: This present emanation has been exhorted, and thus empowered, by all the buddhas.
72. Nuden, vol. 53, 720.2–3, has a slightly different mantra (with explanations): "(The awesome laughter:) Ha ha! (The joyful laughter:) Hi hi! (The dominating:) Hrīḥ! (And bringing under control with body, speech, and mind:) Hu lu hu lu hu lu hūṃ!" The *hrīḥ* syllable is of course the seed syllable of the speech/*padma* family of which Hayagrīva is a representative. From the power of this seed syllable comes the main part of the mantra.

73. Brusha: *jen pa,* "subduer" (Tib. *thul ba*). Nuden, vol. 53, 720.6. Note that this word was translated differently before (see fol. 170).
74. Brusha: *han pa,* "to be in front of" (Tib. *gam du 'dug pa*). Nuden, vol. 53, 721.3.
75. Brusha: *thim par dzams,* "swallowed" (Tib. *gong du mid*). Nuden, vol. 53, 721.3.
76. Nuden, vol. 53, 722.1, explains that he made Rudra suitable for the Path of Accumulation.
77. Here ends the taming by the enhancement activity.
78. Nuden, vol. 53, 724.3 and 737.5, explains that the discussions that follow parallel the nine mistaken views presented in chapter 21 (see fol. 163 above). Note that the first one here, the fault of cessation, came third in chapter 21. *Mun pa'i go cha,* vol. 50, 280.1, notes that the buddha-families' discussions in chapter 24 were for taming in general, whereas the following discussions are for taming by specific activities, in this case those of coercion and violence. KPS suggests that the following short sutra can be understood as a condensation or summary of the meaning of the *Compendium of Intentions* as a whole. We may also consider the possibility that a second discussion is required in order to initiate a shift that parallels that of development stage to perfection stage. We have already seen that the emanation process described in chapter 23 was structured according to the development stage. As we shall see, the narrative that follows involves the generation of the deity within the womb of the consort, whereupon that same deity enacts the violent subjugation. *Mun pa'i go cha,* vol. 50, 280.6–281.1, provides the following topical outline for the discussions: "(1) Who the disciples are, (2) the activities that will not tame them, (3) the exhortation that they should perform in a way that will be effective, (4) that their activities will achieve the purpose is without a doubt, (5) an exhortation to act by manifesting those qualities that are appropriate for the given purpose."
79. These divisions (and the paragraph breaks) follow *Bsdus don* (and therefore also Nuden).
80. Nuden, vol. 53, 724.4, explains, "With the misadapted taming-method of violence, one cannot change someone with a nihilistic view, so it is of no help."
81. Nuden, vol. 53, 724.6, specifies, "the yoga which realizes the selflessness of persons. . . ." Here (as on *Mun pa'i go cha,* vol. 50, 280.4) he explains that the *śravakas* are intended.
82. Nuden, vol. 53, 726.2, following *Bsdus don,* 98, explains that there are two discussions within the *svabhāvikakāya:* First by entitylessness (*ngo bo nyid med pa*) and second by the unchanging entityness (*ngo bo nyi mi 'gyur ba*).
83. I.e., *bodhisattvas* of the Mahāyāna (see Nuden, vol. 53, 726.6).
84. What follows are six discussions: (1) cutting off the discussion by the *vajra* family, (2) by the lord of the families, (3) by the *ratna* family, (4) by the karma family, (5) by the thusness [i.e., *tathāgata*] family, and (6) by the *padma* family. On the distinction between the *vajra* family and the "lord of the families," see n. 53 above and n. 94 below.
85. Nuden, vol. 53, 731.1, explains: "Though these disciples engage in unmistaken teachings, they do so completely mistakenly, doing whatever suits them. Thus they fall into the Incessant Hells."

86. Nuden, vol. 53, 731.3, clarifies that this refers to the four types of hidden intentions (*ldem por dgongs pa bzhi*).
87. Nuden, vol. 53, 731.4: meaning people practicing something that only looks like Secret Mantra.
88. Nuden, vol. 53, 734.2: meaning lazy and only *seeming* to strive at *samādhi*.
89. In other words (following Nuden, vol. 53, 735.4), ". . . we should perform everything in the space of reality within which differences are not clearly distinguished."
90. *Bsdus don* further subdivides this into three: "taming by the practice of general adaptation; taming by the limitless practices of means in action; taming by antidote in this context." Paragraph breaks follow this system.
91. Adds Nuden, vol. 53, 738.1.
92. And now, this second division ("taming by the limitless practices of means in action") is further subdivided into three, corresponding to the following three paragraphs: "(1) an exhortation to guide [beings] to the meaning by various means, (2) the spontaneity of establishing the meaning within the knowledge of beings, and (3) activating the meaning in accordance with what is believed." A discussion follows in Nuden, vol. 53, 740, on whether to use conflicting or similar means for taming, e.g., For a desiring person should one use renunciation or further desire?
93. Nupchen elaborates somewhat, and then Nuden, vol. 53, 744.4, adds more: "From the state of the self-arisen wisdom which is the mass of blazing unbearable fires, the body of the great Bhairava. . . ."
94. Called "Chemchok (Skt. Mahottara) Heruka" by Nupchen (*Mun pa'i go cha*, vol. 50, 285.3). The relationships between the various wrathful emanations that appear for Rudra's taming are unclear, but they might be sorted as follows: Chemchok Heruka seems to be the main emanation, the wrathful aspect of the thusness Vajrasattva. He emanates as the three *vajras* of speech, body, and mind, in that order, i.e., as Hayagrīva, Bhurkuṃkūṭa, and Yangdak (Skt. Viśuddha) Heruka (here called the "Vajra-Demon"). Normally these three are respectively considered emanations of Amitabha/Avalokiteśvara, Vairocana, and Akṣobhya/Vajrasattva (the latter now in his role of head of the *vajra* buddha-family). For each of these three, Chemchok seems to provide the *vajra*/wrathful energy that, when combined with the three buddha-families, results in the three wrathful emanations.
95. Added on the basis of Nuden, vol. 53, 744.5.
96. Nuden, vol. 53, 745.6–746.1, and Nupchen (*Mun pa'i go cha*, vol. 50, 286.1) here comment on this somewhat strange phrase. The phrase is seen elsewhere in Indian narrative literature. It is first introduced within the root text itself at fol. 152.7, where it appears to mark some sort of mythic time. In the present context Nuden and Nupchen note that the time of Rudra's appearance in the world and the time when Vajrapāṇi narrated this mythic account of Rudra's appearance atop Mount Malaya were actually simultaneous.
97. *Mun pa'i go cha*, vol. 50, 286.2, explains that our narrator, Vajrapāṇi, was himself present within the assembly of buddhas that gathered to discuss the problem of Rudra. There, Vajrapāṇi played the role of Holder of Secrets (*gsang ba'i 'dzin pa*), that is, he was the scribe (*sdud pa po*) for the discussions taking place.

98. Nupchen further notes that at the time of this assembly, Vajrapāṇi already knew the entire history of Rudra, but that he asked the following questions in order to check if the bodhisattva, "Capable Intelligence," also present in the assembly, properly understood the situation. Some explanation might help here: This Bodhisattva, Capable Intelligence, is the same Lord of Laṅka whom we saw in chapter 22 as the bodhisattva-king of the demons living in Laṅka. At that time, the reader will remember (see fol. 168–169), he prophesied Rudra's eventual taming by the buddhas and decided (for himself and his followers) to play along with Rudra for the time being in order to receive the Secret Mantra teachings when Rudra's final tamer arrives. In the present context, this same bodhisattva is included in the present assembly of buddhas as a kind of undercover agent, bringing news from Laṅka of Rudra's latest nefarious activities.
99. Nuden, vol. 53, 747.2, explains: "Due to the power of intrinsic and acquired ignorance (*lhan skyes dang kun brtags ma rig pa*), he was ignorant of suchness and karmic causality." Nuden, vol. 53, 747.6, also adds in this context that there are two levels on which this myth can be read, inner and outer: "On the inner level it can also be related to the hindrances to freedom and enlightenment due to self-grasping."
100. Adds Nuden, vol. 53, 748.6.
101. *Mun pa'i go cha*, vol. 50, 287.4, explains that here ends the Lord of the Guhyakas's story of how he and the Lord of Laṅka were involved in that assembly of buddhas in the past. It goes on to explain that the Lord of Laṅka's report on the urgency of the situation in Laṅka was given for three reasons: "That the buddhas gathered there would understand, that the gateway for the Secret Mantra to arise be opened, and that Rudra himself not be left to perish."
102. Also equivalent to Vajrapāṇi, notes Nuden, vol. 53, 751.6.
103. Armor being a common metaphor for the bodhisattva's vow to help others toward enlightenment.
104. *Mun pa'i go cha*, vol. 50, 752.5–753.1, elaborates with striking imagery: "Overlord of the splendorously blazing activities of all the buddhas of the past and all the buddhas of the present, with the sign of not moving from the space of the intention of the great hero, the lord of demons who defeats the demons by creating terror in the demonic hordes, with thick limbs on a huge body that is overwhelmingly splendorous, like a mountain of blue azure color embraced by 100,000 suns, arising in wrath from the state of great compassion which blazes with masses of the fires of wisdom, having a bravery to be feared, with the appearance of the space of reality, the essential aspect of the wrathful mind, in a ferocious body and terrible voice, totally defeat the Lord of Charnel Grounds together with his retinue."
105. Nuden, vol. 53, 753.2, explains that here ends the brief exhortation and begins the extensive one, which will consist of (1) the generation of compassion and (2) the promise to tame.
106. KPS gives the examples of seeds not giving rise to crops or medicines harming rather than healing.
107. What follows is a series of speeches and commands, all coming from the Vajra Holder (i.e., Vajrapāṇi), sending off various buddhas to attend to the various preparations for

the taming. For some reason the order of these paragraphs in the root text is reversed in all the commentaries of Nupchen, Nuden, and *Bsdus don*. The present translation follows these three sources, but my bracketed notes [A.–C.] mark the order as found in the root text, 194.4–195.4.

108. KPS notes that these last four sentences are a common formulation of the tantric vows taken at the time of an empowerment ceremony.

109. Here Avalokiteśvara, whose name literally means "the all-encompassing gaze," is exhorted to play the role of spy (*so ba*), going to see the situation in Laṅka. See, e.g., *Bsdus don*, 99. Hayagrīva is Avalokiteśvara's wrathful form, the Lord of Speech, who will send up the battle cry when the time comes. Concerning his role as the spy, or witness, to the proceedings, note that Hayagrīva appears to have played the same role in certain Yoga tantra rituals. See, e.g., Sharf 2003, 68, where the deity appears in this capacity in a Japanese Shingon rite.

110. Nuden, vol. 53, 757.3, says this song of exhortation is specifically for the purpose of *dbang gis 'dul ba* rather than *drag pos 'dul ba*.

111. Explains Nuden, vol. 53, 758.6.

112. Nupchen and Nuden, vol. 53, 759.2, explain that this refers to "this very tantric scripture of Secret Mantra."

113. As explained in *Bsdus don*, 100, here ends the series of delegations and exhortations, and here begins the buddhas' activities as per exhorted: First, as requested, Vajrasattva exhorts Hayagrīva to go as the watchman; then Hayagrīva goes; then the intention to liberate the universe is activated by all the conquerors; and finally, preparations are made for the taming. Paragraph breaks follow these topics.

114. Listed below in the root text (fol. 204) as follows: "Peaceful (*zhi ba*), stern (*gshe ba*), heroic (*dpa' ba*), terrifying (*'jigs par byed pa*), compassionate (*snying rje*), fearsome (*'jigs su rung ba*), awesome (*rngam pa*), erotic (*sgeg pa*), wildly laughing (*rgod pa/dgod pa*)." Nupchen, 291.2, adds that these nine dances can respectively be related to each of the nine Buddhist vehicles. They are likely based on the nine *rasas* (literally "tastes" or "flavors") of Indian literary theory. On the influence of the latter upon Tibetan writing, see van der Kuijp 1996b and, more recently, Gold 2008, 117–39.

115. As KPS explains, this calls upon a common image of the horse of a wheel-turning (*cakravartin*) emperor, an "all-knowing horse" (*cang shes kyi rta*) that is clairvoyant and able to know its rider's every thought.

116. I.e., "of *vajra* body, speech, and mind . . ." (Adds Nuden, vol. 53, 764.3.)

117. Nupchen (*Mun pa'i go cha*, vol. 50, 293.3) notes this is equivalent to the Great Perfection, *Rdzogs pa chen po*.

118. Nuden, vol. 53, 765.2, and *Mun pa'i go cha*, vol. 50, 293.5, explain that these take the form of Vajrakumāra, *Rdo rje gzhon nu*.

119. Adds *Mun pa'i go cha*, vol. 50, 294.4.

120. This and the following additions are taken from Nuden, vol. 53, 769.5–6. The third goddess in the list, translated here as the Tribal Woman, is called *Gar log ma*. According to the *Tshig mdzod chen mo*, this is a mountain tribe from the region around Kaśmīr. Nuden also specifies that this same goddess sometimes appears with a lion face rather than the hyena face the text suggests.

121. Nuden, vol. 53, 770.1, places each of these at each of the four corners of Mount Meru, the implication being that Mount Malaya is to be identified with Mount Meru. In either case, a kind of anti-mandala is being described here.
122. Addition based on Nuden, vol. 53, 770.2. KPS explains that "Blazing Sky-Iron" (*gnam lcags 'bar ba*) refers to a special kind of very highly treasured metal that appears where lightning strikes the ground. He insists it is quite common in Tibet and that it is sometimes used there to make the ritual dagger (*phur ba*). When lightning strikes near such an object, it sings with a vibrating sound. This would seem to be the substance known today as fulgurite, an excellent example of which can be found in Yale University's Peabody Museum of Natural History.
123. Nuden, who has repeatedly reminded us that this story is "of a meaning requiring interpretation" (*drang don*), here (vol. 53, 770.4–771.1) reinterprets this entire retinue in "inward" terms, as the elements of one's own physical and psychological makeup: "The palace of rotting flesh is one's own body; the swamps of blood and so forth are what exist in that body; the vultures and so forth are the inner organs; the concubines and so forth are self-clinging and the accompanying mind and mental-arisings; the eight *piśācīs* and the eight demonic attendants are the eight consciousnesses; the four door-protectors are the four errors; the four corner-holders are the four egoistic views. These are what will be liberated by the great wisdom of skillful means."
124. *Dbang du mdzad pa,* i.e., to perform the third tantric activity of coercion. It is perhaps worth noting that the Dunhuang liberation rite similarly enacts the activity of coercion before beginning the violence, in order to expel anyone lacking the necessary initiations from the ritual space.
125. Nuden, vol. 53, 772.1, explains that if there is no mother (*yum*), as is the case here, then the emanation is produced from the anus (*snam nas bton pa*) of the father deity. KPS explains that this is considered an unclean birth, made necessary by Rudra's impurities. He also notes that Bhurkuṃkūṭa's mantra is traditionally used as the antidote for impurities.
126. Nuden, vol. 53, 772.4: "*Oṃ āḥ hūṃ sarva pañcāmṛta hūṃ hrī tha.*"
127. Note that these deities are commonly found amongst the one hundred peaceful and wrathful deities of the *Māyājāla.* Thus at this moment the impure goddesses from Rudra's anti-mandala were all transformed into the pure forms of the Buddhist mandala of the Gathered Great Assembly (*Tshogs chen 'dus pa*), the main mandala of the *Compendium of Intentions.* Here and elsewhere it is apparent that the Gathered Great Assembly mandala is based on the standard set of *Māyājāla* deities. On the birth of the purified Buddhist deities of the Gathered Great Assembly out of the sexual union of Bhurkuṃkūṭa and his *Vajra*-Youths with the females in Rudra's horde, Nuden, vol. 53, 773.4–5, notes that the wrathful deities of the mandala in this way emanated from the wisdom of the peaceful deities personified by Bhurkuṃkūṭa and his assembly. This is a standard point in tantric Buddhism, that the wrathful mandala emanates from the primary peaceful mandala.
128. Adds Nuden, vol. 53, 774.5.
129. Nuden, vol. 53, 775.4, divides this into the four stages of approach and accomplishment: "'*Oṃ*' starts it out. '*Bhurkur*' is the [stage of] approach. '*Ichi*' is the [stage of] full

approach. *'Kipi'* is the stage of general accomplishment. *'Ucchuṣma krodha'* is [the stage of] great accomplishment. *'Hūṃ phaṭ'* is the closure."

130. KPS points out that both Bhurkuṃkūṭa and Vairocana belong to the *tathāgata* buddha-family. "*Oṃ*" is the seed syllable for this body-family and here acts as the seed being implanted in the demoness's womb. Nuden, vol. 53, 776.2, calls it the "essential syllable of the Secret Mantra." Here the narrative mirrors perfection-stage visualization practice in which the deity is generated from a seed syllable that is imagined upon a moon-disc within the "womb" of emptiness.
131. "Vajra-Demon," or "Vajra-Rakṣa" (*rdo rje srin po*), is a common epithet for Viśuddha (Tib. Yang dag) Heruka.
132. Thus according to the root text there are three stages in the mantra (*skyed rdzogs 'joms*). *Mun pa'i go cha*, vol. 50, 297.3, adds a final syllable "*phaṭ*" to the mantra as it appears in the root tantra.
133. I.e., the youths that were described above, at the end of chapter 26.
134. In other words, he taught the *Compendium of Intentions* to the now-purified assembly. The *Compendium of Intentions*' prior fame in the three heavens is discussed elsewhere in the same tantra (*Dgongs pa 'dus pa'i mdo*, 347.3). Nuden, vol. 53, 778.4, agrees that the *Compendium of Intentions* is intended here: ". . . the great treasury of Secret Mantra possessing the seven greatnesses . . . this mirror of the secret dharma . . . ," the seven greatnesses being a regularly cited attribute of the *Compendium of Intentions*. Nuden, vol. 53, 778.6 adds, "Thus one should understand this [moment] as a 'way of arising' (*byung tshul*), throughout time without beginning and without end, for the precious teaching of the scripture of the great secret of the conquerors, the realm of the lamp of Vajrasattva." This means the *Compendium of Intentions*, itself containing the story of Rudra's taming, is being taught here in the context of this taming, thus creating a curious doubling of the narrative within itself.
135. Brusha: *'un* means "to come" (Tib. *'ong ba*). Nuden, vol. 53, 779.2.
136. Brusha: *lon 'un* means "to come back" (Tib. *yang 'ong*). Nuden, vol. 53, 779.5.
137. Brusha: *deng hun han phan nyo ba ti/ kho na 'am tsa sma ra tsa/ dpa' bo sgeg po zhe 'am nyid/ ku lan tra tsa bu thra tha* should be translated as above. *Mun pa'i go cha*, vol. 50, 298.5, and Nuden, vol. 53, 780.2. Nupchen translates word for word, while Nuden treats all four phrases together.
138. Brusha: *hon* means "because of saying" (Tib. *smras pa las*). Nuden, vol. 53, 780.6.
139. Nuden, vol. 53, 781.3, says the sound was "*hūṃ!*"
140. Brusha: *lon* means "to wake up" (Tib. *sangs*). Nuden, vol. 53, 781.4.
141. Here begins the violent activity (*drag po'i las*). At this point Nuden, vol. 53, 781.6–782.3, breaks in with a quotation from some notations (*phyag mchan*) by Dampa Deshek: "Adorned with *vajra* wings for the total fulfillment of wishes; adorned with massive metal chainmail for turning away harmful and evil forces; adorned with the resplendent tigerskin for the heroic *samādhi*; adorned with leather armor, laughing and radiant, for power; adorned with supple black snakes clasped around him for magnificent beauty; adorned with a five-spoked *vajra* atop the head for knowing *samādhi*; adorned with an entire crocodile-skin for radiance and clarity, adorned with a *vajra*-fire of burning wisdom." Nuden then adds a still-more-extensive description

drawn from other works such as the *Deity Tantra of Vajra Rakṣa* (*Rdo rje srin po'i lha rgyud*).

142. Nuden, vol. 53, 783.2: "Alternatively, in the first pair are a bell and vajra; with the second pair he drinks from a skull-cup; in the third pair are a corpse and a lasso; then from the fourth pair on it is as above."

143. Nuden, vol. 53, 783.6: "Thus he became the wrathful Vajra-Demon, the great terror (*'jigs byed*)." He also repeats another addition that appears in *Mun pa'i go cha*, vol. 50, 299.4, that is basically the same but adds that there were "nine heads in three tiers of three heads each, all with blazing top-knots." He concludes that although there are some minor differences in the descriptions found in various scriptures, they are not important, citing *The Great Tantra of the Wrathful Deity* (*Khro bo lha rgyud chen po*) to that effect.

144. "A trident with a corpse stuck on it," explains Nuden, vol. 53, 788.6.

145. Thus Hayagrīva's assembly, which has been observing the subjugation from above Mount Malaya since they assembled there at the end of the last chapter (see above, fol. 196), is here exhorting the other billions of youths of Vajra Holder, all of whom have been resting in the womb of the Goddess since dissolving there (on fol. 201).

146. Nuden, vol. 53, 789.6, explains how these nine Blazing Dances became the various aspects of the Vajra-Demon, Viśuddha Heruka: "Because he was ornamented, extremely erotic. He was a demon-destroyer and thus heroic. His massive limbs on a huge body were fearsome. His white faces on the left were wildly laughing. His red faces on the right were stern. His dark blue faces in the middle were terrifying. Since he liberated the six types of beings, compassionate. Since he ate the poisonous, awesome. Since his *dharmakāya* was without signs, peaceful." At this point all the various emanations have dissolved into Viśuddha for the final act: He was already the son of Bhurkuṃkūṭa, empowered by the Vajrakumāras that joined him in the womb of the demoness (201), and now Hayagrīva and his retinue have become inseparable from him through their dances.

147. Here and in several places below, the names of the Hindu gods being subjugated are added upon the basis of *Mun pa'i go cha*, vol. 50, 301.1–302.3.

148. *Mun pa'i go cha*, vol. 50, 301.5, explains that these are "the four Vajra Laughs: 'Ho ho' is the laugh of ferocity and wrath. 'Ha ha' the laugh of majestic severity. 'He he' is the laugh of fearless play. 'Hi hi' is the laugh of delight and satisfaction."

149. Brusha: *(s)ma ra ta*, "completely lead" (Tib. *rab tu drongs shig*). Nuden, vol. 53, 792.4.

150. Additions based on *Mun pa'i go cha*, vol. 50, 303.2. KPS explains that this is a request for the buddha to arise from the supreme of the five wisdoms, the Wisdom of Reality (*chos nyid ye shes*), into the other four wisdoms. Note that this interpretation agrees with Rudra's seventh exhortation in chapter 30 below.

151. Note that the three *herukas* that appear here (Vajra, Padma, and Buddha) represent the mind, speech, and body of the buddha.

152. Adds *Mun pa'i go cha*, vol. 50, 304.1.

153. Nuden, vol. 53, 797.6, adds: "Regarding the inner meaning, the lucid appearances increased within the foundation (*ālaya*), that is, the wisdom of the Path of Meditation,

within which all the obscurations of the three poisons together with their seeds are purified, was born."

154. Closely following Dampa Deshek's *Dka' 'grel*, 240.1–244.2, Nuden, vol. 53, 798.6, discusses two ways of explaining these seeds of the five Rudras. For each of the five stages of teaching and realization that follow, Nuden also includes a more extensive discussion. He concludes (vol. 53, 805.4) by saying that by means of these five interactions Rudra was established in the Path of Preparation (*sbyor lam*). KPS adds that these five instructions (that is, the buddha's five responses to Rudra's displays) can be seen as *ngo sprod* instructions. Note that the five Rudras appear a couple of times in the *Kun 'dus rig pa'i mdo*; see, e.g., 236.1. And finally, note the similarity between the contest of powers that follows and the one seen in the story of Śāriputra defeating Raudrākṣa; see Mair 1995.
155. *Mun pa'i go cha*, vol. 50, 304.5, explains that he responded by adding his heart-syllable, *hūṃ*, to Rudra's mantra: *Rulurulu hūṃ bhyoḥ*.
156. Adds *Mun pa'i go cha*, vol. 50, 304.6. In other words, with this mantra Rudra was reminded that he had broken the vows he had taken alongside Denpak (who is now emanating as his tamer) in the previous aeon.
157. *Mun pa'i go cha*, vol. 50, 305.2, elaborates: "He ate the flesh, drank the blood, and having arranged the bones, ate as offerings the three poisons. He hacked and cut off the limbs, ripping out the heart and sense organs. Drawing out the internal organs, he swallowed them, and all was purified in his stomach. He used the skin [as a cloak], the skull as a cup, and he even wore Rudra's ornaments from the charnel grounds as his signs of triumph, thus purifying the afflictions." Then Nuden, vol. 53, 806.3, further adds, "Here one can also apply these as metaphors for the four demons. His eating the flesh, blood, and bones was a sign of consuming the three poisons. His eating all the inner organs was a sign of the subject-object dualisms being consumed. His eating the sense organs was a sign of freedom from desire. His stealing all the implements—wearing the skin, drinking blood from the skull and adorning himself with all the ornaments—were signs of all the afflictions being completely transmogrified and liberated." Nuden adds that at this moment Rudra attained the path of seeing.
158. Nuden, vol. 53, 808.3, adds that here Rudra is receiving the "great confirmation" (*dbugs chen po phyin pa*). KPS points out that complete joy (*rab tu dga' ba*) is the name of the first level according to the ordinary system of *bodhisattva* levels, and that in the extraordinary system specific to the *Compendium of Intentions* one receives the great confirmation at the level of the third yoga.
159. Meaning this *Compendium of Intentions*, as confirmed by both Nuden, vol. 53, 809.3, and KPS.
160. KPS adds that this female retinue became the twenty-eight goddesses that still today are held to receive the leftovers after the ritual of the offering feast. He also explains that a realized lama can transform his saliva into the nectar of enlightenment and this is what they would receive.
161. Nuden, vol. 53, 812.4, explains, "Thus the five mundane seed syllables and the three supramundane seed syllables were combined, whereby all the *siddhis*, mundane and supramundane, were accomplished." KPS says this is Viśuddha Heruka's mantra.

162. Nuden, vol. 53, 812.6, says they were established in the level of the pure Path of Meditation.
163. KPS says what follows is a "*snying rje po*" confession prayer that commonly appears in ritual manuals, such as those associated with the *Kar gling zhi khro*, the *Bla ma dgongs 'dus*, and the *Bka' brgyad. Bsdus Don*, 103, divides the prayer into seven parts, and the paragraph breaks follow these divisions.
164. An image that emphasizes both the fragility and the physical limitations of the eyes, which are commonly associated with the water element in Buddhist medical treatises.
165. Here ends the first volume (vol. 53) of Nuden's commentary.
166. Thus this paragraph includes a scolding for each of the five afflictions: ignorance, desire, anger, arrogance, envy.
167. Nuden, vol. 54, 12.2, explains that this is a reference to him breaking his vows.
168. *Dgongs pa 'dus pa'i mdo*, 217.5; *ma rtogs pa dang log par rtogs/ ma rtogs phyir yang dag nyid ma rtogs*. Nuden, vol. 54, 12.4, changes *ma rtogs phyir* to *phyogs ma rtogs*, which brings this foursome into line with the lowest four views listed in *Guhyagarbha*. On the relationship between the doxographical systems of the *Compendium of Intentions* and *Guhyagarbha*, see Dalton 2005, 130. As for *Mun pa'i go cha*, vol. 50, 308.6, Nupchen does explain these four and uses *phyogs* in the third, but he mixes the terminology a bit, calling them: *ma shes, log rtog, phyogs shes, yang dag pa'i don ma shes*.
169. Nuden, vol. 54, 14.1, provides a playful threefold reading of this phrase, only partly basing himself on *Mun pa'i go cha*, vol. 50, 309.3, suggesting that this "entrance in the eastern direction" refers to (1) Rudra's being situated in front (and thus to the east) of Viśuddha Heruka, (2) the self-knowing wisdom dawning in the mind (i.e., like the sun in the east), and (3) Rudra's entry into direct realization of no-self, "which stands at the limen between *saṃsāra* and *nirvāṇa*."
170. *Mun pa'i go cha*, vol. 50, 311.1, explains these four mantras separately as follows: "With the hammer of the great emptiness, Rudra is smashed! . . . All the obscurations of grasping at the self of persons are smashed! . . . All the obscurations of conceptualizations clinging to the self of phenomena are smashed! . . . All the obscurations of craving for the objects of grasping at both [me and mine] are smashed!" He goes on to cite another tantra: "This is also seen in such tantras as the *Great Ambrosia Tantra* (*Bdud rtsi chen po'i rgyud*), where it says, ' . . . which combines the feet of subject and object . . . ,' referring to Rudra being smashed underfoot, as *Bsdus don*, 104 explains. Finally, Nuden, vol. 54, 16.4, adds: "In the *Glorious Blazing Wrathful Goddess Tantra* (*Dpal 'bar ba khro mo'i rgyud*) it says, 'Alternatively, the three aspects of Rudra are: the Matraṅgara Rudra, a grasping at objects that apprehends an external object when there is none to be apprehended; the Ākāśa Rudra, a clinging to mind that grasps at an inner mind when there is none doing the grasping; the Khatraṅkha Rudra, establishing the two aspects of subject and object from the expansion (*yul sems brtas pa las*) of object and mind. These three Rudras are also [present within all] sentient beings.'"
171. Nuden, vol. 54, 19.2, adds that at this point Rudra was established in the Path of Seeing. KPS attempts to resolve the possible contradiction between Nuden's statement here and his earlier claim that Rudra had attained the Path of Seeing inside

Viśuddha's stomach (on fol. 208) by saying that before Rudra only attained an insight that had the *extent* (*tshad*) of the Path of Seeing. *Mun pa'i go cha*, vol. 50, 312.2, only says, "The three doors of Rudra were established in the correct level, where they were purified."

172. The first eight lines of this song appear in the Dunhuang *sādhana*, IOL Tib J 331/2, 3v.2–4, suggesting that those lines, if not the entire song, were common in tantric circles.

173. The remaining paragraphs in this chapter describe Rudra's reception of the various initiations. They are arranged so as to proceed according to the following eight ritual stages: (i.) entry into the three mandalas, (ii.) banishing the obstacles, (iii.) conferring the vows: (a) conferring, (b) accepting, (iv.) pouring the reinforcing waters (*chu nan bya ba*), (v.) casting the flower, (vi.) the deity descends, (vii.) displaying the mandala, (viii.) granting the secret name. The translation's paragraph breaks follow these stages. However, while this is the order that appears in most commentaries, the first four stages are scrambled in the root text, so that they appear as follows: (iii.) conferring the vows: (b) accepting, (iii.) conferring the vows: (a) conferring (first part), (ii.) banishing the obstacles, (i.) entry into the three mandalas, (iv.) pouring the reinforcing waters, (iii.) conferring the vows: (a) conferring (second part), (v.) casting the flower, (vi.) the deity descends, (vii.) displaying the mandala, (viii.) granting the secret name. Nupchen simply follows the order of the root text with no reference to any problem, until he makes a brief mention of the disorder below (see note 202). Note that the initiation structure is also scrambled in the *Guhyagarbha-tantra* (see Dorje 1987, 1382), and a similar commentarial correction of ritual order is also seen in Buddhaguhya's commentary to the *Mahāvairocana-abhisaṃbodhi Tantra*; see Hodge 2003, 92 and 97.

KPS's oral commentary on this point may be of some interest, so I translate it here in full: "The order is scrambled like this on purpose. If it were just written in order, people would not need to rely on the *vajrācārya*, and without the *vajrācārya* there would be no benefit. Moreover, to really explain the tantras one needs higher perception (*mngon shes*). A normal scholar, of poetics or logic, for example, would not be able to explain it. The tantras work with *rten 'brel*. It is particularly strange because normally if something is explained clearly it becomes easier to understand, but with the tantras this is not the case. If they were explained simply, they would have no power. They would become like the newspaper that explains lots of events very clearly but is thrown away the next day. The texts of the ancient Indian masters are much more difficult than today's Tibetan commentaries, but they are also much more potent. 'Why is the scrambled order more powerful?' Because it works with, at the level of, *rten 'brel*. For example, once in 1960 in Tibet there was an infestation of insects. At that time there was an accomplished lama living in Chamdo. One man was sent to ask him for help, but the lama did not have the time to come there. So he wrote a note on a small piece of paper to be taken back and read at the infested spot. It read: 'I am Vajrapāṇi! You black bugs, go away!' (*nga ni phyag na rdo rje ste bu nag khyed rnams phyir thon cig*). It was read and the insects went away. A few years later, however, they came again and now this man said, 'I know just what to do.' He read the note as many times as possible, but nothing happened. So the workings of *rten 'brel* are very difficult to see."

174. Nuden, vol. 54, 30.6, adds the extra *phaṭ*. He (and *Mun pa'i go cha*, vol. 50, 319.4) also explains: "By pronouncing the [first] mantra, from within the state of the mandala of the various blazing wrathful *vajras*, the emanated wrathful one with sparks flying out from every pore and from his heart-center burned, purified, and shredded the bodily obscurations of the arrogant one. Then by pronouncing, '*halāhala raṃ*,' all the outer and inner poisons are incinerated" (*halāhala* being the Sanskrit name of a deadly poison).
175. Nuden, vol. 54, 31.2 (based on *Mun pa'i go cha*, vol. 50, 320.1), describes each of these mantras as follows: "(1) The obscurations of arrogant habits were shredded . . . (2) incineration by the fires of wisdom . . . (3) washed away by the waters of reality . . . (4) scattered by the winds of self-knowing. . . . In that way, by expressing that mantra the three elements of wisdom arose with extreme wrath from the seeds of fire, water, and wind."
176. Nuden, vol. 54, 32.3, says this is the mantra of Vajrāmṛta.
177. Nuden, vol. 54, 33.2, explains that the first part of the mantra ("*idante naragante*") is for the pouring of the water of vow-reinforcement. "Then regarding the rest, from '*vāri*' onwards, the Vajra-Demon cut the life-force and, in order to incinerate it in the hells, he poured the five ambrosias."
178. Here Rudra throws a flower onto the mandala, and where it falls determines his tutelary deity.
179. *Mun pa'i go cha*, vol. 50, 321.2, adds that other syllables of light are surrounding this central syllable.
180. *Mun pa'i go cha*, vol. 50, 321.5: His name was Vajra-Zombie (*Rdo rje ro langs*), because he was killed and resurrected, as he explains on 333.1. This later becomes clear in the root text itself, fol. 234. That he "was posted at the secret door" means that, "he was commanded to perform the task of protecting the teachings until he reaches buddhahood."
181. That is, the three realms of desire, form, and formlessness.
182. "That is, the objects of desire and aversion," as explained by Nuden, vol. 54, 40.4.
183. What follow are seven answers to the seven repentances just recited.
184. Nuden, vol. 54, 48.5: "i.e., ignorance, [mistaken] views, cyclic existence and desire."
185. At this point the buddha's compassion for the seven confessions has been produced. Here begins the entry into the mandala, subdivided into two: (1) exhortations for entry, (2) stages of entry (see *Bsdus don*, 106).
186. Note that the names used to refer to this gathering variously combine the elements of the Gathered Great Assembly (*Tshogs chen 'dus pa*), the name of the mandala generally associated with this tantra.
187. Nuden, vol. 54, 55.1, extends this to "*A nu yo ga rnal 'byor grub pa bka'i lung*," perhaps the most-used alternative title for this tantra, particularly by Nupchen in his *Bsam gtan mig sgron*.
188. The stages of entry into the mandala, which begin here, proceed as follows: i. questions and answers on what they want; ii. generating the mind, (a) confessing sins, (b) saying prayers, (c) taking refuge, (d) generating mind; iii. conferring the vows,

(a) requesting conferral, (b) reciting the giving, (c) accepting and the words of the vows; iv. pouring the reinforcing waters, (a) requesting, (b) words of the reinforcing waters; v. reciting the vows; vi. displaying the mandala, (a) requesting, (b) answering. Again, the order is scrambled in the root text, appearing as follows: ii. (d) generating the mind; vi. displaying the mandala: (a) requesting, (b) answering; ii. (c) taking refuge; ii. (a) confessing sins, (b) saying prayers; i. questions and answers on what they want; iii. (c) accepting and the words of the vows; iii. conferring the vows: (a) requesting conferral, (b) reciting the giving; iv. pouring the reinforcing waters: (a) requesting, (b) words of *the reinforcing waters;* v. reciting the vows.

189. *Mun pa'i go cha*, vol. 50, 327.5, changes this to a sun and a moon: "the vajra sun and moon seat, the cause for the non-dual wisdom to arise." On the other hand, in Rudra's private initiation above (end of chapter 30), Viśuddha was also seen standing only on a sun disk. In any case, what is being requested here is the generation of the seat for the deity.

190. Nuden, vol. 54, 61.1, writes, "It appears that in *Bsdus Don* there is a mistake; this and the 'reinforcing waters' stage have been crossed. As the *Ka rta* and [Dampa's] *Notations* are in agreement in ordering it as I have, one can see this is not a mistake." *Bsdus Don* supplies the passage for each subdivision of the text's structure, and for this subdivision he has switched the request for the reinforcing waters for this request for the vows. This is an easy mistake since this passage ends with "*nan tan mdzod.*" Since *nan tan* can be abbreviated as *nan*, it is tempting to read this as a request for the reinforcing waters (*chu nan*). I remain unsure as to the identification of the *Ka rta*. Nupchen gets the order right.

191. *Mun pa'i go cha*, vol. 50, 329.1, explains, "The three seed syllables [*oṃ āḥ hūṃ*], arranged at the crown of the head, the tongue, and the heart, respectively, emanated forth and gathered [into the disciples' corresponding three points]."

192. Nuden, vol. 54, 64.3, says that while the waters are being poured, the same mantra is recited as was in Rudra's initiation above. KPS provides this explanation of this water of reinforcement: The water represents the vows. Having drunk this water, if one keeps the vows, the water goes to one's heart where it becomes the wisdom being. However, if the vows are not kept, the water goes to one's heart where it becomes a nine-headed scorpion that will drink the blood of the heart.

193. Nuden, vol. 54, 65.1, explains that these are "the great secret body, Mahāyoga, the secret speech, Anuyoga, and the most secret mind, Atiyoga."

194. *Mun pa'i go cha*, vol. 50, 330.5–331.5, provides an "uncommon" reading of this whole paragraph, reinterpreting it in terms of subtle body practices. Such readings show that Nupchen had encountered the subtle body practices of the perfection stage during his trips to India in the second half of the ninth century. This is significant, as the Dunhuang documents exhibit little or no awareness of such practices, nor of Nupchen's writings, for that matter. Nupchen emphasizes that this reading is secret and should not be discussed.

195. I.e., the third mandala, the root mandala of the mind of enlightenment, explains Nuden, vol. 54, 67.2.

196. Nuden, vol. 54, 67.3, lists these as: "Emptiness, signless, wishless and the clear light nature." KPS says in the context of sutric teachings there are only the first three, tantra adding the fourth. These are also associated with the "essence, cause, effect and nature" (*ngo bo, rgyu, 'bras bu, rang bzhin*).

197. Thus end the initiations proper. What follows is divided into two: The good qualities of receiving this initiation and then some final speeches bringing the whole myth to its conclusion.

198. These are the five yogas particular to this Anuyoga system. As *Mun pa'i go cha*, vol. 50, 332.3, points out, each is associated with one of the five paths of Anuyoga (*tshogs, sbyor, mthong*, etc.). Mixing the initiation systems of the *Guhyagarbha* and the *Guhyasamāja*, Mun *pa'i go cha*, vol. 50, 331.6, explains that the first group attained "the outer initiations of benefit." The second group attained "the five inner initiations of ability (*nang gi nus pa'i dbang lnga*)." The third group attained "the secret initiation, the initiation of the dissolving *thigle*." The fourth group attained "the knowledge-wisdom initiation." (Note that this knowledge-wisdom empowerment is usually the third of the four empowerments, but here these are being expanded to five.) The fifth group attained, "the empowerment of thoroughly stable great bliss."

199. Nuden, vol. 54, 71.2, here points out that, "Though it may not be clear, the omniscient Dampa Rinpoche says these [names were given to] the leaders of the seven armies listed above [see fol. 223–27]."

200. *Mun pa'i go cha*, vol. 50, 332.6: "Thus the eighteen servants [of the *heruka*] were given various *vajra* names."

201. *Mun pa'i go cha*, vol. 50, 336.3, says, "Thus the yogin should not be apart from the secret substances." Nuden, vol. 54, 81.1, explains the "sacred substances" are human flesh and so forth; the "signs of virtue" are the ritual implements and materials, one's secret name and so forth; the "symbolic supports" are the paintings, statues, and so forth.

202. A strange moment for it, but at this point Nupchen (*Mun pa'i go cha*, vol. 50, 336.3) finally acknowledges that the order of the initiations in both chapter 30 and 31 "was scrambled and should be understood through the oral instructions of one's lama."

203. *Mun pa'i go cha*, vol. 50, 336.5, elaborates on the *sādhana* practice that should accompany the recitation of these mantras: "Illuminating (*gsal ba*) oneself as the great *heruka*, one assembles the secret substances and in an isolated location, for the sake of oneself and others, one recites [the mantras] all at once or in phases."

204. Nupchen (*Mun pa'i go cha*, vol. 50, 337.1) explains the nature of these activities: "Having internalized a confidence in the propitiation, the practice stages of any lower [i.e., mundane or violent] activities, practiced in accordance with one's pith instructions, and whatever activities of liberation or transferring [the consciousness] to another body (*gtan spo ba*) one does will definitely be accomplished unerringly."

205. Chapter 36 describes in detail the vows given to the retinue. I have chosen to stop my translation here because this is where the Rudra-taming myth is traditionally said to leave off, but chapters 36 through 38 bear directly upon the myth, even including some long addresses by the buddha to Rudra and his retinue.

APPENDIX B

1. Here and below, a question mark [?] has been inserted where the text is unclear.
2. As in the translation in chapter 3, the mantra has been removed.
3. Mantra removed.

APPENDIX C

1. The middle pair seems to have been skipped.
2. Mantra removed.
3. Text may have been corrupted here.
4. Mantra removed.

Glossary of Tibetan Titles and Terms

BOOK TITLES

Armor against Darkness (*Mun pa'i go cha*)
Collected Precepts on Maṇi (*Ma ni bka' 'bum*)
Collected Tantras of the Ancients (*Rnying ma'i rgyud 'bum*)
Collected Works (*Gsung 'bum*)
Compendium of Intentions Sutra (*Dgongs pa 'dus pa'i mdo*)
Copper Island (*Zangs gling ma*)
Dangers of Blood Sacrifice (*Dmar mchod nyes dmigs*)
Door for Entry into the Dharma (*Chos la 'jug pa'i sgo*)
An Explanation of the Tantras and Their Narrative Setting (*Rgyud dang rgyud kyi gleng gzhi bshad pa*)
Extensive Edicts (*Bka' shog rgyas pa*)
Flower's Essence: A Religious History (*Chos 'byung me tog snying po*)
Garland of Views (*Man ngag lta ba'i 'phreng ba*)
Grammar in Two Volumes (*Sgra sbyor bam po gnyis pa*)
Great History (*Lo rgyus chen mo*; part of the *Ma ni bka' 'bum*)
A History of How the Mongols Were Repelled (*Sog bzlog bgyis tshul gyi lo rgyus*)
An Invitation to the Great Gods and Nāgas (*Lha klu chen po rnams spyan drang ba*)
Lamp for the Eyes in Contemplation (*Bsam gtan mig sgron*)
Lasso of Means, a Lotus Garland (*Thabs kyi zhags pa padmo'i 'phreng ba*)
Minister Chronicles (*Blon po bka' thang*)
Mirror Illuminating the Royal Genealogies (*Rgyal rabs gsal ba'i me long*)
Padma Chronicles (*Padma bka' thang*)
Pangtangma (*'Phang thang ma*)
Pillar Testament (*Bka' chems ka khol ma*)
Questions and Answers of Vajrasattva (*Rdo rje sems dpa'i zhus lan*)
Sayings of Ba (*Dba' bzhed*)
Seizing and Liberation of the Five Results (*'Bras bu chen po lnga gzung zhing bsgral ba*)

Sutra of the Manifested Teaching on the Methods That Are within the Bodhisattva's Field of Activity (*Bodhisattva-gocara-upāya-viṣaya-vikurvāṇa-nirdeśa-sūtra*)
Words of My Perfect Teacher (*Kun bzang bla ma'i zhal lung*)

PROPER NOUNS

Aklen Dorje Pel (Ag len rdo rje dpal)
Bagyel Tore (Sba rgyal to re; Dba' rgyal to re)
Buddha Star King (Sangs rgyas skar rgyal)
Butön Rinchen Drup (Bu ston rin chen grub)
Chana Dorje (Phyag na rdo rje)
Changi Sertang Yige Khordulma (Byang gi gser tang yi ge 'khor 'dul ma)
Charok Tsang (Bya rog tshang)
Chayul (Bya yul)
Chokden Gönpo (Mchog ldan mgon po)
Choktrul Tsulo (Mchog sprul tshul lo)
Chölo (Chos blo)
Chongye ('Phyong rgyas)
Dakpa Gomtsul Nyingpo (Dwags pa sgom tshul snying po)
Dala Tsenmo (Bda' la btsan mo)
Dampa Deshek (Dam pa bde gshegs)
Dong (Ldong)
Dorje Drak Rigdzin Pema Trinle (Rdo rje 'brag rigs 'dzin padma 'phrin las)
Dorje Dronma (Rdo rje sgron ma)
Dorje Kundrakma (Rdo rje kun grags ma)
Dorje Kunselma (Rdo rje kun gsal ma)
Dorje Kuntu Zang (Rdo rje kun tu bzang)
Dorje Ö Chakma (Rdo rje 'od chags ma)
Dorje Yeshe Chok (Rdo rje ye shes mchog)
Dorje Yudronma (Rdo rje g.yu sgron ma)
Drak (Sgrags)
Drak Yongdzong (Sgrags yang rdzong)
Drakpa Gyeltsen (Grags pa rgyal mtshan)
Dratak Rindor (Gra stag rin dor)
Drenka Pelyon (Bran ka dpal yon)
Drenka Pelgyi Yonten (Bran ka dpal gyi yon tan)
Drikung ('Bri gung)
Drikung Chökyi Drakpa ('Bri gung chos kyi grags pa)
Drigung Gönpa Wön ('Bri gung dgon pa dbon)
Drogön Pakpa Rinpoche (Sgro mgon 'phags pa rin po che)
Drokmi Lotsawa ('Brog mi lo tsA ba)
Drölmawa Samdrup Dorje (Sgrol ma ba gsam 'grub rdo rje)
Dromtönpa ('Brom ston pa)

Druptob Ngödrup (Sgrub thob dngos grub)
Dusum Khyenpa (Dus gsum mkhyen pa)
Dza Patrul Rinpoche (Rdza dpal sprul rin po che)
Ganden Podrang (Dga' ldan pho brang)
Gathered Great Assembly (Tshogs chen 'dus pa)
Gödemchen (Rgod ldem can)
Gö Khukpa Lhetse ('Gos khug pa lhas btsas)
Golok (Mgo log)
Gönpo Namgyel (Mgon po rnam rgyal)
Gugé (Gu ge)
Guru Chowang (Gu ru chos dbang)
Gyalwa Yang Gönpa (Rgyal ba yang dgon pa)
Gyel Lhakhang (Rgyal lha khang)
Jamgön Kongtrul ('Jam mgon kong sprul)
Jamjor Gön (Byams 'byor dgon)
Jamyang Lodrö Gyatso ('Jam dbyangs blo gros rgya mtsho)
Jamyang Sarma ('Jam dbyangs gsar ma)
Jangchup Gyeltsen (Byang chub rgyal mtshan)
Jangchup Ö (Byang chub 'od)
Je Dharma Senge (Rje Dha rma seng ge)
Jigme Lingpa ('Jigs med gling pa)
Kadampa (Bka' dam pa)
Kagyu (Bka' brgyud)
Kangpa Drel Sambho (Gangs pa gral sambho)
Karma Pakshi (Karma Pakshi)
Karma Tensung Wangpo (Karma bstan srung dbang po)
Katsel (Ka tshal)
Kham (Khams)
Khamnyön Dharma Senge (Khams smyon dha rma seng ge)
Kharak Khyungtsun (Kha rag khyung btsun)
Khepa Deu (Mkhas pa lde'u)
Khore (Khor re)
Khyentse Wangpo (Mkhyen brtse'i dbang po)
Kodrakpa (Ko brag pa)
Koka Tangmar (Rko rka thang dmar)
Kongjo (Kong jo)
Kongla Demo (Rkong la de mo)
Kunga Gyeltsen (Kun dga' rgyal mtshan)
Kunga Zangpo (Kun dga' bzang po)
Kyide Nyima Gön (Skyid lde nyi ma mgon)
Kyimolung (Skyid mo lung)
La dong (La dong)
Lang Darma (Glang dar ma)

Lang Pelgyi Senge (Rlang dpal gyis seng ge)
Lerab Lingpa (Las rab gling pa)
Lhade (Lha lde)
Lhalung Pelgyi Dorje (Lha lung dpal gyi rdo rje)
Lhari Yama Kyol (Lha ri g.ya' ma skyol)
Lhato Tori (Lha tho tho ri)
Lhatsun Namkha Jigme (Lha btsun nam mkha' 'jigs med)
Lingme Shabdrung Könchok Chöpel (Gling smad zhabs drung dkon mchog chos 'phel)
Lodrö Gyeltsen (see Sokdokpa Lodrö Gyeltsen)
Longchen Rabjam (Klong chen rab 'byams pa)
Longchenpa (Klong chen pa)
Longdol Lama (Klong rdol bla ma)
Lume Sherab Tsultrim (Klu mes shes rab tshul khrims)
Marpa Lotsawa (Mar pa lo tsA ba)
Mipham Gyatso (Mi pham rgya mtsho)
Namde Ösung (Gnam lde 'od srungs)
Nam Teu Karpo (Gnam the'u dkar po)
Nanam (Sna nam)
Natak (Sna thag)
Ngagi Wangpo (Ngag gi dbang po, Rdo rje brag rig 'dzin)
Ngari (Mnga' ris)
Ngawang Losang Gyatso (Ngag dbang blo bzang rgya mtsho)
Nupchen Sangye Yeshe (Gnubs chen sangs rgyas ye shes)
Nup Namkhe Nyingpo (Gnubs nam kha'i snying po)
Nupyul Rong (Gnubs yul rong)
Nyala Pema Dundul (Nyag bla padma bdud 'dul)
Nyala Sögyel (Nyag bla bsod rgyal)
Nyangrel Nyima Özer (Nyang ral nyi ma 'od zer)
Nyarong (Nyag rong)
Nyemo Chekhar (Snye mo bye mkhar)
Nyen Pelyang (Gnyan Dpal dbyangs)
Nyingma (Rnying ma)
Nyingtig (Snying thig)
Öde ('Od lde)
Ösung ('Od srung)
Otang ('O thang)
Pabongka Peljor Lhundup (Pha bong kha dpal 'byor lhun grub)
Pakmodru(pa) (Phag mo gru pa)
Pakpa Rinpoche—see Drogön Pakpa Rinpoche
Pawo Tsuglag Trengwa (Dpa' bo gtsug lag phreng ba)
Pel Khortsen (Dpal 'khor btsan)
Pema Lingpa (Padma gling pa)
Pema Wangdu (Padma dbang 'dus)

Penyul (’Phan yul)
Pönlop Paṇchen Rinpoche (Dpon slob paN chen rin po che)
Pönsa Rinpoche (Dpon sa rin po che)
*Prajñāgupta (Shes rab gsang ba)
Orgyen Lingpa (O rgyan gling pa)
Pugyal (Spu rgyal)
Ra Lotsawa (Rwa lo tsa ba)
Rasa Trulnang (Ra sa ’phrul snang)
Rateng (Rwa sgreng)
Relpachen (Ral pa can)
Rigdzin Gargyi Wangchuk (Rig ’dzin gar gyi dbang phyug)
Rigdzin Gökyi Demtruchen (Rig ’dzin rgod kyi ldem ’phru can)
Rinchen Zangpo (Rin chen bzang po)
Rinpungpa (Rin spungs pa)
Rok Sherab Ö (Rog shes rab ’od)
Rongzom Chökyi Zangpo (Rong zom chos kyis bzang po)
Sakya (Sa skya)
Samye (Bsam yas)
Śākya Zangpo (Śākya bzang po)
Shamey Gangkar (Sha myed gangs dkar)
Shatreng Sengpu (Sha treng bseng bu)
Shingshak Tseten Dorje (Zhing shag tshe brtan rdo rje)
Shukden (Shugs ldan; Rdo rje shugs ldan)
Sinmo (srin mo)
Sokdokpa Lodrö Gyeltsen (Sog bzlog pa blo gros rgyal mtshan)
Sonam Gyeltsen (Bsod nams rgyal mtshan)
Sonam Rabten (Bsod nams rab brtan)
Sonam Tsemo (Bsod nams rtse mo)
Songtsen Gampo (Srong btsan sgam po)
Taklungpa (Stag lung pa)
Taklung Sangye Yarjön (Stag lung sangs rgyas yar byon)
Tashi Topgyal (Bkra shis stobs rgyal)
Tengyur (bstan ’gyur)
Tenma (brtan ma; bstan ma)
Teu Rang (the’u rang)
Topgyel (Thob rgyal)
Tradrung (Khra ’brug)
Tride Göntsen (Khri lde mgon btsan)
Trisong Detsen (Khri srong lde’u btsan)
Tri Songtsen (Khri srong btsan), another name for Songtsen Gampo
Trisug Detsen (Khri gtsug lde btsan)
Tsana Yeshe Gyeltsen (Tsha na ye shes rgyal mtshan)
Tsang (Gtsang)

Tsangnyön Heruka (Gtsang smyon he ru ka)
Tsangpo (Gtsang po)
Tselpa (Tshal pa)
Tsemo (Rtse mo)
U (Dbus)
Ukpalung ('Ug pa lung)
Upper Hor (Stod hor)
Üru (Dbu ru)
Uyuk ('U yug)
Wui Dumten ('Wu'i dum brtan)
Yangdak Heruka (Yang dag Heruka)
Yangla Shö (Yang la shod)
Yarlha Shampo (Yar lha sham po)
Yazangpa (Gya' bzang pa)
Yeshe Khyungdrak (Ye shes khyung grags)
Yeshe Ö (Ye shes 'od)
Yolmowa Tendzin Norbu (Yol mo ba bstan 'dzin nor bu)
Yoru (G.yo ru)
Yuru (G.yu ru)
Yumten (Yum brtan)
Zhabtrung (Zhabs drung)
Zhangrung (Blon po zhang rung)
Zhikpo Lingpa (Zhig po gling pa)
Zhiwa Ö (Zhi ba 'od)
Zurche Śākya Jungne (Zur che Shākya 'byung gnas)
Zur Chöying Rangdröl (Zur chos dbyings rang grol)
Zurchungpa (Zur chung pa)
Zur Nyima Senge (Zur nyi ma seng ge)
Zur Pakshi Śākya Ö (Zur pakshi shak[y]a 'od)
Zurpa Orgyen Losang Tendzin Drakna Chöje (Zur pa o rgyan bstan 'dzin brag sna chos rje)

BIBLIOGRAPHY

For abbreviations, see list at beginning of the Notes section.

TIBETAN DUNHUANG MANUSCRIPTS CITED

From the Stein Collection: ITJ306, 321, 325, 360, 370, 406, 435, 438, 458, 459, 462, 470, 473, 487, 565, 569, 570, 573, 579, 644, 685, 689, 705, 711, 712, 726, 727, 752, 754, 931, 1236.

From the Pelliot Collection: PT36, 42, 44, 131, 134, 230, 239, 273, 284, 307, 321, 337, 656, 699, 818, 837, 840, 999, 1038, 1042, 1286, 1287, 1289.

OTHER SOURCES IN TIBETAN AND SANSKRIT

Bka' chems ka khol ma. Lanzhou: Kan su'u mi rigs dpe skrun khang, 1989.

Blon po bka' thang. Full title: *Bka' thang sde lnga.* Beijing: Mi rigs dpe skrun khang, 1986.

Bodhisattva-gocara-upāya-viṣaya-vikurvāṇa-nirdeśa-sūtra. Q. 813.

Bodhisattva-yogācāra-catuḥśataka-ṭīkā. Asc. Candrakīrti. Toh. 3865. Bstan 'gyur, dbu ma, ya, 30b.6–239a.7.

'Bras bu chen po lnga gzung zhing bsgral ba. In the *Mtshams brag* edition of the *Rñing ma rgyud 'bum*, 46 vols., ed. Rdo rje thogs med, vol. 34, 26–37. Thimphu, Bhutan: National Library, Royal Government of Bhutan, 1982.

Brgyud pa'i rnam thar. Padma 'phrin las, Rdo rje brag rigs 'dzin II. Full title: *'Dus pa mdo dbang gi bla ma brgyud pa'i rnam thar ngo mtshar dad pa'i phreng ba.* In *Bka' ma mdo dbang gi bla ma brgyud pa'i rnam thar and Rig 'dzin ngag gi dbang po'i rnam thar,* 1–425. Leh, India: S. W. Tashigangpa, 1972.

Bsam gtan mig sgron. Gnubs chen sangs rgyas ye shes. Leh, India: S. W. Tashigangpa, 1974.

Bsdus don. Kaḥ thog dam pa de gshegs. Full title: *Spyi mdo dgongs 'dus kyi bsdus don padma dkar po'i phreng ba.* In *Rnying ma bka' ma rgyas pa*, 56 vols., ed. Bdud 'joms 'jigs bral ye shes rdo rje, vol. 52, 61–206. Kalimpong, West Bengal: Dubjang Lama, 1982.

Byang pa'i rnam thar. Blo bzang rgya mtsho, Dalai Lama V. Full title: *Byang pa rig 'dzin chen po ngag gi dbang po'i rnam par thar pa ngo mtshar bkod pa rgya mtsho.* In *Bka' ma mdo dbang gi bla ma brgyud pa'i rnam thar and Rig 'dzin ngag gi dbang po'i rnam thar.* Leh, India: S. W. Tashigangpa, 1972.

Deb ther sngon po. 'Gos lo tsā ba gzhon nu dpal. New Delhi: International Academy of Indian Culture, 1974.

Dgongs pa 'dus pa'i mdo. Full title: *De bzhin gshegs pa thams cad kyi thugs gsang ba'i ye shes; don gyi snying po rdo rje bkod pa'i rgyud; rnal 'byor grub pa'i lung; kun 'dus rig pa'i mdo; theg pa chen po mngon par rtogs pa; chos kyi rnam grangs rnam par bkod pa zhes bya ba'i mdo.* In the *Mtshams brag* edition of the *Rñing ma rgyud 'bum*, 46 vols., ed. Rdo rje thogs med, vol. 16, 2–617. Thimphu, Bhutan: National Library, Royal Government of Bhutan, 1982.

Dka' 'grel. Kaḥ thog dam pa bde gshegs. Full title: *'Dus pa mdo'i dka' 'grel rdo rje'i tha ram 'byed pa'i lde'u mig.* In *Rnying ma bka' ma rgyas pa*, 56 vols., ed. Bdud 'joms 'jigs bral ye shes rdo rje, vol. 52, 207–78. Kalimpong, India: Dubjang Lama, 1982.

Dkar chag 'phang thang ma. Eishin Kawagoe, ed. Sendai-shi, Japan: Tohoku Indo-Chibetto Kenkyukai, 2005.

Dmar mchod nyes dmigs. Rig 'dzin gar gyi dbang phyug. Full title: *Thar med dmyal ba'i gting rdo srog gcod mchod sbyin gyi nyes dmigs.* Blockprint of unknown origin (Tibetan Buddhist Resource Center W19895).

Dpyid kyi rgyal mo'i glu dbyangs. Ngag dbang blo bzang rgya mtsho. Full title: *Gangs can yul gyi sa la spyod pa'i mtho ris kyi rgyal blon gtso bor brjod pa'i deb ther/ rdzogs ldan gzhon nu'i dga' ston dpyid kyi rgyal mo'i glu dbyangs.* In *The Collected Works (Gsung 'bum) of Vth Dalai Lama Ngag-dbang-blo-bzang-rgya-mtsho*, vol. 19, 1–113a. Gangtok, India: Sikkim Research Institute of Tibetology, 1991–1995.

Dris lan nges don 'brug sgra. Sog bzlog pa blo gros rgyal mtshan. Full title: *Gsang sngags snga 'gyur la bod du rtsod pa snga phyir byung ba rnams kyi lan du brjod pa nges pa don gyi 'brug sgra.* In *Sog bzlog gsung 'bum*, vol. 1 (of 2), 261–601. New Delhi: Sanje Dorje, 1975.

Dukula. Ngag dbang blo bzang rgya mtsho. Full title: *Rgyal dbang lnga pa'i rang rnam du kU la'i gos bzang*, 3 vols. Kawring, H.P., India: Tobdan Tsering, 1979–1983.

Gsang ba'i rnam thar rgya can ma: A Record of the Visionary Experiences of the Fifth Dalai Lama Ṅag-dbaṅ-blo-bzaṅ-rgya-mtsho. Ngag dbang blo bzang rgya mtsho. Leh, India: S. W. Tashigangpa, 1972.

Gsang sngags rig pa 'dzin pa'i sde snod las byung ba'i rgyud sde bzhi'i ming gi rnam grangs. Klong rdol bla ma ngag dbang blo bzang. Chengdu, China, 1991.

Guhyagarbha Tantra. Full title in Tibetan: *Gsang ba'i snying po de kho na nyid nges pa.* In the *Mtshams brag* edition of the *Rñing ma rgyud 'bum*, 46 vols., ed. Rdo rje thogs med, vol. 20, 152–218. Thimphu, Bhutan: National Library, Royal Government of Bhutan, 1982.

Guhyasamāja Tantra. Full title in Tibetan: *De bzhin gshegs pa thams cad kyi sku gsung thugs kyi gsang chen gsang ba 'dus pa zhes bya ba brtag pa'i rgyal po chen po.* Toh. 442. Bka' 'gyur, rgyud 'bum, ca, 90a.1–148a.6.

He ru kaḥ, Nyi zla, and Ye shes 'od zer sgrol ma. 2004. *Reb kong sngags mang gi lo rgyus phyogs bsgrigs*. Beijing: Mi rigs dpe skrun khang.

'Jam dbyangs bsod nams dbang po'i rnam thar. Full title: *Khams gsum gyi 'dren pa dam pa grub pa mchog gi ded dpon 'jam pa'i dbyangs bsod nams dbang po'i rnam par thar pa bcud kyi thigs phreng rab tu 'phel ba'i dgos 'dod 'byung ba'i chu gter*. In 'Jam mgon a myes zhabs ngag dbang kun dga' bsod nams, *The Biographies of Sa-skya Lotshā-ba 'Jam-pa'i-rdo-rje (1485–1533), Sṅgags-'chaṅ grags-pa-blo-gros (1563–1617), and 'Jam-dbyang bsod-nams-dbaṅ-po (1559–1621)*. Dehradun, India: Sakya Centre, 1984: 93–191.

'Jig rten mgon po. *Collected Writings (Gsungs-'bum) of 'Bri-gung Chos-rje 'Jig-rten-mgon-po Rin-chen-dpal*. 5 vols. New Delhi: Khangsar Tulku, 1969–1971.

Kālikā Purāṇa. Śrī Biśwanārāyan Śāstri, ed., *Kālikāpurānaṃ*. Varanasi, India: Chowkhamba Sanskrit Series Office, 1972.

Kauṭilīya Arthaśāstra. R. P. Kangle, ed. and trans. *The Kauṭilīya Arthaśāstra*, part 1 (of 3). Bombay: University of Bombay, 1969.

Kun 'dus rig pa'i mdo; rnal 'byor bsgrub pa'i rgyud ces bya ba theg pa chen po'i mdo. In the *Mtshams brag* edition of the *Rñing ma rgyud 'bum*, 46 vols., ed. Rdo rje thogs med, vol. 15, 321–672. Thimphu, Bhutan: National Library, Royal Government of Bhutan, 1982.

Mahāpratisāravidyārājñī. Q. 179.

Mahāsaṃvarodāya-tantra. Q. 20.

Mahāvairocana-abhisaṃbodhi Tantra. Q. 126.

Manu. In Patrick Olivelle, *Manu's Code of Law*. Oxford, UK: Oxford University Press, 2005.

Mkhas pa'i dga' ston. Dpa' bo gtsug lag phreng ba. Full title: *Dam pa'i chos kyi 'khor lo bsgyur ba rnams kyi byung ba gsal bar byed pa mkhas pa'i dga' ston*. 2 vols. Beijing: Mi rigs dpe skun khang, 1986.

Mkhas pa lde'us mdzad pa'i rgya bod kyi chos 'byung rgyas pa. Mkhas pa lde'u. Lhasa, Tibet: Bod ljongs mi dmangs dpe skrun khang, 1987.

Mun pa'i go cha. Gnubs chen sangs rgyas ye shes. Full title: *Sangs rgyas thams cad kyi dgongs pa 'dus pa mdo'i dka' 'grel mun pa'i go cha lde mig gsal byed rnal 'byor nyi ma*. In *Rnying ma bka' ma rgyas pa*, 56 vols., ed. Bdud 'joms 'jigs bral ye shes rdo rje, vols. 50–51. Kalimpong, India: Dubjang Lama, 1982.

Netra Tantra. Vajravallabha Dvivedaḥ, ed. *Netratantram with the Commentary Udyota of Kṣemarājācārya*. Delhi: Parimal Publications, 1985.

Ngag dbang blo bzang rgya mtsho'i gsung 'bum. Ngag dbang blo bzang rgya mtsho. Full title: *Collected Works (Gsung 'bum) of Vth Dalai Lama Ngag-dbang-blo-bzang-rgya-mtsho*, 25 vols. Gangtok, India: Sikkim Research Institute of Tibetology, 1991–1995.

Nuden, Khenpo. (Mkhan po nus ldan rdo rje.) *Dpal spyi mdo dgongs pa 'dus pa'i 'gel pa rnal 'byor nyi ma gsal bar byed pa'i legs bshad gzi ldan 'char kha'i 'od snang*. In *Rnying ma bka' ma rgyas pa*, 56 vols., ed. Bdud 'joms 'jigs bral ye shes rdo rje, vols. 53–56. Kalimpong, India: Dubjang Lama, 1982.

Nyang ral chos 'byung. Nyang nyi ma 'od zer. Full title: *Chos 'byung me tog snying po sbrang rtsi'i bcud*. Lhasa: Xizang renmin chuban she, 1988.

Padma bka' thang. O rgyan gling pa. Chengdu, China: Si khron mi rigs dpe skrun khang, 1987.

Padma dbang 'dus, *Mkha' mnyam 'gro ba'i rtsug brgyan Padma Dbang 'dus kyi rnam par thar pa gsal bar bkod pa la rmongs mun thib sal ba'i sgron me*. In *Autobiographies of Three Spiritual Masters of Kutang*, ed. Michael Aris, pp. 145–495. Thimphu, Bhutan: Kunsang Tobgay, 1979.

Phun tshogs, Thub bstan. 1997. *Bod kyi lo rgyus spyi don padma rA ga'i lde mig*. Chengdu, China: Si khron mi rigs dpe skrun khang.

Phur pa bcu gnyis. Full title: *Phur pa ki la ya bcu gnyis kyi rgyud ces bya ba'i mdo*. In the *Mtshams brag* edition of the *Rñing ma rgyud 'bum*, 46 vols., ed. Rdo rje thogs med, vol. 19, 785–1013. Thimphu, Bhutan: National Library, Royal Government of Bhutan, 1982.

Rgyal ba thub bstan rgya mtsho'i rnam thar. Phur bu lcog yongs 'dzin sprul sku Thub bstan byams pa tshul khrims bstan 'dzin. Full title: *Lhar bcas srid zhi'i gtsug rgyan gong sa rgyal ba'i dbang po bka' drin mtshungs med sku phreng bcu gsum pa chen po'i rnam par thar pa rgya mtsho lta bu las mdo tsam brjod pa ngo mtshar rin po che'i phreng ba*. In Thub bstan rgya mtsho, ed., *The Collected Works of Dalai Lama XIII*, vols. 6–7 (of 7). New Delhi: International Academy of Indian Culture, 1981–1982.

Rgyud rgyal gsang ba'i snying po'i 'grel pa. Rong zom chos bzang. In *Rnying ma bka' ma rgyas pa*, 56 vols., ed. Bdud 'joms 'jigs bral ye shes rdo rje, vol. 25, 5–435. Kalimpong, India: Dubjang Lama, 1982.

Sa bdag lto 'phye chen po brtag pa'i rab tu byed pa nyes pa kun sel. 'Bri gung chos kyi grags pa. In *Rin chen gter mdzod chen mo*, ed. 'Jam mgon kong sprul blo gros mtha' yas, vol. 65, pp. 97–107. Paro, Bhutan: Ngodrup and Sherab Drimay.

Sarvadurgatipariśodhana-tantra. Q. 116.

Sarvaprajñānta-pāramitasiddhicaitya-nāma-dhāraṇī. Q. 219.

Sarvatathāgata-tattvasaṃgraha-nāma-mahāyāna-sūtra. Horiuchi Kanjin, ed., *Kongocho-kyo no Kenkyu*. Koyasan University, Japan: Mikkyo Bunka Kenkyujo, 1983.

Sba bzhed. Asc. Sba gsal snang. Full title: *Sba bzhed ces bya las sba gsal snang gi bzhed pa*. 2nd printing. Beijing: Mi rigs dpe skrun khang, 1982.

Sbas yul spyi'i them byang. Rgod kyi ldem 'phru can. In *Byang gter lugs kyi rnam thar dang ma 'ongs lung bstan*, 464–96. Gangtok, India: Sherab Gyaltsen and Lama Dawa, 1983.

Sgra sbyor bam po gnyis pa. In *Dkar chag 'phang thang ma/ Sgra sbyor bam po gnyis pa*. Beijing: Mi rigs dpe skrun khang, 2003.

Śiva-purāṇa. J. L. Shastri, ed. Delhi: Motilal Banarsidass, 1970.

Sman pa rnams kyis mi shes su mi rung ba'i she bya spyi'i khog dbubs. Zur mkhar ba blo gros rgyal po. Chengdu, China: Si khron dpe skrun khang, 2001.

Sngags log sun 'byin. 'Gos khug pa lhas btsas. In Chag lo tsā ba *et al.*, *Sngags log sun 'byin gyi skor*. Thimphu, Bhutan: Kunsang Tobgyel, 1979.

Sog bzlog bgyis tshul gyi lo rgyus. Sog bzlog pa blo gros rgyal mtshan. In *Sog bzlog gsung 'bum*, vol. 1 (of 2), 203–59. New Delhi: Sanje Dorje, 1975.

Spyi mdo dgongs 'dus kyi 'chad thabs zin bris nyung ngu rnam gsal. Jamyang Lodrö Gyatso. In *Rnying ma bka' ma rgyas pa*, 56 vols., ed. Bdud 'joms 'jigs bral ye shes rdo rje, vol. 52, 321–34. Kalimpong, India: Dubjang Lama, 1982.

Śrīśambara-maṇḍalavidhi. Asc. Vibhūticandra. Q. 2226.

Susiddhikāra-mahātantra. Toh. 807. Bka' 'gyur, rgyud 'bum, vol. wa, 168a.1–222b.7.

Tattvāloka. Ānandagarbha. Full title: *Sarvatathāgatatattvasaṃgraha-mahāyānābhisamaya-nāmatantravyākhyā-tattvālokakarī-nāma*. Q. 3333.

Theg pa spyi bcings. Dam pa bde gshegs. In *Theg pa spyi bcings rtsa 'grel*. Chengdu, China: Si khron mi rigs dpe skrun khang, 1997.

Vajravidāraṇā-nāma-dhāraṇī. Toh. 750. Bka' 'gyur, rgyud 'bum, vol. dza, 265b.3–266b.7.

Vajrayāna-mūlāṅgāpatti-deśanā. Full title in Tibetan: *Rdo rje theg pa'i rtsa ba dang yan lag gi ltung ba'i bshags pa*. Q. 4626.

Vinaya-vibhaṅga. Toh. 3. Bka' 'gyur, 'dul ba, ca, 21a1-nya, 269a6.

Zangs gling ma. Nyang nyi ma 'od zer gyis gter nas bton. *Slob dpon padma'i rnam thar zangs gling ma bzhugs*. Chengdu, China: Si khron mi rigs dpe skrun khang, 1989.

WESTERN-LANGUAGE SOURCES

Arendt, Hannah. 1970. *On Violence*. New York: Harcourt, Brace and Company.

Aris, Michael. 1979. *Bhutan: The Early History of a Himalayan Kingdom*. Warminster: Aris & Phillips.

Asaṅga. 2001. *Abhidharmasamuccaya: The Compendium of the Higher Teaching (Philosophy)*, French trans. Walpola Rahula; English trans. Sara Boin-Webb. Berkeley: Asian Humanities Press.

Bacot, Jacques, F. W. Thomas, and Ch. Toussaint, eds. 1940. *Documents de Touen-houang relatifs a l'histoire du Tibet*. Paris: Librairie Orientaliste Paul Geuthner.

Bailey, Harold W. 1967. "Altun Khan." *Bulletin of the School of Oriental and African Studies* 30.1: 95–104.

Bakker, Hans. 2007a. "Monuments to the Dead in Ancient and Classical India." *Indo-Iranian Journal* 50.1: 11–47.

———. 2007b. "Human Sacrifice (Puruṣamedha),Construction Sacrifice and the Origin of the Idea of the 'Man of the Homestead' (Vāstupuruṣa)." In *The Strange World of Human Sacrifice*, ed. Jan N. Bremmer, pp. 179–94. Leuven, Belgium: Peeters.

Baumer, Christoph, and Therese Weber. 2005. *Eastern Tibet: Bridging Tibet and China*, trans. Nicole Willock. Bangkok: Orchid Press.

Beal, Samuel. 1993 [1869]. *Travels of Fah-hian and Sung-yun, Buddhist Pilgrims: From China to India (400 A.D. and 518 A.D.)*. New Delhi: Asian Educational Services.

Bentor, Yael. 1995. "On the Indian Origins of the Tibetan Practice of Depositing Relics and Dhāraṇīs in Stūpas and Images." *Journal of the American Oriental Society* 115.2: 248–61.

———. 2000. "Interiorized Fire Rituals in India and in Tibet." *Journal of the American Oriental Society* 120.4: 594–613.

Bhattacharyya-Panda, Nandini. 2008. *Appropriation and Invention of Tradition: The East India Company and Hindu Law in Early Colonial Bengal*. Oxford, UK: Oxford University Press.

Bischoff, F. A. 1978. "Padmasambhava est-il un personnage historique?" In *Proceedings of the Csoma de Körös Symposium*, ed. Louis Ligeti, pp. 27–33. Budapest: Akadémiai Kiadó.

Bischoff, F. A., and Charles Hartman. 1971. "Padmasambhava's Invention of the Phur-bu: Ms. Pelliot Tibétain 44." In *Études tibétaines dédiées à la mémoire de Marcelle Lalou*, pp. 11–27. Paris: Adrien Maisonneuve.

Blaquiere, William Coates. 1799. "The Rudirādhyaya, or Sanguinary Chapter; translated from the Calica Puran." *Asiatick Researches* 5:371–91.

Boord, Martin. 1993. *The Cult of the Deity Vajrakīla, according to the Texts of the Northern Treasures Tradition of Tibet.* Tring, UK: Institute of Buddhist Studies.

Bose, Nirmal Kumar. 1932. *Canons of Orissan Architecture.* Calcutta: R. Chatterjee.

Bremmer, Jan N., ed. 2007. *The Strange World of Human Sacrifice.* Leuven, Belgium: Peeters.

Cantwell, Cathy. 1997. "To Meditate upon Consciousness as *Vajra*: Ritual 'Killing and Liberation' in the Rnying-ma-pa Tradition." In *Tibetan Studies: Proceedings of the 7th Seminar of the International Association for Tibetan Studies, Graz 1995*, ed. Helmut Krasser, et. al., pp. 107–18. Vienna: Verlag der Österreichischen Akademie der Wissenschaften.

———. 2005. "The Earth Ritual: Subjugation and Transformation of the Environment." *Revue d'Etudes Tibétaines* 7:4–21.

Cantwell, Cathy, and Robert Mayer. 2008. *Early Tibetan Documents on Phur pa from Dunhuang.* Vienna: Verlag der Österreichischen Akademie der Wissenschaften.

Chandler, Edmund. 1905. *The Unveiling of Lhasa.* London: Edward Arnold.

Chandra, Lokesh. 1990–1998. *Cultural Horizons of India: Studies in Tantra and Buddhism, Art and Archaeology, Language and Literature.* 7 vols. New Delhi: International Academy of Indian Culture and Aditya Prakashan.

Charpentier, S., and P. Clément. 1975. *L'habitation lao dans les régions de Vientiane et de Louang Prabang.* Paris: Thèse de 3e cycle.

Childs, Geoff H. 1997. "Householder Lamas and the Persistence of Tradition: Animal Sacrifice in Himalayan Buddhist Communities." In *Tibetan Studies*, ed. Helmut Krasser, pp. 141–55. Vienna: Verlag der Österreichischen Akademie der Wissenschaften.

———. 1999. "Refuge and Revitalization: Hidden Himalayan Sanctuaries (Sbas-yul) and the Preservation of Tibet's Imperial Lineage." *Acta Orientalia* 60:126–58.

Coomaraswamy, Ananda K. 1993. *Yakṣas: Essays in the Water Cosmology.* Oxford, UK: Oxford University Press.

Cuevas, Bryan J. 2006. "Some Reflections on the Periodization of Tibetan History." *Revue d'Etudes Tibétaines* 1:44–60.

Dalton, Jacob P. 2002. *The Uses of the* Dgongs pa 'dus pa'i mdo *in the Development of the Rnying-ma School of Tibetan Buddhism.* Unpublished Ph.D. diss., University of Michigan.

———. 2004. "The Early Development of the Padmasambhava Legend in Tibet." *Journal of the American Oriental Society* 124.4: 759–72.

———. 2005. "A Crisis of Doxography: How Tibetans Organized Tantra during the 8th–12th Centuries." *Journal of the International Association of Buddhist Studies* 28.1: 115–81.

———. 2011. "The Questions and Answers of Vajrasattva." In *Yoga in Practice*, ed. David G. White. Princeton: Princeton University Press.

Dalton, Jacob, Tom Davis, and Sam van Schaik. 2007. "Beyond Anonymity: Paleographic Analyses of the Dunhuang Manuscripts." *Journal of the International Association of Tibetan Studies* 3:1–23.

Dalton, Jacob, and Sam van Schaik. 2006. *Tibetan Tantric Manuscripts from Dunhuang: A Descriptive Catalogue of the Stein Collection at the British Library.* Leiden: E. J. Brill.

Das, Sarat Chandra. 1902. *Journey to Lhasa and Central Tibet.* London: J. Murray.

Dash, Mike. 2005. *Thug: The True Story of India's Murderous Cult.* London: Granta Books.

Davidson, Ronald. 1991. "Reflections on the Maheśvara Subjugation Myth: Indic Materials, Sa-skya-pa Apologetics, and the Birth of the Heruka." *Journal of the International Association of Buddhist Studies* 14.2: 197–235.

———. 1995. "The Bodhisattva Vajrapāṇi's Subjugation of Śiva." In *Religions of India in Practice,* ed. Donald S. Lopez, pp. 547–55. Princeton: Princeton University Press.

———. 2002. *Indian Esoteric Buddhism: A Social History of the Tantric Movement.* New York: Columbia University Press.

———. 2003. "The Kingly Cosmogonic Narrative and Tibetan Histories: Indian Origins, Tibetan Space, *bKa' 'chems ka khol ma* Synthesis." *Lungta* 16:64–83.

———. 2005. *Tibetan Renaissance.* New York: Columbia University Press.

Decaroli, Robert. 2004. *Haunting the Buddha: Indian Religions and the Formation of Buddhism.* New York: Oxford University Press.

Decleer, Hubert. 1996. "Atiśa's Journey to Tibet." In *Religions of Tibet in Practice,* ed. Donald S. Lopez, Jr., pp. 157–77. Princeton: Princeton University Press.

de la Vallée Poussin, Louis. 1991. *Abhidharmakośabhāṣyam.* Trans. Leo M. Pruden. 4 vols. Berkeley: Asian Humanities Press.

Demiéville, Paul. 1952. *Le concile de Lhasa. Une controverse sur le quiétisme entre bouddhistes de l'Inde et de la Chine au VIII siècle de l'ère chrétienne.* Bibliothèque de l'Institut des Hautes Études Chinoises, vol. 7. Paris: Imprimerie Nationale de France.

Denwood, Phillip. 1990. "Some Remarks on the Status and Dating of the Sba bzhed." *Tibet Journal* 15.4: 135–48.

Dietz, Siglinde. 1984. *Die buddhistische Briefliteratur Indiens.* Wiesbaden, Germany: Otto Harrassowitz.

Doniger O'Flaherty, Wendy. 1975. *Hindu Myths: A Sourcebook Translated from the Sanskrit.* New York: Penguin Classics.

Dorje, Gyurme. 1987. *The Guhyagarbhatantra and Its XIVth Century Tibetan Commentary, phyogs bcu mun sel.* Unpublished Ph.D. thesis, London: School of Oriental and African Studies.

———, trans. 2005. *The Tibetan Book of the Dead.* New York: Penguin Classics.

Dotson, Brandon. 2006. *Administration and Law in the Tibetan Empire: The Section on Law and State and Its Old Tibetan Antecedents.* Unpublished Ph.D. diss., Oxford University.

———. 2007. "Divination and Law in the Tibetan Empire: The Role of Dice in the Legislation of Loans, Interest, Marital Law and Troop Conscription." In *Contributions to*

the Cultural History of Early Tibet, ed. M. Kapstein and B. Dotson, pp. 3–77. Leiden: Brill.

——. Forthcoming. "At the Behest of the Mountain: Gods, Clans and Political Topography in Post-Imperial Tibet." *Proceedings of the Tenth International Association of Tibetan Studies at Oxford University*, 2003.

Drake, Richard. 1989. "Construction Sacrifice and Kidnapping Rumor Panics in Borneo." *Oceania* 59.4: 269–79.

Dreyfus, Georges. 1998. "The Shuk-den Affair: History and Nature of a Quarrel." *Journal of the International Association of Buddhist Studies* 21.2: 227–70.

Dudjom Rinpoche. 1991. *The Nyingma School of Tibetan Buddhism*. Trans. Gyurme Dorje. 2 vols. Boston: Wisdom Publications.

Eastman, Kenneth M. 1983. "Mahāyoga Texts at Tun-huang." *Bulletin of Institute of Buddhist Cultural Studies (Ryukoku University)* 22:42–60.

Edgerton, Franklin. 1953. *Buddhist Hybrid Sanskrit Grammar and Dictionary*. 2 vols. Delhi: Motilal Banarsidass.

Edou, Jerome. 1996. *Machig Labdron and the Foundations of Chöd*. Ithaca, NY: Snow Lion Publications.

Ehrhard, Franz-Karl. 1997. "A 'Hidden Land' in the Tibetan-Nepalese Borderlands." In *Mandala and Landscape*, ed. A. W. Macdonald, pp. 335–64. New Delhi: D. K. Printworld.

——. 1999a. "The Role of 'Treasure Discoverers and Their Search for Himalayan Sacred Lands." In *Sacred Spaces and Powerful Places in Tibetan Culture*, ed. Toni Huber, pp. 227–39. Dharamsala, India: The Library of Tibetan Works and Archives.

——. 1999b. "Political and Ritual Aspects of the Search for Himalayan Sacred Lands." In *Sacred Spaces and Powerful Places in Tibetan Culture*, ed. Toni Huber, pp. 240–57. Dharamsala, India: The Library of Tibetan Works and Archives.

——. 2001. "Concepts of Religious Space in Southern Mustang: The Foundation of the Monastery sKu-tshab gter-lnga." In *Kagbeni: Contributions to the Village's History and Geography*, ed. P. Pohle, pp. 235–46. Giessen, Germany: Institut für Geographie der Justus-Liebig-Universität.

——. 2005. "The Mnga' bdag Family and the Tradition of Rig 'dzin zhig po gling pa (1524–1583) in Sikkim." *Bulletin of Tibetology* 41.2: 11–29.

——. 2008a. "Addressing Tibetan Rulers from the South: mChog-ldan mgon-po (1497–1531) in the Hidden Valleys of Bhutan." In *Chomolangma, Demawend and Kasbek. Festschrift für Roland Bielmeier (Beiträge zur Zenztralasienforschung, 12)*, ed. B. Huber, M. Volkar, and P. Widmer, vol. 1, pp. 61–91. Halle: International Institute for Tibetan and Buddhist Studies.

——. 2008b. *A Rosary of Rubies: The Chronicle of the Gur-rigs mDo-chen Tradition from South-Western Tibet*. Munich: Indus Verlag.

English, Elizabeth. 2002. *Vajrayoginī, Her Visualizations, Rituals, and Forms*. Boston: Wisdom Publications.

Everding, Karl-Heinz. 2002. "The Mongol States and Their Struggle for Dominance over Tibet in the 13th Century." In *Tibet, Past and Present: PIATS 2000*, ed. Henk Blezer, vol. 1, pp. 109–28. Leiden: Brill.

Frankfurter, David. 2006. *Evil Incarnate: Rumors of Demonic Conspiracy and Satanic Abuse in History.* Princeton: Princeton University Press.

Gardner, Alexander. 2006. "The Sa Chog: Violence and Veneration in a Tibetan Soil Ritual." *Études mongoles et sibériennes, centrasiatiques et tibétaines* 36–37:283–323.

Gentry, James. 2010. "Representation of Efficacy: The Ritual Expulsion of Mongol Armies in the Consolidation and Expansion of the Tsang." In *Tibetan Ritual,* ed. José I. Cabezón, pp. 131–63. Oxford, UK: Oxford University Press.

Germano, David. 1998. "Re-membering the Dismembered Body of Tibet: Contemporary Tibetan Visionary Movements in the People's Republic of China." In *Buddhism in Contemporary Tibet: Religious Revival and Cultural Identity,* ed. Melvyn C. Goldstein and Matthew Kapstein, pp. 53–94. Berkeley: University of California Press.

———. 2005. "The Funerary Transformation of the Great Perfection (Rdzogs chen)." *Journal of the International Association of Tibetan Studies* 1:1–54.

Germano, David, and Janet Gyatso. 2000. "Longchenpa and the Ḍākinīs." In *Tantra in Practice,* ed. David G. White, pp. 239–65. Princeton: Princeton University Press.

Gernet, Jacques. 1995. *Buddhism in Chinese Society.* Trans. Franciscus Verellen. New York: Columbia University Press.

Gethin, Rupert. 2004. "Can Killing a Living Being Ever Be an Act of Compassion? The Analysis of the Act of Killing in the Abhidhamma and Pali Commentaries." *Journal of Buddhist Ethics* 11:168–202.

Giebel, Rolf W. 1995. "The *Chin-kang-ting ching yü-ch'ieh shih-pa-hui chih-kuei*: An Annotated Translation." *Journal of Naritasan Institute for Buddhist Studies* 18:107–201.

———. 2001. *Two Esoteric Sutras.* Berkeley: Numata Center for Buddhist Translation and Research.

Gold, Jonathan C. 2008. *The Dharma's Keepers: Sakya Paṇḍita on Buddhist Scholarship in Tibet.* Albany: State University of New York Press.

Goudriaan, Teun. 1978. *Māyā Divine and Human: A Study of Magic and Its Religious Foundations in Sanskrit Texts.* Delhi: Motilal Banarsidass.

———. 1983. "Some Beliefs and Rituals concerning Time and Death in the *Kubjikāmata.*" In *Selected Studies on Ritual in the Indian Religions. Essays to D. J. Hoens,* ed. Ria Kloppenborg, pp. 92–117. Leiden: E. J. Brill.

Granoff, Phyllis. 1992. "The Violence of Non-Violence: A Study of Some Jain Responses to Non-Jain Religious Practices." *Journal of the International Association of Buddhist Studies* 15.1: 1–43.

Gray, David B. 2005. "Eating the Heart of the Brahmin: Representations of Alterity and the Formation of Identity in Tantric Buddhist Discourse." *History of Religions* 45.1: 45–69.

———. 2007. "Compassionate Violence?: On the Ethical Implications of Tantric Buddhist Ritual." *Journal of Buddhist Ethics* 14: 239–71.

Gregory, Peter. 1983. "The Teaching of Men and Gods: The Doctrinal and Social Basis of Lay Buddhist Practice in the Hua-yen Tradition." In *Studies in Ch'an and Hua-yen,* ed. Robert M. Gimello and Peter N. Gregory, pp. 253–319. Honolulu: University of Hawai'i Press.

Grönbold, Günter. 2001. "'Saptavāra': A Dhāraṇī Collection from Nepal." In *Le Parole e i Marmi*, ed. Raffaele Torella, vol. 1, pp. 369–75. Rome: Istituto Italiano per l'Africa e l'Oriente.

Gyalbo, T., G. Hazod, and P. K. Sørensen. 2000. *Civilization at the Foot of Mount Sham-Po: The Royal House of Lha Bug-Pa-Can and the History of G.Ya'-Bzang*. Vienna: Verlag der Österreichischen Akademie der Wissenschaften.

Gyatso, Janet. 1987. "Down with the Demoness: Reflections on a Feminine Ground in Tibet." *Tibet Journal* 12.4: 38–53.

———. 1999. *Apparitions of the Self: The Secret Autobiography of a Tibetan Visionary.* Princeton: Princeton University Press.

Gyatso, Thubten Legshay. 1979. *Gateway to the Temple.* Trans. David Jackson. Kathmandu, Nepal: Ratna Pustak Bhandar.

Haarh, Erik. 1969. *The Yar-luṅ Dynasty.* Copenhagen: G. E. C. Gad.

Hamerton-Kelly, Robert, ed. 1987. *Violent Origins: Walter Burkert, René Girard, and Jonathan Z. Smith on Ritual Killing and Cultural Formation.* Stanford: Stanford University Press.

Harper, Katherine Anne. 1989. *Seven Hindu Goddesses of Spiritual Transformation*. Lewiston, NY: Edwin Mellen Press.

Harris, Clare. 1999. *In the Image of Tibet: Tibetan Painting after 1959*. London: Reaktion Books.

Harvey, Peter. 2000. *An Introduction to Buddhist Ethics*. Cambridge: Cambridge University Press.

Hatley, Shaman. 2007. *The Brahmayāmalatantra and Early Śaiva Cult of Yoginīs.* Unpublished Ph.D. diss., University of Pennsylvania.

Hazra, R. C. 1963. *Studies in the Upapurāṇas.* 2 vols. Calcutta: Sanskrit College.

Heller, Amy. 2006. "Archeology of Funeral Rituals as Revealed by Tibetan Tombs of the 8th to 9th Century." In *Eran ud Aneran. Studies Presented to Boris Il'ic Marsak on the Occasion of His Birthday*, ed. M. Compareti, P. Raffeta, and G. Scarcia, pp. 261–74. Venice: Cafoscarina.

Hodge, Stephen. 1995. "Considerations on the Dating and Geographical Origins of the *Mahāvairocanābhisambodhi-sūtra.*" In *The Buddhist Forum*, ed. Tadeusz Skorupski and Ulrich Pagel, vol. 3, pp. 57–83. London: School of Oriental and African Studies.

———. 2003. *The Mahā-vairocana-abhisaṃbodhi Tantra, with Buddhaguhya's Commentary.* London: Routledge Curzon.

Hopkirk, Peter. 1983. *Trespassers on The Roof of the World.* Oxford, UK: Oxford University Press.

Horner, I. B., trans. 1938. *The Book of the Discipline (Vinaya-Piṭaka).* Vol. 1. London: Humphrey Milford, Oxford University Press.

———. 1963–1964. *Milinda's Questions.* 2 vols. London: Luzac & Company.

Huber, Toni. 1999. *The Cult of Pure Crystal Mountain: Popular Pilgrimage and Visionary Landscape in Southeast Tibet.* Oxford, UK: Oxford University Press.

Huber, Toni, and Paul Pederson. 1997. "Meteorological Knowledge and Environmental Ideas in Traditional and Modern Societies: The Case of Tibet." *Journal of the Royal Anthropological Institute* 3.3: 577–97.

Huntington, C. W. 2007. "History, Tradition, and Truth." *Journal of the History of Religions* 46:187–227.

Imaeda, Yoshiro. 1979. "Note préliminaire sur la formule *oṃ maṇi padme hūṃ* dans les manuscrits tibétains de Touen-houang." In *Contributions aux études sur Touen-Houang*, ed. Michel Soymié, pp. 71–76. Geneva and Paris: Librairie Droz.

Iwasaki, Tsutomu. 1993. "The Tibetan Tribes of Ho-Hsi and Buddhism during the Northern Sung Period." In *Acta Asiatica: Bulletin of the Institute of Eastern Culture* 64:17–37.

Iyanaga, Nobumi. 1985. "Récits de la soumission de Maheśvara par Trailokyavijaya, d'après les sources chinoises et japonaises." In *Tantric and Taoist Studies in Honour of R. A. Stein*, 3 vols, ed. Michel Strickmann, vol. 3, pp. 633–745. Brussels: Institut Belge des Hautes Études Chinoises.

Jenkins, Stephen. Forthcoming. "On the Auspiciousness of Compassionate Violence." *Journal of the International Association of Buddhist Studies.*

Jinpa, Thubten. 2008. *The Book of Kadam: The Core Texts.* Somerville, MA: Wisdom Publications.

Johnson, W. J. 1998. *The Sauptikaparvan of the Mahabharata: The Massacre at Night.* New York: Oxford University Press.

Jones, Sir William. 1799. *The Works of Sir William Jones. In Six Volumes.* London: Printed for G. G. and J. Robinson; and R. H. Evans.

———. 1869 [1794]. *Institutes of Hindu Law; or, The Ordinances of Menu.* London: W. H. Allen.

Jordaan, Roy E., and Robert Wessing. 1999. "Construction Sacrifice in India, 'Seen from the East.'" In *Violence Denied: Violence, Non-violence and the Rationalization of Violence in South Asian Cultural History*, ed. Jan E. M. Houben and Karel R. van Kooij, pp. 211–47. Leiden: E. J. Brill.

Kane, Pandurang Vaman. 1968. *History of the Dharmaśāstra.* 5 vols. Poona, India: Bhandarkar Oriental Research Institute.

Kapstein, Matthew T. 1992. "Samantabhadra and Rudra: Innate Enlightenment and Radical Evil in Tibetan Rnying-ma-pa Buddhism." In *Discourse and Practice*, ed. Frank E. Reynolds and David Tracy, pp. 51–82. Albany: State University of New York Press.

———. 2000. *The Tibetan Assimilation of Buddhism.* Oxford, UK: Oxford University Press.

———. 2006. *The Tibetans.* Malden, MA, and Oxford, UK: Blackwell Publishing.

Karmay, Samten. 1988a. *The Great Perfection.* Leiden: E. J. Brill.

———. 1988b. *Secret Visions of the Fifth Dalai Lama.* London: Serindia Publications.

———. 1998. *The Arrow and the Spindle: Studies in History, Myth, Rituals and Beliefs in Tibet.* Kathmandu, Nepal: Mandala Book Point.

———. 2003. "The Fifth Dalai Lama and His Reunification of Tibet." In *Lhasa in the Seventeenth Century: The Capital of the Dalai Lamas*, ed. Françoise Pommaret, pp. 65–80. Leiden: E. J. Brill.

———. 2005. *The Arrow and the Spindle: Studies in History, Myth, Rituals and Beliefs in Tibet.* Kathmandu, Nepal: Mandala Book Point.

Kohn, Richard J. 2001. *Lord of the Dance: The Mani Rimdu Festival in Tibet and Nepal.* Albany: State University of New York Press.

Kramrisch, Stella. 1976. *The Hindu Temple.* 2 vols. Delhi: Motilal Banarsidass.

Kwanten, Luc. 1977. "Chio-ssu-lo (997–1065): A Tibetan Ally of the Sung." *Rocznik Orientalistyczny* 39.2: 97–105.

Lalou, M. 1939. *Inventaire des Manuscrits tibétains de Touen-houang conservés à la Bibliothèque nationale (Fonds Pelliot tibétain nos. 1–849).* Paris: Adrien-Maisonneuve.

——. 1952. "Rituel Bon-po des Funérailles Royales." *Journal Asiatique* 240:339–61.

Lessing, Ferdinand D., and Alex Wayman. 1978. *Introduction to the Buddhist Tantric Systems.* Delhi: Motilal Banarsidass.

Linrothe, Rob. 1999. *Ruthless Compassion: Wrathful Deities in Early Indo-Tibetan Esoteric Buddhist Art.* Boston: Shambala Publications.

Lopez, Donald S. 1992. "Paths Terminable and Interminable." In *Paths to Liberation: The Mārga and Its Transformations in Buddhist Thought,* ed. Robert Buswell and Robert Gimello, pp. 147–92. Honolulu: University of Hawai'i Press.

——, ed. 1995. *Curators of the Buddha: The Study of Buddhism under Colonialism.* Chicago: University of Chicago Press.

——. 1996. *Elaborations on Emptiness: Uses of the Heart Sūtra.* Princeton: Princeton University Press.

Macdonald, Ariane. 1971. "Une lecture des Pelliot tibétain 1286, 1287, 1038, 1047 et 1290. Essai sur la formation et l'emploi des mythes politiques dans la religion royale de Sroṅ-bcan sgam-po." In *Etudes tibétaines dédiée à la mémoire de Marcelle Lalou,* ed. Ariane Macdonald, pp. 190–391. Paris: A. Maisonneuve.

——. 1980. "Creative Dismemberment among the Sherpas and Tamangs of Nepal." In *Tibetan Studies in Honour of Hugh Richardson,* ed. Michael Aris and Aung San Suu Kyi, pp. 199–208. Westminster, UK: Aris & Phillips.

Macdonald, Ariane, and Yoshiro Imaeda. 1978–2001. *Choix de documents tibétains conservés à la Bibliothèque nationale.* Paris: Bibliothèque nationale.

Macdonald, A. W., and Anne V. Stahl. 1979. *Newar Art,* pp. 83–105. Warminster, UK: Aris & Phillips.

Mair, Victor. 1995. "Śāriputra Defeats the Six Heterodox Masters: Oral-Visual Aspects of an Illustrated Transformation Scroll (P4524)." *Asia Major,* 3rd Series, 8.2: 1–53.

Malamoud, Charles. 1996. *Cooking the World: Ritual and Thought in Ancient India.* Trans. David White. Oxford, UK: Oxford University Press.

——. 1999. "Modèle et réplique. Le sacrifice humain dans l'Inde védique." In *Archiv für Religionsgeschichte,* ed. J. Assman, et al., pp. 27–40. Stuttgart and Leipzig: B. G. Teubner.

Mani, Lata. 1998. *Contentious Traditions: The Debate on Sati in Colonial India.* Berkeley: University of California Press.

Martin, Dan. 1990. "Bonpo Canons and Jesuit Canons: On Sectarian Factors Involved in the Ch'ien-lung Emperor's Second Goldstream Expedition of 1771–1776. Based Primarily on Some Tibetan Sources." *Tibet Journal* 15.2: 3–28.

——. 1994. "Tibet at the Center: A Historical Study of Some Tibetan Geographical Conceptions Based on Two Types of Country-Lists Found in Bon Histories." In *Tibetan Studies: Proceedings of the 6th Seminar of the International Association for Tibetan*

Studies, ed. Per Kvaerne, vol. 1, pp. 517–32. Oslo: The Institute for Comparative Research in Human Culture.

———. 1996. "The Star King and the Four Children of Pehar: Popular Religious Movements of 11th- to 12th-Century Tibet." *Acta Orientalia Academiae Scientiarum Hungaricae* 49.1–2: 171–95.

———. 1997. *Tibetan Histories: A Bibliography of Tibetan-Language Historical Works.* London: Serindia Publications.

———. 2002. "Gray Traces: Tracing the Tibetan Teaching Transmission of the *Mngon pa kun btsu* (*Abhidharmasamuccaya*) through the Early Period of Disunity." In *The Many Canons of Tibetan Buddhism,* ed. Helmut Eimer and David Germano, pp. 335–58. Leiden: E. J. Brill.

Mayer, Robert. 1991. "Observations on the Tibetan *Phur-pa* and the Indian Kīla." In *The Buddhist Forum II,* ed. Tadeusz Skorupski, pp. 163–92. London: School of Oriental and African Studies.

———. 1996. *A Scripture of the Ancient Tantra Collection: The Phur-pa bcu-gnyis.* Edinburgh, Scotland: Kiscadale.

———. 2007. "The Importance of the Underworlds: Asuras' Caves in Buddhism and Some Other Themes in Early Buddhist Tantras Reminiscent of the Later Padmasambhava Legends." *Journal of the International Association of Tibetan Studies* 3:1–31.

Meinert, Carmen. 2006. "Between the Profane and the Sacred? On the Context of the Rite of 'Liberation' (*sgrol ba*)." In *Buddhism and Violence,* ed. Michael Zimmermann, pp. 99–130. Lumbini, Nepal: Lumbini International Research Institute.

Meister, Michael W. 1979. "Maṇḍala and Practice in Nāgara Architecture in North India." *Journal of the American Oriental Society* 99.2: 204–19.

Mill, James. 1817. *The History of British India.* 3 vols. London: C. Baldwin.

Mumford, Stan R. 1989. *Himalayan Dialogue: Tibetan Lamas and Gurung Shamans in Nepal.* Madison, WI: University of Wisconsin Press.

Nandi, Ramendra Nath. 1973. *Religious Institutions and Cults in the Deccan.* Delhi: Motilal Banarsidass.

———. 1979. "Client, Ritual and Conflict in Early Brāhmaṇical Order." *Indian Historical Review* 6:64–118.

Nattier, Jan. 1990. *Once upon a Future Time: Studies in a Buddhist Prophecy of Decline.* Berkeley: Asian Humanities Press.

Nebesky-Wojkowitz, René. 1976. *Tibetan Religious Dances: Text and Translation of the 'Chams yig.* The Hague: Mouton.

———. 1996 [1956]. *Oracles and Demons of Tibet.* Delhi: Book Faith India.

Obeyesekere, Gananath. 2005. *Cannibal Talk: The Man-Eating Myth and Human Sacrifice in the South Seas.* Berkeley: University of California Press.

Ohnuma, Reiko. 2005. "Gift." In *Critical Terms for the Study of Buddhism,* ed. Donald S. Lopez, Jr., pp. 103–23. Chicago: University of Chicago Press.

———. 2007. *Head, Eyes, Flesh, and Blood: Giving Away the Body in Indian Buddhist Literature.* New York: Columbia University Press.

Olivelle, Patrick. 2008. *Life of the Buddha by Aśvaghoṣa.* New York: New York University Press & JJC Foundation.

Oppitz, Michael. 1993. "On Sacrifice." In *Nepal: Past and Present*, ed. Gérard Toffin, pp. 99–116. New Delhi: Sterling.

———. 1997. "The Bull, the Ox, the Cow and the Yak: Meat Division in the Himalaya." In *Les Habitants du Toit du Monde*, ed. Samten Karmay and Philippe Sagant, pp. 515–42. Nanterre: Société d'ethnologie.

Owens, Bruce. 1993. "Blood and Bodhisattvas: Sacrifice among the Newar Buddhists of Nepal." In *The Anthropology of Tibet and the Himalayas*, ed. Charles Ramble and Martin Brauen, pp. 258–69. Zurich: Ethnological Museum of the University of Zurich.

Padel, Felix. 1995. *The Sacrifice of Human Being: British Rule and the Konds of Orissa*. Oxford, UK: Oxford University Press.

Panikkar, Shivaji K. 1989. *Saptamātṛka Worship and Sculptures*. New Delhi: D. K. Printworld.

Pathak, Suniti K. 1974. *Indian Nītiśāstras in Tibet*. Delhi: Motilal Banarsidass.

Patrul Rinpoche. 1994. *The Words of My Perfect Teacher*. New York: Harper Collins.

Paul, Robert A. 1982. *The Tibetan Symbolic World: Psychoanalytic Explorations*. Chicago: University of Chicago Press.

Pelliot, Paul. 1961. *Histoire Ancienne du Tibet*. Paris: Librairie d'amérique et d'orient.

Petech, Luciano. 1990. *Central Tibet and the Mongols: The Yüan-Sa-skya Period of Tibetan History*. Rome: Istituto Italiano per il Medio ed Estremo Oriente.

———. 1994. "The Disintegration of the Tibetan Kingdom." In *Tibetan Studies: Proceedings of the 6th International Seminar of the International Association for Tibetan Studies, Fagernes 1992*, ed. Per Kvaerne, vol. 2, pp. 649–59. Oslo: The Institute for Comparative Research in Human Culture.

Przyluski, Jean. 1923. "Les Vidyārāja: Contribution à l'histoire de la magie dans les sectes Mahāyānistes." *Bulletin de l'École Française d'Extrême Orient* 23:301–18.

Ramble, Charles. 1990. "How Buddhist Are Buddhist Communities? The Construction of Tradition in Two Lamaist Villages." *Journal of the Anthropological Society of Oxford* 21.2: 185–97.

Richardson, Hugh. 1985. *A Corpus of Early Tibetan Inscriptions*. London: Royal Asiatic Society.

———. 1993. "Mention of Tibetan Kings in Some Documents from Tunhuang." In *Richardson Papers Contributed to the Bulletin of Tibetology (1965–1992)*. Gangtok, India: Sikkim Research Institute of Tibetology.

———. 1998. *High Peaks, Pure Earth: Collected Writings on Tibetan History and Culture*. London: Serindia Publications.

Robbins, Jill. 1998. "Sacrifice." In *Critical Terms in the Study of Religion*, ed. Mark C. Taylor, pp. 285–97. Chicago: University of Chicago Press.

Robson, James. 2009. *Power of Place: The Religious Landscape of the Southern Sacred Peak [Nanyue 南嶽] in Medieval China*. Cambridge: Harvard University Asia Center.

Rock, Josef. 1930. "Seeking the Mountains of Mystery." *National Geographic* 57.2: 131–85.

Roerich, George N. 1996. *The Blue Annals*. Delhi: Motilal Banarsidass.

Ruegg, David Seyfort. 1995. *Ordre spirituel et ordre temporel dans la pensée Bouddhique de l'Inde et du Tibet*. Paris: Collège de France.

Said, Edward W. 1978. *Orientalism*. New York: Random House.

Samuel, Geoffrey. 1993. *Civilized Shamans: Buddhism in Tibetan Societies*. Washington, DC: Smithsonian Institution Press.

Sanderson, Alexis. 1995. "Vajrayāna: Origin and Function." In *Buddhism into the Year 2000. International Conference Proceedings*, pp. 89–102. Bangkok: Dhammakāya Foundation.

———. 2004. "Religion and the State: Śaiva Officiants in the Territory of the King's Brahmanical Chaplain." *Indo-Iranian Journal* 47.3–4: 229–300.

———. Forthcoming. "Religion and the State: Initiating the Monarch in Śaivism and the Buddhist Way of Mantras." In *Ethno-Indology, Heidelberg Studies in South Asian Rituals*. Wiesbaden, Germany: Harrassowitz Verlag.

Schaeffer, Kurtis. 2005. "The Fifth Dalai Lama." In *The Dalai Lamas: A Visual History*, ed. Martin Brauen, pp. 65–91. Chicago: Serindia Press.

Scharfe, Harmut. 1993. *Investigations in Kauṭalya's Manual of Political Science*. Wiesbaden, Germany: Harrassowitz Verlag.

Scherrer-Schaub, Cristina. 1999–2000. "Prière pour un apostat: Fragments d'histoire tibétaine." *Cahiers d'Extrême-Asie* 11:217–46.

———. 2001. "Contre le libertinage. Un opuscule de Tabo adressé aut tantrises héretiques?" In *Le Parole e i Marmi*, ed. Raffaele Torella, pp. 693–733. Roma: Istituto Italiano per l'Africa e l'Oriente.

———. 2002. "Enacting Words: A Diplomatic Analysis of the Imperial Decrees (*bkas bcad*) and Their Application in the *Sgra sbyor bam po gnyis pa* Tradition." *Journal of the International Association of Buddhist Studies* 25.1: 263–340.

Schlieter, Jens. 2006. "Compassionate Killing or Conflict Resolution? The Murder of King Landarma according to Tibetan Buddhist Sources." In *Buddhism and Violence*, ed. Michael Zimmermann, pp. 131–57. Lumbini, Nepal: Lumbini International Research Institute.

Schmithausen, Lambert. 1999. "Aspects of the Buddhist Attitude towards War." In *Violence Denied: Violence, Non-violence and the Rationalization of Violence in South Asian Cultural History*, ed. Jan E. M. Houben and Karel R. van Kooij, pp. 45–67. Leiden: E. J. Brill.

Schopen, Gregory. 1985. "The Bodhigarbhālaṅkāralakṣa and Vimaloṣṇīṣa Dhāraṇīs in Indian Inscriptions." *Wiener Zeitschrift für die Kunde Südasiens* 29:119–49.

———. 1997. *Bones, Stones, and Buddhist Monks*. Honolulu: University of Hawai'i Press.

———. 2004. *Buddhist Monks and Business Matters*. Honolulu: University of Hawai'i Press.

———. 2007. "Cross-Dressing with the Dead." In *The Buddhist Dead: Practices, Discourses, Representations*, ed. Bryan J. Cuevas and Jacqueline I. Stone, pp. 60–104. Honolulu: University of Hawai'i Press.

Sharf, Robert. 2003. "Thinking through Shingon Ritual." *Journal of the International Association of Buddhist Studies* 26.1: 51–96.

Sheehan, Jonathan. 2006. "Altars of the Idols: Idolatry, Antiquarianism, and the Polemics of Distinction in the Seventeenth Century." *Journal of the History of Ideas* 67:648–74.

Shen, Weirong. 2004. "Magic Power, Sorcery, and Evil Spirits: The Image of Tibetan Monks in Chinese Literature During the Yuan Dynasty." In *The Relationship Between Religion and State (chos srid zung 'brel) in Traditional Tibet*, ed. Christoph Cüppers, pp. 189–227. Lumbini, Nepal: Lumbini International Research Institute.

Shizuka, Haruki. 2008. "An Interim Report on the Study of *Gaṇacakra:* Vajrayāna's New Horizon in Indian Buddhism." In *Esoteric Buddhist Studies: Identity in Diversity*, pp. 185–97. Koyasan: Koyasan University.

Sihlé, Nicolas. 2001. *Les tantristes tibétains (ngakpa), religieux dans le monde, religieux du rituel terrible: Etude de Ch'ongkor, communauté villageoise de tantristes du Baragaon (nord du Népal).* Unpublished Ph.D. diss., University of Paris-Nanterre.

Skorupski, Tadeusz. 2002. *Kriyāsaṃgraha: Compendium of Buddhist Rituals.* Tring, UK: Institute of Buddhist Studies.

Slusser, Mary S. 1982. *Nepal Mandala: A Cultural Study of the Kathmandu Valley.* 2 vols. Princeton: Princeton University Press.

Snellgrove, David. 1959. "The Notion of Divine Kingship in Tantric Buddhism." In *The Sacred Kingship: Contributions to the Central Theme of the Eighth International Congress for the History of Religions*, pp. 204–18. Leiden: E. J. Brill.

Snodgrass, Adrian. 1988. *Matrix and Diamond World Maṇḍalas in Shingon Buddhism.* 2 vols. New Delhi: Aditya Prakashan.

Sørensen, Per K. 1994. *Tibetan Buddhist Historiography: The Mirror Illuminating the Royal Genealogies.* Wiesbaden, Germany: Harrassowitz Verlag.

Sørensen, Per K., and Guntram Hazod, eds. 2005. *Thundering Falcon: An Inquiry into the History and Cult of Khra-'brug, Tibet's First Buddhist Temple.* Wien: Verlag der Österreichischen Akademie der Wissenschaften.

———, eds. 2007. *Rulers on the Celestial Plain: Ecclesiastic and Secular Hegemony in Medieval Tibet: A Study of Tshal Gung-thang.* Vienna: Verlag der Österreichischen Akademie der Wissenschaften.

Sperling, Elliot. 1990. "Hülegü and Tibet." *Acta Orientalia Academiae Scientiarum Hungaricae* 45:147–53.

Stablein, William G. 1976. *The Mahākālatantra: A Theory of Ritual Blessings and Tantric Medicine.* Unpublished Ph.D. diss., Columbia University.

Stapelfeldt, Sylvia. 2001. *Kāmākhyā, Satī, Mahāmāya: Konzeptionen der Großen Göttin im Kālikāpurāna.* Frankfurt: Peter Lang.

Stearns, Cyrus. 2007. *King of the Empty Plain.* Ithaca, NY: Snow Lion Publications.

Stein, Rolf A. 1970. "Un document ancien relatif aux rites funéraires des Bon-po tibétains." *Journal Asiatique* 258:155–85.

———. 1972. *Tibetan Civilization.* Stanford: Stanford University Press.

———. 1986. "La tradition relative au début du bouddhisme au Tibet." *Bulletin de l'École Française d'Extrême-Orient* 75:169–96.

———. 1995. "La soumission de Rudra et autres contes tantriques." *Journal Asiatique* 283.1: 121–60.

Steinkellner, Ernst. 1999. "Notes on the Function of Two 11th-century Inscriptional Sūtra Texts in Tabo." In *Tabo Studies II: Manuscripts, Texts, Inscriptions, and the Arts,* ed. C. A. Scherrer-Schaub and E. Steinkellner, pp. 243–74. Rome: Istituto Italiano per l'Africa e l'Oriente.

Stoddard, Heather. 2004. "'Rekindling the Flame,' A Note on Royal Patronage in Tenth Century Tibet." In *The Relationship between Religion and State (chos srid zung 'brel) in Traditional Tibet*, ed. Christoph Cüppers, pp. 49–104. Lumbini, Nepal: Lumbini International Research Institute.

Strenski, Ivan. 2002. *Contesting Sacrifice: Religion, Nationalism, and Social Thought in France*. Chicago: University of Chicago Press.

Strickmann, Michel. 1983. "Homa in East Asia." In *Agni, the Vedic Ritual of the Fire Altar*, ed. Frits Staal, vol. 2, pp. 418–55. Berkeley: Asian Humanities Press.

Strong, John S. 1983. *The Legend of King Aśoka: A Study and Translation of the Aśokāvadāna*. Princeton: Princeton University Press.

Suzuki, Daisetz Teitaro. 1957. *The Tibetan Tripitika: Peking Edition*. Tokyo and Kyoto: Tibetan Tripitika Research Institute.

Tachikawa, Musashi. 2004. *Mother-Goddesses in Kathmandu*. Delhi: Adroit.

Takakusu, Junjirō, and Kaigyoku Watanabe, eds. 1924–1934. *Taishō shinshū daizōkyō*. Tokyo: Taishō issaikyō kankōkai.

Takeuchi, Tsuguhito. 2004. "Sociolinguistic Implications of the Use of Tibetan in East Turkestan from the End of Tibetan Domination through the Tangut Period (9th–12th c.)." In *Turfan Revisited—The First Century of Research into the Arts and Culture of the Silk Road*, ed. Desmond Durkin-Meisterernst et al., pp. 341–48. Berlin: Reimer.

Tanemura, Ryugen. 2004. *Kuladatta's Kriyāsaṃgrahapañjikā*. Groningen, The Netherlands: Egbert Forsten.

Tatz, Mark. 1986. *Asanga's Chapter on Ethics with the Commentary of Tsong-kha-pa, The Basic Path to Awakening, the Complete Bodhisattva*. Lewiston, NY: Edwin Mellen Press.

———. 1994. *The Skill in Means (Upāyakauśalya) Sūtra*. Delhi: Motilal Banarsidass.

Tauscher, Helmut. 2007. "The *Rnal 'byor chen po bsgom pa'i don* Manuscript of the 'Gondhla Kanjur.'" In *Text, Image and Song in Transdisciplinary Dialogue*, ed. Deborah Klimburg-Salter, Kurt Tropper, and C. Jahoda, pp. 79–103. Leiden: Brill.

Terwiel, B. J. 1985. "The Rotating Nāga: A Comparative Study of an Excerpt from the Oldest Tai Literature." *Asie du Sud-Est et monde insulindien* 16.1–4: 221–45.

Thomas, F. W. 1935–63. *Tibetan Literary Texts and Documents concerning Chinese Turkestan*. 4 vols. London: Royal Asiatic Society.

Thomas, Lowell. 1950. *Out of This World: Across the Himalayas to Forbidden Tibet*. New York: Greystone Press.

Toganoo, Shōun. n.d. *Shingon: The Japanese Tantric Tradition*. Trans. Leo M. Pruden. Unpublished translation of *Himitsu Jisō no kenkyū* (1935).

Trungpa, Chogyam. n.d. "Vajrayāna." Unpublished transcript of teachings delivered December 3, 1973.

Tsering, Pema. 1978. "*Rñiṅ ma pa Lamas am Yüan-Kaiserhof*." In *Proceedings of the Csoma de Körös Memorial Symposium*, ed. Louis Legeti, pp. 511–39. Budapest: Akadémiai Kiadó.

Tsogyal, Yeshe. 1993. *The Lotus Born: The Life Story of Padmasambhava.* Trans. Erik Pema Kunsang. Boston: Shambala Publications.

Tsomu, Yudru. 2006. *Local Aspirations and National Constraints: A Case Study of Nyarong Gonpo Namgyel and His Rise to Power in Kham (1836–1865).* Unpublished Ph.D. diss., Harvard University.

Tsonawa, Lobsang Norbu. 1984. *Indian Buddhist Pandits from "The Jewel Garland of Buddhist History."* Dharamsala, India: Library of Tibetan Works & Archives.

Tucci, Giuseppe. 1932. *Indo-Tibetica,* vol. 1. Rome: Reale Accademia d'Italia.

——. 1949. *Painted Scrolls.* 2 vols. Rome: Libreria dello Stato.

Türstig, Hans-Georg. 1985. "The Indian Sorcery called *Abhicāra.*" *Wiener Zeitschrift für die Kunde Südasiens* 29:69–117.

Uebach, Helga. 1990. "On Dharma-Colleges and their Teachers in the Ninth Century Tibetan Empire." In *Indo-Sino-Tibetica: Studi in onore di Luciano Petech,* ed. Paolo Daffinà, pp. 393–417. Rome: Università di Roma.

Ui, Hakuju, Munetada Suzuki, Yenshô Kanakura, and Tôkan Tada, eds. 1934. *A Complete Catalogue of the Tibetan Buddhist Canons (Bkaḥ-ḥgyur and Bstan-ḥgyur).* Sendai: Tôhoku Imperial University.

Uray, Geza. 1972. "The Narrative of the Legislative Organisation of the mKhas-pa'i dga-ston." *Acta Orientalia Scientiarum Hungarica* 26:11–68.

——. 1992. "The Structure and Genesis of the *Old Tibetan Chronicle* of Dunhuang." In *Turfan and Tun-huang, the Texts: Encounter of Civilizations on the Silk Route,* ed. Alfredo Cadonna, pp. 123–43. Florence: Leo S. Olschki.

van der Kuijp, Leonard W. J. 1991. "On the Life and Political Career of Ta'i-si-tu Byang-chub Rgyal-mtshan (1302–?1364)." In *Tibetan History and Language. Studies Dedicated to Uray Géza on His Seventieth Birthday,* ed. E. Steinkellner, pp. 277–327. Vienna: Arbeitskreis für Tibetische und Buddhistische Studien Universität Wien.

——. 1992. "Notes Apropos of the Transmission of the Sarvadurgatipariśodhana tantra in Tibet." *Studien zur Indologie und Iranistik* 16:109–25.

——. 1996a. "Tibetan Historiography." In *Tibetan Literature: Studies in Genre. Essays in Honor of Geshe Lhundup Sopa,* ed. José Ignacio Cabezón and Roger R. Jackson, pp. 39–56. Ithaca, NY: Snow Lion Publications.

——. 1996b. "Ornate Poetry and Poetics. Tibetan *Belles Lettres*: The Influence of Dandin and Ksemendra." In *Tibetan Literature: Studies in Genre: Essays in Honor of Geshe Lhundup Sopa,* ed. José Ignacio Cabezón and Roger R. Jackson, pp. 393–410. Ithaca, NY: Snow Lion Publications.

Van Kooij, Karel R. 1972. *Worship of the Goddess according to the Kālikāpurāṇa.* Leiden: Brill.

van Schaik, Sam. 2006. "The Tibetan Avalokiteśvara Cult in the Tenth Century: Evidence from the Dunhuang Manuscripts." In *Tibetan Buddhist Literature and Praxis,* ed. R. M. Davidson and C. K. Wedemeyer, pp. 55–72. Leiden: Brill.

——. Forthcoming. "Red Faced Barbarians, Benign Despots and Drunken Masters: Khotan as Mirror to Tibet." In *Religions on the Silk Road,* ed. Max Deeg. Lumbini, Nepal: Lumbini International Research Institute.

van Schaik, Sam, and Jacob Dalton. 2004. "Where Chan and Tantra Meet: Buddhist Syncretism in Dunhuang." In *The Silk Road: Trade, Travel, War and Faith*, ed. Susan Whitfield, pp. 61–71. London: British Library Press.

van Schaik, Sam, and Kazuo Iwao. 2008. "Fragments of the Testament of Ba from Dunhuang." *Journal of the American Oriental Society* 128.3: 477–87.

Vasudeva, Somadeva. 2004. *The Yoga of the Mālinīvijayottaratantra*. Pondicherry, India: Institut Français de Pondichéry.

Vitali, Roberto. 1990. *Early Temples of Central Tibet*. London: Serindia Publications.

———. 1996. *The Kingdoms of Gu-ge Pu-hrang*. Dharamsala, India: Tho.ling gtsug.lag. khang lo.gcig.stong 'khor.ba'i rjes.dran.mdzad sgo'i go.sgrig tshogs.chung.

———. 2004. "The Role of Clan Power in the Establishment of Religion (from the *kheng log* of the 9th–10th Century to the Instances of the dByil of La stod and gNyos of Kha rag)." In *The Relationship between Religion and State (chos srid zung 'brel) in Traditional Tibet*, ed. Christoph Cüppers, pp. 105–57. Lumbini, Nepal: Lumbini International Research Institute.

Waddell, L. Austine. 1972 [1895]. *Tibetan Buddhism: With Its Mystic Cults, Symbolism and Mythology*. (Originally published under the title *Buddhism of Tibet or Lamaism, With Its Mystic Cults, Symbolism and Mythology*.) New York: Dover Publications.

Walshe, Maurice, trans. 1995. *The Long Discourses of the Buddha: A Translation of the Dīgha Nikāya*. Boston: Wisdom Publications.

Walter, Michael. 2004. "The Persistence of Ritual: Continuities in the Execution of Political Religion in Tibet." In *The Relationship between Religion and State (chos srid zung 'brel) in Traditional Tibet*, ed. Christoph Cüppers, pp. 159–88. Lumbini, Nepal: Lumbini International Research Institute.

Wangdu, Pasang. 2002. "King Srong btsan sgam po According to the Dba' bzhed: Remarks on the Introduction of Buddhism into Tibet and on the Greatest of the Tibetan Royal Ancestors." In *Territory and Identity in Tibet and the Himalayas*, ed. Katia Buffetrille and Hildegard Diemberger, pp. 17–32. Leiden: Brill.

Wangdu, Pasang, and Hildegard Diemberger. 2000. *dBa' bzhed: The Royal Narrative Concerning the Bringing of the Buddha's Doctrine to Tibet*. Vienna: Verlag der Österreichischen Akademie der Wissenschaften.

Weber, Max. 1965. *Politics as a Vocation*. Philadelphia: Fortress Press.

Wedemeyer, Christian. 2007. "Beef, Dog, and Other Mythologies: Connotative Semiotics in Mahāyoga Tantra Ritual and Scripture." *Journal of the American Academy of Religion* 75.2: 383–417.

———. 2008. *Āryadeva's "Lamp That Integrates the Practices" (Caryā-melāpaka-pradīpa)*. New York: Columbia University Press.

Weinberger, Steven. 2003. *The Significance of Yoga Tantra and the* Compendium of Principles (Tattvasaṃgraha Tantra) *within Tantric Buddhism in India and Tibet*. Unpublished Ph.D. diss., University of Virginia.

Weinstein, Stanley. 1987. *Buddhism under the T'ang*. Cambridge: Cambridge University Press.

White, David G. 2003. *Kiss of the Yoginī: "Tantric Sex" in Its South Asian Contexts*. Chicago: University of Chicago Press.

Wu Hung. 1992. "What Is *Bianxiang?*—On the Relationship between Dunhuang Art and Dunhuang Literature." *Harvard Journal of Asiatic Studies* 52.1: 111–92.

Xinguo, Xu. 1996. "The Tibetan Cemeteries in Dulan County: Their Discovery and Investigation." *China Archaeology and Art Digest* 1.3: 7–12.

Yamaguchi, Zuihō. 1996. "The Fiction of King Dar-ma's Persecution of Buddhism." In *Du Dunhuang au Japon: Études chinoises et bouddhiques offertes à Michel Soymié*, ed. Jean-Pierre Drège, pp. 231–58. Geneva: Droz.

Zimmermann, Michael. 1999. "A Mahāyānist Criticism of *Arthaśāstra:* The Chapter on Royal Ethics in the *Bodhisattva-gocaropāya-viṣaya-vikurvaṇa-nirdeśa-sūtra.*" *Annual Report of the International Research Institute for Advanced Buddhology at Soka University for the Academic Year* 1999 3: 177–211.

——, ed. 2006. *Buddhism and Violence*. Lumbini, Nepal: Lumbini International Research Institute.

INDEX

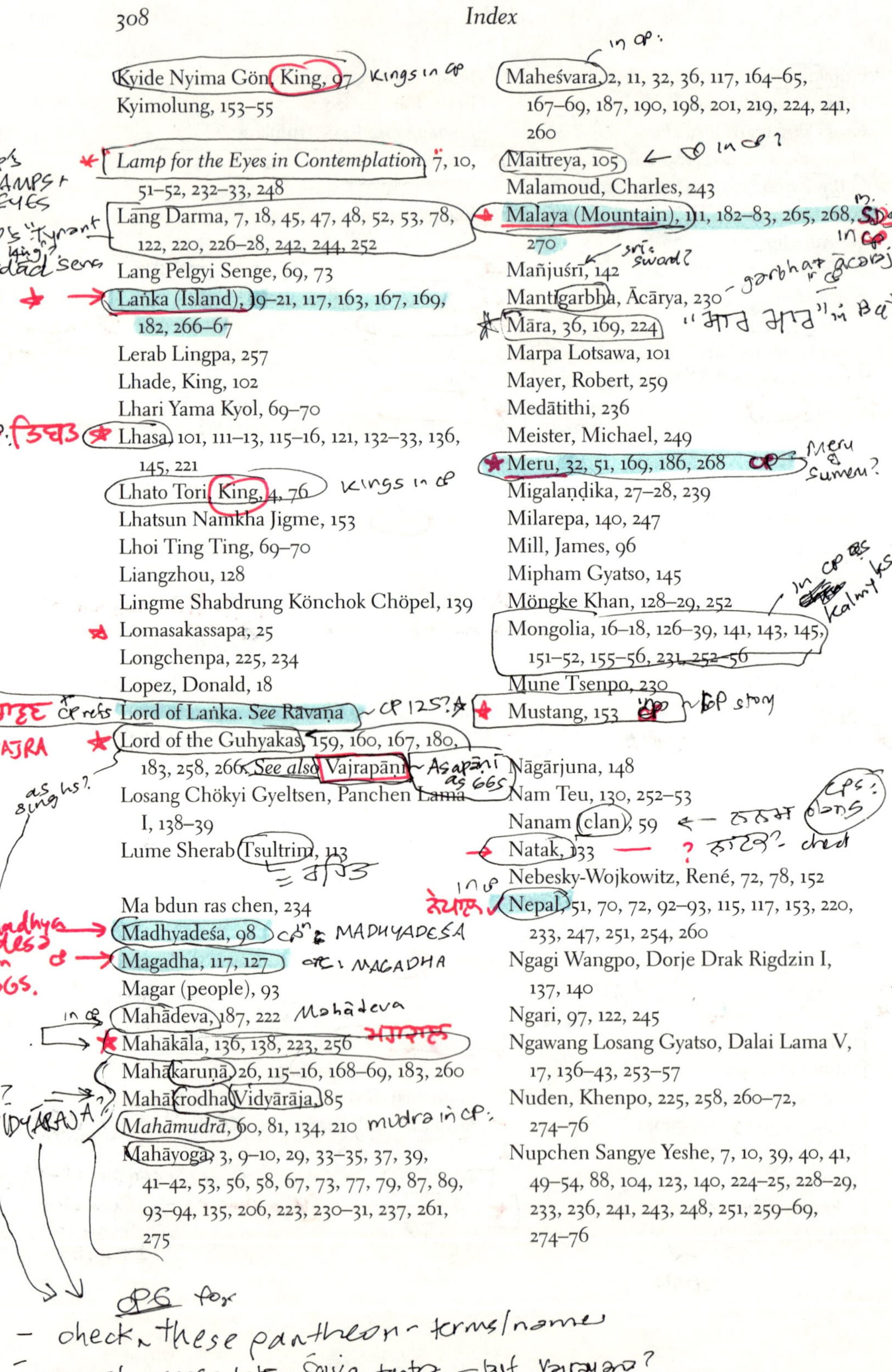